# Leg over Leg

*Volumes One and Two*

## Letter from the General Editor

LIBRARY OF
المكتبة
ARABIC
العربية
LITERATURE

The Library of Arabic Literature series offers Arabic editions and English translations of significant works of Arabic literature, with an emphasis on the seventh to nineteenth centuries. The Library of Arabic Literature thus includes texts from the pre-Islamic era to the cusp of the modern period, and encompasses a wide range of genres, including poetry, poetics, fiction, religion, philosophy, law, science, history, and historiography.

Books in the series are edited and translated by internationally recognized scholars and are published in parallel-text format with Arabic and English on facing pages, and are also made available as English-only paperbacks.

The Library encourages scholars to produce authoritative, though not necessarily critical, Arabic editions, accompanied by modern, lucid English translations. Its ultimate goal is to introduce the rich, largely untapped Arabic literary heritage to both a general audience of readers as well as to scholars and students.

The Library of Arabic Literature is supported by a grant from the New York University Abu Dhabi Institute and is published by NYU Press.

Philip F. Kennedy
*General Editor, Library of Arabic Literature*

## About this Paperback

This paperback edition differs in a few respects from its dual-language hardcover predecessor. Because of the compact trim size the pagination has changed, but paragraph numbering has been retained to facilitate cross-referencing with the hardcover. Material that referred to the Arabic edition has been updated to reflect the English-only format, and other material has been corrected and updated where appropriate. For information about the Arabic edition on which this English translation is based and about how the LAL Arabic text was established, readers are referred to the hardcover.

# Leg over Leg

*Volumes One and Two*

BY

Aḥmad Fāris al-Shidyāq

TRANSLATED BY
Humphrey Davies

FOREWORD BY
Rebecca C. Johnson

VOLUME EDITOR
Michael Cooperson

NEW YORK UNIVERSITY PRESS
*New York and London*

NEW YORK UNIVERSITY PRESS
*New York and London*



Library of Congress Cataloging-in-Publication Data
Shidyaq, Ahmad Faris, 1804?-1887.
Leg over leg or The turtle in the tree concerning the Fariyaq : what manner of creature might he be / by Faris al-Shidyaq ; edited and translated by Humphrey Davies.
volume cm — (Library of Arabic literature)
Includes bibliographical references and index.
ISBN 978-1-4798-0072-8 (vols. 1-2 : ppk ) — ISBN 978-1-4798-1329-2 (vols. 3–4 : ppk : alk. paper) — ISBN 978-1-4798-3288-0 (ebook) — ISBN 978-1-4798-8881-8 (ebook)
1. Shidyaq, Ahmad Faris, 1804?-1887. 2. Shidyaq, Ahmad Faris, 1804?-1887—Travel—Middle East. 3. Arabic language—Lexicography. 4. Middle East—Description and travel. I. Davies, Humphrey T. (Humphrey Taman) translator, editor. II. Shidyaq, Ahmad Faris, 1804?-1887. Saq ʻala al-saq. III. Shidyaq, Ahmad Faris, 1804?-1887. Saq ʻala al-saq. English. IV. Title. V. Title: Turtle in the tree.
PJ7862.H48S213 2015
892.7'8503—dc23 2015021915

Series design and composition by Nicole Hayward
Typeset in Adobe Text

Manufactured in the United States of America
10 9 8 7 6 5 4 3 2 1

# Contents

# Foreword

REBECCA C. JOHNSON

> While I do not claim to be the first writer in the world to follow this path or thrust a pinch of it up the noses of those who pretend they are dozing, I do notice that all the authors in my bookcase are shackled to a single stylistic chain . . . . Once you've become familiar with one link of the chain, you feel as though you know all the others, so that each one of them may truly be called a chain-man, given that each has followed in the footsteps of the rest and imitated them closely. This being established, know that I have exited the chain, for I am no chain-man and will not form the rump of the line; nor do I have any desire to be at its front, for the latter is an even more calamitous place to be than the former.
>
> —*Leg over Leg* (1.17.10)

For most Anglophone readers, this will be their first introduction to the writing of Fāris al-Shidyāq (later Aḥmad Fāris al-Shidyāq, born in 1805 or 1806 and died in 1887), a foundational figure in Arabic literary modernity.[1] For, although he is the author of at least four published works of literary prose, ten linguistic studies of Arabic, Turkish, English, and French, over 20,000 lines of poetry, and at least four unpublished manuscripts (not to mention his many translations, journalistic and critical essays, or those works that have been lost), his work has never appeared in English until now. For specialists in Arabic literature and many native readers of Arabic, however, he needs little introduction. As belletrist, poet, travel writer, translator, lexicographer, grammarian, literary historian, essayist, publisher, and newspaper editor, he is known as a pioneer of modern Arabic literature, a reviver of classical forms, the father of Arabic journalism, and no less than a modernizer of the Arabic language itself. His masterwork, *Al-Sāq ʿalā l-sāq fī mā huwa al-Fāriyāq* (*Leg over Leg or the Turtle in the Tree concerning the Fāriyāq, What Manner of Creature Might He Be*, 1855), is acknowledged as one of the most distinguished works of the nineteenth century and an inaugural text of Arab modernity. It is also among the most controversial: generically impossible to characterize, it is a critical, self-referential, learned, and irreverent book of observations on the lives and manners of "The Arabs and their Non-Arab Peers" that includes scathing attacks on authority, both ecclesiastical and worldly, as well as liberal and libertine discussions of relations between the sexes.

Yet, while virtually all studies of Arabic literature acknowledge his central place in literary history, the works of al-Shidyāq, as Nadia Al-Bagdadi writes, have largely been "merely read, but not seriously known" in Arabophone and Anglo-European academies alike.[2] Although a growing number of essays on his work has been published in English, no monograph on his work has yet been written, and, although several biographies and studies exist in Arabic, his oeuvre was still so little known in 1995 that an edited volume of his selected works could be published in a series entitled *Unknown Works*.[3] *Leg over Leg* itself has been seldom reprinted and often abridged (as often for moral as for aesthetic reasons), making a thorough study of its contents difficult. Moreover, it has suffered from more general scholarly neglect, as the nineteenth century has, until recently, remained one of the lesser-studied periods of Arabic literature. Known as the *Nahḍah*, a term derived from the verb meaning "to rise" or "to stand up," it is commonly translated as the "awakening" or "revival" of Arabic literary culture—a flowering often attributed to the salutary influence of European culture, for which reason it has also been called the "Arab rediscovery of Europe," beginning with Napoleon's invasion of Egypt in 1798.[4] Following a clearly Eurocentric paradigm, scholarship has tended for many years to emphasize the innovative aspects of the period—most notably the introduction of European genres and styles—and to sideline works following classical models, as well as works that fall between the two. Works such as *Leg over Leg* have been overlooked by those scholars who have seen it as a transitional curiosity between the "intellectually frivolous" and decadent post-classical literary age and the twentieth-century flowering of the modern novel.[5]

Looking at al-Shidyāq's complete work, however, helps scholars to re-evaluate this assessment, to engage critically with the *Nahḍah* and its output, to understand the importance of both translation and philology to modern Arabic literature, and to reconceptualize global frameworks of literature and Arabic's place in them. As al-Shidyāq writes, he is no "chain-man" and does not seek to replicate the style of those authors who have come before him. Yet he has as much distaste for appearing at the front of the chain as he does for appearing at its rear. For this reason, *Leg over Leg* can be seen as a portrait in miniature of Arabic literary modernity, if we understand that modernity as it has been described more recently in scholarship: a contested category marked by self-interrogation and a "constant reworking of the meaning of community" through language, created not by being imported from the West, but through interaction with Europe.[6] Historically contingent rather than inevitable and ambivalent in its relationship to both universalist claims and Eurocentric enunciations, Arabic modernity in *Leg over Leg* appears not as a stage on a single linear trajectory of history but as the name given to all of the competing "discrepant histories" which are themselves intertwined.[7]

Engaged with both the literary heritage of the past and the social and political conditions of the present, written in conversation with European languages and literature, and following the path of a burgeoning print industry, *Leg over Leg* is a portrait of a world where material and literary culture are in simultaneous flux. As al-Shidyāq writes:

> I tell you, the world in your late grandfather's and father's day was not as it is now. In their day, there were no steamboats or railway *tracks* to bring close far-off *tracts* and create new *pacts*, to connect the *disconnected*, and make accessible what was *once protected*. Then, one didn't have to learn many languages. It could be said of anyone who knew a few words of Turkish—Welcome, my lord! How nice to see you, my lord!—that he'd make a fine interpreter at the Imperial court. (1855 4.1.9)

The "new age" [*al-ʿaṣr al-jadīd*], the subject of many *Nahḍah*-era writings, was one in which the disconnected were being rapidly and frequently connected—through technologies of travel, of course, as well as through imperialist military expansion, missionary activities, and trade. Yet as al-Shidyāq hints here, these connections were formed as much by the production of knowledge and literature as they were by material innovations. Languages, translation, and even print culture—as printing presses gradually replaced the scriptoria of the imperial court—are what draw distant places closer in *Leg over Leg*, as it follows its protagonist from his native Lebanon to Malta, Egypt, Tunisia, France, and England, while he searches for gainful employment in the literary sphere, as a scribe, then poet, translator, editor, and author.

. . .

*Leg over Leg* is not only emblematic of his age; it is also largely autobiographical and, in this sense, irreducibly idiosyncratic. Al-Shidyāq followed the same peregrinations as his protagonist, whose name, al-Fāriyāq (or "the Fāriyāq," as he retains the definite article from his family name), is a condensation of his given and last names.[8] In the absence of consistent historical records, biographers have even gone so far as to use *Leg over Leg* as a historical document, although this practice—considering the text's satirical and highly stylized mode of narration—seems to obscure more than it illuminates.[9] It cannot, for example, help settle the question of al-Shidyāq's birth date (which is variously given as 1801, 1804, or 1805), as the Fāriyāq is only specified as being "born with the misfortune of having misfortune in the ascendant everywhere, the Scorpion raising its tail to strike at the Kid, or Billy Goat, and the Crab set on a collision course with the horn of the Ox" (1.1.13). What is known is that Fāris al-Shidyāq was probably born in the village of Ashqūt, in what is now Lebanon, to a prominent family in the Maronite community. Like many in his family, which had for generations provided clerks, teachers, and secretaries for local emirs and their sons, al-Shidyāq entered the local village school in Ḥadath, where the family later moved. An intelligent child of a literary family, he learned in large part at home and afterward took up the family profession as copyist and instructor in the service of the emir Ḥaydar al-Shihābī and helped him to compile his family chronicle and history of Lebanon, *Al-Ghurar al-ḥisān fī tārīkh ḥawādith al-zamān.*

Al-Shidyāq might have kept to this well-trodden path had he not come into contact with some of those forces that "connect the disconnected." In 1825 his older brother Asʿad began working as an Arabic instructor and translator for two American evangelical missionaries in Beirut and eventually converted to Protestantism and declared his desire to interpret the Gospel independently and preach it to others. Distraught and probably fearful of the social and financial repercussions of his leaving the church, his family begged him to renounce his new faith and his vocal skepticism of what he called their "custom and upbringing"; when he did not, he was taken into Patriarchal custody.[10] In the Qannūbīn monastery in Mount Lebanon, whether from torture or poor living conditions—he was kept for some time in a small cell that was blocked entirely by earth and stone except for a small window through which rations were passed to him—Asʿad died in 1830.[11] In the meantime Fāris al-Shidyāq—who "anticipated trouble," according to a missionary account of As'ad's case, but possibly also out of disgust for the general approbation among the elites in his community for his brother's punishment—fled with several of the Americans to Alexandria and then British-protected Malta, where he entered their employ.[12]

This would mark al-Shidyāq's exile from Lebanon and the beginning of his lifetime of wandering, as he would return only once, in 1840, to visit his family in secret. He stayed in Malta from early 1827 to 1828 and again from 1834 to 1848, working primarily for the London-based Church Missionary Society (CMS). At first, he was employed as a tutor in Arabic for several of the missionaries, but they soon recognized the full extent of his abilities and enlisted him in their most precious and frustrating project—their Arabic printing press, which they hoped would produce translations of religious materials but was stalled by the lack of printing materials and qualified personnel. Al-Shidyāq soon began translating texts, as well as editing and correcting others' translations; as Jurjī Zaydān remarks in the biographical entry for al-Shidyāq in his *A History of Arabic-Language Literature*, "he was responsible, as the author, translator, or editor, for every single Arabic book printed at the Malta press" during his tenure there.[13] Zaydān's description, as later scholars have pointed out, is probably an exaggeration—there were other translators employed by the press, and the missionaries themselves took an active role in the production of literary materials. But it is nonetheless clear that al-Shidyāq became essential to the operations of the press, as the missionaries found him indispensable, despite the fact that he remained unconvinced of the truth of Protestant Christianity and the validity of the missionary project as a whole.

Upon his arrival, as his supervisor notes, al-Shidyāq was "very much in need of a sound knowledge of the truth of the Gospel, and . . . gives good hope of receiving it."[14] But if they hoped that they would find him to be like his brother, open to evangelical teachings and eager to join the missionary ranks himself, then they were deeply disappointed. Al-Shidyāq maintained a steadfast skepticism in matters ecclesiastical, which is evident in his sometimes ambivalent adoption of Protestantism.[15] As one of the American missionaries writes, "Fares has always expressed a wish to be free, and loudly sometimes."[16] Yet he was also the most qualified and learned of any of those they could find to work with them; he "probes things to the very bottom," as his supervisor wrote of him, an often vexing quality—as it meant long sessions of debate (as the same missionary also wrote, "were it not for his disputing I scarcely knew labours more pleasant to me than those I perform with him")—but one that was ultimately beneficial.[17] Al-Shidyāq translated religious tracts, secular educational materials, and grammars for the CMS and was often the only translator in their employ.

Al-Shidyāq was unhappy in Malta. In *Leg over Leg* he calls it as "the Island of Scoundrels" (*Jazīrat al-mulūṭ*, a word-play with the root letters of Malta) and "the Island of the Foul of Breath" (an allusion to the Maltese language, which he sometimes referred to as a corrupt version of Arabic). In his *Travel Narrative of the Known Conditions of Malta* he found fault with almost every aspect of Maltese culture and geography, describing the climate as so inhospitable that vegetables, even when grown abroad, lose their taste when eaten there.[18] He likewise bristled under missionary life: he could not tolerate the missionaries' food or austere lifestyle—he visited taverns, to the missionaries' chagrin, and was rumored to have had "conversation with bad women"[19]—and wished to be more fairly compensated for his work.

Yet his years in Malta also gave him his first opportunity to work in print, allowing him to develop skills and interests in many aspects of the printing process, all of which would allow him to hold editorial and managing positions in Arabic presses throughout the region. In Egypt, where he traveled when he left CMS employ between 1828 and 1834, he worked on the editorial staff of the first Arabic periodical, *Al-Waqāʾiʿ al-Miṣriyyah* (*Egyptian Events*), and he would later found his own journal and printing press in Istanbul. Little is known about his life in Egypt, except that he seemed dissatisfied with his government position—he approached the missionaries in 1829 to return to Malta, and in 1832 was employed as an Arabic instructor in a missionary school. When his replacement translator left to participate in an expedition to the Euphrates, he returned to Malta and resumed his former post, remaining there from the end of 1834 until the press closed in 1842.

When al-Shidyāq finally left CMS employ, it was to complete a translation of the Bible under the auspices of the Society for Promoting Christian Knowledge (SPCK), another Anglican mission organization operating in Malta. In 1845, this brought al-Shidyāq to the small village of Barley, in Hertfordshire, and then (after a brief return to Malta) to Cambridge, in order to work with Professor Reverend Samuel Lee (d. 1852), an Orientalist and missionary. After Lee's death, al-Shidyāq continued to work on the Bible, while living alternately in London and Paris until its publication in 1857. This was the first of his periods of great literary productivity, enabled by the steady salary he received from the SPCK (and supplemented by a job as the commercial correspondent for the trading company of Butrus Ḥawwā, to whom he dedicates *Leg over Leg*).[20] In England, he lived near the Cambridge University Library and the British Museum and their substantial Arabic manuscript holdings—he was impressed by the access readers were granted to rare and important manuscripts—and came into contact with scholars of Arabic literature there and in Paris (including Thomas Jarrett at Cambridge, John Nicholson at Oxford, and Caussin de Perceval in Paris). In Paris he also met Arab litterateurs and reformers on their travels (including Fransīs Fatḥallah Marrāsh and Khayr al-Dīn al-Tūnusī). It was in this atmosphere of intellectual stimulation (as opposed to the "Panegyricon," or "praise factory," of the Egyptian press office) that al-Shidyāq wrote and published *Leg over Leg* (at the Paris press of Benjamin Duprat, in 1855) and began his travel narratives of Malta and Europe and several other minor projects, including a French grammar for Arabic students and an Arabic grammar for English students.

Although he worked with Protestant missionaries for nearly half of his career, he rigorously maintained an independent-minded scholarly agenda. While translating texts in Malta, he held a post as lecturer in Arabic at the university in Valletta. In Egypt, while working for Muḥammad ʻAlī's state-run newspaper and then a CMS-run school, he began to attend Muslim scholarly and literary circles, studying jurisprudence, grammar, and literature with al-Azhar shaykhs, as well as acquiring or copying "as many classical texts as he could find."[21] Later, when he moved to England in order to collaborate on a translation of the Bible, he not only copied manuscripts of some of the most important works produced during the golden age of Islam but also began to compose a refutation of the Gospels.[22] That is, during the same years that al-Shidyāq worked to establish a faithful and correct translation of the Bible, in accordance with the Hebrew and Syriac source texts, he was also working on a treatise arguing for the unreliability of the Gospels on the very basis of source criticism. In this treatise, al-Shidyāq presents the contradictions of source criticism and faith as irresolvable—a gesture that perhaps most concretely points to his own resolute skepticism that remained the basis of his literary and scholarly endeavors, whether he worked under Christian or under Ottoman Muslim patronage, which he did after leaving Europe in 1857.

The year 1857 marks al-Shidyāq's final departure from missionary employment (though it may be argued that the true break came in 1855, with the publication of his scathing depiction of the missionaries in *Leg over Leg*). In 1842, while in Malta, he had written a poem in praise of the ruler of Tunis, Aḥmad Bāy, and had received a diamond in recognition of it. Later, in Paris, on one of the Bāy's journeys there, al-Shidyāq wrote another laudatory poem; this one elicited an invitation from the Bāy to Tunis to establish a state printing press and newspaper. While this project was eventually realized by one of his contemporaries, al-Shidyāq remained in Tunis for nearly two years, where he continued to work on his European travelogue, *Uncovering the Hidden Arts of Europe* (published in Tunis in 1863).

Scholars believe that it was here that he converted to Islam, taking the name Aḥmad—though evidence in *Al-Sāq* seems to point to his having converted even earlier, while still in Europe.[23]

Soon afterward, he was invited by the Sublime Porte to the capital, and it was there, as *Aḥmad* Fāris al-Shidyāq, that he would attain the greatest recognition. He arrived in Istanbul/Constantinople in 1859, where he was first employed as chief corrector at the imperial press, and, in 1861, he became the founder and editor in chief of *Al-Jawāʾib* (*Tidings from Afar*), the first Arabic periodical to be published there and perhaps the most influential Arabic publication to be produced in the *Nahḍah*. *Al-Jawāʾib* ran weekly from 1861 to 1883, and for the first nine years it was subsidized by the imperial ministry of finance and printed at the government press.[24] Thus beholden, as were most other periodicals of the time, to "our master, the great sultan," as al-Shidyāq puts it, *Al-Jawāʾib* reproduced government bulletins and produced news reports that corresponded with official accounts of events and yet maintained a partial independence, for which it was occasionally punished.[25] More than merely a mouthpiece for the Ottoman sultan and his provincial governors, *Al-Jawāʾib* was also a source for domestic and international news and might have been best known as a venue for cultural and literary debates. A lover and defender of the Arabic language, al-Shidyāq used *Al-Jawāʾib* as a vehicle for his philological scholarship and as a place where he could hold fierce linguistic debates with his contemporaries and publish poems satirizing his critics. He engaged in international debates about Arabic usage with the editors of the Paris journal *Birjīs Bārīs* (*The Paris Jupiter*, 1858–63) and an intergenerational argument about orthography with Ibrāhīm al-Yāzijī and the editors of *Al-Jinān* in Beirut. These were so heated as to inspire a critic to launch a periodical devoted entirely to satirizing al-Shidyāq, *Rujūm wa-ghassāq ilā Fāris al-Shidyāq* (*Fire and Brimstone upon Fāris al-Shidyāq*, 1868); it only lasted a few issues.

During this period, al-Shidyāq launched the Jawāʾib Press; in 1870 he began printing his periodical himself (with the assistance of his son, Salīm), as well as his book-length works, the works of his supporters and friends, and classical works on Arabic language and literature. Many of these were devoted to philological inquiry, including works on the morphology, lexicography, and phonology of Arabic, most notably *Al-Jāsūs ʿalā l-Qāmūs* (*Spying on the Dictionary*, 1884) and *Sirr al-Layāl fī l-qalb wa-l-ibdāl* (*The Secrets of Morphology and Metathesis*, 1884) as well as a comparative study of Arabic, French, and Turkish (*Kanz al-lughāt*; *The Treasury of Languages*, 1876). As Geoffrey Roper notes, al-Shidyāq "did not just passively accept and make use of the printing press" but was "an active protagonist and propagandist of the print revolution."[26] Al-Shidyāq helped to establish many of the norms of modern printing—from language to typesetting—including the addition of tables of contents and title pages with dates. As he argued, "all the crafts that have been invented in this world are inferior to the craft of printing."[27]

Al-Shidyāq operated the Jawāʾib Press from 1870 until three years before his death, when he was perhaps able to devote his full attention to his final project—a critical edition and introduction to the seventh/thirteenth-century dictionary, *Lisān al-ʿArab* (*The Arab Tongue*, 1883–89) of Ibn Manẓūr. Published in twenty volumes at the Bulāq Press in Cairo, it remains one of the largest dictionaries in Arabic and a near-exhaustive source for rare words—one of al-Shidyāq's particular passions, as evidenced in *Leg over Leg*'s extensive lists of synonyms and near-synonyms. His final journey, in a life of traveling, was to Cairo in 1886, in order to confer with the press about its publication. A fellow author and literary biographer described his visit:

> Old age had overtaken him, dimmed his eyes, and bent his back; but he had lost nothing of his keenness or intelligence. He was, until the last of his days, a pleasant conversationalist with graceful expressions, amiable—with a tendency towards profanity.[28]

Eloquent and profane until the last, al-Shidyāq died, shortly after his return from Egypt, in the village of Kadiköy, on September 20, 1887. Some biographers claim that he converted back to Maronite Catholicism on his deathbed, but his own final wishes seem to contradict this. Never one to settle such questions simply, he requested to be buried in a Christian cemetery near his family home in Hazmiyyah, Lebanon, in a grave marked not by a cross but by a crescent.[29]

Al-Shidyāq, then, was paradoxical even in death, as is fitting, considering the broadest strokes of his biography. In the (perhaps understated) words of the missionary society's annual report, "Fāris is a man of excellent mind, but strong and wayward passions"—an apt way to describe many of his political and religious affiliations. He wrote poems in praise of Aḥmad Bāy of Tunis but also of Queen Victoria and the rebel leader ʿAbd al-Qādir of Algeria, and he became a British citizen before leaving England to work as a subject of the Ottoman Empire. To quote Kamran Rastegar, he was a "Muslim Christian. A sedentary traveler. An ascetic sensualist. A modernist classicist. A literary gutter-mouth. A pious unbeliever."[30] He was, intellectually and personally, a series of irresolvable paradoxes.

. . .

Al-Shidyāq's body of work—seen as a whole—is equally difficult to categorize neatly. Most frequently, al-Shidyāq is seen as a modernizer, a renovator of Arabic letters who "had little regard for literary tradition" and who instead looked to Europe for literary modes that would replace those discredited indigenous ones.[31] In a certain sense this is true: he was a pioneer of narrative forms new to the Arab public sphere, including the modern travelogue and experimental narrative prose such as we find in *Leg over Leg*. Known as the father of Arabic journalism for his work on *Al-Waqāʾiʿ al-Miṣriyyah* and *Al-Jawāʾib*, he was invested in the modernization of the Arabic language, so as to preserve its usefulness and expressiveness in modern daily life. Thus, he introduced many surviving neologisms that described his contemporary reality, including *jarīdah* "newspaper," *intikhāb* "election," and *jawāz* "passport," and he translated and edited English translations of religious, geographical, pedagogical, natural historical, and narrative works. His literary career, that is, showed a sustained engagement with European languages, scholarship, and literary forms.

And yet much of his published work consists of works one might classify as neo-classical, or even "revivalist," including influential studies in classical lexicography and critical editions of classical Arabic texts, as well as original compositions in neo-classical style, such as his poetry and his examples of *maqāmāt* (a rhyming prose form that originated in the fourth/tenth century but that was produced by many during the *Nahḍah*).[32] These works, comprising much of his prolific production, signal that al-Shidyāq was not interested simply in abandoning inherited Arabic literary modes and rhetorical styles: he was equally interested in reviving classical rhetoric and forms and publishing them for the new reading public.[33] His modernity, that is, was pioneered precisely *through* an interest in Arabic literary pre-modernity.

In this sense, al-Shidyāq's oeuvre exemplifies the diverse trajectories of the *Nahḍah*. Yet, despite the diversity of its output, the *Nahḍah* had for many years been seen as an enlightenment movement with its primary origins in "Western influences, the introduction of unknown or barely known genres such as the theatre or the European-style novel" or which "loosened the attachment of Arab societies to traditions reckoned inappropriate to modern civilization."[34] In recent years, however, scholars have looked at the production of the *Nahḍah* as more ambivalent in its attitude toward Western literary and cultural models and less categorical in its rejection of indigenous ones. Studies of translation and literary contact in the *Nahḍah* now tend to see experimentations in Western forms not as admiring imitations of a dominant culture but as creative acts of cultural resistance or indifference that "cared nothing for origins and genealogies."[35] And intra-regional studies have questioned the extent to which these works should be viewed solely in conversation with the West. These studies point to more continuities than discontinuities with the literary heritage of the East, and show us that looking at the literature of the *Nahḍah* solely in the context of its relationship with the West writes out a significant part of the period's output: not only "revivalist" literature (classical and neoclassical publications) but also those works that lie between revivalist and "modernist," such as *Leg over Leg*.[36]

The *Nahḍah*, in light of these recent studies, might more precisely be understood as a period of dynamic social and literary change, which oriented its modernity simultaneously inward, toward a classical heritage, and outward, in the direction of Europe. Indeed, Samah Selim has gone as far as to suggest abandoning the singular term *Nahḍah*, in order to "speak of two intertwined literary *Nahḍah*s": "one that, partly looking backwards to an antediluvian 'golden age,' was invested in an act of genetic and linguistic recuperation (re-naissance) and another that was strictly materialist in the play of its textual and social articulations."[37] That is, one *Nahḍah* that recovers a *literary* past and another that *represents*, in varying degrees of realism, a material present, which included goods and people from both inside and outside the Arabic-speaking world, or the "Arabs and their non-Arab peers" of *Leg over Leg*'s subtitle, or those disconnected and newly connected by steamships and railways, to paraphrase the Fāriyāq.

Al-Shidyāq's—and the Fāriyāq's—steamship fare to England was, of course, paid by missionaries. The missionary presence in the Middle East, mostly American and British, began in Egypt and the eastern Mediterranean in the early nineteenth century and was aimed mainly toward the conversion of Eastern Christian sects such as the Maronites in Lebanon and the Copts in Egypt (and, to a lesser extent, Jewish Ottoman subjects). While they failed to convert many—in 1830, the entire "Protestant community" of the Ottoman empire reportedly consisted of six people[38]—they did establish important institutions of learning and foster intellectual relationships with several influential literary figures. Yet missionary societies are just one example of international contact in the Middle East; far more influential and commonplace than the "Biblemen," as they were sometimes called—or "bag-men," as al-Shidyāq satirizes them, because they, like itinerant merchants, would hawk their wares in the spiritual marketplace—were European merchants and manufacturers, who appeared more often in the region during the nineteenth century.

During this period, economic ties between European countries and the larger Ottoman Empire (of which modern-day Syria and Lebanon were a part) deepened: beginning in the 1840s with a series of laws called the *tanẓīmāt*, Istanbul rapidly opened its empire to foreign investment and trade. In Egypt this meant that European banks began to establish themselves in Alexandria as early as the 1850s, lending money to the soon-to-be bankrupt Egyptian government.[39] In Lebanon the consequence of these changes was the rapid growth in the export of agricultural products in the 1850s and 1860s; the silk-thread trade alone accounted for over eighty percent of the region's exports to Europe.[40] At the same time, the quantity of European manufactured goods consumed in the region increased: the Middle East became incorporated into the new world economic system as a dependent region, with prices and exports determined by demand in Europe, and with locally-based European merchants reaping much of the profit.[41]

Foreign travel and immigration to the Middle East rose apace; the silk trade brought French capitalists and merchants (especially from Lyon) to Mount Lebanon to set up silk factories, and a booming cotton industry and transport construction lured workers and investors to Egypt. (The number of Europeans who came into Egypt alone rose from between 8,000 and 10,000 in 1838 to 30,000 in 1861 and 80,000 by 1865.)[42] At the same time that foreign travel and immigration to the Middle East became more frequent, so did Arab migration and travel to Europe. While it was once a scholarly commonplace to consider Muslims and Arabs as generally uncurious about Europe—a view popularized, at least in academic contexts, by Bernard Lewis in *Islam and the West* and *The Muslim Discovery of Europe*—recent work has made lesser-known travelogues of the seventeenth through nineteenth centuries known and available to English readers.[43] Putting this period's travel literature into the long history of Arab contact with Europe makes it clear that there was no sudden nineteenth-century "discovery" of Europe.

Nonetheless, a new dimension to this contact emerged in the nineteenth century—national consolidation, with the goal of strengthening Arab scientific and military capabilities in the wake of European encroachment. After Napoleon's short-lived occupation of Egypt, from 1798 to 1801, Egypt's ruler, Muḥammad ʿAlī, launched his own scientific campaign to Europe by dispatching educational missions in various disciplines.[44] First sending a group of students to Italy to train as printers and type-founders, he later sent missions to France and England to study shipbuilding, engineering, medicine, law, diplomacy, and languages. During what Muḥammad ʿAlī envisioned as a cultural and technical revival, these missions stood at the core of a national education project—as they not only brought home valuable skills and information, but also disseminated them through university teaching and the translation of technical textbooks.[45] Printing presses, then, including the press that Napoleon brought to print his military bulletins and the still-operating Bulāq Press (founded in 1821), were instrumental to Muḥammad ʿAlī's modernizing agenda, as they published official news and the scientific and academic works that Egyptian delegates translated upon their return.

Not all publishing, however, was produced in the service of the state. Any author could have a book printed at Muḥammad ʿAlī's press, provided that the costs were paid, and private presses began to compete with state publishing houses for the emerging print market.[46] By mid-century, there were more than a dozen presses operating in the Levant alone, with six privately owned commercial presses opening in the 1850s.[47] In addition to missionary presses like the CMS Press in Malta, authors themselves also became printer-publishers, founding their own presses and publishing their own writing or journals. In Cairo, Alexandria, Beirut, Baghdad, Mosul, Aleppo, Damascus, Jerusalem, and Valletta, authors and translators published a range of texts for the emerging commercial market.[48] The nineteenth-century Arabic print sphere emerged as one that was profoundly heterogeneous, producing editions of classical Arabic texts as well as translations from English and French literature. Alongside these, original Arabic prose works appeared, some in neoclassical style, and others written in a form called *riwāyah*, the word now used to mean "novel" but which then signified a category more fluid, such as "narrative" (literally, it is the verbal noun for "telling"), as well as works in between.

In doing so, the *Nahḍah*'s print market forged new alliances, not simply within the imagined community of the nation, but intra-regionally—creating, in effect, something that could for the first time be called a public Arabic print sphere, where "the sounds from Beirut, Cairo, and Alexandria reached other Arab provinces, and educated groups in the towns of Syria, Palestine, Iraq, and even the Hejaz became involved in the new exchange in print across provincial boundaries."[49] Periodicals published in Beirut would advertise or review novels written by Egyptian colleagues, and journals of various affiliations would engage each other in debate about the correct use of Arabic, the relative merits of different literary translators, or editorial policy. The picture that emerges is of an Arabic print sphere that was intricately interlinked, making alliances across provincial borders, confessional boundaries, and even across continents. Early journals and newspapers were sometimes the product of either foreign investment (as was the case with the Franco-Egyptian ventures of *L'Echo des Pyramides*, 1827, and *Al-Tanbīh*, founded in 1800) or direct intellectual exchange,[50] and featured an international news section often translated from European newspapers and wire services, thanks to the widespread use of the telegraph and the establishment of Reuters's first office outside Europe, in Alexandria in 1865.[51] Their audience, too, was international—composed not just of readers in Beirut or Cairo but also immigrant readers and Orientalists in Europe and, later, in North America.[52] An English traveler to the Arabian Peninsula in the 1870s, Charles Montagu Doughty, remarked that al-Shidyāq's *Al-Jawā'ib* was "current in all countries of the Arabic speech" and that he had seen it even "in the Nejd merchants' houses at Bombay."[53]

The links established by trade and travel, then, were formed simultaneously in the print sphere, and it was there that they were debated. What was shared in print, perhaps even more than a sense of a bounded national or imperial space, was the *Nahḍah* reader's relationship to the world around him, the sense both of being a local actor and participating in global phenomena. Indeed, by the end of the nineteenth century it was possible to see journalists referring an international or even global *Nahḍah*, consisting of Arab authors or litterateurs who traveled and published abroad.[54] The *Nahḍah*, then, might be understood as an attempt to negotiate Arab modernity, identity, and enlightenment in the context of what authors identified as a new age of technological, social, literary, commercial, and even moral change, which they were joining by virtue of a new sense of global interconnectedness.[55] One intellectual project that concerned the writers and thinkers of the *Nahḍah*, then, was how—and on what terms—to understand their participation in this global process. Debates about modernity, oriented toward the issue of *tamaddun* (loosely translated as "progress toward civilization"), emerged. Journalistic essays asked, "Who are we?" as a way to seek answers to the larger question of what it means to be Arab (and not necessarily an Egyptian or a Lebanese) and modern, or Arab and enlightened, in the cross-currents of global capitalism, empire, and the trans-regional and potentially global community of the faithful, the *umma*.[56] To do so was to demarcate local specificity within the global, rather than against it. Thus *Nahḍah* intellectuals did not necessarily seek either to preserve or to abandon authentic traditions in the face of foreign encroachment. The common understanding of the choice intellectuals made, between the position of "reformer" and "reactionary," might be a false dichotomy. As Shaden Tageldin writes, "For most of the elite Egyptian intellectuals of the *Nahḍah*, becoming modern was never a question of abandoning Arabic and writing in the languages of their European colonizers—in French or English. The *Nahḍah* unfolded in translation: it transported French or English into Arabic. Thus it appeared to 'preserve' Arabic—all the while *translating* it."[57] In other words, these intellectuals theorized modernity as a comparative project, as something taking shape alongside Europe.[58]

. . .

One can see this comparative tendency in the title page of *Leg over Leg*. As its subtitle announces ("Days, Months, and Years spent in Critical Examination of the Arabs and their Non-Arab Peers"), the narrative takes the outward form of a travelogue that follows the Fāriyāq between Europe and the Arab Middle East. In his "critical examination," he looks outward at a cultural other, but he also reflects inwardly upon his own social background, leaving no society safe from his satirizing gaze. It takes place on the road between cultures; though influenced by Laurence Sterne and François Rabelais, it takes equal interest in the wandering scholars of the classical Arabic tradition, such as Badīʿ al-Zamān al-Hamadhānī (d. 398/1008), who—like the Fāriyāq—traveled in search of literary patronage. Though nominally Christian at the time of its publication (he added "Aḥmad" several years later), he invokes Islamic motifs and values that seem to identify him ambivalently as already Muslim.[59] And though avowedly a work devoted to linguistic preservation—and indeed taking antiquarian delight in stringing together lists of rare words and in lampooning authors and orators for using incorrect language—he also claims to eschew the dominant rhetorical tendencies of the preceding centuries that produced texts "marinated in the spices of paronomasia and morphological parallelism, of metaphor and metonymy" (1.1.11).

This final contradiction helps to describe the work's complex prose style. *Leg over Leg* contains many elaborate displays of linguistic erudition—in the form of its lists of synonyms but also his repeated demonstrations of rhetorical and generic mastery. Al-Shidyāq intersperses his narrative with original verse compositions and sections in rhymed prose (*sajʿ*), as well as the four *maqāmāt* he includes, along with other more occasional usages. These passages, combined with his quotations and intertextual references to poets and linguistic scholars, give the reader a full sense of his scholarly abilities and qualifications—he makes clear that he could hold his own with the literary masters of his time. In this sense, we can see *Leg over Leg* as "a last glance at a fading language," in which the author is conscious of "the precarious state written classical Arabic reached under the growing impact of European languages and local attempts at reforming the Arab language in the Ottoman world."[60] One cannot help but wonder, however, if this final glance did not contain a glint of irony. In the opening pages, as the reader will see, he preserves classical erudition by recalling over 250 synonyms and euphemisms for "penis," "vagina," and "sexual intercourse." He may have aimed to unseat literary authority even as he claimed it for himself.

In other sections, he renders events in clear and direct language that can approach the style of present-day Arabic novels. He even, on rare occasions, writes in colloquial Arabic—an act that remains controversial even today. For many scholars, the shifting of registers between formal and informal Arabic and between ornate and simple styles, marks *Leg over Leg* as a text produced during the transition to modernity and is one of the sources of the notorious difficulty in categorizing the work. While its title seems to present it as a travelogue, and its story follows the author's real-life travels, its characters and events are abstracted and stylized, with rhetorical acrobatics often seeming to take precedence over attempts at ethnographic verisimilitude. Long philosophical and literary digressions frequently interrupt the plot, so that the narrative often takes on the form of a miscellany. As the narrator admits, "I committed myself to writing a book that would be a repository for every idea that appealed to me, relevant or irrelevant, for it seemed to me that what was irrelevant to me might be relevant to someone else, and vice versa" (1.10.6).

Despite this hint at formlessness, the author's preface gives two possible generic possibilities: to "give prominence to the oddities of the language, including its rare words" (0.2.1) and to "discuss the praiseworthy and blameworthy qualities of women" (0.2.12). Yet no study exists that treats the work as either a linguistic treatise or a sociology of gender. Instead, scholars have categorized it as belonging to a variety of literary genres. Luwīs ʿAwaḍ and Shawqī Ḍayf, for example, classify it as a *maqāmah* or neo-*maqāmah*, Radwa ʿAshour as a novel ("the first and most important Arabic novel"), Matityahu Peled as Menippean, and Paul Starkey as fictional autobiography or a "voyage of self-definition."[61] For Nadia Al-Bagdadi, the work transcends categorization: she argues that it should be understood both as a novel and as "a unique literary expression of its time," or "a genre of its own."[62] Al-Shidyāq might have agreed with this characterization. As he warns in his prefatory poem, his art is "an orphan" and "unique"; "so be well disposed toward it," he begs his reader (0.4.5). In this verse description (and anticipatory list of complaints) of *Leg over Leg*, he identifies what might be the central difficulty in characterizing it: it appears as if he "pieced it together and cobbled it up by hand" (0.4.2). It might not be categorizable because it is pieced together from many genres and literary modes, as it contains passages in verse (*madīḥ*, *hijāʾ*, *ghazal*, *rithāʾ*), prose (with passages that imitate or make reference to historical writing, sermons, aphorisms, ethnographic writing, linguistic studies, and philosophical critiques), and prosody (it includes four original *maqāmāt*, as well as other passages written in rhyming prose, or *sajʿ*). Alongside these Arabic exemplars, he includes sections translated from European authors, such as the travel narratives of Chateaubriand and Lamartine, and original passages written in "the Frankish way"

(1.7.5). And he intersperses in these lists (many quoted, as Humphrey Davies notes in his Afterword, from *Al-Qāmūs*), anecdotes, and typographical jokes which punctuate the text.

In cobbling together this multigeneric work, he renders no mode privileged over any other. Instead, he incorporates all into his narrative archive, to praise and discredit equally. As a result, there is no stable position of narrative authority in *Leg over Leg*, a fact perhaps announced by the work's title itself. In a text abounding in sexual puns and innuendos, "leg over leg" could refer to an intimate union of limbs or the detached posture of an armchair academic. Moreover, this single phrase signals the linguistic and structural play built into all aspects of the work: "*al-sāq ʿalā l-sāq*" also appears within the text in a list of the conventional topoi of courtship narratives, which interrupts the very courtship story that the narrator is trying to tell:

> It is the custom of my fellow writers sometimes to go back and leap over a period of time and connect an event that happened before it to an event that happened after it. This is called analepsis (*tawriyah*), that is, "taking backward (*warāʾ*)." They also may start by mentioning everything about the protagonist, from his first whisperings into his beloved's ear until his reappearance as a married man. In the course of this, the author will relate such long and tedious matters as how his face paled and his pulse raced when he met her, how he was reduced to a tizzy and felt ill while he waited for her answer, how he sent her an old woman or a missive, how he met with her at such and such a time and place, and how she changed color when he spoke to her of the bed, of drawing her close, of embracing, of *leg over leg*, of kissing, of kissing tongue to tongue, of intercourse, and the like. (3.4.1)

The "and the like" that mockingly ends this list opens it up to parodic criticism, gesturing simultaneously toward infinite substitutability on the one hand and the impossibility of precise equivalence on the other—signaling both the mechanisms and limits of representation that will be explored throughout the text (which reaches the absurd in the secondary reading of the title, "The Turtle in the Tree"). Thus al-Shidyāq, in his display of mastery over these genres, also leads the reader through a series of generic parodies, anatomizing literary forms—interrupting his *maqāmah* to talk about the limitations of *saj*ʿ (likening it to walking with a wooden leg), interrupting his protagonist's poetry with literary-critical commentary, or (as above) disrupting the narrative episodes to discuss the conventions of the narrative discourse.

Furthermore, these interruptions, digressions, and lists create an endless leg after leg of narrative, where text seems to generate only more text. This itself points to the work's operative hermeneutic mode: it is contiguity, not equivalence, that serves as the driving force behind meaning. It is by the juxtaposition of events, characters, and even adjectives that the plot, as nonlinear as it is, moves forward (or sideways, which is often the case). Al-Shidyāq even goes so far as to reject explicitly the very notion of equivalence, in the form of synonymity, in its opening pages. He writes:

> In addition, I have imposed on the reader the condition that he not skip any of the "synonymous" words in this book of mine, many though they be (for it may happen that, on a single road, a herd of fifty words, all with the same meaning, or with two meanings that are close, may pass him by). If he cannot commit to this, I cannot permit him to peruse it and will not offer him my congratulations if he does so. I have to admit that I cannot support the idea that all "synonyms" have the same meaning, or they would have called them "equi-nyms." (1.1.7)

As al-Shidyāq points out here, the Arabic root for "synonym," *r-d-f*, does not necessarily connote equivalence. The verbs derived from it can mean to pile up in layers, to become stratified, to flock, to throng, to form a single line, or to follow one after another. Or, to put one foot after another, follow leg upon leg, as another reading of *al-sāq ʿalā l-sāq* allows.[63] Thus does *Leg over Leg*, in its very title, "lay bare the device," as Victor Shklovsky wrote of *Tristram Shandy*.[64]

*Leg over Leg*, then, might be more precisely characterized as meta-generic—as al-Shidyāq seems to comment *on* genre more often than he writes *in* a generic mode. Yet his interruptions of literary convention are not only a commentary on style; they are also the foundation of his larger social and political critiques. The linguistic authority that al-Shidyāq undermines is always tied to political authority: he lampoons emirs for their misguided over-confidence in grammatical studies, satirizes Maronite priests for their hypocritical lack of scholarly goals—when staying at a monastery and in need of a dictionary to compose poetry, he inquires after a copy of the *Qāmūs*, Muḥammad ibn Yaʿqūb Fīrūzābādī's lexicon, and is given answers about *jāmūs* and *kābūs*, or buffaloes and nightmares—ridicules Protestant missionaries for their inability to communicate with their congregations in their native language, and criticizes Orientalist scholars for their errors in translation (he devotes an entire appendix to correcting the errors found in the works of the French scholars he came into contact with in Paris). Yet his attacks on ecclesiastical authority should not be seen solely in light of his well-known disagreements and injuries. His position against ecclesiastical authority is more than a reaction to his brother's treatment in Lebanon, just as his critiques of Orientalist scholarship are more than simply a reaction to his reported failure to find an academic post in Europe.[65] Both are part of a sustained critique of institutionalized interpretations of sacred texts, canonical works of literature, and even social conventions—and especially of any person who blindly accepts them. Instead, al-Shidyāq subtly suggests skepticism—based on individual perception and self-improving study—as the guiding principle for spiritual enlightenment, political leadership, judicial decisions, and moral principles, as well as for scholarly research. Or, as his narrator tells us early on: "Observe, then, how people differ with regard to a single word and a single meaning!" (1.2.7) The linguistic indeterminacy that reigns in *Leg over Leg*—with simple definitions of words seeming to collapse under the weight of his lists of subtly differentiated synonyms—does not establish him as the ultimate linguistic authority as much as it shows that language itself is the key to dissidence. It is not a coincidence, in this sense, that his protagonist's name also means "he who distinguishes."

It might not be possible to tease a coherent political doctrine from his work, but al-Shidyāq expressed in his writings values that today would be associated with liberalism. He repeatedly advocated a separation of religious and political life and a respect for "personal freedoms" (so long as they are in the interest of society). Both in his travels and in his observations on life within the Ottoman Empire, he called attention to the need to improve working conditions for farmers and workers, approaching (but never wholly identifying with) some of the socialist ideas being debated in Europe during his sojourn there, chief among them the responsibility of the ruling classes toward the poor and the importance of equality under the law.[66] His promotion of the value of equality, in fact, might be considered among his most radical, as he advocated for it not only among religious sects and social classes but also between genders. In *Leg over Leg* and elsewhere he promotes absolute equality between men and women, advocating—nearly fifty years before Qāsim Amīn's *The Liberation of Women* (1899)—for the right of women to be educated. (As he explains in *Al-Jawā'ib*, "knowledge and education are the light of the mind . . . and if you cannot entrust this light to woman, then you cannot trust her with any light whatsoever, for fear that she might use it to burn down the house.")[67] Unlike many of his contemporary reformers, however, he did not write of an idealized woman whose education was in the service of a better performance of her domestic duties or the education of a new generation of children. As he writes in *Leg over Leg*, if one reads him in order to hear about women "possessing peculiar skills in terms of the excellent management of such household tasks as sewing, embroidery, and the like, these are mentioned in many a book and you'll have to look them up yourselves" (2.16.72). In his book, women appear not as angels of the house but as full and equal participants in society who have a right to work as well as stay at home. "There can be no *Nahḍah* in the East," al-Shidyāq is reported to have said, "without a *Nahḍah* of women."[68]

In *Leg over Leg*, written, as he claims, with so much interest in women and sympathy for them that one might believe his protagonist had been transformed into one, his interest in women's equality is centered less on female education than on female emotional and sexual fulfillment. Through conversations with the protagonist's wife, the Fāriyāqiyyah, al-Shidyāq decries sexual double standards, advocating for the right of women to choose their own husbands, to divorce, and to demand sexual pleasure (see Volume Three). These conversations reveal her as a witty social satirist in her own right, or, as al-Shidyāq writes in the preface, one who "argues with theorist and practitioner alike and provides excellent critiques of the political issues and conditions, mundane and spiritual, of the countries she has seen" (0.2.12). Rastegar argues for reading "the Fāriyāqiyyah" not as a name—if it were a feminization of Fāriyāq, it would be Fāriyāqah, as he points out—but as "Fāriyāq-ness," rendered in the feminine form.[69] She might thus be thought of not as a stand-in for a historical personage (al-Shidyāq's wife, Wardah al-Ṣūlī) but as a second apparition of the self. Writing not simply *about* women but *as if a woman*, al-Shidyāq uses gender as another permutation of his thought-experiment in radical difference and belonging. And he reveals that above all, it is an experiment in subjectivity—which does not result in a definition of the self or of something one might call the modern Arab subject, but examines "the ways the self cannot be accommodated by social frameworks the world around."[70] The self, in *Leg over Leg*, seems always to exceed its narrative frame and multiply. As if to see himself from the inside and out, he appears as the author on the title page ("Fāris al-Shidyāq") and as his textual doubles: the unnamed narrator (who narrates in the first person), the Fāriyāq, the Fāriyāqiyyah, and the interpolated narrator of the four *maqāmāt* that appear in the work.

But even the lisping narrator of these *maqāmāt,* "al-Hāwif ibn Hifām," has his own textual doubles, in the form of the narrators of the most famous series of *maqāmāt,* ʿĪsā ibn *Hishām* and *al-Ḥārith* ibn Hammām. Indeed, as Humphrey Davies points out, the name in its "lisped" form is no name at all but may be translated as "Masher, son of Pulverizer." At every turn, al-Shidyāq does violence to the very presumption of verisimilitude; word and thing never correspond neatly, even in the attempt simply to name a character. Instead, he holds up art and artifice as the substance that underlies the world and even constitutes it. To navigate it, one must travel not only through space but through texts; when one reads *Leg over Leg* one also reads those innumerable authors he quotes or invokes, like the authors of the *maqāmāt,* al-Hamadhānī and al-Ḥarīrī ("men who have rendered their reputations white by covering pages in black," 1.1.1), or the English and French authors whom he quotes. It is no wonder that the text begins with eleven synonyms for the command, "be quiet!" (1.1.1), as al-Shidyāq attempts to speak alongside, and often over, the voices that crowd the text.

This multi-register and multi-lingual cacophony sets the stage for many of the travel narrative's comic scenes, where intercultural encounters are not always entirely fungible. As in *Tristram Shandy,* its closest English analogue, communication more often leads to misunderstanding and misinterpretation than to understanding. The result can hardly be used as a guide for East–West relations but instead parodies intercultural communication and its institutional forms—chief among them Orientalist scholarship. If this period's literature was partly looking to the West, what it saw was the West looking at it. Perhaps, then, there was no other way to write about that encounter than as a self-reflexive one. It looks to the West as a way to reflect on itself, not to imitate it but to critique and reformulate it. If we see *Leg over Leg* as an archive of Arabic literary modernity, we must take this double refraction into account.

What al-Shidyāq ultimately gives us in *Leg over Leg* is a theory of world literature—from a particular, *Nahḍawī* perspective. It imagines and constructs the world anew, through an omnivorous textuality, absorbing texts and literary forms through juxtaposition, quotation, imitation, and parody. Far from holding up Sterne or Lamartine as culturally distinct and inviolable paradigms, he incorporates them into Arabic literary categories, aligning *Tristram Shandy* with the *maqāmāt*. Rather than a choice between the two, or a straight line of filiation connecting them, literary history in al-Shidyāq appears as a winding one—modernity is staged on the road and does not always appear in the guise of "progress" (to use the language of modernity's evil twin, modernization). It sometimes appears to move sideways, to digress.

As an alternative translation of the work's subtitle allows, al-Faryāq's travels track the *ʿujm*, or mistakes, of the Arabs and "non-Arabs" (*al-ʾaʿjām* can also be translated as "barbarians," or those whose speech is unintelligible to Arabic-speakers). Traveling along linguistic boundaries, al-Shidyāq pieces together an unruly patchwork of a text whose unity is in danger of disintegration, threatening to dissolve into mere *ʿujmah*, or "babble." *Leg over Leg* thus creates a literary sphere that reminds us that the "world" in world literature is not a given; it must be manufactured. It is not merely "there" to be observed but is itself a dynamic constitutive process. It creates trouble—generic and otherwise—and it is always in danger of collapse. That is, world literature during the *Nahḍah* age is constructed out of the migrations and cross-fertilizations that define the era. Or, as the Fāriyāq reminds us, it was produced in the time of steamboats and railways, of "connecting the disconnected."

Rebecca C. Johnson
*Northwestern University*

# Notes to the Frontmatter

Al-Shidyāq's biographers differ as to the date of his birth, with dates ranging from 1801 to 1805. We have used Geoffrey Roper's calculations, based on al-Shidyāq's British naturalization record submitted September 26, 1851, which lists his age as 45. Public Record Office, Home Office Papers—Naturalisation, 1278A, 26.9.1851.

1 Nadia Al-Bagdadi, "The Cultural Function of Fiction: From the Bible to Libertine Literature. Historical Criticism and Social Critique in Aḥmad Fāris al-Šidyāq," *Arabica,* 46, no. 3 (1999): 377.

2 ʿAzīz al-ʿAẓmah and Fawwāz Ṭarābulsī, *Aḥmad Fāris al-Shidyāq: Silsilat al-aʿmāl al-majhūlah* (London: Riad El-Rayyes Books, 1995).

3 See Ibrahim Abu-Lughod, *The Arab Rediscovery of Europe: A Study in Cultural Encounters* (Princeton: Princeton University Press, 1963).

4 Examples of this opinion abound; see, for example, M. M. Badawi, *A Critical Introduction to Modern Arabic Poetry* (Cambridge: Cambridge University Press, 1975), 25.

5 Samah Selim, *The Novel and the Rural Imaginary in Egypt, 1880–1985* (New York: Routledge, 2004), 90.

6 Timothy Mitchell, "The Stage of Modernity," in *Questions of Modernity,* edited by Timothy Mitchell (Minneapolis: University of Minnesota Press, 2000), 24; see also Stephen Sheehi, *Foundations of Modern Arab Identity* (Gainesville: University of Florida Press, 2004).

7 The following biographical information is taken largely from M. B. Alwan, "Aḥmad Fāris ash-Shidyāq and the West" (PhD diss., University of Indiana, 1970) and Geoffrey Roper, "Arabic Printing in Malta 1825–1845: Its History and Its Place in the Development of Print

Culture in the Arab Middle East," supplemented by archival research in the CMS Archives in Birmingham, UK.

8 See, e.g., Muḥammad al-Hādī al-Maṭwī, *Aḥmad Fāris al-Shidyāq, 1801–1887: Ḥayātuhu wa-āthāruhu wa-ārā'uhu fī l-nahḍah al-ʿarabiyyah al-ḥadīthah*, 2 vols. (Beirut: Dār al-Gharb al-Islāmī, 1989) and ʿImād al-Ṣulḥ, *Aḥmad Fāris al-Shidyāq: Āthāruhu wa-ʿaṣruhu* (Beirut: Sharikat al-Maṭbūʿāt li-l-Tawzīʿ wa-l-Nashr, 1987).

9 Ussama Makdisi, *Artillery of Heaven: American Missionaries and the Failed Conversion of the Middle East* (Ithaca: Cornell University Press, 2008), 114. For a complete account of the Asʿad al-Shidyāq affair, see Makdisi, 103–37, Buṭrus al-Bustānī, *Qiṣṣat Asʿad al-Shidyāq* (1860; Beirut: Dār al-Ḥamrā', 1992) and Isaac Bird, *The Martyr of Lebanon* (Boston: American Tract Society, 1864).

10 Makdisi, *Artillery of Heaven*, 127.

11 Bird, *Martyr of Lebanon*, 145.

12 Jurjī Zaydān, *Tārīkh ādāb al-lugha al-ʿarabiyyah*, vol. 16 of *Mu'allaffāt Jurjī Zaydān al-Kāmilah* (Beirut: Dār al-Jīl, 1982), 222. Originally published in 1911–13 by Maṭbaʿat al-Hilāl.

13 Christopher Schlienz, letter to Society Secretary, 18 May 1827, Church Missionary Society Archives CMS/CMO 65/1, University of Birmingham Special Collections.

14 The matter of al-Shidyāq's two conversions is difficult to settle using archival sources. Though Theodor Müller writes that he has received a "confession of belief with which [he] was satisfied" from al-Shidyāq in 1832, his colleague, William Krusé, writes three years later that, in his opinion, "Fares . . . is not yet converted." Theodor Müller to Christopher Schlienz, April 2, 1832, Church Missionary Society Archives CMS/CMO/65/20; William Krusé to Lay Secretary, January 25, 1835, Church Missionary Society Archives CMS/CMM 5/39. For references to the Fāriyāq's beliefs, see 1.19.4 and 1.19.5: "[H]e concluded that, in view of his said perseverance and mild manners, the Bag-man must be following the right path and that the metropolitan, with his vehemence and eagerness to do evil, must be among the misguided. (1.19.4) So he said to the Bag-man, 'Sir, I have heeded everything with which

you've filled my ears and believe the truth to lie with you alone. I am your partisan, your follower, and the co-carrier of your bag.'" (1.19.5)

15 Daniel Temple to William Jowett, July 25, 1828, Church Missionary Society Archives CMS/CMO/ 39/121; emphasis Temple's.

16 Christopher Schlienz to Society Secretary, February 3, 1836, Church Missionary Archives CMO/65/44A; Christopher Schlienz to William Jowett, May 20, 1828, Church Missionary Society Archives CMO/65/4A.

17 Aḥmad Fāris al-Shidyāq, *Al-Wāsiṭah fī maʿrifat aḥwāl Mālṭa* (Beirut: al-Mu'assasah al-ʿArabiyyah li-l-Dirāsāt wa-l-Nashr, 2004), chap. 2.

18 Theodor Müller to Christopher Schlienz, June 15, 1830, Church Missionary Society Archives CMS/CMO 73/47.

19 Buṭrus Yūsuf Ḥawwā: one of a group of Lebanese merchants living in London, on whom al-Shidyāq depended for financial and moral support during his third sojourn there, between June 1853 and the summer of 1857, during which period he was also visiting Paris to oversee the printing of *Al-Sāq*; Ḥawwā provided al-Shidyāq with employment as a clerk in his offices.

20 See Geoffrey Roper, "Aḥmad Fāris al-Shidyāq and the Libraries of Europe and the Ottoman Empire," *Libraries & Culture* 33, no. 3 (Summer 1998), 235. For the names of the scholars with whom al-Shidyāq made contact, see Alwan, 42–45.

21 Aḥmad Fāris al-Shidyāq, *Mumāḥakāt al-ta'wīl fī munāqiḍāt al-injīl* [*Altercations of Interpretation: On Contradictions in the Gospels*] (Amman: Dār Wā'il li-l-Nashr wa-Tawzīʿ, 2003). For a discussion of its contents and technique, see Al-Bagdadi, 375–401.

22 There is no empirical evidence for the exact date or place of his conversion, which might also have occurred while he was in Tunis, Paris, or London. Al-Shidyāq, in fact, began an intellectual relationship with Islamic scholars while in Egypt and continued to pursue, in the libraries of Cambridge and London, his interest in linguistic and literary texts produced during Islam's golden age. And, as Humphrey Davies notes in the translator's Afterword, his invocation of Islamic motifs in *Leg over Leg* might indicate that he converted before its

1855 publication—as he deploys specifically Islamic formulae on more than one occasion, even going so far as to say, regarding a Christian woman, that "she had converted to Islam, praise be to God, Lord of the Worlds" (2.4.16). For more on al-Shidyāq's textual studies in England see Roper, "Aḥmad Fāris al-Shidyāq and the Libraries of Europe and the Ottoman Empire," 236–41.

23 Ami Ayalon, *The Press in the Arab Middle East: A History* (Oxford: Oxford University Press, 1995), 30.

24 Ayalon, 30.

25 Geoffrey Roper, "Fāris al-Shidyāq and the Transition from Scribal to Print Culture," in *The Book in the Islamic World: The Written Word and Communication in the Middle East*, edited by George N. Atiyeh (Albany: State University of New York Press, 1995), 214.

26 Al-Shidyāq, *Al-Wāsiṭah*, 382. Cited in Roper, "Scribal to Print Culture," 214.

27 Jurjī Zaydān, *Tarājim mashāhīr al-Sharq fī l-qarn al-tāsiʿ ashar* (Cairo: Maṭbaʿat al-Hilāl, 1922), 2:87.

28 Walid Hamarneh, "Ahmad Fāris al-Shidyāq," *Essays in Arabic Literary Biography: 1850–1950*, edited by Roger Allen (Wiesbaden: Otto Harrassowitz, 2010), 327.

29 Kamran Rastegar, *Literary Modernity between the Middle East and Europe: Textual Transactions in Nineteenth-century Arabic, English, and Persian Literatures* (New York: Routledge, 2007), 109.

30 Sabry Hafez, *Genesis of Arabic Narrative Discourse: A Study in the Sociology of Modern Arabic Literature* (London: Saqi Books, 1993), 47.

31 The *maqāmah* (plural *maqāmāt*), or "session," is a genre popularized by Aḥmad Badīʿ al-Zamān al-Hamadhānī in the fourth/tenth century. Considered the first avowedly fictional literary genre in Arabic, al-Hamadhānī's *maqāmāt* narrated, in rhyming prose, the adventures of Abū l-Fatḥ al-Iskandarī, a vagabond trickster figure who earns his living by outwitting his companions with his verbal dexterity. For an introduction to the *maqāmāt*, see Abdelfattah Kilito, *Les séances* (Paris: Sindbad, 1983).

32 These include a commentary on al-Fīrūzābādī's *Al-Qāmūs*, entitled *Al-Jāsūs ʿalā l-Qāmūs* (Istanbul: al-Jawāʾib, 1882), an edition (with introduction) to Ibn al-Manẓūr's fourteenth-century lexicon, *Lisān al-ʿArab*, 20 vols. (Cairo: Bulāq, 1883–9), and a lost commentary on classical Arabic poetry, *Malḥūẓāt ʿalā l-shiʿr al-ʿarabī*. For a complete bibliography of the works of al-Shidyāq, see al-ʿAẓmah and Ṭarābulsī, 408–40.

33 Robert Brunschvig, *Classicisme et déclin culturel dans l'histoire de l'Islam: Actes du symposium international d'histoire de la civilisation musulmane, Bordeaux 25–29 juin 1956*, organized by R. Brunschvig and G. E. Von Grunebaum (Paris: Chantemerle, 1957), 284; cited in Nada Tomiche, "Nahḍah," in *Encyclopaedia of Islam*, edited by P. Bearman et al., 2nd ed. (Leiden: E. J. Brill, 2008), 7:900.

34 Samah Selim, "The People's Entertainments: Translation, Popular Fiction, and the Nahdah in Egypt," in *Other Renaissances: A New Approach to World Literature*, edited by Brenda Deen Schildgen et al. (New York: Palgrave Macmillan, 2006), 38.

35 See Rastegar, *Literary Modernity*, and the essays in "The Novelization of Islamic Literatures: The Intersections of Western, Arabic, Persian, Urdu, and Turkish Traditions," a special issue of *Comparative Critical Studies*, 4, no. 3 (2007), guest editor Mohamed Salah Omri.

36 Samah Selim, "The Nahda, Popular Fiction, and the Politics of Translation," *MIT Electronic Journal of Middle East Studies* 4 (Fall 2004): 71.

37 Henry Harris Jessup, *Fifty-three Years in Syria* (New York: Fleming H. Revell, 1910), 2:713.

38 Roger Owen, *The Middle East in the World Economy, 1800–1914* (London: Methuen, 1981), 116.

39 Akram Fouad Khater, *Inventing Home: Emigration, Gender, and the Middle Class in Lebanon, 1870–1920* (Berkeley: University of California Press, 2001), 22–29.

40 Owen, *Middle East in the World Economy*, 160.

41 Roger Owen, "Egypt and Europe: From French Expedition to British Occupation," in *The Modern Middle East*, edited by Albert Hourani et al., 2nd ed. (London: I. B. Tauris, 2005), 117, and Fritz Steppat,

"National Education Projects in Egypt before the British Occupation," in *Beginnings of Modernization in the Middle East: The Nineteenth Century*, edited by William R. Polk and Richard L. Chambers (Chicago: University of Chicago Press, 1968), 283–4.

42 See Nabil Matar, *Europe through Arab Eyes, 1578–1727* (New York: Columbia University Press, 2009), Nabil Matar (ed.), *In the Lands of the Christians: Arabic Travel Writing in the Seventeenth Century, First English Translations* (New York: Routledge, 2003), and Roxanne L. Euben, *Journeys to the Other Shore: Muslim and Western Travelers in Search of Knowledge* (Princeton: Princeton University Press, 2006).

43 On these early educational missions, see Ibrahim Abu-Lughod, *The Arab Rediscovery of Europe* (Princeton: Princeton University Press, 1963), Alain Silvera, "The First Egyptian Student Mission to France under Muhammad Ali," *Middle Eastern Studies*, 16, no. 2 (May 1980): 1–22, and Lisa Pollard, "The Habits and Customs of Modernity: Egyptians in Europe and the Geography of Nineteenth-Century Nationalism," *The Arab Studies Journal*, 7–8, no. 2/1 (1999/2000): 52–74.

44 Headed by Rifāʿa Rāfiʿ al-Ṭahṭāwī, the scholar selected to accompany the first *Mission égyptienne* to Paris in 1824, Muḥammad ʿAlī opened the School of Languages [Kulliyat al-Alsān] in Cairo in 1837 in order to centralize these translation efforts that were earlier performed out of individual schools and institutes. (Al-Ṭahṭāwī himself had worked as a translator out of the School of Medicine and the Artillery School.) While the purview of the school was by no means strictly literary—they published more than 2,000 scholarly and scientific books—al-Ṭahṭāwī himself is commonly considered the initiator of what became known as the "Translation Movement" of Arabic literature (*ḥarakat al-tarjamah*) with his 1867 translation of François Fénelon's *Aventures de Télémaque*.

45 John Heyworth-Dunne, "Printing and Translations under Muhammad Ali of Egypt: The Foundation of Modern Arabic," *Journal of the Royal Asiatic Society*, no. 3 (1940): 332.

46 Heyworth-Dunne, 332; see also Ayalon, 565.

47 These presses were international also in their day-to-day operations, with translators sometimes working with the European authors (who were employed in government schools, for example) to produce Arabic versions of textbooks; Heyworth-Dunne, 346.

48 Ayalon, 561.

49 Elisabeth Kendall, "Between Politics and Literature: Journals in Alexandria and Istanbul at the End of the Nineteenth Century," in *Modernity and Culture: From the Mediterranean to the Indian Ocean*, edited by Leila Tarazi Fawaz, Christopher Alan Bayly, and Robert Ilbert (New York: Columbia University Press, 2002), 332.

50 Kendall, 350.

51 See for example Stephen Sheehi, "Arabic Literary-scientific Journals: Precedence for Globalization and the Creation of Modernity," *Comparative Studies of South Asia, Africa, and the Middle East,* 25, no. 2 (2005).

52 Charles Montagu Doughty, *Travels in Arabia Deserta* (Cambridge: Cambridge University Press, 1888), 2:371.

53 In an article entitled "Al-Jarā'id al-ʿarabiyyah fī Amrīkā" ("Arabic Periodicals in America"), appearing in Ibrāhīm al-Yāzijī's journal *al-Ḍiyā',* for example, the author refers to Arab writers in the United States as part of a worldwide *Nahḍah*: "Al-Jarā'id al-ʿarabiyyah fī Amrīkā," *Al-Ḍiyā': Majallah ʿilmiyyah adabiyyah ṣiḥḥiyyah ṣināʿiyyah* 16 (Cairo, April 30, 1899): 502.

54 As Lital Levy puts it, *Nahḍah* authors "viewed themselves as local agents of this global process" of historical change; Lital Levy, "Jewish Writers in the Arab East: Literature, History, and the Politics of Enlightenment, 1863–1914" (PhD diss., University of California Berkeley, 2007), 23.

55 Both of these are titles of articles in Buṭrus and Salīm al-Bustānī's biweekly *Al-Jinān* (Beirut, 1870), 1:160–4.

56 Shaden Tageldin, *Disarming Words: Empire and the Seductions of Translation in Egypt* (Berkeley: University of California Press, 2011), 5.

57 This description is not exclusive to Arab modernity. As the essays in Timothy Mitchell's *Questions of Modernity* make clear, modernity in

Western and non-Western contexts alike "had its origins in reticulations of exchange and production encircling the world," making it "a creation not of the West but of an interaction between West and non-West;" Mitchell, "The Stage of Modernity," 2.

58 For an example, see the translator's Afterword in Volume Four, and Rastegar, 113–25.

59 Al-Bagdadi, 392.

60 Luwīs ʿAwaḍ, *Al-Muʾaththirāt al-ajnabiyya fī l-adab al-ʿarabī al-ḥadīth* (Cairo: 1962), 28, and Shawqī Ḍayf, *Al-Matāmāt* (Cairo: 1964), both cited in Mattityahu Peled, "Al-Sāq ʿalā al-Sāq: A Generic Definition," *Arabica* 32, no. 1 (March 1985): 35; Raḍwah ʿĀshūr, *Al-Ḥadātha al-mumkina: Al-Shidyāq wa-l-Sāq ʿalā l-sāq, al-riwāyah al-ūlā fī l-adab al-ʿarabī al-ḥadīth* (Cairo: Dār al-Shurūq, 2009), 10; Paul Starkey, "Voyages of Self-definition: The Case of [Ahmad] Faris al-Shidyāq," in *Sensibilities of the Islamic Mediterranean: Self-Expression in a Muslim Culture from Post-Classical Times to the Present Day*, edited by Robin Ostle (London: I. B. Tauris, 2008), 118–32.

61 Al-Bagdadi, 394–95.

62 Lexically, the adverbial phrase *sāqan ʿalā l-sāq* is also a figurative way of saying "one after another"—which is fitting for the text's self-conscious attention to narrative sequence. Lane gives the example, "So-and-So had three children one after the other [*sāqan ʿalā l-sāq*]." Edward Lane, *Arabic-English Lexicon* (Beirut: Librairie du Liban, 1968), 4:1472.

63 Viktor Shklovsky, *Theory of Prose*, translated by Benjamin Sher (Normal IL: Dalkey Archive Press, 1991), 147.

64 For a reading of *Leg over Leg* in the context of al-Shidyāq's intellectual challenge to ecclesiastical authority, see Al-Bagdadi, 391–401.

65 See al-Ṣulḥ, 109.

66 Aḥmad Fāris al-Shidyāq, in *Kanz al-raghāʾib fī muntakhabāt al-Jawāʾib*, edited by Salīm Fāris (Istanbul: Maṭbaʿat al-Jawāʾib, 1288–98/1871–81), cited in al-Ṣulḥ, 215.

67 ʿAẓmah and Ṭarābulsī, 34.

68 Rastegar, 104–5.

69 Rastegar, 104–5.

# Leg over Leg

OR

# The Turtle in the Tree

CONCERNING

# The Fāriyāq

*What Manner of Creature Might He Be*

OTHERWISE ENTITLED

# Days, Months, and Years

SPENT IN

# Critical Examination

OF

# The Arabs

AND

# Their Non-Arab Peers

BY

*The Humble Dependent on His Lord the Provider*

Fāris ibn Yūsuf al-Shidyāq

The writings of Zayd and Hind these days speak more to the common taste
Than any pair of weighty tomes.
More profitable and useful than the teachings of two scholars
Are what a yoke of oxen from the threshings combs.

## Contents of the Book

# The Dedication of This Elegantly Eloquent Book

*Praise Be to God*

It being the custom of Frankish authors to dedicate their works to those distinguished in their day by virtues and praiseworthy qualities and of whom great achievements are reported regarding the patronage of scholarship and its servants, I have decided here to follow their example by dedicating this elegantly eloquent book to the esteemed and honorable Khawājā Buṭrus Yūsuf Ḥawwā,[1] of London, for he is well known in this age of ours for all the commendable merits with which the eulogist adorns his songs and the author his words, while he is now also head of that house[2] so long celebrated for its pedigree, pride, and elevated status. Many a time has he assisted in the attainment of virtuous qualities and provided those of his race, and others, with the means to obtain their highest hopes and realize their most distant goals, so that they leave him uttering *praise*, grateful to him for his generous *ways*. Moreover, albeit his standing exceeds what little may be contained in *summary* form in this book, it is nevertheless fitting that the latter be dedicated to him in *sum*. We ask that he accept it, take it under his wing, promote it, and grant it his approval, for whatever is unworthy regains, through appurtenance to him, its worth, and all that is incomplete is made whole. 0.1

From Fāris al-Shidyāq
Who Prays for His Honorable Person

# Author's Notice

0.2.1 Praise be to God, who each happy thought *inspires*, and to guide man to righteous acts *conspires*. To proceed: everything that I have set down in this book is determined by one of two concerns. The first of these is to give prominence to the oddities of the language, including its rare words.[3]

0.2.2 Under the category of oddities fall words that are similar in meaning and words that are similar in lexical association. Here I have included the most celebrated, important, and necessary items that need to be known, and in elegantly eloquent form, for, had they been set out in the style typical of our books on language, divorced from any context, the effect would have been wearisome. I have also taken care on some occasions to present them in alphabetical order and on others to arrange them in paragraphs of rhymed prose and morphologically parallel expressions.[4]

0.2.3 Another consists of substitution and swapping,[5] as in *tu'rūr*, *thu'rūr*, *tu'thūr*, and *turtūr* ("police officer or his assistant"),[6] or *tamaṭṭā*, *tamattā*, *tamaṭṭaṭ*, and *tamaddad* ("to stretch"). Another is the production of numerous words of similar sound and meaning from a single letter of the alphabet, such as *ghaṭash* ("going blind from hunger") and *ghamash* (ditto), and *bahz* ("shoving"), *baḥz* (ditto), *baghz* ("striking with the foot or a stick"), and *ḥafz* ("pushing from behind"), for it is to be noted that each letter is associated with a specific meaning distinct from that of every other letter—a peculiarity of the Arabic language of which few have taken note. I have written a book devoted to this topic entitled *Muntahā l-ʿajab fī khaṣāʾiṣ lughat al-ʿArab* (*Wonder's Apogee Concerning Every Arab Linguistic Particularity*).[7]

Thus, among the characteristic associations of the letter *ḥ*, for example, are amplitude and expansiveness, as in the words *ibtiḥaḥ* ("affluence and abundance"), *badāḥ* ("broad tract of land"), *barāḥ* ("broad uncultivated tract of land"), *abṭaḥ* ("wide watercourse"), *iblindāḥ* ("widening out (of a place)"), *jaḥḥ* ("leveling out (of a thing)"), *raḥraḥ* ("wide and spread out"), *murtadaḥ* ("scope, freedom"), *rawḥ* ("breeze"), *tarakkuḥ* ("spaciousness"), *tasṭīḥ* ("roof-laying"), *masfūḥ* ("spreading (of water)"), *masmaḥ* ("ample room") as in the saying "Keep thou to the truth, for in it is ample room, i.e., space,"[8] *sāḥah* ("courtyard"), *insiyāḥ* ("bigness of belly"), *shudḥah* ("roominess"), *sharḥ* ("laying open"), *ṣafīḥah* ("slab of stone"), *ṣaldaḥ* ("wide stone"), *iṣlinṭāḥ* ("widening out (of a valley)"), *muṣalfaḥ* ("large-headed"), *ṭaḥḥ* ("spreading"), *mufalṭaḥ* ("large-headed"), *fashḥ* ("standing astraddle"), *fatḥ* ("broadening"), *falṭaḥah* ("flattening"), and so on to the end of that rubric. To these may be added numerous words whose connection to the idea of amplitude and expansiveness is not obvious and can be detected only with careful scrutiny, such as *sujāḥ* ("air"), *tasrīḥ* ("divorce"), *samāḥah* ("generosity"), and *sunḥ* ("good fortune and blessing"). 0.2.4

Among characteristic associations of the letter *d* are softness, smoothness, and tenderness, as in the words *burakhdāh* ("a smooth, limp woman"), *tayd* ("kindness"), *thaʾad* ("soft, tender plants"), *thaʿd* ("soft dates"), *muthamʿidd* ("clear-faced (of a boy)"), *muthamghidd* ("fatty (of a kid)"), *thawhad* ("fat and well-formed (of an adolescent boy)"), *thahmad* ("large and fat"), *khabandāh* ("fat and full (of a woman)"), *khawd* ("young and well-formed (of a girl)"), *raʾdah* ("early matured due to good nourishment (of a girl)"), *rakhwaddah* ("soft (of a woman)"), *rahādah* ("softness and pliancy"), *ʿubrud* ("white and soft (of a girl)"), *furhud* ("plump and handsome (of an adolescent boy)"), *umlūd* ("soft and pliable"), *fulhūd* ("fat and comely (of a youth)"), *qurhud* ("smooth, fleshy, and soft"), *qishdah* ("clotted cream"), *maʾd* ("large and fat"), *murd* ("boys with downy 0.2.5

upper lips but no beards"), *maghd* ("smooth and fleshy"), *malad* ("youthfulness, softness, and wobbliness"), and so on to the end of the rubric. To these may be added, under the heading of figurative usages, such words as *raghd* ("generous and kindly"), *sarhadah* ("ease of living"), *majd* ("glory, generosity"), and so on.

0.2.6 It may be that the ancient Arabs sought to bring a balance to certain letters or, in other words, took care to give the opposite meaning full play too, for the letter *d* also encompasses many words indicating hardness, strength, and force, as in *ta'addud* ("harshness"), *ta'kīd* ("asserting"), *ta'yīd* ("confirming"), *jal'ad* ("hard and strong"), *jalmad* ("a rock"), *jamad* ("ice"), *ḥadīd* ("iron"), *suḥdud* ("strong and rebellious"), *sukhdūd* ("a man of iron"), *samhad* ("a thing hard and dry"), *tashaddud* ("harshness, severity"), *ṣafad* ("shackle"), *ṣald* ("hard and smooth"), *ṣalkhad* ("a tall, strong, aged camel"), *ṣimaghd* ("hard"), *'ajrad* ("thick and strong"), *ta'ajlud* ("to grow large and strong"), *'ard* ("erect, strong, and hard"), *'irbadd* ("strong"), *'arqadah* ("to twist tightly"), *'aṣlad* ("strong and hard"), *'aṭawwad* ("harsh and difficult"), *'aṭarrad* ("4harsh and difficult"), *'ald* ("hard and strong"), and so on.

0.2.7 Among the characteristic associations of the letter *m* are cutting, uprooting, and breaking, as in the words *arama* ("to seize and bite"), *azima* ("to bite hard using the whole of the mouth"), *tharima* ("to be gap-toothed"), *thalama* ("to nick or notch (a blade or the like)"), *jadhama* ("to chop off"), *jarama* ("to bone (meat)"), *jazama* ("to cut short"), *jalama* ("to clip"), *ḥadhama* ("to cut quickly"), *ḥadhlama* ("to sharpen to a point"), *ḥasama* ("to sever"), *ḥaṭama* ("to smash"), *ḥalqama* ("to cut the throat of (s.o.)"), *khadhama* ("to cut"), *kharama* ("to pierce"), *khazama* ("to thread (pearls)"), *khaḍama* ("to bite into (s.th.)"), and so on to the end of the rubric. To these may be added, under the heading of figurative usages, *ḥumma* meaning "it (a certain matter) was decreed," *ḥaruma* ("to be forbidden"), *ḥatama* ("to declare necessary") and *ḥazuma* ("to be resolute"), in all of which the sense of "cutting" is clearly observable. Also common in this letter are the meanings "darkness" and "blackness."

0.2.8 Among the characteristic associations of the letter *h* are stupidity, heedlessness, and *rathʾ*, or lack of native wit, examples being *aliha* ("to be perplexed"), *umiha* ("to become demented"), *baliha* ("to be stupid"), *būhah* ("a stupid, inconstant, and disordered man"), *tafiha* ("to become stupid"), *tawh* ("disturbance of the mind"), *dalh* ("being maddened by love"), *sabah* ("senile dementia"), *shudiha* ("to become amazed and confused") (a dialectal variant of *duhisha*, or formed from it by metathesis), *ʿutiha* ("to lose one's mind"), *ʿaliha* ("to become confused and amazed"), *ʿamiha* ("to hesitate as though lost and confused (in an argument or on a road)"), *namiha* ("to become somewhat confused"), and *wariha* ("to become stupid"). It is the same with the rest of the letters.

0.2.9 Another oddity of the language is that certain patterns are associated with a specific meaning, examples being *ijrahadda* ("to hasten one's pace when walking") and *ismaharra* ("to become hard and strong").[9]

0.2.10 All these things are alluded to in this book and must be quickly grasped. I have perused what Imam al-Suyūṭī[10] (God show him mercy) has to say on the distinguishing characteristics of the language in his *Al-Muzhir fī l-lughah* (*The Luminous Work on Language*),[11] copying from the master linguist Ibn Fāris,[12] and found that it fails to deal at any length with this type of association of form and sense; even worse, it sometimes seems to provide examples of "associations" that shouldn't be considered as such—for example, the application of the term *ḥimār* ("donkey") to a dim-wit.[13]

0.2.11 Among other such oddities are the rare words, as when I use *akhā* to describe a man shivering with cold; in the *Qāmūs*, it states that "*akhā* means 'he warmed the ends of his fingers by blowing on them'." Further examples are *ʿinqāsh* for "the man who goes around the villages selling things," *ḍawṭār* for "one who enters the market without capital and swindles people for gain," *dhubābah* meaning "the amount outstanding on a debt," *tharmala* as in *tharmala l-ṭaʿām* meaning "he ate messily, so that it was scattered over his beard and mouth," *yatakaẓkaẓ* meaning that a person "straightens up in his seat every time he feels his belly is full." Further examples are *jalhazah* ("pretending ignorance of something of which one is aware"), *talaḥḥuz* ("drooling from the mouth on eating a pomegranate or the like"), *wadham* ("a penis with its testicles"), *arghāl* ("orache plants"), and so on. Some such words are explained while others have been left without explanation to avoid inflating the size of the book.

0.2.12 My other concern has been to discuss the praiseworthy and blameworthy qualities of women. One such praiseworthy quality is the distance a woman may advance in knowledge and education depending on the varying circumstances to which she is subjected, as will appear in my reports on the Fāriyāqiyyah,[14] for the latter, who once didn't know the difference between a beardless boy and a clean-shaven one, or between the ocean and the Nile, has made such progress in education that she now argues with theorist and practitioner alike and provides excellent critiques of the political issues and conditions, mundane and spiritual, of the countries she has seen. If it be said that the book attributes to her rare words that are little-known either in speech or in books and which she could not have uttered, I reply that such attributions do not, in this case, have to be literal; the thought is what matters. Other praiseworthy qualities of women are their alluring ways of moving and all their various charms, no imaginable form of which have I left unmentioned in this book. Nay, I have put into it most of their thoughts and ideas as well, and everything else that has to do with them.

## An Introduction by the Publisher of This Book

0.3.1 To Almighty God be *praise*, for the blessings with which He has showered us throughout our *days*. To proceed: Rāfāʾīl Kaḥlā, of Damascus,[15] humble seeker of the mercy of his Lord the Preserver and Protector, declares: When I perused this book entitled *Leg over Leg*, I found it provided a wealth of useful information through its enumeration of many synonymous and lexically associated words in a style clear and *admirable*, presented in a manner both fascinating and *delectable*. This is especially so, given that it encompasses all the names of instruments and tools that need to be known and provides a complete reckoning of all types of foods, drinks, perfumes, clothes, furniture, shoes, jewelry, and gems, the like of which is to be found in no other book in this form, while any items that may have been omitted in the relevant chapter—and they are few—have been mentioned by the author in the table enumerating synonyms.[16] I also found that a further excellent feature of the book is its inclusion of prose and poetry, sermons and *maqāmah*s, aphorisms and philosophical critiques, conversations and idioms, double entendres and puns, and amusing dialogues and expressions, so that the reader will never grow bored perusing it, even if he reads it over and over again.

0.3.2 Among the most entertaining of the aforesaid conversations are those to be found in Chapter 9 of Book One, chapters 18 and 20 of Book Three, chapters 2, 6, and 10 of Book Four, and elsewhere, and of the idioms, those to be found in chapters 18 and 20 of Book One, in the sermon in Book Two,[17] and in Chapter 5 of Book Two, as well as in many other places. The puns are almost too many to count; anyone reading the book is asked to turn the pages slowly and focus closely in order to uncover the hidden meanings conveyed through jokes and the other excellent features that have been placed within its separate chapters. Another of the book's excellent qualities is that, when it mentions something, it says everything there is to say about it, while also taking into consideration every aspect of any similar words.

0.3.3 In sum, I would make so bold as to say that the author, having once opened the door to this strange style of writing, has as quickly shut it again and that hereafter the book will never be challenged, for it has covered all the most celebrated oddities of the language that the reader might want to know. This being the case, when I saw the abundant useful literary items and linguistic rarities that it contained and became convinced that it would appeal to scholars and people of sound taste, I asked God for proper guidance as to its printing and promotion, so that its benefits might be generally enjoyed and it might be easy to obtain.

0.3.4 As to what it contains at the beginning by way of disrespectful comments directed against persons named by the author, I would have preferred that those names "had not been mentioned,"[18] but the author imposed the condition on me—before printing went ahead—that I should leave nothing out of the book, and he has imposed the same on all his readers, a fact to which he alludes in the *Proem* when he says, "[Beware lest you] . . . think of using it in abbreviated form." I decided therefore that the small amount of condemnation that might result from making those names explicit was no reason—when measured against the many benefits that would accrue from the book as a whole—to stop its promotion and acceptance.

0.3.5 Here then, Reader, is a novel and unprecedented treasure for you, a precious gift to be treated with care. Scrutinize it closely when reading it and give it your undivided attention, so that its veiled meanings may *appear*, its enigmatic constructions become *clear*, and do not treat it as you would any other well-known work, for it is an innovation singular beyond *compare*.

Finally, we apologize to you for certain mistakes that occurred during printing, most of which are limited to the vowelling of little known words and are, anyway, very few. Nor do they occur in all the copies printed, as we managed to catch and correct some. Few books on the oddities of language are completely without such errors and we hope you will be gracious enough to match them against the table of corrigenda and correct them with your pens; the author confesses his shortcomings, confession erases commission, and none is perfect but God alone, from whom we ask forgiveness and aid. 0.3.6

*Praise Be to God Almighty*

## PROEM

0.4.1 This book of mine to the sophisticate will be sophisticated
And smooth-tongued, while to the foolish it will be foolish.
I have set down in it words and lexical items to bejewel it
And filled it with dots that shine[19] and letters,
With natural style, humor, and purity of intent
As well as with license, temperance, and abstinence.
Like a body, it has more than one member. Those that are concealed
May earn your passion, those that are in plain sight your praise.
I have tailored it, but to fit my own way of thinking, for
The measure of yours is to me unknown.
0.4.2 I beat a path for it with the hooves of my thoughts
To make it wide enough for the words and forced it to be hollowed out.
I pieced it together and cobbled it up by hand. Say then,
"What a well-pieced-together and cobbled-up book it is!"
I emptied into it every sort of ink that might make it appealing
And for it I sharpened thousands of pens.
One might almost say that with my very hands I shaped it, down to the last detail,
So that it came out tightly constructed and compactly built.
I composed it on a night black as pitch
Which is why it emerged so filled with animus and darkling allusion.
0.4.3 Outdoing the best of cooks, I seasoned it for you with pulicaria
Plants, for these will dispel the bad breath of fasting from your mouths[20]

And set right whatever misfortunes may afflict you and whatever
Sets your teeth on edge; after which you'll be ready to gobble up the pellicle of a date stone.
It will allow you to dispense with doctors' lies and their fees—
Nor on its account will you have to face a struggle to feed your children.
From the clayey ground of its lines has sprouted
A meadow, and gardens excelling in luxuriance.
From them will come to you the scent of statuesque girls,[21]
Ruddy-colored, whose beauty charms the comely youth.
At her side you will see tall plump girls 0.4.4
And well-endowed ones, white and tall, and tall smooth women
While behind them and to their fore are smooth girls whose flesh wobbles
And fair women, ever proud.
And should there emerge before you from among its letters
Heavy-haunched women, fat and ready to be bedded, then propose marriage to a girl whose saliva is sweet and vagina dry.
Should you lack what it takes to do so and excuse
Yourself from this obligation, you will find, hot on their tails, slim-bellied lasses;
So choose, God guide you, what you desire
And be not lazy in pursuing and realizing cunsummation.[22]
Other describers of such things have made their categorizations, 0.4.5
But did not do so well,
For what they said was trite and not one
Among them studied minutely what was to be described.
My book, however, or I myself, have done the opposite:
We save the enquirer the task of delimiting and defining.
We have no blemish, though you will not find
Any like us in our art nor any co-worker.
For this art is an orphan to find whose brother is impossible,
And it is unique, so be well disposed toward it.

0.4.6 To me and to the author of the *Qāmūs* must go the credit
Since it is from his fathomless sea that my words have been scooped.
Unlike a woman, my head was pregnant with it
For a year, and the whole year was a season of storms.
But it took only three months to be born
And quickly it learned to crawl and grew into a delightful youth.
I could not tell if my head gave birth to it feet first or blew it out of its nose or
Spat it out or dumped it there at the latrine.
I suffered over it in groans, may the Lord protect
You, suffering such as cannot be measured haphazardly
And cut its umbilical cord to suit only the people of discernment
To whose name alone it is dedicated.
0.4.7 It had no wet nurse other than
My thoughts, and even so I thought it too well suckled.
From days of old, my soul had craved it, like a pregnant woman, and
Its longing could not be distracted
And I sweated with pleasure just before it was born,
So much so that when I ejaculated the book, I was left drained.
I fathered two sons for myself, not for you, O Reader, then this one
Which is for you—a third, not for me, so lend it your ears.
My behest to my two true sons is that they should emulate
Its style and make a ritual circuit around its covers
So that they make keep it safe from burning, should any
Grow hot with anger against it, because of its spiciness.
I wash my hands of the doings of both, should they turn aside
From it and take an ally against it.
0.4.8 Any who longs to find it will be granted success,
Or if not and he loses his way and is stricken,
At night he will hear a burbling sound coming from it
That will sweeten his slumber with its unceasing gurgling—
And how many a shining light will appear if
You find yourself faced with it on a gloomy day!

How many a one large of belly has given up on it in dudgeon!
How many a murderous killer recoils from it, now weak!
To him like elusive mercury it seems and he cannot
Grasp any of the wool on its nape.
It falls like the wind in the valley when 0.4.9
Stirred up, and wears the mountain peak down to a bump.
It is the best of levelers for any who has found no humming top
Among Fate's toys and games to please him.
If you recite it, the beauty of its sound, like a gazelle calling to its young, will delight you
And if you seek to drown it out with your talk, it will give out a musical sound to which you will have no choice but to hearken.
In it you will find a winter refuge in the cold; then,
When the burning wind of summer gusts, a summer resort.
If you grow tired of food and other things, 0.4.10
You will find in it relief for your boredom
And if you acquire a garden, plant there
Little words from it that will give you yet more posies
That will relieve you of having to erect a scarecrow in it;
Should even Shiẓāẓ[23] come to steal them, he'll be affrighted.
I guarantee[24] you will find it so absorbing that you will lose all interest in sex,
But no one thereafter will think you're strait-laced or no longer able—
No indeed!—nor that you're one who doesn't want to sleep or is kept awake
By insomnia, or because he suffers thirst or hunger.
Make not bold to mount life's challenges 0.4.11
Unless you are ready to take them as your companion and pillion rider,
So that, should you be shaken in your seat, it may protect
You from slipping and so missing . . . summation.[25]
Well I know, and common sense instructs me,
That Your Honored Self finds monks frightening.

Scare them yourself, then, using every cutting character[26]
That's in it inscribed, and any monk will pull back from you blinded.[27]
It is sour grape juice in the eye of its calumniator,
Whose eye, if its title is ever mentioned, will weep and weep.
It is the sharp cutting steel that
Slices bones and cleaves cartilage.
0.4.12 If you wish to dress yourself in it, despite its shortcomings,
Then enjoy it; if not, then leave it be, still clean.
I have licensed you to swallow it whole or to lick it
Or, if afraid of vomiting, to take it diluted.
Beware, though, lest you add to it or
Think of using it in abbreviated form,
For no place in it is susceptible
To abbreviation, or to addition, to make it better.
0.4.13 If an inanimate object may be fallen in love with for its beauty,
Then all humanity will be enamored of it.
After I have bidden mankind farewell,
They will find their way to it, wherever it be, in droves.
And if two liars quarrel, the hair of the beard
Of the more unjust will end up plucked out
And finally the hair on both their jawbones will be like
Mattress cotton, smooth and carded.
By the life of your head, my head knows that
I'll never benefit from it by even a loaf—
No indeed!—nor cottage cheese, nor poor-quality dates,
Nor silk mixed with wool to hang on my peg, nor a cotton wad for my inkwell.
0.4.14 But on my pate I had an itch that spurred me
To practice writing, if only once,
Though he who is hired to compose a sermon for money,
Such a one is well suited to be considered a laborer of no worth.
Take of my words such as will find a market, and what you find
Counterfeit, leave for me in their wrappings.

The money changers are bound on occasion to find
Among the silver coins one that is of bad metal.
Many a gold coin will drag to you by his beard one whom you
May love, even if its face cannot be clearly read.
The old patina that you see thick 0.4.15
Upon it will not adhere to the glass of your mind.
He whose nature is refined, be he where he may,
Will believe what is gross in his beloved to be as refined as he.
Do not spurn what has gladdened you in him just because of what
Has hurt you. Nay, turn not your back on him in disgust.
The classifier is no classifier
If he doesn't put things into classes.
Isn't "of a certain stamp" the same in meaning as
"Of a certain type," with the addition of the thwack of a stick?[28]
God forbid that you should judge me incoherently 0.4.16
Before you have properly studied it
And say, "The author has committed blasphemy, so gather,
You people—your friend has uttered unbelief,"
Causing the masters of the churches to rise up in dread
Outrage and unsheathe their swords against it.
The bonds of affection between you and me are such
As to cut short any accusations of my being either a sinner or a saint.
Raise not your hackles in preparation for a quarrel, or a complaint,
And let there be between us no dogfight.
If I have come with good intentions, you should acclaim 0.4.17
Me. If not, at least do not calumniate me.
Do not let my father, my mother, or my
Honor be insulted, and do not get used to doing so.
My sin is suspended, dangling, from my nose.
It does not strike the noses of other mortals.[29]
Many a foul-tongued loud-mouth
Has become, when the chaste have become sinners, himself chaste,

And many a man of pure soul, if he visits a man who has a wife,
Becomes, if she smiles at him, a rascal.

0.4.18 One rabid for young girls with firm breasts infects none but himself
And his medicine's a breast abreast of him that's well-risen.
What blame can attach to one who gives to his brethren
Something more delicious than wine, something exquisite?
He spent the nights carefully crafting its details
While they were sleeping, snoring loudly as they did so.
Did you ever see a noble man return a gift,
Humiliating the one who gave it to him with harsh words?

0.4.19 Could it not be that Fate has taken to playing the fool,
To raving and making jokes unfairly?
It derives *kharif* ("dotard") from *kharf al-janā* ("the gathering in of the harvest") and
From the *ḥaṣaf* ("mange") that weakens the fingernails it derives *ḥaṣīf* ("man of clear judgment").
Avoid making the lion frown, and be a brother
To the fox, a crafty fellow, of iron will.
He the sound of whose bow-string when plucked makes the sultan laugh
Is the one whom the people consider an expert.
My proem finishes with this line,
Which I have made as a roof to complete its construction.
Read nothing after this, even should you be
Charged with reading a single letter of any other book,
For then you'll be on a slippery path, where you'll go wrong foot first
And so slide across the line.
(Though I think that the scented air of my advice,
Like wind is in your ears—passing, leaving no trace, as though it were nought.)

# Book One

# Chapter 1

## Raising a Storm[30]

Gently! Hush! Silence! Quiet! Cock an ear! Listen up! Hold your tongue! Quit talking! Hear! Hark! Hearken!—and know that I embarked upon the composition of this four-book opuscule of mine during wearing, grinding nights that had me praying to God standing and seated, until finally I found no further impediment to stop the faucet of my thoughts from emptying like rain clouds into the drainpipe of my pen and onto the surfaces of these pages; and that when I found the pen obedient to my fingertips and the inkpot to the pen, I said to myself, "There can be no harm to my following in the footsteps of that company of men who have rendered their reputations white by covering pages in black, for if they did well, then I too may be considered to have done well, and if they did badly, it may be that one more book is needed to add to their efforts, in which case my book, at least, may be described as perfect, for whatever has perfected something else must be capable itself of being perfect." Taking this as my starting point, I never paused in the pursuit of my goal and felt no compunction in consigning to it all such words attractive and *fascinating* and figures admirable and *scintillating* as bring pleasure to the *ear* and to the constitution *cheer*; this, despite knowing that scarce an author can please everyone. 1.1.1

I picture myself, then, as one confronted by some picky fault-finder who says to himself, or to another, "If the author had put his 1.1.2

talent to work to compose a book that was of some use, he'd deserve to be praised for it; but it seems to me he has wasted his time for nothing by mentioning on some occasions things that should not be mentioned and on others things that yield no benefit." My reply to the first point is "How many a pot has called the kettle black!,"[31] and "You've made a bad business worse!,"[32] and "Make the most of what you're given!,"[33] and "So what are you going to do about it?!,"[34] and "Mind your own business!," and "The accepting eye to every fault is blind!," while to the second it is to point out that one who limps (a) should go easy on himself, (b) shouldn't try to climb mountains, (c) should tend to his own limp before anyone else's, and (d) shouldn't call attention to his limping;[35] or as though confronted by someone else who says, "Another of Khurāfah's tales, Umm 'Amr!,"[36]—to which I reply, "Many a true word has been spoken by the less than perfect!"

1.1.3 Next, I am confronted by a mighty crowd of priests, abbots, and monks, bequeathers of pious bequests, churchwardens, and sacristans, board-beaters,[37] patriarchs, and hegumens, before whom goes the Great Catholicos[38] with, before him, the Supreme Pontiff,[39] all of them clamoring and havering, mooing and snorting, raging and roaring, shouting and shrieking, fuming and furious, threatening and fulminating, complaining and calumniating, venting, ventilating, and hyperventilating, yelling and gasping, praying and spittle-spraying, thus causing me to say, "*Hold your horses! Hold your horses!* You have spent your whole lives in the craft of exegesis, so what harm would it do if you were to explain away what it is you don't like about my book from the get-go, making arguments, as is your wont, that whatever is malformed is in fact comely and whatever seems hideously phrased is in fact elegant? This is something Abū Nuwās made incumbent on you hundreds of years ago, when he said,

Be not stingy in forgiveness if you be a pious man
For your illiberality is but contempt of religion

"and

Be as you wish, for God is kind—
No harm shall befall you if you sin.
Two things alone you must eschew in full—
Ascribing partners[40] to God and injuring men."

If, on the other hand, you say, "Its words are too plain to explain away," I say to you that only yesterday you were making mistakes, mispronouncing, and maledicting, uttering solecisms and stuttering, erring and aberring, speaking randomly and raggedly, misspeaking and randomly mouthing off, rambling and roaming, raving, ranting, and talking irrationally, faltering and floundering, babbling like foreigners, bumbling as though you had plums in your mouths and mumbling as though your mouths were covered, dragging out your words and wagging your tongues mischievously (and at great length too), stammering, yammering, and pronouncing letters like Qur'ān readers,[41] tripping over your *t*s, prattling, faltering,[42] and battologizing, hemming and hawing and hawing and hemming, talking as though you had a bone in your throats, swallowing your words, lifping your *f*s, mumbling as though you'd lost your teeth, speaking as though you were belching and vomiting, prattling incoherently, burbling like emptying water jars and squawking like parrots, talking nonsense, snarling like wolves tearing at their prey, howling, and ending up running out of breath like winded horses—so at what point did you acquire the knowledge that would allow you to understand it? 1.1.4

And if you say that one part (the bad part) is comprehensible and the other part incomprehensible, I reply, "Perhaps the part you don't understand consists of precisely those good fẹatures that compensate for the work's bad, and, anyway, under no circumstances do you have the right to burn the book." I swear by my life, even if the 1.1.5

only thing it had to intercede for it and give it currency with the literati, and with you too, as a literary work, were its enumeration of so many synonyms, that would be enough! Yet, in fact, there is more: the book contains sufficient discussion of beauty and beautiful women—God prolong their glory!—to require that it be extolled and its author be lauded while alive and eulogized when the time comes for him, unwillingly, to part their company.

1.1.6 In addition to which, I know many a noble churchwarden whose virtues are acknowledged among men and yet has no compunction about referring to "things quivering," "things rounded," "things tightened,"[43] "things huge," "things 'the size of mountains,'" or "things hard and vigorously thrusting," nor about making mention of the pudendum big, the pudendum large, the pudendum swollen, the pudendum huge, enormous, the pudendum vast, the thick, raised pudendum and the raised, thick pudendum,[44] the pudendum thick of lip, the vulva huge, the vulva mighty, the vulva long of clitoris, the buttocks, the vulva's inner chamber and space, the wide wet one and the bulgy one, the big brutish one and the just plain large one,[45] the genitals of either sex, the woman's droopy one, the skinny one, the buttocks but with a slightly different spelling,[46] the anus, the flabby vulva, the pudendum shaven, the woman whose vulva is huge, the woman with a huge vulva with widely separated edges, the woman whose vulva squeaks when it's entered, the woman with the dry little scrawny one, the woman with the emaciated one, the woman with the tiny vagina a man can't get at, the woman who holds the man's semen inside her womb, the woman who flashes her "thing" and her belly folds, the woman the clefts at the head of whose womb are narrow and who holds herself rigid on her side for the man,[47] the woman whose vagina makes a sound when entered, the woman broad-buttocked as a donkey whose vulva also makes a sound, the one whose vagina makes another kind of sound, the woman who swoons during intercourse and the woman who faints during intercourse, the woman who menstruates from her anus, the woman with a wide vagina, the woman the meaty parts of whose vagina are tight, the woman whose vagina is wide open and the woman whose vagina is open wide,[48] the woman whose vagina may be either small or capacious, the woman whose vagina and rectum have been torn so that they have become one, the broad-vagina-ed and debauched woman, the uncircumcised woman with torn vagina and rectum who is also incontinent, the women so much fucked that, like an overused she-ass, she's developed a medical condition in her womb, the woman with the tiny vagina a man can't get at (again, but a different word),[49] the woman who covets the man during intercourse,[50] the woman who wets her bed, the woman who excretes when laid, the tight woman, the woman who whinnies through her nostrils during intercourse like a lunatic, the woman who derives her pleasure from the edges of her vagina, the woman who gushes water during intercourse, the woman whose belly's so big they say, "Bravo!", the woman who's no good at intercourse, the woman whose vagina is droopy with large edges, the woman with the long clitoris, or the woman who doesn't keep herself covered when alone with her husband; nor about the thick clitoris, the clitoris *tout court*, the prepuce of the clitoris or that of the girl before she's been cut, the semen in the womb, the woman's womb itself,[51] the folds that protect the clitoris, the part between the backside and the front, the side of the vagina, the back of the vagina, the edges or sides of the womb, the testicles, the clitoris said with a funny accent,[52] the pelvic bone, the navel, the flabby belly between the navel and the pelvis, the tip of the clitoris, the glans, the "knotty rod," the man with a strong penis, the "thick stick," the large glans, the tip of the glans if it's broad, the edges of the glans, the donkey's glans, the donkey's penis, the fly's penis, the large limp penis, the large glans, the foreskin of a boy if it widens so far that the glans emerges, and a vein in the penis; nor about extra hard erections, ordinary erections, pricks that commit fornication, women's stuffing of their vaginas with rags so that their wombs won't come out, women's spreading their legs wide during coitus, a man's practicing coitus with one woman and then another before ejaculating and a man's practicing coition with one women and then another before ejaculating,[53] one slave-girl's hearing the sounds made by her master when he's with another slave-girl, and a little-used word for plain copulation,[54] the spontaneous leaping of she-camels by he-camels, emaciation resulting from incessant intercourse, lusting for intercourse, sleep taken after intercourse, having intercourse with one's slave girl by merely inserting and withdrawing because not wishing to ejaculate, withdrawing before ejaculation because not wanting children, thrusting it into her the whole way, ejaculating into the womb, people who fuck frequently, men with long genitalia, vaginas that excite, men intercourse with whom is sure to result in pregnancy, men who find it difficult to have intercourse with a woman, the hard man who keeps on fucking, the deflowering of pre-pubescent girls, sitting between a woman's thighs in order to have intercourse with her, women's emptying a man of all his seed, a noun meaning copulation from which no verb is formed,[55] something white that comes out of the vulva, the curing of the thing resembling a scrotal hernia that emerges from a woman's vulva and makes intercourse impossible, having protuberant buttocks (of a woman), the nympha at the base of the clitoris, to push forth its penis (of a donkey), women voracious as lionesses, dashing water on one's vagina,[56] the external parts of the vulva, the thing resembling a scrotal hernia that emerges from a woman's vulva and makes intercourse impossible, the protuberant part of the womb, and the flesh of the inner part of the vulva;[57] nor about the vulva (especially when large), the vulva said four other ways,[58] the flabby vagina,[59] the vagina that dries the liquid from the surface of the penis,[60] the gaping vagina, the tight vagina, and another name for the vagina,[61] the large ugly vagina with long womb flaps, the large wet squeaky vagina, the women's sexual parts in general, the "bulge," the "sprayer," the fleshy vagina, the bizarrely spelled,[62] the "shrunken," the "gripper," the "nock,"[63] the woman sent mad by the cravings of her crevice, the woman's "wide well," and the vagina again in another exotic spelling,[64] the large floppy one, and other "instruments of erection";[65] nor about mentioning the backside, the posterior, "the thrower,"[66] "the catapult," "the podex," "the bellower," "the dunger," "the winnower," "the currycomb," "the sickle," the *khabanfatha*,[67] "the fontanel,"[68] "the dry and sweaty-smelling,"[69] "the slimy," "the watermelon," "the heater," "the howler," "the draining vent,"[70] "the toothless one," "the black one,"[71] "the exploder," "the whistler," "the greatly swollen," "the gusher," "the prominent," "the swallower," "the blackener," "the betrayer," "the flintstone," the bunghole, the butthole,[72] and other "instruments of cutting off,"[73] nor about mentioning the penis, "the falcon's stand," "the little bolter," the huge penis, the huge long penis, the flaccid penis incapable of erection, "the lengthener," "the little man," "the big spider," another rare word for the penis,[74] "the strong, crafty wolf,"[75] the erect but not very hard penis, "the mast," "the thimble,"[76] "the snub nose," "the plumb line," the prick,[77] the penis distended and erect, the *qaṣṭabīr*,[78] "the tassels,"[79] "the short ugly thing," "the straight, thick lance," the huge, strong penis, the hard, dry thing, and other "instruments of attraction",[80] nor about using words meaning to lie with, to have sex with, to compress, to lie with one's slave girl, to have intercourse, to perform coitus, to have sex with in or out of wedlock, "to prod," to copulate with, to "push," to "jab," to shtup,[81] another word of similar form but dubious status,[82] to double up like a she-goat during mating, to "bridge,"[83] to fuck hard,[84] to "string her bow," to "fill her up,"[85] to "kick"[86] her, to "nibble" her and a variant,[87] to "chafe" her, to "cut" her, to "suckle" her, to "stick the kohl-stick in her kohl-pot," to "furrow" her, to "push" her, or to "ram it in all the way to the hilt." I would stare into their faces while they were using such words and see there no trace of either embarrassment's *red* or the yellow of *dread*. On the contrary, their faces would be verdant and *cheerful*, radiant and *joyful*—and should anyone, out of sheer pigheadedness, deny that what I say is true and demand of me a list of their names, I'll tell him, "Here it is, beginning with *alif* and ending with *yāʾ*.[88] Just think of me as a churchwarden like them."

1.1.7 In addition, I have imposed on the reader the condition that he not skip any of the "synonymous" words in this book of mine, many though they be (for it may happen that, on a single road, a herd of fifty words, all with the same meaning, or with two meanings that are close, may pass him by). If he cannot commit to this, I cannot permit him to peruse it and will not offer him my congratulations if he does so. I have to admit that I cannot support the idea that all "synonyms" have the same meaning, or they would have called them "equi-nyms." They are, in fact, synonymous only in the sense that certain of them may take the place of certain others. Proof of this lies in the fact that beauty, length, whiteness, smoothness, and eloquence differ in kind and in collocation, depending on the differences among the objects they describe. The Arabs,[89] therefore, assigned to each type of beauty, length, etc., a specific name, and it is only our distance from their days that makes us think they all mean the same; how much more so, then, in the case of words relating to jewelry, food, drink, dress, household furnishings, and footwear. Indeed, in my opinion—and I am not afraid of anyone saying, "Aren't you being opinionated?"—if two words derive from the same base form and refer to the same object (as is the case for example with *khajūj* and *khajawjāh*, meaning "wind that passes violently"),[90] the longer of the two forms must involve an extension of meaning. Grant me this, if you wish, or be stubborn—it makes no difference to me. Bear in mind, too, that I composed the work at a time when the only book in Arabic I had to refer to or depend on was the *Qāmūs*, for my books had taken against me as a wife does her husband, and I'd decided to have nothing more to do with them—though it must be acknowledged that the author of the work in question, God rest his soul, did not fail to record a single word descriptive of women; it is almost as though he knew by divine inspiration that someone would come along after him and dive into his "ocean"[91] in order to collect such pearls into a single work where they could be so arranged as to lodge more firmly in the mind and become more deeply rooted in the memory.

1.1.8 And, did I not fear the wrath of these beauties against me, I would have made mention of many of their crafty ways, their stratagems, and their artifices too; however, my intention in writing the book has been to approach closer to them and use it to appease, not anger, them. I am indeed extremely sorry that they will be incapable of understanding it—as a result of their ignorance of reading and not of the recondite nature of its language, for nothing that involves the union of souls, love, or passion, is too hard for them to understand; they take it all in and grasp it without hesitation, deficiency, or incomprehension. Enough for me that the rumor should reach their ears that so-and-so has written a book about women in which he gives them precedence over all other creatures, declaring them to be the adornment of the universe, the comfort and pride of this world, the joy and hope of life, the soul's pleasure(1) and its desire, the heart's jewel and the eye's apple, the breast's refreshment and spirit's refection, the mind's elucidation and thought's preoccupation, a distraction for the head and paradise for the soul, good cheer for the constitution and limpidity for the blood, pleasure for the senses and diversion for the intellect, the embellishment of the age and the glory of every place and dwelling.

(1) Al-Fīrūzābādī is wrong in deriving *surriyya* (concubine) from *sirr* meaning "coition." In reality, the word derives from *surr* meaning "pleasure" (*surūr*).

1.1.9 Indeed, I declare unabashedly that they have about them a whiff of the divine, for one can scarce behold a beautiful woman without glorifying the Creator. At their mention, the tongue breaks into praise while the foot runs to serve them, bearing burdens and taking on hardships, and in their service what is difficult seems easy, colocynth may be drunk, injury borne. To please them, what is dear is treated with contempt, what is precious is not spared, what is sacred is trodden underfoot. Without them, a man's lot of what is good in this world is turned into deprivation, his triumphs become disappointments, his happiness displeasure, his sense of companionship loneliness; where once he was full he hungers, and where once he was watered he thirsts; where once he slept he suffers from insomnia, and where once he was strong he is in tribulation; his felicity turns into misery, Paradise to him is become like the fruit of the *zaqqūm* tree[92] and its nectar like pus.

1.1.10 Thus, if God should ordain that this intoxicating news reach the ears of one of these beautiful mistresses of mine and she is pleased and made happy and dances and is merry, I beg of her, extending the hand of supplication, that she communicate it to the ears of her lady neighbor too, who will show it in turn, I hope, to a friend, so that not a week passes before news of the book has spread throughout the whole city. This will be sufficient reward for the trouble that I have gone to for their sakes. Indeed, they must know that, were I able to write their praise with all my fingers and proclaim it with all my limbs, it would still not be equal to their virtues. How much I owe them for appearing in their finest garb, strutting in the best of their jewelry, and casting me such darting looks that I returned to my little house barely able to hold my thoughts and fancies in check! Then, no sooner did my hand touch the pen than the ideas gushed from it and spread themselves over the paper. Thus women have earned me repute and honor among the public and raised my status above that of the unemployed and idle. True, one among them refused to let her specter visit me in sleep, thinking me unworthy, but she is to be excused because she was unaware that I, in fact, was only feigning sleep,[93] after my mind had been dazzled and my brain discombobulated by her beauty.

1.1.11 If, on the other hand, someone should insist that my language is devoid of rhetorical devices—which is to say, not marinated in the spices of paronomasia[94] and morphological parallelism, of metaphor and metonymy—I'd say to him, "When I undertook to serve His Honor[95] by composing this work, the last persons on my mind were al-Taftazānī,[96] al-Sakkākī,[97] al-Āmidī,[98] al-Wāḥidī,[99] al-Zamakhsharī,[100] al-Bustī,[101] Ibn al-Muʿtazz,[102] Ibn al-Nabīh,[103] and Ibn Nubātah.[104] My thoughts were exercised exclusively by the description of beauty, my tongue tied to the praise of those on whom the Almighty has bestowed this egregious blessing, to the expression of happiness for those to whom He, Great and Glorious, has accorded the glory of comeliness, and to mourning over the fate of those whom He has deprived of it, and this was enough to distract one from everything else. Nevertheless, I hope that the scintillation, the luster, and the decorative nature of the description of beauty will, in and of itself, relieve the book of the need for any such rhetorical embellishments, just as a beautiful woman is relieved of any need for jewelry (which is why she is called a *ghāniyah*).[105] In addition, experience has shown me that these rhetorical embellishments in which authors so freely indulge often draw the reader's attention to the words' outward forms and away from their inner meanings."

I swear that this book contains nothing reprehensible, unless you 1.1.12
find the Fāriyāq's[106] sometimes pushing his way through a troupe of *ghāniyas* or forcing himself upon them as they rest safe in their bridal pavilions or in a garden or in the corner of a house or on their beds to be so. This was, however, something I was unable to avoid, for the book has been compiled as an account of his doings and to provide knowledge of the circumstances that influenced him, it having come to my attention that many people have denied that the above named even exists and claimed that he belongs to the same category as the ghoul and the phoenix, while others have asserted that he appeared but once throughout the *age* and thereafter vanished from the *stage*, and more than one has held that he was transmogrified a few days after his birth and that it is not known what shape he adopted or into what form he mutated. Another party has claimed that he joined the race of the monopods and another that of the monopodettes.[107] Still others have said that he joined the *ḥinn*.[108] Some have insisted that he was transformed into a woman, for when he saw that the female enjoys a happier state in this world—this "women's world," as it is known—he let not a night go by without praying to his Lord to turn him into a female and God accepted his prayer (and He is capable of all things). This being the case, it seemed to me that one of my duties should be to acquaint these same people, with their differing opinions, with the fact of his presence in the very form

that he bore when he was brought into being, due exception made for the changes wrought on him by the efforts he has expended in the pursuit of a living, his difficult circumstances, the hardships of his travels and of consorting with foreigners and learning their languages, and, especially, the graying of his hair and his passage from the borders of youth to the age of maturity.

1.1.13 This now being known, I declare: the Fāriyāq was born with the misfortune of having misfortune in the ascendant everywhere, the Scorpion raising its tail to strike at the Kid, or Billy Goat, and the Crab set on a collision course with the horn of the Ox. His parents were people of notability, nobility, and righteousness (Bravo! Bravo!) but while their prospects for the world to come were *expansive*, their prospects in the world in which they lived were not with these *co-extensive,* and their reputations were, of their *purse*, the *inverse* (Boo! Boo!). The thunder of their names resounded far and *wide*, while the whirlwinds of their circumstance kicked up a cloud of praise as audible on plain as on *mountainside*, and so frequent were the visits of those seeking solace for their *plight*, so often did petitioners seek out their campfires by *night*, that the fountains of their income had run *dry*, the end of their bounty's wellspring come *nigh*, and all that was left there was a little seepage from which the destitute and deprived might derive provision against want—and still they were generous with this to those who wanted for provisions (Boohoo!). Thus it was that they no longer found themselves with the means to send him to Kufa or Basra[109] to learn the Arabic language, placing him instead with the teacher at the *kuttāb* of the village in which they dwelt (Alas! Alas!).

1.1.14 The teacher in question, like all other teachers of children in that country, had never in his life perused any book but that of the psalms, and it was that and that alone that the children studied there (Faugh! Faugh!) though to say they studied it doesn't imply that they understood it. God forbid! Given its antiquity, it is no longer within anyone's capacity to understand that book (Snore! Snore!), and the inaccuracy of its Arabic translation and the lameness of its language have made it yet more obscure and mysterious, to the point that it has almost come to consist of no more than word puzzles and riddles (Have at it! Have at it!), despite which, the tradition of the people of the country is to use it to train their children to read, without understanding what it means. Furthermore, in their opinion, it is forbidden to understand its meanings (For shame! For shame!) which makes one think that they don't understand the meaning of the letters *s-t-u-p-i-d*,[110] for example; neither, by the same token, do they understand the purely linguistic components of the book in question when they read it (Belly laugh!).

It seems that our masters, lords of the next world as of this, do not want their wretched subjects either to understand or to open their eyes but instead try as hard as they can to leave them wandering in the labyrinths of ignorance and stupidity (Barf! Barf!). If they wanted otherwise, they would bestir themselves to establish a printing press for them there[111] to print useful books, whether written originally in Arabic or translated into it (Forward! Forward!). How, O mighty masters, can it please you that your abject slaves should raise their children in ignorance and confusion (Too bad! Too bad!) and their teachers not know Arabic or penmanship or arithmetic or history or geography or anything else of the things that a teacher ought to know? (So sad! So sad!) On how many of these children has the Almighty bestowed faculties of capacity and quickwittedness, despite which, for loss of the means to knowledge and lack of the instruments to discipline and raise them, the spark is so thoroughly extinguished in them when young that the tinder of achievement can no longer ignite it in them once grown (Ah! Ah!). What is more, you are, praise God, numbered among the well-heeled and wealthy, and it would not be beyond your means to spend a few purses on the construction of schools and the printing of useful books (Well? What about it?). 1.1.15

The income of the Maronite patriarch is of great *weight* and massive *aggregate*, so much so that with it he could bring life to the hearts of this desiccated sect of his that has lost any interest in competing 1.1.16

with or challenging in any area those who, in earlier generations, attained to every science and virtue (On! On!) and whose only concern now is to learn a few rules of the Arabic and Syriac[112] languages simply for the sake of knowing them and not for any benefit (Oh dear! Oh dear!). To date, not one of them has been known to have translated a book or beneficial pamphlet into either of these two languages, nor is the patriarch known to have ordered the printing of a language-teaching book in either (Tee hee! Tee hee!). If he were to spend half his annual income on acquiring the means to knowledge instead of on all those feasts and banquets that they put on for his visitors, or if each emir and noble shaykh were to make an annual gift of a certain amount toward this charitable end or were to send agents to the lands of the Franks to collect from the charitable there a sum that could be allocated to such things, everyone, east and west, would praise him for his deed (Hooray! Hooray!).

1.1.17 However, if one of our masters were to go to the trouble of sending Ḥanna or Mattā or Lūqā to his Frankish brethren[113] to collect money, he would do so only for the building of a church or a hermitage (Ugh! Ugh!) overlooking the fact that, from birth to the age of twelve, no one can properly comprehend anything that comes to him from church or hermitage, though he can, during the same period, be learning useful things in a school or *kuttāb* (Blech! Blech!). Will you then, my masters, promise me to build libraries and print books, so that I don't have to make this chapter too long for you?

1.1.18 My heart with rancor against you *burns*, while my breast with accusations against you *churns* (Ach! Ach!) because under your auspicious reign, my dear friend the Fāriyāq was unable to learn anything in his village other than the psalms, which is a book that they have stuffed with vulgar usages, mistakes, and lame language (Yech! Yech!) because its translator didn't know chaste Arabic, and you can well imagine what the rest of the books printed in your country and in Great Rome are like (Retch! Retch!).

It is well known that, if error becomes rooted in the mind of the child, it grows up with him and is thereafter impossible to root out. Is there any other cause for this disgrace and shame than your neglect and mismanagement of civil and clerical affairs? (Ptui! Ptui!) Do you reckon lameness of language to be part of religion's rites and *lineaments*, duties and *requirements*, or that chasteness of language will lead you to unbelief and *heresy*, reprehensible innovation and *errancy*? (Tut-tut!) Or did you reckon that those verses *inastute* might confound the learned Muslim in *dispute*? (Forget it! Forget it!) Is there no blood in your veins to rouse you to a love of eloquent, stately language, of rhetoric and fluency, of the arrangement of the words in accordance with set rules, of the expression of what passes through the mind without grammatically incorrect padding and boring *interpolation*, sickening complexity and phthisic *expatiation*? Without saying "et cetera" in mid-sentence or turning triliteral verbs into quadriliterals and vice versa,[114] without using *fī* instead of *bi-* after a verb and the other way round,[115] without making transitive verbs intransitive and the reverse, or the glottal stop into an elision and the contrary, or failing to distinguish between the active and the passive participles—for you say "They are *envied* of me" when you mean "are *envious* of me" and the like? (Ha-ha!) This book of mine is no *Durrat al-thīn fī awhām al-qissīsīn* (*Prize Pearl of the Fishery concerning the Delusions of the Clerisy*)[116] that I have to include in it a mention of every one of your errors and delusions (My! My!). My intention is simply to use it to demonstrate to you that your brains have been fed with incorrect and lame language from the days when you went to the *kuttāb* and read the psalms there until you became grown, and then old, men (Hold your tongue! Hold your tongue!) and that if you remain in this state, no cure is to be hoped for (Woe! Woe!). 1.1.19

Thereafter the Fāriyāq remained with his teacher, where he completed his study of the aforementioned book, after which the teacher became concerned lest the Fāriyāq get him caught up in 1.1.20

matters that were beyond him and through them expose him, so he indicated to his father that he should remove him from the *kuttāb* and put him to work copying books at home (Wow! Wow!), which he continued to do for a long while, gaining therefrom as much as the likes of him could by way of improving his hand and memorizing certain words (Good for you! Good for you!). The people of that land gave precedence to good writing over anything else the hand might make, and, to them, one who wrote a good hand had achieved more than any of his peers. Despite this widespread attitude, the country's ruler[117] employed as scribes only those whose writing was ugly to the eye and whose words were disgusting to good taste (Oy! Oy!), this being a kind of public declaration that good fortune is not dependent on good handwriting, that to administer the *law* does not call for language without *flaw* (Abtholutely not!),[118] and that they themselves have often attained lofty rank and exalted position though barely able to sign their noble names (Aiee! Aiee!).

1.1.21 The Fāriyāq, however, was not elated at having to practice this craft, believing that any earnings that might reach him through a slit as narrow as that in the nib of a pen must themselves be straitened (Alack! Alack!).[119] True, many a person has obtained a living expansive and *agreeable*, as well as good fortune unabated and *reliable*, from a wellspring that, though broad by comparison with the pen's nib, when measured against their greed and extravagance, was narrow (What a pity!). However, the Fāriyāq was then a greenhorn, with neither practice nor experience, given to judging what is distant by what is close—and nothing is closer to the eye of the scribe than the nib of his pen and the paper before him, or closer to his heart than the words he is writing. A clever fellow is he who accepts the craft that he practices, to whom the shame of hard work is no burden, and who does not crane his neck to look out for things at which he does not excel (No to the flesh! No to the flesh!).

## Chapter 2

# A Bruising Fall and a Protecting Shawl

It was in the Fāriyāq's nature, as is normal among the young, to imitate in dress, behavior, and speech those in his time distinguished by merit and knowledge. One day, he saw a wretched poet wearing a large round turban. The said wretched poet then being numbered among the masters, the Fāriyāq set his heart on having just such a turban, small as was his head, and he would walk along nodding under the weight of it to right and left, like a judge passing through the markets on his way home after Friday prayers saluting the people. 1.2.1

Now it happened once, when his father went to the ruler's house, that he took him along with him, mounting him on a filly of his, while he rode a stallion. There they stayed for a number of days, on one of which the Fāriyāq got it into his head to take his filly for a gallop in the square, where the stallion was tied up to one side. He'd raced her one length of the square when his filly, passing the place where her friend was picketed, turned her head toward him as though to indicate that her dashing cavalier was unworthy to ride her past the prince's steeds. The Fāriyāq promptly flew off and landed on his head, while the filly set off running, leaving him flat on the ground, though, had he been an expert horseman, she'd never have left him in such a state but would have waited for him to get up. He then arose, thanking God for the size of his turban, for it was that 1.2.2

which had protected his head from receiving any of "the ten head wounds"[120] (to wit, the bloodless abrasion and the bloodless graze, the break in the skin that brings blood but does not make it flow, the one that makes the blood flow, the one that enters the flesh without reaching the periosteum, the one that reaches the periosteum, the one that cuts to the bone, the one that breaks the bone, the one that shifts the bone, the one that leaves only a thin layer of skin over the brain, and the one that cuts to the brain).

1.2.3 However, he arose, having taken a blow to his loins, and that day made the discovery that there are benefits and advantages to a large turban, and he conceived the idea that the people of his country had taken to wearing large turbans simply to protect their heads and not to beautify their faces, for a huge turban hides the good qualities of the face and makes a small face look bad, not to mention that it hurts the head and blocks the ascent of vapors from the pores, something the Great Christian Master Physician[121] prescribes.

1.2.4 If it be said,[122] "If the sole reason for adopting large turbans is to protect people's heads, not to adorn or beautify them, how do you explain the people who wear their turbans when they go to bed at night? Are they afraid their heads will roll off their pillows and fall into a chasm inside their houses, even though their bedding is placed on the floor?" I reply, "The origin of this custom lies in the fact that the women of that land are given to wearing on their heads those 'horns' that they there call *ṭanāṭīr*.[123] These are made of silver or gold, and are as long as a forearm in height and as wide as a wrist. Now, if a man spends the night with his wife with nothing, or only a thin covering, on his head, he will be in danger of being bashed on his pate by her 'horn' and receiving from her one of the ten head wounds referred to above."

1.2.5 If you were to insist on being argumentative and say, "What is the reason for these veritable horns? Are they placed there to remind one of the figurative horns that a man acquires when he goes against his wife's wishes or is stingy with her or breaks off relations with her, or as a kind of adornment, or as a sign of women's wantonness and greed, in that, when they catch the smell of riches on their husbands, they think that every inch of their bodies should be decorated and ornamented, believing as they do that, while such things should be concealed from the eyes of others, they should not be concealed from their eyes or those of their husbands (albeit there is many a difference over the matter, with some forbidding it and some taking an attitude of acquiescence), for the mere knowledge that something valuable is safely hidden away may give pleasure to its owner, just as, if a person squirrels away treasure in a concealed hoard, he may revel in it even though he cannot see it?" I would reply, "The idea that they are there to provide a reminder of the figurative horns is not to be entertained, for the women of that country maintain their honor and preserve their chastity, and especially the women of the Mountain. In addition, the husband's cudgel, the hooked staffs of his own and his wife's families, and the eyes of the neighbors prevent her from having the full range of marital traits ascribed to her; in the cities, on the other hand, such traits are stronger and more widespread."

In origin, these "horns" were merely a device from which to suspend the face veil and, when first used, were small and short. Then they grew taller and larger as time went by and people got richer, a wife's horns getting taller and larger the richer and better off her husband became. And this brings us to a bit of useful information that we have to mention: the word *qarn* ("horn") is one that is common to all languages,[124] like *ṣābūn* ("soap"),[125] *qiṭṭ* ("cat"),[126] *mazj* ("mixing"),[127] and so on and has become famous among writers as a metonym for you-know-what on the part of the wife against the husband, except where Jewish writers are concerned, for in their books the horn has a positive significance, which is why you often hear in the Book of Psalms, "My horn has been exalted" and "You have exalted my horn" and "I shall butt with my horn" and so on.[128] 1.2.6

Both usages contain a certain incomprehensibility and ambiguity. The incomprehensibility of the use of "horn" by non-Jewish 1.2.7

writers as a metonym for women's infidelity to their husbands lies in the fact that the shape of the horn does not bring to mind any specific human member and neither do its actual manifestations bring to mind any specific animal, for the ox, the mountain goat, the billy goat, and the rhinoceros all have one. Similarly, the word itself is not derived from any verb that might indicate a woman's being unfaithful or taking a lover.[129] What, then, lies behind this usage? I have asked many married men of lengthy experience about this prickly issue, and all of them changed color on hearing my question and, embarrassed and despondent, stammered, got up, and left me. Should God, then, grant any of those who peruse this book of mine a sudden insight as to the meaning of this word, both in common usage and as a technical term, let him be so good as to respond, out of kindness and charity. As to its usage among the writers of the Jews as a metonym for high rank, power, strength, and victory, what is true of the preceding is true of that too, namely, that it is common to many animals, some of which are possessed of neither power nor might. Observe, then, how people differ with regard to a single word and a single meaning!

1.2.8 As for "turban" (*ʿimāma*), I believe it derives from *ʿamma* meaning "to embrace," for it embraces the head. It comes in various forms, among them the spiral, the cake-shaped, the wheel-shaped, the globular, the coil-shaped, the conical, the basket-shaped, and the cup-shaped, and all of these, whatever the type, are better than the baptismal fonts that the Maronite religious leaders wear. Let them just take a look at their faces in a well-polished mirror!

## Chapter 3

# Various Amusing Anecdotes

From childhood, the Fāriyāq had felt an instinctive disposition to read and assiduously study the classical language, picking out the rare words that he came across in books, of which his father had amassed a large number in a variety of disciplines. He, that is, the Fāriyāq, was also, from his youth, wild about poetry, even before he had learned anything about the requirements of that craft; thus sometimes he would hit the mark and other times miss it. He also believed poets were the best people and poetry the most magnificent thing with which a man could occupy himself. 1.3.1

Then one day he read in some chronicle of a poet who in his youth had been stupid and artless but had grown up to excel and to shine at composing lengthy odes. The story is told of him that one day he got drunk and sat down beside a monk's cell(1)[130] 1.3.2

(1) Metropolitan Jirmānūs Farḥāt is misguided in his statement in his *Bāb al-Iʿrāb* (*Gateway to Grammar*) that "*ta'mūr* means 'container' and 'soul' and 'heart' *and 'the monk's cell' and 'the monastic rule'* (*qānūn al-rāhib*)." The wording of the original [from which Farḥāt took this, sc. the *Qāmūs*] is "and the monk's cell *and his hide* (*ṣawmʿat al-rāhib wa-nāmūsuhu*)" and Farḥāt was deluded enough to imagine that *nāmūs* here means "rule" or "path" as is the common usage among Christians. In fact, the author of the *Qāmūs* intends the original meaning, which is "[a hunter's] hide." The common people say *nāwūs* [when they mean *nāmūs*], and this widespread sense in which they use the word is either a figurative extension of the meaning "one who holds a secret" [a further meaning listed in the *Qāmūs*] or an Arabization of the Greek [*naos* ("temple")].

from whence he set about delivering the sermon of Abū l-ʿIbar Ṭarad Ṭabak Ṭalandī Bak Nak Yak[131] from the drain.[132] Also that one day, he wanted to scale a wall so that he could reach some dates, and he fell into an animal trap set by the owner of the orchard.[133] And that one day he told his mother that such and such a woman had an excellent maid who had "washed the door of her house today till it was shining black." And that one day he caught sight of a boy who had had one of his molars removed, so he went and borrowed a dirham and told the cupper, "Take my molar out too because it doesn't cut my food; maybe another, sharper, molar will grow in its place."

1.3.3 And one day someone said to him, "Many stories have been recorded of your stupidity," to which he replied, "I wish someone would read them to me so I could have a laugh!" And one day his brother fell ill and his father said to his wife, "The food he ate yesterday was bad for him," and the poet said, "Yes, the food was bad for him and so was the maid." "What has the maid got to do with it?" his father asked him, and he said, "Maybe she gave him something he didn't like." And his mother noticed blood on his clothes and asked him, "What's that blood?" and he answered, "I fell over and my blood ran, which is for the good, for it is said, 'If someone falls over and his blood runs, he gets well and is strengthened.'" And he cut his hand with a knife and threw it away, saying, "This knife is worthless"; his father said to him, "If it really were, it wouldn't have cut your hand," to which the man replied, "Everyone in the world cuts his hand, if not with a knife then with something else."

1.3.4 And he said, "Once I saw cheese as white as tar in the market." And someone said to him, "Why don't you wash your hands?" He replied, "I do, but they get dirty again straight away; I can't get them clean because my blood is dirty." And one day he saw some men who had been crucified and he asked his mother, "Mother, if those men survive, can those who crucified them re-crucify them?" And a company of people once asked after someone's house and he said,

"I know where it is located." "How do you know?" he was asked and he replied, "I saw the man going through the market on foot." And one day he said, "Time moves faster between eight and nine than between six and seven." And someone asked him, "Which do you like better, meat or fish?" and he replied, "Really, I think I like this one better."[134]

And his father said to him, "If you were away from us, would you be able to write us a letter?" and he replied, "Yes. I'd write it and bring it to you, too." And he heard his father singing the praises of some silk-wool he'd bought and with which he was delighted, so the man said, "It would have been a fortunate hour if you hadn't bought it." And he saw his father writing a letter and said to him, "Father, can you read what you write?" and the father replied, "How could I not when I am the one who wrote it?" "For my part," the man said, "I cannot." And he saw that his father was upset over a bird he had lost and told him, "God bless the hour in which it flew away!," so his father said to him, "You imbecile, I'm upset at its loss." "So why didn't you build it a house?" responded the man. "Can one build a house for a bird?" asked the father. "All I mean," said the man "is two sticks going from here to there." 1.3.5

And once he described some animals he'd seen, saying, "They included a pig that was larger than me." And he complained of a pain in his foot and said, "I wish this foot would rot away." And his father was explaining to him the meaning of "to save" and said to him, "If someone fell into the fire, for example, and you went and pulled him out, that would be saving him," to which the man replied, "But he would have burned up, so how could I save him? Suppose I stuck this skewer into the fire and pulled him out with it, would that be saving?" And once another was explaining to him the meaning of "to reproach" and said to him, "If someone was slow in doing something for you and you said to him, 'Why were you so slow? Why were you so slothful?' that would be reproaching," and the man said, "And I'd tell him too, 'Why did you grow large? Why did you grow small? Why did you grow short?'"[135] 1.3.6

1.3.7 And his mother reproached him for snorting when he spoke, and he replied, "You should reproach not me but my breath." And his father wanted to go out one day when it was raining but decided against it because of the rain, so he said to his mother, "Mother, it's a blessing from God that we didn't go out today, for the weather was fine." And his mother bought him a length of cloth and when she had had it made up he said to her, "Will the color of this cloth fade?" "I don't know," she replied. "I hope that it does," he said, "because it might look better." And once in the winter, when he was wearing only a shift, his mother said to him, "Wear your robe over your shift!" and he told her, "No. It'll make me colder."

1.3.8 And his father reproached him for shrieking as he read out loud, and he said, "I can't shout any louder." And one day he couldn't think of the meaning of the word "visit," so his mother said to him, "If I were to go today to such and such a lady to see her, I would be visiting her." He responded, "I deduce from this that you're going to her to play a trick on her."[136] And his mother said to him, "Such and such a lady who was kind to you has died," and he was silent for a while and then said, "I have mourned for her as I would for my mother. May God send her and her husband to Heaven this minute!" And one day he told his father, "Today our teacher bought a rod to beat the children, and now they are making him angry in order to make him beat them with it till it breaks, which will be a relief to me too."

1.3.9 And he told his mother, who had fallen sick, "If we brought you a doctor and God wasn't willing to cure you, what would be the point of the medicine?" And on another occasion he said to her, "Use this medicine. It may make you sick." And one day he wanted to light the fire, so he said, "I wanted to put it out but it wouldn't go out." And his mother told him, "Go to such and such a woman and ask her, 'Why are you afraid of my mother? She's a human being like you,'" so he told her, "I'm going to tell her, 'My mother asks you, "Why will you have nothing to do with her when she's an animal just like you?"'" And once he said of something he admired, "May God be protected from every eye!"[137] And once he was told, "So and so wants to take you to his school to teach you" and he replied, "May God send him to Heaven!" His father asked him, "Do you want to kill him?" "What should I say then?" he asked. His father replied, "Say, 'God prolong his life!'" "He already has," said the man. And he asked his mother, "Will you give me some of that halvah tonight?" and she said to him, "If we live to see the night." He responded, "We're going to live to see the morrow, so how could we not see the night?" End.

An intelligent person of his country came to learn of these things and said to the Fāriyāq, "It appears to me that these sayings are dumb and disturbed, or dotty and deranged, or feather-brained and feeble-minded, or confounded and befuddled, or bedazed and confused, so how could he have gone on to become a poet?" The Fāriyāq told him, "Probably he intended, with these sayings of his, to make his parents laugh, or maybe his first impulses were slow-minded but his more carefully thought-out responses quick-witted. Some people are so put off their stroke by a question that they can only answer wrongly, but if they put their brains to work when they're on their own, they perform excellently. Or maybe his intention in doing so was to become noted and celebrated among men, if only for foolishness and folly, for most people seek fame by any means possible. 1.3.10

"Some practice the translation of books and teaching when they know nothing, despite which they derive pleasure from putting their names at the beginning of the book and stuffing it with feeble phrases and stupid statements that they make up themselves, or in having others report their sayings so that it may be said, 'So and so said thus and such,' the statement itself being erroneous and pointless. Others sit cross-legged at the forefront of the salon among their brethren and peers and suddenly start telling tales of far-away countries, mixing their words with a few phrases from foreign languages that they have learned. Thus they will say to them, for example, *sans façon*, and *pardon, monsieur*, and *dunque*, and *very well* to show that they have spent a lot of time touring France, Italy, and England and 1.3.11

have learned their languages, though they are ignorant of the language in which they were brought up.

1.3.12 "Some wear large turbans like those worn by certain scholars of religion, for a large turban is supposed to indicate a large head and a large head is supposed to indicate an excellent mind and sound judgment. Some affect to imitate some nasal intonation of those who are known for the chasteness of their speech, and you find them using high-sounding terms and chewing their words inside their mouths and using words inappropriately.

1.3.13 "But, to return to your original question: the poet does not have to be sensible, or a philosopher. Many madmen were poets. Examples are Abū l-ʿIbar, Buhlūl, ʿUlayyān,[138] Ṭuways,[139] and Muzabbid.[140] The philosophers have stated that poetry is the first product of rapture and that the best of it is that which has its origins in rapture and amorous infatuation, which explains why the poetry of sedate scholars is always feeble."

1.3.14 When the Fāriyāq[141] heard this, he renounced poetry in favor of committing rare words to heart. It wasn't long, however, before he reverted to his first nature, the reason being that his father took him with him to a certain distant village to collect the taxes imposed on its inhabitants and deliver them to the ruler's treasury. The people of the village put his father up in grand style, and, living close to where he was staying, was a girl of surpassing beauty. Despite his tender age, the Fāriyāq began to look on her with the eyes of the star-struck paramour, according to the custom of novices in love of first falling in love with girls who are their neighbors, because they believe the goal is easily reached and because they can make use of their relationship as neighbors to plead their cause. Similarly, the girl neighbors usually sigh over their boy neighbors and wink at them as a way of signaling that there's no need to go looking for a distant physician when the cure is close at hand. Old hands at love, however, look far afield and cruise the most distant grazing grounds, for, having made it their custom and habit to give in to every fancy of their souls, they feel it an obligation and a duty to make things difficult for themselves, and they find enormous pleasure in distancing themselves from the beloved and falling sick over her; any who opens his mouth in the hope that the fruit will fall into it can only be regarded as impotent.

In short, the Fāriyāq fell in love with his neighbor because he was new to the game, and she welcomed his love and gave him hope of success because she was a neighbor and because the prestige that he derived from being with his father disposed people well toward him. His stay did not last long, however, and he was compelled to return with his father. He had fallen very much in love with the girl and, when the time for separation came, he wept and mourned and heaved mighty sighs, and passion prompted him to compose a poem to express his love, one of whose verses went 1.3.15

I part from her against my will and
Leave, I swear, my soul with her

—which is much like the poetry of the rest of the poets of his day, who would swear mighty oaths that they had given up food and drink out of yearning and passion, had spent long nights awake out of love and longing, were dead men, and had died and been put in their shrouds and embalmed and buried, while at the same time indulging themselves in any sport that might be going. When his father took a look at these valedictory verses, he reproached him and forbade him to write poetry anymore, though this seems to have made it the more attractive to him, for it is, generally speaking, in the nature of sons to do the opposite of what their fathers want. Then he left that village sad, *forlorn*, bewitched, *lovelorn*.

## Chapter 4

# Troubles and a Tambour

1.4.1 The Fāriyāq's father was involved in matters as difficult in point of *extrication* as they were uncertain in terms of outcome and *implication*, given their ability to set people at one another's *throats* and the bad feeling between ruler and ruled that this *promotes*. He had a close relationship with a faction of Druze shaykhs famous for their doughtiness, valor, and generosity, whose hands, money pouches, coffers, cupboards, waist-bands,[142] and houses were, however, empty. It is no secret that the world, being round in shape, favors none unless they lure it with something equally round, namely the golden dinar, without which nothing happens. To serve it, sword and pen stand to *arms*, while knowledge and beauty throng to service its *demands*. Anyone endowed with an ample physique or excellent qualities will find that tallness and talent benefit him nothing without the dinar, which, despite its small size, can bend any large and weighty ambition or care of the soul to its will. Round, well-minted faces thus submit to it when e'er it appears, tall figures are drawn to it no matter where it wanders, shining brows bend o'er it, and the sunniest of dispositions darkens when it's lost.

1.4.2 As to what they say about the Druze being lazy and slow and about their knowing neither covenant nor compact, the truth is entirely otherwise. Their characterization as lazy is more akin to a compliment, for it springs from their moderation, abstention from dishonorable acts, and renunciation of the world. On the other hand, the most praiseworthy characteristics become indistinguishable from their opposites when men compete in making a show of them and they exceed by even a little their proper bounds. Thus, excessive clemency, for example, becomes indistinguishable from weakness, generosity from prodigality, courage from impetuosity and recklessness. Indeed, even excessive worship and religiosity become indistinguishable from obsession and insanity. This being the case, and given that the Druze are excessive in their moderation—so that you will not find any of them braving the desert wastes or setting forth upon the seas to seek their sustenance (*izāʾ*)(1) or aspiring to elegance in clothing or food or stooping to or becoming deeply involved in any base occupation or practicing the toilsome crafts—they are thought to be lazy and sluggish. It is also well known that as a person's appetites and greed increase, so too do his ill health, his hard work, and his cares. Frankish merchants, for all their wealth and riches, are worse off than the peasants of our country: you find them on their feet from morning until ten at night.

(1) *Izāʾ* means "means of sustenance, or whatever ease of living has been created through work."

As for the Druze knowing no agreements or covenants, this is mere slander and falsehood, for they have never been known to undertake to do something and then to break their word, unless they sensed foul play on the other's part. Nor is it known for an emir or shaykh of theirs to see his Christian neighbor's wife bathing one day and, finding her fair-skinned plumpness, her buttocks, and her fine silks pleasing, to send someone to flatter or abduct her. Also, as you are well aware, there are many Christians living under their patronage who have requested and received their promises of protection and who, if given the choice of abandoning their protectors in favor of having their security provided by the Christian shaykhs, would refuse. In my opinion, anyone who takes care to preserve the sanctity of the neighbor who is under his protection deserves every good thing and will not betray him in other matters. As for the factionalism and conspiracies among the Druze and other 1.4.3

communities, these are purely political matters, some wanting this emir to rule them and some that, and they have nothing to do with religion.

1.4.4 The Fāriyāq's father was one of those who sought to depose the emir who was, at the time, entrusted with the political affairs of the Mountain; he took the side of his enemies, who were the emir's relatives.[143] More than once, commotions and skirmishes broke out. Then the tide turned against the emir's enemies, and they fled to Damascus begging for aid from its governor, who gave them promises and raised their hopes. On the night of their escape, the emir's troops attacked the Fāriyāq's home town, so he fled with his mother to a fortified house nearby belonging to another emir. Looters took all the silver and household possessions that they found in his house, among them a tambour[144] that he used to play in his spare time. When these convulsions quieted down, the Fāriyāq and his mother returned to their house and found it stripped bare. A few days later, the tambour was returned to him; the person who'd stolen it, seeing no benefit in carrying it about and unable to sell it—for players of musical instruments in those parts were very few—had given it to the village priest to make amends for what he had stolen, and the priest returned it to the Fāriyāq.

1.4.5 Do I hear someone objecting here and asking, "What is the point of this banal tale?" I respond: as we said, a tambour was a very rare item on the Mountain, for composing tunes and playing musical instruments are regarded as shameful, because they induce ecstatic pleasure and amorousness and incite desire. The natives there are fanatical about religion and warn against anything capable of causing sensual pleasure. Consequently, they do not want to learn to sing or play an instrument or to use the latter in their places of worship and their prayers, as do their Frankish shaykhs,[145] lest this lead them into disbelief. Thus, every one of the gentle arts, such as poetry and harmony, for example, or painting, is an abomination. Could they but hear the hymns sung in the churches of their aforementioned shaykhs or the tunes on the organ that people are so fond of and that are played in places of entertainment, dance halls, and cafés to attract men and women, they'd find no sin in the tambour.

1.4.6 The tambour is to the organ as the branch is to the tree or the thigh to the body, for the only sound that it makes is a strumming, while the organ produces strumming and humming, mumbling and rumbling, jangling and jingling, squeaking and creaking, chirping and cheeping, burbling and barking, clicking and clacking, gnashing and crashing, chinking and clinking, gurgling and gargling, purring, cooing, and bleating, thrumming and drumming, roaring and guffawing, glugging and gabbling, la-la-ing and lullabying, horses' neighs and the roaring of waves, blubbing of billy goats and cricking of cradles, cries of men at war, call of merlins and raven's caw, old women moaning and heavy doors groaning, snores and stertors, huffing and soughing, water boiling and grief-stricken bawling, frogs ribbiting and ears tinky-tinkling, bulls bellowing and gaming-house reprobates roaring, reverberations and crepitations, pots gently bubbling and chilly dogs whimpering, pulleys squeaking and crickets chirruping, milk flowing, chickens crowing, and cats mewing, not to mention caw-caw and hubble-bubble and wham-bam and slurp-slurp and baa-baa and tee-hee and keek-keek and buzz-buzz and schlup-flup[146]—after all of which, what's wrong, God guide you, with plinkety-plink? If it be said that that aversion to playing the organ derives solely from its resemblance to the buttocks, reply may be made, "What do you make then of the fact that their women enter their churches with those silver 'horns' that resemble pigs' snouts (God exalt you above any contamination by their mention!) on their heads, given that pigs' snouts (God exalt you above any contamination by their mention!) resemble you-know-whats?" This should prove to you that your objection is baseless and mention of the tambour appropriate.

1.4.7 If you insist on being obstinate, are bent on catching me out in error and exposing me for slips (and non-slips) of the pen, and want to show people how clever you are by criticizing me, then I won't go through with this book. I swear, if you knew the reason why I embarked on it—namely, to relieve your dudgeon and entertain your mind—you wouldn't utter a word of reproach against me about anything. Meet, then, good deeds with good and be patient with me till I finish my tale. Afterward, if it crosses your mind to throw my book into the fire, or the water, go ahead.

1.4.8 Let us return now to the Fāriyāq. We declare: he lived with his mother in the house and practiced the copyist's trade, but news of his father's demise in Damascus soon reached him. He was heartbroken and wished the tambour were still with the one who stole it. Each morning his mother would go off by herself, utter laments for her husband, and grieve for him, the tears gushing for his loss, for she was one of those righteous women who love their husbands with honest affection and true loyalty. She thought that, if she went off by herself, her son wouldn't see her and her sorrow would not then be compounded by seeing him weep at her grief, but the Fāriyāq would look on her in her private place and weep bitterly over her desolation and loneliness. Then when she returned he would hold back his tears and busy himself with writing or anything else. It was now that he realized that he had nothing he could rely on, after God, but the sweat of his own brow, so he devoted himself to copying. However, since the day that God created the pen, that profession has never been enough to support those who practice it, especially in countries where the appearance of a piaster is cause for rejoicing and the sight of a dinar is greeted with plaudits of "God is great!" and "We seek refuge with God from lapidated Satan!" It did, however, give him a good hand and refine his thinking.

## Chapter 5

# A Priest and a Pursie, Dragging Pockets and Dry Grazing[147]

If anyone read the end of the previous chapter and then his servant came and called him to dinner, causing him to leave the book and rise and turn toward glasses and goblets, tumblers and tankards (in all their different shapes and sizes), and then his friends dropped in to pass the evening with him, one saying, "Today I beat my slave girl and went down to the market with her intending to sell her, even at half price, because she'd given my wife a pert answer" and another, "And I too today beat my son because I found him playing with the neighbors' children and then I locked him up in the latrine and he's still there" and another, "And today I insisted to my wife that she make me privy to every thought and worry that goes through her head or troubles her breast and every dream she dreams at night—such dreams coming from the food vapors that fill her brain or from the smoke of passion consummated before sleeping—and I told her, 'If you don't tell me every detail, I'll set the priest on you and he'll declare you a disbeliever and ban you from the church and then he'll get out of you everything you're hiding and harboring and take a good look at everything you're concealing and secreting and holding out on, that you're on guard against, have taken measures to prevent, feel at ease with, have a liking for, and have taken it upon yourself to do,' and I left my house in a rage against my wife, uttering threats, and swore I'd only make up with her if she told me her 1.5.1

dreams" and another, "My problem with my eldest daughter is even worse, to wit, today, after she had coiffed, hatted, perfumed, scented, bedecked, painted, made-up, arrayed, displayed, rouged, bedizened, bejeweled, tricked out, beautified, decorated, adorned, dandified, prettified, primped, preened, prinked and pranked herself, donned her saffron-dyed dress and girded her loins for battle, she went and sat by the window to watch the people going in and out. I forbade her to do so, so she left, but then she disobeyed me and returned to her place and tricked me into thinking that she was sitting there to darn some of her clothes, but for every stitch she made, she stole two looks, so I went to her burning with anger and tugged her by the hair that she'd dressed and braided and curled, and a tress came off in my hand (here it is!), and, if she doesn't put an end to her wicked ways, I'll pull it all out, for she's like an unruly filly without reins: boxing her ears doesn't stop her, and nor do beatings with sticks"—if anyone, I say, filled his bowels with all kinds of food and his ears with talk of this sort, he will certainly have forgotten all the physical and moral incidents that have befallen the Fāriyāq (*his grief at hearing of his father's death, his devoting himself to the copying of books, and how he thereby acquired an excellent hand*) which is why I have just been compelled to repeat them.

1.5.2 Though here I would add that, when his excellence as a copyist became bruited abroad, a certain man whose name rhymes with Baʿīr Bayʿar[148] summoned him to copy out the ledgers in which he would enter everything that had happened during his day. His purpose in doing so was not to benefit any scholar but derived from a simple desire to hold onto events lest they escape the orbit of the days or become detached from the chain of circumstance, for many believe that to summon up the past and make it a visible entity is in itself a great thing. This is why the Franks have been keen to record everything that happens in their lands; the exit of an old woman from her house in the morning and her return to it at ten o'clock, leading a dog of hers, with the wind blowing and the rain coming down hard, neither escapes their pens nor is foreign to their thoughts.

There is material of this sort in the introduction to the verse collection *Méditations poétiques* of Lamartine,[149] the greatest French poet of our day, which I translate as follows: "The Arabs smoked tobacco in their long pipes in silence, watching the smoke rising like graceful blue columns until it dispersed into the air in a way beguiling to the observer, the air at the time being transparent, gentle." Later he goes on: "Then my Arab companions put the barley in goat's hair nosebags and placed these around the necks of the horses that were around my tent, their feet tethered to iron rings, and which stood motionless, their heads lowered to the ground and shaded by their heavy forelocks, their coats a glossy grey and smoking beneath the hot rays of the sun. The men, having gathered in the shade of an enormous olive tree, had spread out beneath them on the ground mats from Damascus, and set about talking and telling tales of the desert as they smoked their tobacco. They recited verses by ʿAntar, one of those Arab poets celebrated for their valor,[150] husbandry"—by which he means, "animal husbandry"—"and eloquence, his verses having as much effect on them as the Persian tobacco in their nargilehs. When a verse cropped up that appealed particularly to their feelings, they would raise their hands to their ears, bow their heads, and cry out over and over again, '*Allah! Allah! Allah!*'"[151] Later, describing a woman whom he saw weeping at the grave of her husband, he says, "Her hair hung down from her head, enveloped her, and brushed the ground. Her entire bosom was exposed, as is the custom among the women of this part of Arabia, and when she bent to kiss the carved turban that topped the gravestone or press her ear against it, her exposed breasts would touch the ground and press their shapes into the dust, as though they were molds" (end; p. 24). The rest of this introduction is of the same character, even though he calls it *Poetry's Destiny*, meaning, "what God Almighty has ordained for poetry and poets."[152] 1.5.3

1.5.4 Similarly, the *Voyage en Amérique* of Chateaubriand,[153] also one of the greatest poets of his day, contains the following: "The residence of the president of the United States was a small house built in the English style, with neither a guard of soldiers round it nor servants inside. When I knocked on the door, a young girl opened to me, so I asked her if the general was at home. She replied that he was. I said I had a letter that I wanted to deliver to him, so she asked me my name, which she found hard to remember. Then she said, *Walk in sir*." (He gives these words in English to show that he knows the language.) "Then she walked in front of me, down a long walkway like a corridor and took me into a private apartment and indicated to me that I should sit down there and wait," etc. (p. 25). Elsewhere he writes that he saw an American Indian woman with a thin cow and said to her, bewailing its state, "Why is this cow so thin?" and the woman answered him, "She eats little," and again he provides these words in English, to wit, *She eats very little*. In yet another place he writes that he observed fragments of clouds, some in the shape of animals and others in that of a mountain or a tree or similar things. Knowing this, you will appreciate that, in objecting to my talking of things that are of no interest to you but are to me, you are simply being stubborn.

1.5.5 These two great poets wrote what they did fearing the censure of none, and none of their race opposed them. Indeed, the acknowledgment of their worth and their reputations grew to such dimensions that Our Lord the Sultan, may God preserve his rule, awarded Lamartine vast estates in the area of Izmir, even though no one has ever heard of a Frankish king awarding an Arab, Persian, or Turkish poet a single field, sown or barren. As for the person-whose-name-rhymes-with-Baʿīr-Bayʿar imitating the Franks in his history when he was an Arab, both his parents were Arabs, and his paternal uncle and aunt were both Arabs—the reasons remain unclear to me to this day. Maybe I'll find out after finishing this book and then, God willing, let the reader know. All I ask is that no reader stop reading just because he's ignorant of the reasons behind this imitation, important as they may be.

Here now is an example of the sort of thing the Fāriyāq used to write concerning the legends of Baʿīr Bayʿar: "On this day, the eleventh of the month of March 1818, So-and-so, son of Mistress So-and-so daughter of Mistress So-and-so, cut the tail of his grey stallion, which had been so long it swept the ground. That very day, he mounted it and it threw him off." If you ask, "Why does he give the man's ancestry via the female line?" I reply, "Baʿīr Bayʿar was religious, godly, and pious, and it is more proper and precise to trace a man's ancestry via his mother than his father, for there can be only one mother—which is not the case with the father—because the fetus has only one possible exit point." Further: "Today a ship was seen on the sea, plowing along. It was thought to be a man-o'-war come from one of the ports of France to bring freedom to the people of the land. On investigation, however, it turned out to be just a rowing boat loaded with empty barrels coming to take water from the spring at such-and-such a place." If it be said that this contradicts the normal state of affairs, for large things appear small at a distance and not the opposite, reply may be made that when a person gives himself over to his fancies, he sees things differently from how they really are. Thus, for example, someone in love with a short woman will fail to notice her shortness, and if someone finds himself alone with his beloved in a hunter's hide, he'll think it more spacious than the pavilion of Bilqīs;[154] furthermore, a small light seen from a distance will appear to us as a large one. Small wonder, then, that a rowing boat should look like a man-o'-war or a frigate. The people there still dream that their heads have been crowned with the bonnets of the French and their honor welded to theirs, to the degree that they see their womenfolk to be like those described by the poet when he says: 1.5.6

Our gazelles along the paths
    The raging lions hunt with word and glance.
And the gazelles of the Franks hunt too, with both of those,
    But by adding hands the hunt they enhance.

1.5.7 Baʿīr Bayʿar was a big-buttocked, short-legged, round, waddling little glutton, but he was also mild-mannered and loved peace and self-effacement. To a great extent he was a simpleton. He had delegated his worldly affairs to a base man of vicious morals, conceited, proud, arrogant, uncouth, boastful, and haughty. An hour or two would pass without his uttering a word, so the poor simpleton thought he must be exercising his wits on setting the world to rights or syncretizing the different sects, for it has become a habit to regard the man of elevated status, if he be inarticulate and at a loss to answer questions, as serious and dignified, and if he be a prattler, as a sound counselor.

1.5.8 Baʿīr Bayʿar's spiritual affairs, on the other hand, rose and fell, waned and waxed, came apart at the seams and were mended up again through the scheming of a jolly, cheerful, smiling, jovial priest, short and fat, white and plump. This goodly Father had gained an unshakeable control over the man's womenfolk, having found his niche with one of the man's daughters, who was comely of face, dulcet of tongue, and had been married to a man who had gone insane and become a madman; leaving him to his madness, she had sought the sanctuary of her father's household, where the priest had become her master and *commander*, her conscience and *reprimander*. Anything that was delivered to her or that she dispatched she would give him to look at, for she was one of those who made no distinction between the domains of this world and the next. She confessed her transgressions to him in private, and he would question her concerning every slip and lapse, asking her, "Do your buttocks *shake* and your breasts *quake* as you climb the stairs or when walking? And does this shaking produce a pleasurable sensation? I ask only because it is mentioned in a chronicle that a certain sensualist found relief in any shaking whatsoever, even praying many a time that the earth would quake beneath his feet and the mountains above him move from side to side. And did you ever see yourself in your dreams struggling with some *bed-mate*, or shaking the hand of some *profligate* (there being in God's eyes no difference between the waking and the sleeping *state*, the strongest realities being but built upon dreams)? And did the Recoiler ever whisper in your ear and leave you with a desire to be a hermaphrodite (which is to say, both male and female, and not, as the common people say, neither male nor female, the latter being a definition that has found no favor with erudite and learned scholars who make sure of their facts)?"

Thus spoke he, and of other matters that this chapter is not large enough to hold. He could do no wrong in her father's eyes because the latter was so convinced that all who wore black had weaned their appetites off worldly pleasures and cut themselves off from sensual desires, that, when one day he saw the following line of verse in a book[155]— 1.5.9

To us they condemned the world while they themselves on it
suckled
Till they'd drained the milk that collects between milkings, so
that even the supernumerary teats could yield us nought—

he imagined that this had been written to run the clergy down and make insinuations against them and ordered that it be burned, which it was, and its ashes scattered. And one day he saw another two verses in a book, which went like this—

How is it that mine eye ne'er sees
A skinny man among those mortals who wear black?
Of what they have by way of flesh or any other thing
The hardest bit is that which stands erect, the rest is slack—

so he ordered that that book be burned too and sent spies out into the town to find out who its author was, the call going out over hill and dale, "Let him who can point out the author of this book come forward, for he will be rewarded with the best of rewards and raised to an elevated state!" When the poet heard this, he was obliged to go into hiding for a while, until his name was forgotten. If you say, "This contradicts your description of him as mild-mannered," I reply, "It is the custom of the people of the country to regard mildness as praiseworthy in all things but two—the sanctity of women's honor and the sanctity of religion, for the sake of which a man will deliver his brother to perdition."

1.5.10 The Fāriyāq resided with this mild-mannered man for a while, during which he made not a sou. Too proud to complain when asked, he was driven one night to gather large quantities of firewood and straw and set fire to them. The flames leaped toward the private apartments of Baʿīr Bayʿar, who, thinking that the fire had engulfed his palace, roused everyone. They came, each trying to be the first to reach the fire, and there they found the Fāriyāq adding fuel to it by the armful. When they asked him what he thought he was doing, he said, "This is one of those fires that take the place of a tongue, even if it doesn't have the form of one. Among its virtues, it alerts the *slack-twisted* and gives warning to the *tight-fisted* that behind it stand words that are *strong*, and an iron *tongue*!" "Woe unto you!" they said. "This is one of your godless innovations! Who speaks through fire? We've heard of people speaking to one another using a trumpet, or by beating on something with a stick, or by making a sign with a finger, or by winking an eye, or by moving an eyebrow, or by raising a hand in the air, but fire is a godless innovation and a deviation."

1.5.11 Just as they were about to declare him a heretic and a disbeliever and call him a Magian[156] and throw him into the fire, one man said to the others, "Before you do anything rash, report his answer to the one who sent you." When they informed Baʿīr Bayʿar of what they had seen and heard, he demanded to see the Fāriyāq and asked him to tell him about the blaze in question, so the latter said to him, "God better Our *Lord* and more blessings and power to him *accord*! Once I had a little pursie that was of no more use to me than I was to it. Now pursies, and other things that have similar-sounding names,[157] have a way with them that goes against all other ways, for, when they're light they're a drag, and when they're heavy, they're delightful. When my pursie grew light while within your Happy Purlieu, which is to say, when it grew to be a drag, I burned it in this fire, which I only made this big because when that pursie was in my pocket it felt as big to me as Mount Raḍwā,[158] to the point that it often prevented me from standing up and going out on some important errand."

When Baʿīr Bayʿar heard his words, he laughed at his fanciful invention and squeezed from his tight fist something equal in its exiguousness to what the Fāriyāq had copied out in his ledgers. The Fāriyāq then hopped and skipped all the way home, swearing he would never again write anything that wasn't worth writing or yielded no profit, with the hope that the fee would be in proportion to the quantity of the work—which is, of course, a ridiculous notion, as those who work hardest and whose work deserves the geatest *consideration* receive the lowest wages and *remuneration*, while for those who can do no more than sign their *names* are reserved the highest *planes*, and the hands and feet of such as these are gobbled at, much as the breast is gobbled at by the suckling child. 1.5.12

## Chapter 6

# Food and Feeding Frenzies

1.6.1 While the Fāriyāq's head and feet stayed put in his house, his mind was climbing mountains and hills, scaling walls, conquering castles, descending into valleys and *caves*, plunging into mire, roaming deserts and launching itself upon the *waves*, for his dearest desire was to see a land other than his own and people other than his family, which is everyone's first concern while growing up. It occurred to him therefore to visit one of his brothers who was a scribe working for a Druze notable, and he set forth, with nothing for baggage but his dreams. When he was united with him and beheld how coarse and rough were the people and how at variance with his own nature were the conditions there, he rejected some of those things and resigned himself to putting up with the rest.

1.6.2 At the same time, he didn't want to find himself at some point about to return without first having got to know them better, albeit had he been wiser, he would have had nothing to do with them from the first day on, for it is not to be expected that the people of a city or a village will change their manners and the ways in which they've been raised for the sake of a stranger who has entered among them, especially if they be hulking fellows of great height and strength while he's a little titch. The less work people have to do, though, the more their curiosity gets the better of them; this being the case, it wasn't enough for him to make do with what his ears had heard: he had to see it with his own eyes.

The better the Fāriyāq got to know these folk through experience and close examination, the less he liked them and the less he wanted to do with them, for they were coarse-natured, full of boorishness, and horrid to *excess*, their clothes and bedding filthy, they themselves ever prey to shortage of provisions and *distress*. The filthiest of all was the emir's cook: his shirt was fouler than a *cum-rag*, and his feet bore more dirt than one could scrape into a *vomit bag*. When they sat down to eat, such rumbling and mumbling and teeth-gnashing and lip-smacking was to be heard you would have thought they were wild beasts at a carcass. They ate like animals, taking huge bites, burying their front teeth in the food, stripping off the meat down to the bone, sucking out the marrow, licking their lips and smacking them, polishing off the desserts, licking the plates with their tongues, and throwing half-eaten food down on the table, all the while seated on the ground with their legs crossed under them at their ease. You might think that on each one's brow was inscribed the proverb "Eat your fill and you'll never be ill." When they stood up, one beheld their beards strewn with *rice*, their clothes dripping with *grease*. When the Fāriyāq ate with them, he'd get up hungry from the *table* and his guts would rise against him, so that till late at night to sleep he'd be *unable*. 1.6.3

To his brother he'd say, amazed at how any with *wits* could live in the company of these barbarous *twits*, "What distinguishes the Druze from the beasts save their beards and their turbans? For sure, their very way of life leads to the closing of their eyes and *minds*, the opening of their mouths and *behinds*. Scarce one of them can credit that God Almighty has created a race of men to which they are not superior. They're unaware that a man isn't better than a dumb *animal* or distinguishable from an inanimate *mineral* simply because he has the power of speech. Words are but the Matter pertaining to the Form in which various meanings may be *expressed*, 1.6.4

and this Matter alone is of no use if the Form, which is the second stage of existence, has not within it been *impressed*.[159] It has been said that 'a silver coin covers the fool's shortcomings,' but these people have been deprived of both brains and *ease* and are content to take from this whole world nought but the *breeze*. How can you bear to live alongside such *kine*, and at a time when your own gifts have just begun to *shine*?"

1.6.5 His brother replied, "They often envy me for my standing with the *emir*, but I bear the wiles of my enviers with patience, however hard they be *to bear*. As it is said:

Many things men think a blessing
To those who have them, when in fact they bring them down.
Did not the envious plot to take them from them,
They'd disavow them with a frown.

"In addition, these people are endowed with pride and *chivalry*, courage and *gallantry*, and though ill-mannered at the *board*, they're well-mannered in deed and *word*. They never utter a word *obscene*, and among them sodomy and adultery are nowhere to be *seen*."

1.6.6 The Fāriyāq, however, could appreciate no manners but those of the dining table, as though he'd been gently raised by *Franks* or belonged somehow to their *ranks*. Summoning, then, his native wit to mock them and being *obeyed*, calling for rhymes to describe them and being not *gainsaid*, he composed on them an ode in which he exposed the wretchedness of their daily *grind* and their coarseness of *mind*, one line of which went:

When each one holds knife and cutter
In his mouth, what's left for him to eat with?

1.6.7 He showed this to his brother (to whose knowledge of literature all bore *witness*, as they did to his grammatical *fitness*) and the latter thought it well done—even though the Fāriyāq's age was still *tender*—and was impressed by the skill with which his art he did *render*. In no time, however, the ode became *celebrated*, and much *debated*, the reason being that his brother, so proud, recited it to many of those whom he *knew*, at which one of the envious communicated it to the emir of the *crew*. This informer was a Christian—envy being a quality found only among Christians—even though many of those to whom it had been read out were among the Druze who were the object of the satire.

When the emir heard about it, he was greatly offended and told his brother, "*Forsooth*, your brother's committed an act *uncouth*! How can he satirize us when he's our guest whom we've dealt with as one of high *station*, and to whom we've alloted generous *compensation*? I swear to God, if he doesn't cancel out his attack with a poem of praise, I shall vex him greatly." This emir was, of the Arab qualities of chivalry and courage, the *epitome*, and would do anything in his power to attract a *eulogy*, though he submitted his affairs to *fate*, giving little thought to his current or future *state*. Now, however, he feared this threat might invite further *attacks*, should the Fāriyāq leave his service while in a *wax*, and thus decided that to disregard the slight was the best path to *placation*, flattery the surest route to *reconciliation*. As a consequence, he discreetly asked a friend of his, a scholar of his *sect*, a member of the community's *elect*, to put on a feast, to which he was to invite him, the Fāriyāq, and his brother. 1.6.8

When all had been gathered by the public crier in one *place*, the sweets brought in on dishes like a herd of camels heading up a *race*, the emir made an oath and swore, "I shall not taste of these, till Abū Dulāmah"[160] (meaning the Fāriyāq) "has composed two lines of praise *impromptu*!" The Fāriyāq, not slow to respond, came up with the following, *in situ*: 1.6.9

Abū Dulāmah by nature can scarce forbear to mock
  For mockery's in his nature fixed.
But this date-and-butter pudding stopped him in his tracks
  When his sour tongue with its sweetness mixed.

The company went into transports over the lines, to the point that the emir couldn't restrain himself from shaking the Fāriyāq's hand

and kissing him between the eyes. This sealed their mutual *conciliation* and all returned home in *jubilation*, though our friend went to his house and swore he'd never again tie his forelock to any great man's skirts and would block his ears to the reverberations of their *reputations*, though they rang louder than any church bells' *tintinnabulations*.

## Chapter 7

# A Donkey that Brayed, a Journey Made, a Hope Delayed

Thereafter the Fāriyāq continued to practice his first profession, becoming, in the process, as sick of it as the invalid of his *bed*. He had a true friend who kept an eye on how he was; once they met and embarked on a discussion of how a person might keep himself *fed* and cut a dash before others by dint of wearing the best *thread*, both concluding that the people of their day judged others not by their virtue and *discrimination* but by their attire and its *decoration*, that those who were born to the wearing of the silk-wool, silk, cotton, and linen that are hung on the pegs of merchants' stores were of greater account than those who were without of such things, and that a person, be he petty and *dumb*, so long as his pantaloons and drawers were baggy, was the one man all would point to as noble and learned and who'd be praised by every *tongue*. They ended up agreeing that they'd acquire some goods for trade and try to sell them in certain towns, as a way to observe how their inhabitants lived and to dispel the rancor from their minds. 1.7.1

They hired a donkey to carry their wares, though the donkey was so thin and emaciated he could barely carry his own carcass, let alone whatever might be put on top of him. Nothing of any force was left him but his bray and his fart. The first of these was an appeal for *fodder*, the second directed at any who threw a pack-saddle on him and at any *prodder*. Then they set off, cutting the cloth of success 1.7.2

to fit the figure of *hope*, measuring out the carpet of triumph to fit fate's *scope*. By the time they reached their destination, however, the donkey was at the edge of a crumbling dike of *prostration*, while the Fāriyāq too was about to give up the ghost from fatigue and *vexation*, remorseful at having abandoned his pen, however *ungiving*, along with the little it spat out by way of a *living*.

1.7.3 That day he discovered the consequence of *greed* and where cupidity can *lead*. He realized how foolish he'd been to lust after that which brings with it physical *contusion* and mental *confusion*. It is also true, though, that the wise man is he who extracts some benefit from each *reverse*, some advantage from each circumstance *adverse*. Even in loss of health there's benefit to him whose path is *straight*, good fortune for him who doesn't *deviate*, for the soul of the sick man stretched out head upon pillow is too constrained to pursue *depravity*, forbidden lusts, or mortal *iniquity*. As the disease makes him weaker, his insight becomes *stronger*, and he sees things more plainly as the pain lasts *longer*, thus pleasing both God and men with his behavior. This was how things stood with the Fāriyāq, after he had suffered through these *travails*, for when he became sensible of the hardships of *travel*, and saw what it had to offer by way of *trials*, it became clear to him that the slit of the pen nib was more capacious than the salesman's *sack*, colored wares less gay than ink, however *black*, while to the marketing of goods there pertained a *stigma* no less great than that of buboes or of *goiter*. He determined, therefore, that, on returning to his hometown, he'd rest content with whatever ease or discomfort life might *bring*, not caring if he were a man of *note*, wore an elegant *coat* or lived like a *king*, and that never again through the world's cities would he *pass*, walking behind an *ass*.

1.7.4 Now, were I to describe the donkey after our *fashion*, my dear Arab *nation*, I'd say he was a slow-witted beast with a vicious *kick*, balky, stubborn, and shaggy, with a hide that was *thick*, scarce willing to move without the *stick*. Catching sight of a drop of water on the ground, he'd think it a flotsam-covered *ocean* and, as scared as though it promised death, shy from it like an ostrich and make a *commotion*.

Were I, though, to describe him in the Frankish way, I'd say he was a donkey son of a donkey, born of a she-ass all of whose ancestors were donkeys. His color tended toward the *black* and his hair felt like thorns when you touched his *back*; his ears were cropped and *listless*, his legs stiff, his coat starting to fall, and he was *toothless*; wide-mouthed, slack-lipped, and with hide discolored, he kicked out when goaded and when driven walked with buttocks *splayed*, not to mention that he sniffed at she-asses' pee, rolled on the ground, smeared his dung everywhere and *sprayed*. The stick on him had no effect, nor did rebuke, when he *disobeyed* and he never *moved* unless he sensed *food*, be it only darnel. No trace of animal nature would he show until a she-ass he *espied*; then you'd see him frisk and gambol, show vigor and pull the bridle to one *side*, so that he often overturned his load or sent it *askew*; and another peculiarity he had *too*, which was that, rarely though his molars were put to work, everywhere he *defecated* and incessantly over hill and dale he *flatulated*, making him seem yet more *ill-fated*. He'd been raised in lands where there was an abundance of cabbage, radish, rape, turnip, and cauliflower, as there is in certain foreign *parts*, and was therefore accustomed from his youth to producing *farts*, and this condition had only grown worse as he'd grown older. Thus any who walked behind him had, *perforce*, to hold his nose and keep saying "*How coarse!*" In any case, whichever of the two descriptive modes you choose, of all the pains of the journey and its injuries, keeping company with this *beast* was by no means the *least*. 1.7.5

After touring a number of villages offering neither bed nor *board*, and after long debates with customers and hagglings and chafferings they could ill *afford*, the Fāriyāq and his partner returned with *nowt*, deciding to cut their losses and return to whence they'd set *out*, well aware that "the empty well cannot be filled by *rain*," that any further toil at this affair would be in *vain*. They were thus compelled to sell their goods for the price they'd *paid* to forestall from gloating any 1.7.6

who might see them returning with the very stuff they'd taken to *trade*, and spent the night as though stunned from all the *rout*, for there are people who'll buy a thing only after they've turned it inside *out* and called the seller a fool and a *gyp*, leaving him no choice but to bite his *lip*, to the likes of these paying no *attention* but turning, rather, a blind eye and offering no *contention*. This talent, though, was not one possessed by either the Fāriyāq or his *friend*, each of whom sought to bend the world to his own *end*.

1.7.7 Thus they returned with the cost of the goods and the donkey and handed the money over to his owner, who offered them other goods, which they refused. They did, however, agree to meet again to work as partners on some business of greater import, preferring that this be in selling and buying too, for it is usual, when someone does a job and does not at first succeed, that his avarice insist he try again, since no one will accept that he was born to be unlucky or suffer dire fortune; rather, he attributes his bad luck in his chosen profession to certain accidents and unexpected incidents that have befallen him, telling himself, "The same will not occur this time around." The root of all this is man's dependence on his own intelligence, his confidence in his own efforts, and his reliance on his own intuitions. Many of God's creation have done so *fecklessly*, most hurting themselves in the process and destroying their livelihoods *recklessly*.

## Chapter 8

# Bodega, Brethren, and Board

After a long discussion between the Fāriyāq and his companion, they settled on renting an inn on the road to the city of al-Kuʿaykāt, where are to be found the caravans that leave for the city of al-Rukākāt.[161] They stocked up on what they needed by way of provisions and equipment and settled there, doing business with whatever *cap*ital (and *ass*ets)[162] they'd been able to muster. It wasn't long before their renown spread among all who came and went *thence*, all travelers learned of their good *sense*, and people started seeking them out for their reasonable prices, so that their inn was so much frequented by the better and more skilful class of *men*, those possessed of means and *gravamen*, that it became as a garden where the distressed could find relief. 1.8.1

Now, it is typical of the people of that district that they can hardly meet together in any place without passing back and forth among them the chalice of discussion and *debate*, plunging into matters that both to this world and the next *relate*. If one asserts a *proof*, the next denies its *truth*, and if the first believes that it is *well*, the other condemns it and claims it'll send you to *Hell*. The people thus divide into opposing *factions*, the place filling with clamor and disastrous *actions*. Sometimes the discussion ends with boasting over noble *extraction* and high degree of influential *connection*, one saying, for example, to his fellow, "Would you answer me back, 1.8.2

when my father's the companion of the *emir*, sits with him of an evening to maintain his good *cheer*, is his partner at *board* and at *bar*, the frequenter of his salon and his *mate*, his special friend and *intimate*? Not a night goes by without him summoning him to *socialize*, and he makes no decisions without first asking his *advice*. Plus, my people have been known since time immemorial as ambassadors to many a *land* and confidential advisors to the *grand*. Never has any man vied with him in glory, honor, plenty, pride, or virtue without being beaten, thrashed, trashed, outdone and undone." At this, cudgels might be set to work and take the place of arguments, he who hadn't lost his temper losing it, and *all*, drunk and sober alike, setting down to *brawl*. In the end, news of the affair would come to the ear of the emir of the local *lands*, who would send men to exact punishment by dealing out to them slaps with their *hands*, and woe betide any who dragged the name of the emir into the *discussion*: pardon for him was out of the *question*. Where grave matters were concerned and the aggressor fled in fear of retribution, a member of his family or a neighbor, or his cattle and stores, would be taken to pay for his crime, his trees would be felled, and his house burned.

1.8.3 Our company, however, never crossed the line between debate and donnybrook, for the Fāriyāq and his companion took on the role of arbiter, and, this being the case, the number of those who frequented them became great. Many a time, family men would spend the night with them, each the other with wine *plying*, songs succeeding one another, faces radiant,[163] turbans *flying*—which led to conflict between the women and their husbands. It is in the nature of women generally, should anyone keep their husbands from them, to scheme till, by one of their wiles, they can get close to that person. If the man is *handsome*, they promptly make a deal of barter and exchange with him, to exact revenge, taking every limb of his as their husband, every hair as their boon *companion*; should he be of the type to which the eye's *averse*, they get him into trouble, plotting to wrest their husbands from him and thus their loss of goods *reverse*.

The women of those lands,[164] however, do not oppose their husbands, keeping the latter's infidelities to themselves and regarding it as permitted for their husbands to replace them. They have been raised to feel affection for their fathers and be obedient to their husbands, and their disputes with them go no further than reprimands—and how pleasurable a reprimand can often be! To this day no one has heard of any of them taking a dispute with her husband to the legal authorities or an emir or a bishop, though many members of these three groups would like that to happen in certain circumstances, either so that they could boast of their imposition of justice and fair dealing upon their subjects, or for some other reason. Also part of the nature of these blessed creatures is the purity of their intentions, the sincerity of their belief, and their capacity to create intimate relationships with men without hint of debauchery. One may observe one of these women, married or a widow, sitting beside a man and taking his hand, or putting her hand on his shoulder and resting her head on his chest, smiling at him, holding friendly converse with him, and making him a present of something that has come her way, and all that with sincere intent and uncomplicated affection. The best qualities to be observed in them are their simplemindedness and naiveté, which, in women, are to be preferred to guile and cunning, so long as they do nothing to bring them dishonor or destroy their sanctity as women. When things get serious, however, simplemindedness will not do. 1.8.4

In addition, given their habit of exposing their chests and their use of nothing, from childhood on, to support their breasts, theirs are mostly pendulous. Most of them think that the longer they breastfeed their children, the healthier it is for them, and some breastfeed them for two whole years, or even longer. Their affection for their children and their kindness to them and tenderness toward them are too great to describe. I have known many girls who, on their wedding days, wept at being separated from their fathers, mothers, and siblings as other women do at funerals, or more. The claim that their husbands eat on their own, without their wives, is 1.8.5

completely without basis; this happens only if the husband has a guest who is not a member of the family, on which occasion, even if he should wish to have his wife sit down with the guest, she would refuse, believing that such a thing would indicate lack of respect for her and a violation of her sanctity.

1.8.6 Overall, there is nothing for which they can be blamed save ignorance, and in that they are to be excused. Ignorant Frankish women add to their ignorance cunning and baseness, so how much the worse is their shame! It pains me greatly to hear of the beloved women of Lebanon growing discontented with these virtues and adopting other ways. If this is indeed the case, I shall be obliged to change my description of their virtues, or give the reader permission to write in the margin either "Lies, lies, lies!" or the following lines of verse:

Women, where'er they be, are all the same—
They incline to love from wherever it may appear.
Let not piety, right guidance, reason, or shame on their part
Take the gullible unaware!

Or these:

Walk the length of the world and its breadth—
You'll see women selling their honor like market wares.
They clap with feet, not hands, once the sale is made,
And every judge[165] "It's legal!" declares.

Or these:

Beg a young maiden, a virgin, to let you love her
If you see her prowling on the hunt
And if she invites you to satisfy some urgent need she feels,
Comply with her and shake up her c . . . .[166]

Or the words of Di'bil:[167]

Let not the harsh words of a chaste lady,
Though wounding, make you refrain.

Women's recalcitrance leads to complaisance:
After bolting once, the prancing steed submits to the rein.

You should know too that in those countries where their honor is traded without constraint, apart from a small levy paid to the treasury for the building of temples and so forth, without regard to the words of him who said, "O feeder of the orphans . . ." etc.,[168] women are rarely courted with words of love, for it would never occur to a man in such a place that the sight of a charming face could dispel his worry and put paid to his *unrest*, alleviate his burdens and relieve his *distress*, from his heart polish the *rust*, from his blood remove the *dust*. Since he leaves the house and finds what he's looking for waiting for him right there on the other side of the door, he has no need of a lover's complaints, reproaches, and passionate protestations, or of saying, "Sleepless night after sleepless night!" or "Such as I can never sleep!" or "I have lost enough weight! I am a man and have melted away with burning desire and love!" and so on. 1.8.7

In countries, however, in which this trade is forbidden, you'll find that talk of women exceeds all bounds, which is why you find the same bawdiness in the poetry of the ancient Franks as in the works of the Arabs, the sole reason being that this commerce was, in their day, banned. Once it became common, bawdiness became rare among them. On the Mountain, however, you'll find neither commerce of this sort nor bawdiness. It is said of the Fāriyāq that he once fell in love with one of the women who used to visit him, and all she granted him was a kiss on the hollow of her foot. When he got up the next morning, he recited to his companion 1.8.8

Any who's kissed her foot thenceforth's too good
To kiss the hands of priests or of emirs,
Such women are the bachelors' charmers, and all the treasures of this world
Are worth less than one of their hairs.

## Chapter 9

# Unseemly Conversations and Crooked Contestations[169]

1.9.1 It would be well to provide here an example of the kind of conversations that used to take place among this company. Thus we declare: Once, when this company of ours had gathered, the cup was on its rounds, joy *unconfined*, the chastest among them in speech and most dogged in debate posed the following question: "Which person, in your opinions, is the best-off and has the greatest peace of *mind*?" Replied the one with cup in hand, "He who's in this same state as *I*, holding his vessel *high*." The first told him, "It is not so at all, nor is it *he* on whom men may *agree*, for his condition's one that will not *last* and his joy, it follows, will soon be *past*. Moreover, it rests on but a partial *proof*, is but a part of a greater *truth*, of which the rest remains to be considered—namely there's no denying that imbibing wine can make a man *ill* and stop him from eating his *fill*, which is why it's called *qahwah*;[170] no man can use it regularly without *disaster*."

1.9.2 Another now declared, "He who enjoys the greatest peace of mind is the emir when on his sofa he sits at *ease*, a party of servants and scions at his *knees*. His living comes to him without a *care*, for his Provider relieves him of any effort regarding daily *fare*. When he takes himself off to his harem, he closets himself with the most gorgeous of women on the softest of beds (and how true the words of him who said, 'There's nothing more wonderful than to bed on a comfortable bed'!). What's more, with a different dish each day his table's *laid*, in soft garments he's *arrayed*, his orders are *obeyed*, his judgment never *gainsaid*." Another then declared, "That's not how things *are*. The truth from that is *far*. The emir never sees his *wife* but his head's full of *strife*, his heart with worries *rife*, for he's always thinking how he's been betrayed over his *wealth*, cheated by his agents of his *pelf*. His income's consumed by his *court*, which yet finds *fault*. He places his affairs under their *sway* and yet they *betray*. He treats them with *generosity* and yet they accuse him of *illiberality*. In addition, they watch every step he *takes*, criticize him for every move he *makes*. He'd love to travel, but has to *stay*, longs to see new lands but can never have his *way*. He's jealous of those who walk aimlessly hither and *yonder* and looks with envy on all who whimsically *wander*."

Now rose another to *criticize*, saying, "Listen now, all you who're 1.9.3
*wise*. The happiest of God's creation is the monk who remains in his cell to *read*, who from work on his land or in his village is *freed*; he eats of what others labor to *earn*, providing prayers in overflowing measure in *return* (so relieving them of any need for *light*, in the darkness of the *night*), and he takes his steed from among whatever beasts to their lot may be *counted*, so that he is, as the saying has it, 'Fed, watered, and *mounted*.' Thus equipped, it matters not to him whether the world flourish or go to *pot*, mankind be resurrected or left to *rot*." One of those wise men then said, "These words are far from true. The monk and his like, should they see men setting forth on their *labors*, occupied in their *endeavors*, are far from happy to be reduced to living off their *toil*, taking their ease at the expense of others' exhausting labor on the *soil*, idly waiting till they bring him their gifts. On the contrary, he'd rather take on a part of their *chores* than be a partner in what they've set aside as *stores* (this if he be of blameless soul and noble *stock*, honest in his striving, his conscience not *ad hoc*). Nay more—on seeing men with their wives and children he suffers agonies and sorrows too great to *tell*, especially when, alone in his *cell*, he sees his plumpness going to waste

and doing him no *good* while others, weakened by toil and fatigue, enfeebled by effort, sickness, and lack of *food*, are more capable than him of realizing the *desires* to which all mankind, Arab and non-Arab alike, *aspires*."

1.9.4 Another, who the last man's opinion *shared* and was at ease with his view, *declared*, "This, I swear, is the revealed *truth*! The monk and those like him are better counted among those who live in *ruth*. However, it seems to me that the happiest of men where livelihood's concerned is the merchant. He sits in his store for a few hours of his day and earns in one hour, with his mighty oaths, enough to pay his expenses for a month. By means of constant *hype*, he converts loss to gain, the unwanted into things desired, the shoddy into goods of superior *stripe*. Plus, when he goes home at *night*, Daʿd and Laylā[171] are waiting there to treat him *right*; thus by day he earns his *monies*, and by night he spends it on his ankleted *honies*."[172] One who the truth of these words *denied* and wished to prove that the man before had *lied* now said, "The merchant can attain this pleasant life, enjoy this ample ease, only if he be ambitious, a rolling *stone*, with dealings in lands far from his *own*, a master of risks, one who boldly seizes what he wants. This being so, the realization of the results of his greed and toil must put paid to his *leisure*, the burgeoning of his ambitions must spoil his *pleasure*; what he must do to please customers and *family* must fill his soul with *anomie*. He fears for his goods at sea whenever the wind *blows* and, when dawn breaks, worries that someone will come to inform him of *woes*, some letter arrive to inform him of damage or loss, of stagnant markets or *embargoes*. Thus in thought his brow he ever *furrows*, gulping down regret and *sorrows*."

1.9.5 One of his audience now said, "Verily, your words are true. As for me, I'd have no desire to engage in *trade*, even if each day a hundred golden dinars I *made*. Any who engages in that profession spreads gossip, tells lies and absurdities, schemes, practices craft and deception, and *betrays*, not to mention that I'd be stuck there in the store for a quarter of my *days*. I'd have no idea of what was afoot in my nest: perhaps some watcher would go there and make *hay* while I was *away*, while I was lying to a buyer and *wangling*, flattering, and *wrangling*. Sin's rope would then be round my neck both for what I did in the *store* and for being a means to the commission of forbidden acts behind my very own *door*. For my part, I believe the man who most deserves to be envied for his way of life, whose craft and profession most deserve our *praises*, is none other than the cultivator, who labors to do good to both himself and others with what he *raises*, thus gaining both health for his body and provender for his dependants, which is the best of the many blessings by him *enjoyed*, though in addition his wife goes back and forth with him to work and keeps him company when times are hard and he's *unemployed*. If he falls sick, she nurses him herself and looks after his *mead*; if he's absent, she watches out for his interests and waits, hoping he'll return with *speed*. What's more, the tired man savors his *meat* and finds his slumbers *sweet*. Do you not observe that the children of those who strive and toil have healthier bodies and are quicker *witted* than the children of those who live a life of ease and are better *outfitted*? The sole reason for this is that they go to sleep when tired, eat when hungry, and drink when thirsty." The one closest to him now answered, "I must take issue with what you *say*, for you look at the picture in only one *way*, while the other side escapes you. The cultivator, I swear, over and above his body's hard work, is captive to care and *woe*, bedfellow to anxiety and *sorrow*, for he's a slave to the *elements*, at the bidding of the great families and of *accidents*. If a storm blow, he fears his fruit will *fall* and he feel *gall*; if the rain's too little or too *savage*, he fears lest what he's sown be *ravaged*; if a great man in his town *dies*, he worries he won't be able to market his *supplies*. If he be a man of insight and sensibility, it hurts him that his family should see him poorly clothed and *shod*, abject and submissive, wretched and *downtrod*, as does their grief at having nothing by way of food that's *tasty* nor by way of clothes that's *comfy*, at being unable to raise his son as he would have *desired*, unable to visit any town but the one in which he was *sired*, for that is his cradle and his *tomb*, his prison and sole dwelling *room*. In addition, he is the object of the designs of his leader in religion, and a stick on which any may lean who has more money than *he*, or any ruler or wielder of *authority*. He barely escapes the snare set for him by the one before he falls into the trap set by the other, and should one evil pass him *by*, he'll find another, yet greater, *nigh*. Given his burdens and lack of *education*, he finds no escape for himself or for any *relation*. Should he ever desire to follow a path for his family that's of his own choosing and he believes *correct*, but which is not what his imam, emir, or other high-ranking person would *elect*, he may not be spared a fine, or the lopping of his *nose*, or the breaking of his neck, and in no time his friends will be his enemies, his boon companions his dogged *foes*. In short, he's a pawn to *subjection*, a prisoner to *supplication*."

1.9.6 Said a companion, who held that what the former had outlined was correct, "Indeed, we may say with *certitude* that there is no abjection worse than *servitude*. Now, after all this scrutiny and *reflection*, interrogation and *investigation*, I see that the happiest of men in *kind* is he to whom God has allotted wealth, and a good *mind*, and who makes it his habit to travel to foreign *places* and observe new *races*. Each day some fresh matter he *discovers*[173] new homelands of every sort and new *brothers*." Said one who'd understood his *tenor*, and attributed his views to dotage and *error*, "You've gone off track as you well *know*, and what you say is not thought *through*. The *lot* of any exposed to travel is suffering and danger, is it *not*? With the change of air and strange surroundings, awful diseases often *strike*, not to mention that he's forced to drink things that bring chronic sickness and to eat what he doesn't *like*. Thus he consumes what eats his body *away* and drives any wink of slumber from his *eye*. When these Franks come to our lands, their mood is ruined by the absence of *swine*, as by their innocence of turtle, rabbit, and other creatures of this sort to which they *incline*, for they claim to mix the grease and blood of the pig into each dish, every soup, and all their *sweets*, and make from turtle flesh a broth that all ills *treats*. They fault us because our milk's neither watered nor thinned, our bread too salty, our food not with salt *saturated*, our water not mixed with chalk, our wine not *adulterated*, because we slaughter our animals by cutting their throats and eat the meat fresh, while they strangle theirs and eat it wormy and almost *raw*, because our weather's never overcast, our rain's not always pelting down and it doesn't always *pour*, because our land's not covered with a *tilth* of excrement, dung, and other *filth*. Our legumes they say are *tasteless*, our fruits *flavorless*. They blame us that our winter doesn't last two-thirds of the *year* and in our summers no booming thunder fills the *ear*. Having made their way to our land to learn our *tongue* and after living among us a decade only to return as ignorant of it as they *come*, they blame the *weather* and say, 'It gave me consumption and *fever*, or terrible *diarrhea*, or a cough that drove me to *despair*.' Moreover, because of the foreigner's ignorance of the language of those among whom he *dwells*, he cannot learn their customs and ways and one and the same to him are their outer and their inner *selves*. He sees what he sees and learns nothing, hears what he hears and understands *nought*; thus the traveler has no choice but to hire a dragoman, depending on him for business of every *sort*. Soon, however, he develops an unappreciative *attitude* and decides the man seeks to burden him with a debt of *gratitude*. Should he try to dispense with him, however, he can no longer the meaning of events *discern*, and he lives on among the people, a victim of loneliness and *concern*. He may yearn to see his family, to be reunited with his *kin*, in which case longing will make him sick, separation from the beloved *thin*. One can only have fun being *peripatetic* if one travels with a companion *sympathetic*, a confidant with whom one can share a *lot*—especially if each is *polyglot*, fancy-free, preconceptions quite *forgot*. How difficult it is, though, for *two* to agree on any one *view*, or for there to be any pleasure without strenuous *objection* or constraining *reflection*!"

Now spoke the least of those present in terms of good sense 1.9.7
and scholarly *renown*, the one most likely to play the *clown*. "Dear

*friends*!" said he. "I have something to say—forgive me if it *offends*. The happiest and most favored of persons, the best-off among them and most *content*, is the beautiful whore who opens her door to visitors and makes herself available to any who accosts her, for *rent*. She wins her visitor's companionship as well as his *wealth* and drives him so wild with love he thinks groveling before her an honor to *himself*. Once she has a *band* of men who'd sell their eyes for her in *hand*, they provide her with all she needs of 'the two best things,'[174] and she's no longer obliged to look for custom on the *roads* or be exposed to anything that harms or *discommodes*. When she grows old, she finds she'd saved a lot when young, and so, with open hand, she *spends* and, with the money, for her earlier misdeeds she makes *amends*, living blamelessly the *while*, all praising her for her radiant repentance and large *style*. *Man* is by nature *amn*esiac. He thinks only of what's present, not what's passed, especially if the current situation yield a mighty *dividend* and the good life on which all hopes *depend*. The clergy have only to praise her high and low, to exonerate her of all debaucheries and *abominations*, to be given non-stop gifts and abundant *donations*. With each *present* she gets from them *prayers*, with each *banquet blessings*. Let any who doesn't believe me, ask his consort and master his *irritation*, till such time as I can furnish proofs from both this and any earlier *generation*."

1.9.8 When the company had heard his *claim* and seen through to his hidden *aim*, they laughed at his raving and decided that the correct response to his misleading words, simply for the sake of the *wrangle*, should be to address the matter from a different *angle*, so they snubbed him, saying, "Shame on your opinion and God damn you! If all the people of a place sang the same *refrain*, the land would become corrupted, honor be blighted, and no vestige or smidgen of decent behavior *remain*. But the fault is the cup's, which has made off with your *brain* and revealed the corrupt thinking of your *kind*, the ignominy of your mischief-ridden *mind*. Perhaps, when you sober up, you'll be guided to what's *right*, and, after your gross falsehood and irresponsibility, see the *light*." The man decided then that silence was a safer *course* for him than discussion and back-and-*forth*, or bickering and getting cross, and that the mass outranks the *one*, even if the latter's well-guided and full of wisdom, the former in the *wrong*. He swallowed therefore their rebuttals and took fearful account of their *monitions* and the company dispersed without having come to a consensus as to who is the happiest of men or which the most easeful of *conditions*, finding that for each trade there was a fly in the *ointment*, for every state a *disappointment*, and every dish was accompanied by its own form of *indigestion*, albeit to many a condition of men they'd paid no *attention*, the time being too short to allow its *mention*, just as this chapter has been too short to allow a *computation* of all the arguments they made or their *enumeration*. Halt with me, then, at this portion that I've *outlined*, and let us return together to the story of the one I've *left behind*. Farewell.

## Chapter 10

# Angering Women Who Dart Sideways Looks, and Claws like Hooks

1.10.1 Rhymed prose is to the writer as a wooden leg to the walker. I must be careful therefore not to rest all my weight on it every time I go for a stroll down the highways of literary expression lest its vagaries end up cramping my style or it toss me into a pothole from which I cannot crawl. Indeed, it seems to me that the difficulties of rhymed prose are greater than those of poetry, for the requirements regarding linking and correspondence set for lines of verse are fewer than those for the periods of rhymed prose. In rhymed prose, the rhyme often leads the writer from his original path to a place he would never have wanted to reach had he not been subjected to its constraints. Here our aim is to weave our story in a way acceptable to every reader. Anyone who likes to listen to language that's entirely *rhymed* and *chimed*, with metaphors and metonymies adorned and *primed*, should go to the *Maqāmāt* of al-Ḥarīrī[175] or the *Nawābigh*[176] of al-Zamakhsharī.

1.10.2 Thus we declare: after our friend the Fāriyāq had lived for a while in the state that we've described, he was obliged by the conflicts and quarrels that occurred between him and his grandfather[177] to abandon what he was at and adopt another means of making a living. Fate ordained he should become tutor to the daughter of an emir, and a bonny lass was *she*, her features pleasing to a *degree*, with a body in which naught was *awry*, and a sleepy *eye*[178] (which doesn't mean that she was unable to see anyone who loved her, as would be the case with one who was actually sleepy; it means that she had an eye that was "dried up."[179] And even that doesn't fully express what I'm trying to say, because it gives the false impression that *she* was dried up, when, in fact, she was tender and full of sap. No, what I'm trying to get at is that she would seem to be, as we say, "given to looking through half-closed eyes [*taḥshīf*]"—but the whole entry for *ḥ-sh-f* in the dictionary is repugnant to me: it contains the senses "dryness," "baseness," and "mediocrity," plus something else that pretty girls are too dignified to speak of.[180] What I really mean is that, when looking, she would open her eyelids a crack—but even "crack" isn't the right thing here. In the end, I don't know how to to convey to the reader what I'm trying to get at. Perhaps the most appropriate way of saying it would be "she shot arrows from her eyes.")

Her youth was no impediment to her "tenderizing" a man's heart with her glance, for the heart attaches itself as easily to the small-breasted girl as to the big-busted grown woman, not every passion being a prelude to prostitution. Men have fallen in love with pictures, with the remains of the beloved's campfire, with her footprints in the *sand*, with outward forms, with a beloved *land*. Some have fallen in love at the sight of a hennaed hand, a lock of hair, a dress, a pair of drawers, a drawstring, or whatever. I know a man who fell in love with a woman's cat and would play with it, led by passion to imagine that he was playing with its owner; often it would fasten its claws in him and draw blood, which pleased and delighted him, either because he took pleasure in being tormented as part of his love for the beloved or because of his belief that toying with a woman was likely to lead to scratches and blood-letting so in the end it would come to the same thing, whether the wound was inflicted personally or by proxy. One who had loved was asked to what lengths his ardor had gone and he said, "I used to find pleasure in the wind if, coming to me from the direction of the beloved, it carried with it the smell of carrion." Most loves of the people of 1.10.3

these lands are of this sort: when one of them is in love he goes into ecstasies over anything associated with the beloved, such as a handkerchief, a flower, a letter, or, especially, a lock of hair, which he will sniff and hug, kiss, turn over in his hands, and hold to his chest, in accordance with the words of the poet who said,

Verses, like hair, are summoners to love,
  A lock of hair, like a line of verse, a relic to be hoarded.
The only way to feel him close when he's not there
  Is through a verse or through a lock (the latter the less oft accorded).

1.10.4 If it be said that they only love such relics out of hope of union with the beloved who has been so generous as to give them these favors, not because they feel any fondness for them in and of themselves, I reply, "There's nothing wrong in loving a young girl in the hope and expectation that she will grow into a mature woman. Without hope's broad horizon, how narrow life would be, and many a hope is sweeter than a triumph. People of experience know that he to whom God has denied beauty for a purpose of which he is unaware is more than equally recompensed by Him with sharpness of intellect and insight, powers of visualization and imagination, and acuity of intuition, and as a result is quicker to fall in love and more solicitous of those who possess beauty, for the further a person finds himself from the desired object, the greater his longing for it and the more powerful his infatuation with it." The point of all of this is to provide an opportunity to say that the Fāriyāq was aware, from an early age, that he was himself far removed from beauty, that from his childhood he venerated those who possessed it and favored them above all others, and that the ugly man is to be excused for loving pretty girls. As the poet says,

"Ugly fellow," they asked, "wouldst thou love
  A pretty girl, access to whom dusky slaves will stymie?"

"Am I not a literary man?" I replied.

"Never could I let such a 'contrast' get by me!"[181]

("They asked"—or I do on their behalf.)[182]

Young love can be big, too, just as grown-up love can be little. 1.10.5
A young person, being still without the emotional and intellectual maturity that might inhibit him from the unaffected and extreme expression of his affections, may be led by such unaffectedness to a wildness of passion that knows no restraint. Have you not observed how, when a child becomes infatuated with some toy or game, he may become intemperate in its pursuit and abandon himself to it entirely? How much more so, then, if he inclines to that thing that is stronger than anything else to which temper may incline or for which soul may yearn? True, the adult calculates the benefits of what he wants from his lover more carefully than the child and is therefore more solicitous of him and demands more from him; however, self-esteem, strength of character, and the instinct for self-preservation may prevent him from surrendering the reins of his will to love; thus on the road of his longing and desire he takes one step forward, one back. The child, having once abandoned himself to his natural spontaneity, believes that everything will be easy.

To return to our topic: I committed myself to writing a book 1.10.6
that would be a repository for every idea that appealed to me, relevant or irrelevant, for it seemed to me that what was irrelevant to me might be relevant to someone else, and vice versa. If you're of a mind, submit—if not, so be it: this is no time for quibbling and quarreling. The long and the short of it is that the Fāriyāq continued to tutor his young mistress, making a habit of gaining her affection by forbearing to correct her mistakes. In fact, he couldn't see how anyone so beautiful could be refused anything, as a result of which she fell behind in her education while he progressed in his obsession. One poem he wrote about her went as follows:

My soul I'd give, and heart, for him I teach!
The prisoner of his love ne'er can patience know.
Passion makes me jealous of every letter
He mouths and that kisses his lips as he does so.

Thank God the Arabic language lacks the Persian *p* and Frankish *v*,[183] or our friend's jealousy would have been even greater and might have driven him insane: jealousy and madness issue from the same place, as learned scholars familiar with marriage tell us.

1.10.7 This brings us to a nice point, to wit, that certain of the people known as *'atāwil* (plural of *'itwal* and meaning "men who can see no good in women") find it irksome to use the feminine gender in amorous and erotic poetry and so turn it into the masculine instead, and others invoke it only implicitly. The words of the Fāriyāq "for him I teach" conform to this practice.[184] It seems likely that the implicit referent of such masculine pronouns is the word *shakhṣ* (person). Would that the word referred to in our language by the pronoun were feminine, as it is in French and Italian, so that the erotic poet would find no impediment to using that gender![185]

1.10.8 On the question of whether the women of our country should be taught reading and writing, in my opinion, it's a good idea, provided it be according to certain conditions, namely that reading be confined to the perusal of books that refine their moral conduct and improve their writing skills, for if women are kept busy learning, they will find no time to work up schemes and concoct stratagems, as we shall see below. There would be nothing wrong with married women reading this book of mine or its like, for, just as certain sorts of food are reserved for married people only, so it is with ideas. It seems that the Arabic language is a snare for love, for it contains words of passion and amorousness found in no other.

1.10.9 Any woman who reads, in Ibn Mālik's *Sharḥ al-mashāriq*,[186] for example, that the stages of love are eight—the lowest of which is liking, which has its starting point in seeing and hearing and is then strengthened through cogitation, which turns into friendly regard, which is an inclination toward the beloved person (meaning the beloved *woman*), which in turn becomes stronger and turns into affection, which is the congenial intercourse of spirits, which grows stronger and turns into intimate companionship, which is affection's taking control within the heart to the point at which the couple start to share secrets, and then grows stronger until it turns into full-blown love unmixed with shifts of mood and not subject to change, which then grows stronger until it turns into passion, which is an affection so extreme that the passionate lover's mind is never empty of thoughts of the passionately loved person (meaning the passionately loved *woman*), which then grows stronger until it turns into lovesickness, in which condition the only thing that can satisfy the lover's soul is the image of the person whom he passionately loves (by whom I mean, of course, the *woman* he passionately loves), which then grows stronger until it turns into love-crazed distractedness, which is when he goes so far over the edge that he no longer knows what he's saying or where he's going, at which point the doctors are powerless to treat him—and noting in addition, as I do, that there are also different varieties of love, such as *ṣabābah*, which is love and longing in their most delicate form; *gharām*, which is love as surrender; *huyām*, which is insanity born of passion; *jawā*, which is the love one holds inside oneself; *shawq*, which is the struggle with the self; *tawaqān*, which means the same; *wajd*, which is the affection that the lover receives from the beloved person (by which I mean, again, of course, the beloved *woman*); *kalaf*, which is craving; *shaghaf*, which is what happens when love reaches the pericardium, which is to say the tissue that enwraps the heart or the fat that surrounds it or the kernel or core of it; *shaʿaf*, which is when love coats the *shaʿafah* of the heart, which is the top of it, where the aorta is attached, or *shaʿf*, which means the same; and *tadlīh*, which is when one loses one's mind from love—will be able to refrain from experiencing all these sublime stages one condition after the other. This contrasts with the languages of the non-Arabs, in which there is only one word meaning love, which they apply to Creator and created alike.

1.10.10 It seems to me that many qualities considered praiseworthy in men are considered blameworthy in women. Take liberality, for example. Liberality in a man covers all faults, but the same quality is considered blameworthy in a woman, and the same applies to truculence, craftiness, praising people hypocritically, horsemanship, bravery, heroism on the field of battle, callousness, and coarseness, as well as zeal in the pursuit of high office, difficult affairs, distant journeys, hard-to-achieve purposes, impossible ambitions, and so on. The reason for this is that the woman inclines by nature to deviation and excess, as evidenced by those of them who develop a taste for worship and self-abnegation. Such women never know where to draw the line; on the contrary, they go to such lengths that they become obsessed and demented, claiming miracles and supernatural gifts, getting caught up in visions and dreams and imagining that angels are speaking to them and voices whispering in their *ears*, or that they can bring mortal remains back to life and raise the dead with their *prayers*. Sometimes they kill their children when they're still young, in the hope that they will enter Heaven without being held to *account*, or give birth to twins and claim they were conceived with no father *about*. Some have a weakness for love and leave their mothers and fathers who bore them and raised them and run off after a man of whose qualities they know nothing except that he's a male. Everything, then, that women set their hearts on they go to greater lengths over than men, and if they set their hearts on reading, who knows where it will end? What drives them to such exaggeration and excess is their innate awareness that they are stronger in resisting sensual pleasures than men; having extra capacity in this area, they go to excess in it, and from there it has spread to other states, affairs, and contingent conditions, as also to certain instinctual matters. These states and so forth include talking and laughing, bustling about and physical exercise. What one of them lacks in a particular area you'll find immeasurably compensated for in another. What I say may displease women if they come to hear of it when they're among men, but I'm certain they'll laugh behind their hands at it in approbation and amazement.

It even seems to me that they'll decide that I must have lived for a while as a woman and learned their secrets, until such time as God, blessed and almighty, turned me into a man, or that I learned these things from Hind and Suʿād, Mayyah and Zaynab,[187] when, as a youth, I would write them love sonnets and lie to them that I'd gone without sleep all *night* and, complaining of our separation, make up maxims about my *plight*, saying my soul had been *bewitched*, my heart from its moorings become *unhitched*. In fact, we can be sure that it never left me, for if it had, it would never have returned, so often had I burdened it with cares and sorrows of a kind that had never previously bothered anyone in my country. These included mourning if a trope proved uncooperative when I tried to compose in the "novel" style[188] something that no one had ever said before, believing it would be accorded the same status as those inventions on which everyone prides himself so much these days, and it wouldn't come out right for me, causing me to spend the night in torment and despair. I swear before God, "Hind" never spoke to me and I never spoke to her. I just learned what I did from truth-telling dreams, for I spent the nights in sincere repentance and obedience to God, and if they don't believe me, let them spend a night or two in repentance and obedience as I did and I guarantee them that He'll send them down enough truth-telling dreams to provide them with a complete overview of men's affairs. 1.10.11

## Chapter 11

# That Which Is Long and Broad[189]

1.11.1 Let us now return to the Fāriyāq, just as he returned to his profession—namely, the copying of manuscripts—albeit against his will. It happened that at that time two young emirs of the region had decided to study works of grammar at the feet of a grammarian, and the Fāriyāq was present at these classes, bent over his copying. One of the two pupils was slow to understand, quick to answer. He'd yawn and stretch, fidget and fart, slack off and snore, stick out his bum and sneeze. If he thought he'd understood a point, he'd scratch himself under his armpit and smell the scent, sniffing at it with bared teeth and smacking his lips like someone savoring a piece of cottage cheese. Then, out of delight at his own cleverness, he'd kick up a rumpus and tongue-lash the one next to him, saying, "Shame indeed on those of slow *comprehension* and dim *apprehension*! How is it that not all men can master grammar's *rules*, which is easier than scratching your *balls*? If all the sciences were like *that*, I swear I'd have them down *pat*. I've heard, though, that grammar, while being 'a key to the sciences' is not regarded as one of them, so the others must be harder."

1.11.2 Then his tutor would tell him, "Say not so! Say rather, 'Grammar is the basis of the sciences' and all the rest are as much in need of it as a building is of a foundation. Have you not observed that the people of our land learn only this and do not stray from it to any other? They think that he who has a command of grammar commands a knowledge of all aspects of the universe. That's why it's the only thing they write books about and why the only disputes that arise among them are about which chapters to put before others and the clarification of the ambiguities of that science with proofs and citations. They also disagree over the latter, some saying that they're fabricated, others that they are determined by the meter or anomalous, though it all comes to the same in the end, namely that a scholar cannot be considered such unless he has acquired a command of grammar and gone deeply into all its finer points, and that almost no business can go smoothly without it. If you were to say, for example, 'Zayd struck ʿAmr'[190] without putting Zayd in the nominative and ʿAmr in the accusative, he would not in fact have struck him, and it would be wrong to depend on the information thus conveyed, for a true understanding of the nature of the act of striking is dependent in this instance on knowing that Zayd is in the nominative. Any language that has no markers for the nominative is utterly worthless, people understanding one another in the absence of these only by virtue of custom or convention; their books cannot therefore be relied on, however they may *multiply*, and neither can their sciences, however they *ramify*. Even though I might toil over this science by day and would often go to bed racking my brains over one of its knotty points or fiendish difficulties, I'd have to spend the whole night awake, unable to find my way to the proper solution to whatever was giving me such trouble. I did, however, derive one great benefit from it that made me eternally grateful to the daughter of Abū l-Aswad al-Du'alī (since she was one of the reasons for its invention)."[191] (To which I would add that all the other rhetorical sciences owe their existence to women, too.)

"And what was that benefit, master?" asked his pupil. Replied the 1.11.3
tutor, "I had long harbored doubts over the question of the immortality of the soul and inclined toward the dictum of the philosophers to the effect that whatever has a beginning must have an end. But when I found that grammar has an 'inchoative' but no 'terminative,'

I drew an analogy between that and the soul and ceased to be confused, praise God. Similar to grammar or greater in difficulty is the science of topoi and rhetoric." "That I have never ever heard of before," said the pupil. "I, however, have," said his teacher, "and I know what it covers, which is metaphor, metonymy, figurative usage, punning, morphological parallelism, and more than a hundred other things. Laying all that out in detail takes an age, and one could spend his whole life just on the science of figurative usages and then die and still know little about it, or forget by the end of the book or books what he'd learned at the beginning.

1.11.4 "The reason for this is that the inventor of this magnificent science was no sultan with the authority to force everyone to follow up on it and unceasingly pursue it. On the contrary, he was a just poor man who fell in love with the subject and whose heart God had made receptive to the laying out of its principles. Thus his eyes had only to fall on a particular thing for his mind to come up with a way of dealing with it. If, for example, he saw the sun rising, he'd say, 'How are we to understand the "rising" of the sun here? Is it "literal" or "metaphorical," and would the metaphor here be "conventional" or "linguistic"?' Likewise, if he were to see green plants sprouting in the spring, he'd say, 'How should we analyze the words of the one who said, "The spring caused the plants to sprout"? Can we correctly trace the sprouting back to the spring, which itself is born of the revolution of the earth around the sun, this revolution being without doubt a contributing factor? At the same time, however, there can be no doubt that the one who makes the earth revolve is God, Mighty and Majestic, in which case his words "the spring caused the plants to sprout" would be a two-step metaphor, for the spring is caused by the revolution of the earth and the revolution of the earth is caused by the ordinances of the Almighty Creator. The same applies to the expressions "the ship sails" or "the mare runs."'"[192] There are also three- and four-step metaphors and some with more steps than the stairway of a minaret. Some of these stairways are smooth, some spiral, some winding, and others something else.

"The originator of this science went on thinking about these rhetorical figures until he came to the end of his life, and he died leaving much undecided. After him, another, similarly enamored, arose and fleshed out many areas left by his predecessor, continuing to debate with and contradict him until he too passed away, making room for others. Next came someone who reconciled the two with regard to a number of cases, while declaring them both at fault with regard to others, but he died without finishing what he'd set out to do, and after him another came along, who did to him what he'd done to the rest, and thus it is that the doors of criticism have remained open down to these days of ours. One will say, 'This expression belongs to the category of "subordinate metaphorization,"' while another will claim that it is 'propositional.' Certain scholars have said that metaphors may be divided into the literal and the analogical, the literal into the categorical and the presumptive, and the categorical firstly into the make-believe and the factual, secondly into the primary and the subordinate, and thirdly into the abstracted and the presumed, with some claiming that this last may be sub-divided into the aeolian,[193] the ornitho-sibilant,[194] the feebly chirping, the tongue-smacking,[195] the faintly tinkling, the bone-snapping, the emptily thunderous, and the phasmic, while the aeolian itself may be sub-divided into the stridulaceous, the crepitaceous, and the oropharyngeal, the crepitaceous may be sub-sub-divided into the absquiliferous, the vulgaritissimous, the exquipilifabulous, the seborrhaceous, the squapalidaceous, and the kalipaceous, the crepitaceous into the panthero-dyspneaceous,[196] the skrowlaceous[197] and the skraaaghhalaceous,[198] as well as the transtextual and the intertextual,[199] and the oropharyngeal into the enteric, the dipteric, the vermiculo-epigastric, the intestinal, the audio-zygo-amatory, the anal-resonatory, the oro-phlebo-evacuative, the capro-audio-lactative, the ovo- (or assino-) audio-lactative, and other 'may-be-sub-divideds.' A book's prologue[200] is required to bring together all of these kinds of metaphor, just as attention should be paid, there and throughout, to the specific kind known as 'opposition.'[201] For 1.11.5

example, if someone writes in a certain paragraph 'he went up,' in the next he has to write 'he went down,' and if he says 'he ate' he has to say afterward, without let up, 'he vomited' or '** ****.' Over all, the prologue should be as difficult as possible to understand; a prologue that isn't serves notice that the book as a whole is poorly written and not worth the reading."

1.11.6 The pupil, who by now had turned pale, asked his teacher, "Did all the grammarians too die before completing the rules for that science? And does the fact that I've studied it at your hands relieve me of the need to go over it all again with someone else here? And is the student obliged to learn grammar as it is understood by the people of every country he travels to, or is it a science that has to be learned only once?" The shaykh told him, "As far as the first's concerned, my response would be that the story of the rhetoricians is that of the grammarians. Al-Farrāʾ[202] said, 'I shall die still pondering the meaning of *ḥattā*,'[203] and Sībawayhi died still unsure as to certain questions relating to when **nna* should be realized as *anna* and when as *inna*.[204] Al-Kisāʾī died of tetters he was so exercised over the difference between connective *fāʾ*, causative *fāʾ*, clarifying or deductive *fāʾ*, consequential *fāʾ*, and binding *fāʾ*,[205] while al-Yazīdī[206] died of a headache (and what a headache!) caused by connective *wāw*, resumptive *wāw*, affirmative *wāw*, supplemental *wāw*, and negative *wāw*.[207] Al-Zamakhsharī died with ulcers on his liver from the differences between the right-related, ascriptive, proprietorial and semi-proprietorial, purposive, emphatic-negative, and other uses of *lām*,[208] and al-Aṣmaʿī[209] died with a goiter on his neck from worrying about the glottal stop. In sum, if a student wants to acquire an in-depth knowledge of just one of these particles, he will have to give up all other concerns and interests and devote himself to what has been said about it and the refutations thereof, which is why we have such proverbs as 'You may give all of yourself to scholarship but it will give only part of itself to you.'

1.11.7 "As to your question whether you should study grammar with others than myself here, meaning in this country of ours, that will not be necessary. None of our countrymen have read any books other than the very one you are reading. Indeed, few are those who have read that and understood it or can apply its rules. As for your third question, I'd say that it is not necessary for you to go over the same science in every country. However, wherever you go and in whichever direction you head, you will find people who will criticize you for your way of speaking. Thus, if you use *wāw*, for example, they will say that *fā'* is the more correct, and if you use *aw*, they will say that *am*[210] is preferable, while in some countries, if you put dots below the letter *yā'* in the words *qā'il* or *bā'i'*,[211] you will lose all respect in people's eyes. I read in some work of *belles lettres* that a certain scholar paid a visit to a friend of his who was sick in bed and caught sight of a notebook in which the word *qā'il* was written with two dots below the *yā'*, so he turned on his heel and said to his companion, 'We have wasted our steps in coming to see him.'

"This is why so few people write works on grammar in this day and age: under such circumstances, the writer exposes himself to criticism, vilification, and tribulation and no one will pay any attention to the useful information and maxims in his book, unless it be replete with every kind of stylistic embellishment and linguistic nicety. It's as though a virtuous man were to go into a gathering dressed in rags and tatters; they wouldn't see his inner refinement, only his outer clothing and attire. Thank God there are so few writers in our country these days: if they were to increase—and, along with them, their criticism and fault-finding—the occasions for their mutual hatred and quarrelsomeness would increase in proportion. People have substituted for serious writing the concoction of a few paragraphs in rhymed prose that they put in letters and the like, as when they say 'salutation and veneration' or 'the splendid and resplendent,' these being easiest to take when pronounced without vowels at the end.[212] As far as poetry in this day and age is concerned, it consists merely of describing a man who is the subject of a eulogy as generous and brave or of a woman as having a slender *waist*, heavy *nates*, and an eye with collyrium *laced*. Anyone who 1.11.8

sets out to compose a poem fills up most of its lines with amatory and erotic or plaintive and querulous material and keeps the rest for eulogy."

1.11.9 This brilliant pupil continued to read grammar with his shaykh until he got to the chapter on the "doer" and the "done,"[213] when he objected to the fact that the doer was "raised" while the done was "laid,"[214] claiming that the terminology was corrupt, for if the doer was raised then someone else must have raised him, whereas in fact it was the doer who did the work, the evidence being that we may observe a man working on a building raising a stone or the like on his shoulder, in which case the stone is the thing raised and the doer is the raiser, and likewise the doer of the . . .[215] is the one who raises his leg. At this point, the tutor told him, "Steady on! Steady on! You're being foul-mouthed. In the scholarly gathering—which is quite different from the princely—you're supposed to demonstrate good manners." Then the two pupils concluded the reading of the book, neither having benefited in any way, and the commentary might as well have been directed entirely at the Fāriyāq who, from then on, took to improving his speech by following the rules of grammar till he came to scare the pants off the rabble as will become clear in the following chapter.

## Chapter 12

# A Dish and an Itch

I must go on at some length in this chapter, just to test the reader's endurance. If he gets to the end of it at one go without his teeth smoking with rage, his knees knocking together from frustration and fury, the place between his eyes knitting in disgust and shame, or his jugulars swelling in wrath and ire, I shall devote a separate chapter to his praise and count him among those readers "who are steadfast."[216] And because the Fāriyāq had become prone in those days to making a long tongue at people—even though his brains remained quite short and his head quite small and exiguous at the occiput—and I had taken a vow to follow along behind him step by step, mimicking the way he walked, if I saw him doing something stupid I would do the same, wandering off the path if he did, and matching too anything sensible he did, for otherwise I'd be his foe, not the writer of his life story or the reporter of his sayings. An injunction to do the same should be hung around the necks of all writers, who, in fact, are very far from obeying it. I observe that most of them depart from this approach, and you suddenly find such a writer, in the middle of describing a disaster that has affected some mortal's sanity, wife, or wealth, going to the trouble of inserting paragraphs in rhymed prose and expressions full of parallelisms, padding his story with all sorts of metaphors and metonymies, and forgetting all about his subject's worries, thus indicating that he 1.12.1

doesn't care about them. As a result you find the victim moaning and wailing, objecting and complaining, while the author is rhyming and using paronomasia, making parallel constructions and puns, going off on tangents, switching persons,[217] and playing with unlikely topoi, as when he reaches out his hand now to the sun, now to the stars, trying to bring them from the zenith of the heavens down to the lowly level of his words, or, on some occasions, plows across *oceans* and at others plucks *orchids* while bounding around in garden and thicket from trunk to branch and from hollow to hill. Such, though, is not my way of doing things, for if I introduce the words of an idiot, I put every kind of silly expression in his mouth, and if I report something said by an emir, I use, to the extent possible, polite language, as though I were sitting with him in this salon; or by a priest, for example, or a bishop, I make him a gift of every variety of lame and defective phrase so that it isn't too difficult for him to express himself, which, should it happen, would undermine the purpose of writing this book.

1.12.2 Know, then, that after the Fāriyāq's brains had boiled over following the application of the heat of grammar, which came on top of his desire to be a poet, he set off one day to take care of some business. On the road he passed a monastery and, it being evening, thought it would be a good idea to spend the night there. Turning off to it, he knocked on the door, at which a young monk appeared before him. "Can you provide a guest with bed and *board*?" the Fāriyāq asked, to which the young monk replied, "He'd be most welcome so long as he has no *sword*." The Fāriyāq was delighted with this response and amazed to find in the monastery someone who was good at repartee. The young monk had only said what he did because numbers of the large-gulleted, omnivorous, gluttonous, voracious, craving, dyspeptic, ravenous, loudly swallowing followers of the emir afflicted the monastery with their demands for lodging, and, whenever one of them spent the night there, he would charge the monks with providing fine dishes that they knew nothing of, for these folk live a life of short commons and *abnegation*, surviving on the most meager *ration*, regarding, as they do, this world and its pleasures as their foe; it is to them the arch-rival of the life to come, and the further mortal man distances himself from it, the closer he approaches Paradise. Even their bread, which they often eat plain, is unlike other people's, for after they've baked it in thin layers, they expose it to the sun for several days in rows until it dries and gets so hard that if one were to take a loaf in each hand and strike them against each other, the din would panic all the rats in the monastery, or they could use them in place of the wooden plank they strike to mark the times of prayer, and they can eat it only after it's been soaked in water so long it has turned back to dough. The emir's followers wear swords to terrify those who pay them less than total respect and to warn them of the consequences, in just the same manner as the Fāriyāq terrified the young monk with his question. If one of them doesn't have a sword, he borrows his friend's or takes a thin stick and puts it in a scabbard. The people of the Mountain find nothing shameful about borrowing provisions or other things; on the contrary, they often borrow jewelry and apparel for the bride for her procession and borrow clothes and a turban for the groom to make him look smart.

When dinnertime came, the same young monk brought a dish of 1.12.3
lentils cooked in oil and three "cymbals" of that bread and placed them before the Fāriyāq, who then sat down to eat, taking a piece of bread and whacking it against another until it broke. When he took the first mouthful a sliver of the bread caught against a tooth and almost carried it off. The Fāriyāq tried to prop it up and fill the holes in the tooth with lentils but hardly had he finished his meal before the heat of the lentils started to grow in his body and he took to scratching with his fingernails and fragments of the loaf until his skin was in shreds. This upset him greatly and he said to himself, "That crust almost dislodged my tooth, so I'm going to dislodge one of the monastery's," and he cudgeled his brains to compose a couple of lines of verse on lentils to avenge himself for what it had done to him, in imitation of the custom of poets of getting their own back

by rebuking fate for any ill-fortune or depression, wretchedness or oppression they may have suffered.

1.12.4 Searching for a certain word, he rose and went looking for a copy of the *Qāmūs* and knocked on the door of his neighbor, who was one of those particularly zealous in religion, and asked him, "Do you have, sir, a *Qāmūs*?" to which the other replied, "In the monastery we have neither *qāmūs* nor *jāmūs* ('buffaloes') nor oxen, and what would you be needing them for at this hour, anyway?" So he knocked on the door of another who was even coarser and asked him, "Would you mind lending me the *Qāmūs* for an hour?" to which he replied, "Hang on till midnight, for the *kābūs* ('nightmare') never comes at any other time." So he went to another and asked him the same question and the man replied, "What *qāmūṣ*, you *māghūṣ*?"[218] So he returned to his cell, saying, "I'll have to compose the lines and leave a space for the missing word," and he wrote,

I ate lentils in a monastery of an evening,
Then spent the night with an itch that my mind did almost derange.
Had I not set my nails to working,
Men would have said, "The Fāriyāq's got *****!"

1.12.5 When it was midnight and the Fāriyāq was sleeping, one of the monks suddenly knocked on his door. Thinking that he'd brought the book he wanted, he opened the door in expectation of finding what he'd been looking for, only for the monk to tell him, "Get up and come to prayers. Lock your door and follow me." Then the Fāriyāq recalled what his neighbor had said about the nightmare not coming till midnight and said to himself, "The man spoke truly, for this summoner is harder on the sleeper than a nightmare. Damn this for a wretched night for me: the bread almost pulled out my tooth and the lentils made me scratch, and now I'd barely started to doze off when this miserable scald-headed door-striker comes and summons me to prayer. Was my father a monk or my mother a nun, or have I incurred some other obligation, to have to give thanks and perform prayers for the sake of a dish of lentils? All the same, I shall endure until morning."

Next day, the same young monk came to ask him how he was, for he had joined the monastery only a little while before and still retained some traces of finer feeling and kindness. "I beg you," said the Fāriyāq, "do sit with me a little," and when the man had taken his seat, he asked him, "Tell me, if you'd be so kind, do you do that every day?" The young monk frowned at him and thought his question odd. Then he said, "What are you alluding to?" The Fāriyāq replied, "Eat lentils in the evening and get up at midnight to pray." "Yes indeed," he answered. "Such is our custom every day." "What imposed this duty upon you?" said the Fāriyāq. "The need to worship God and become closer to him," he replied. The Fāriyāq responded, "God, Blessed and Mighty, doesn't care whether a person eats lentils or meat, and he didn't command any such thing in His Book, as there is no benefit therein, for the soul of the eater or for the eaten." "This is the way of the contemplative ascetics," said the other, "for a life of abnegation and chastisement of the body through eating the worst foods and reduction of sleep drives away the appetites." 1.12.6

"On the contrary," said the Fāriyāq, "it is inconsistent with God's will, for had He wanted to chastise your body and free it of its appetites, He would have created you emaciated and sickly. What say you about those whom God has created beautiful? Is such a person allowed to disfigure his face, gouge out an eye, pierce his nose, slit his lip, or pull out his teeth—as you wanted to pull out my teeth yesterday with that hard bread of yours—or to blacken his appearance?" Said the other, "In my opinion, that would not be allowed." Said the Fāriyāq, "Isn't the body as a whole analogous to the face? I swear, God cannot have created a well-muscled forearm without wanting it to remain a well-muscled forearm, or a leg rippling with muscles without wanting it to stay that way for ever. Nor would he have made it permissible to people to eat good foods unless he had wanted them to eat them in blooming good health. True, 1.12.7

some eccentric religions have forbidden these good foods, but the Christian religion permits them and they only came to be prohibited because of a few aging dodderers who didn't care for meat or anything else. What is your objection to eating them every day?"

1.12.8 "I don't know," said the other, "but I heard our scholars say it was so, so I imitated them, and to tell you the truth, I've grown sick of this life. I see my body wasting away day by day and my spirit becoming dejected, and if I'd known beforehand how I'd end up, I never would have taken this path. My father and mother, though, are poor and were afraid I'd end up unemployed and idle, for there are no useful crafts in our land for a person to learn and live by, so they painted me a pretty picture of the monk's life. They told me that if I stuck to the path in the monastery for a few years, I might be promoted to a high rank, 'and do yourself some good and us too.' They kept on at me until I agreed, and if I hadn't done so of my own free will, they would have forced me into it."

1.12.9 The Fāriyāq told him, "It's true: the monastic life is a refuge from unemployment, for anyone who's too idle to have acquired any knowledge or a craft makes a beeline for it. But you're still a young man like me, so you can go to any person of good will and charity and he will direct you to something that will help you. The Almighty created the *jaws* and He's guaranteed the daily bread to fill those *maws*, just as He's made *action* the key to *benefaction*. Moreover, you will be aware that the word *rahbāniyyah* ('monasticism') derives from *rahbah* ('fear'), meaning fear of Almighty God. It you adopt a profession, make your living from it among your fellow men, marry, and are blessed with a child, you will have manifested fear of God and will then be *rāhib* ('god-fearing/a monk'). True *rahbāniyyah* doesn't depend on eating lentils and dry bread. Isn't it the case that there's more quarreling, name-calling, and grudge-bearing among the monks of your monastery than among other people, that their chief never stops trying to humiliate them and force them to submit to him, that they never stop grumbling and complaining about him, and that there's as much envy and competitiveness between him and the other heads of monasteries as there is among the ministers of the world's countries? Most of them obtain their posts by flattering the ruling emir or the patriarch, and when they feel their terms are approaching their end and fear dismissal, you find them showering people of influence with gifts and presents such as the ordinary people of our land would never give and continuing to do so until they are confirmed in their positions as heads of their monasteries.

"If anyone invites their monks—who have to put up with lentils and abstain from meat—to a feast, you can hear the roar as they swallow, for they dive into their food, gnaw on the bones using their whole mouths, lick their lips by sticking out their tongues like snakes, fill their waterskins to the brim, and drink them dry until their eyes start from their sockets. The thing that I hold most against them, though, is that you can hardly say hello to one of them without his stretching his hand out for you to kiss, and often enough it's defiled and filthy—how am I to kiss the hand of one who is more ignorant than me and good for nothing? See how many monasteries there are in our land and how many monks each monastery holds—and yet I haven't come across a single one of them who excels in scholarship or has left behind him anything to boast of. 1.12.10

"On the contrary, all you hear of them are things that are a disgrace to the mind and morals of mankind. I was in the service of Baʿīr Bayʿar for a time and discovered that one of these preachers had acquired as much control over his daughter as a husband over a wife. Among the things he'd ask her were, 'Do your buttocks shake and your breasts quake?' What has a monk got to do with the quivering of women's buttocks and the jiggling of their breasts? Another was head of a monastery. He conceived an affection for a girl in a village near to the monastery and it wasn't long before she conceived a child by him. Because his brother was highly regarded by the ruler, the girl's father was afraid to stand up to him and expose him; indeed, it has become an accepted fact in the minds of the ignorant people of our land that it's a sin to disclose a matter of this sort that might expose one of these so-called ascetics to scandal. I 1.12.11

swear by God, concealing such things is a sin, for exposure would deter others!

1.12.12 "I know another, too, who came to our village pretending to be at death's door. To show how righteous and pious he was, he wore his sleeves long and had pulled his cowl down till almost nothing could be seen but his mouth and beard. The first thing he did was to set himself up as a preacher to the local laity, and he took to preaching and sermonizing and uttering warnings of coming judgment in a basso profundo, weeping as hard as he could the while, tear ducts overflowing, for he had put something pungent, I know not what, on the handkerchief with which he wiped his face. Eventually he ended up spending days and nights in seclusion with a pretty young widow of the princely class, justifying himself by saying that she was making plenary confession to him, meaning starting from the time when her breasts swelled and her hair sprouted and going all the way up to that very day.

1.12.13 "And I know of another who went to Rome. Being a simpleton, he would go to bed in his monk's habit just as he did at his monastery and thus dirty the sheets, so the owner of the house forbade him to do so. When the monk discovered that all the priests of Rome, from the cardinals to the monks, slept naked, with nothing to cover their shame but a thin linen sheet, he renounced his faith and started declaring that everything, sinful or not, was permitted. Observe, then, how none of these 'contemplative' worshippers of God turns out to be anything but base and *hypocritical* or ignorant and *hysterical*. A righteous man among them is rarely to be *descried* and with regard to scholarship they're all equally *deprived*.

1.12.14 "There's nothing, nothing at all, wrong with becoming a monk of one's own free will; it is a praiseworthy path—on condition that one is over fifty and that those who join the monastic ranks be people of virtue and knowledge who occupy themselves with scholarship and improving the writing skills of their brethren and acquaintance, spurring them to noble morals and the adoption of praiseworthy qualities, writing useful books and laying down for their people the roads that lead to good fortune and *salvation*, triumph and a happy *termination*, unlike those ignoramuses who know nothing but mortification of the flesh and ragged clothes. To demonstrate their ignorance it's enough to say that I asked the most zealous of them to lend me the *Qāmūs* and he thought I said *jāmūs*, while another thought I said *kābūs*, and a third *qāmūṣ*. Set to, then, my friend, and have done with them: God guide you right, or you'll end up as a man of neither this world nor the next, for God doesn't give a fig for the religion of the ignorant. Then, when you reach sixty, you'll find the monastic life awaiting you."

"How am I to get free?" the man asked him. "If you have belong- 1.12.15
ings in the monastery," said the Fāriyāq, "I'll help you carry them." "I have nothing but what you see upon me," said the other. "Let's be off, then," said the Fāriyāq, "for the monks are presently occupied with their prayers," and they set off through the door of the monastery, and no one noticed. When they had gone a little way, the Fāriyāq congratulated his friend on his escape from the noose of ignorance and told him, "I swear, if I were to free a monk or a novice, or at least a nun or a novice nun, every time I ate lentils, I'd want to eat nothing else so long as I should live, even if the lentils consumed my body. May God reward the monastery well!"

## Chapter 13

# A *Maqāmah*, or, a *Maqāmah* on "Chapter 13"

1.13.1 A while has passed now since I tasked myself with writing in rhymed prose and patterned period, and I think I've forgotten how to do so. I must therefore put my faculties to the test in this chapter, which is worthier than the rest—because it's higher in number than the twelfth and lower than the fourteenth—and I shall continue to do so in every chapter branded with this number till I've finished my four books. The total number of *maqāmah*s in it will therefore, I believe, be four. Thus I declare:

1.13.2 Faid al-Hāwif ibn Hifām in lifping tones:[219] "Sleepless I lay on a night on which the stars were *concealed*, the clouds *revealed*, a night never-*ending*, full of worries to anguish *trending*. Now on my back to sleep I *tried*, now on any other *side*, placing before my eyes the image of a person drowsing or yawning or *snoring*, or of another into a drunken stupor *falling*. Imagination, they say, is conducive to the doing of the thing for which you *burn*, and stimulates the achievement of that for which you *yearn*, despite which sleep to my eyes not a drop of salve *applied*, not a yawn spread wide my mouth, from top to bottom or from side to *side*. Meseemed the people of the earth, without exception, were fast *asleep*, while I alone among them all no repose could *reap*, that all my neighbors were at *rest*, while I alone remained *distressed*. So I arose to take a *nip* and took indeed a *sip*, but all this brought was an *oscitation*, something barely more than a lapse of *attention*, after which I awoke once more quite *overwrought*, in a desperate agony of *thought*, cares thronging toward me from every *side*, my worries ranging far and *wide*. All things possible and impossible to my mind *occurred*, every situation over which I'd ever worried (if only once and many years before) *recurred*.

"When I grasped that slumber had escaped me, even though sleep I *feigned*, and that I'd have to witness dawn whether I resisted or was *resigned*, I stretched out my hand for a book to read, with the following *hope*, that, 'If it doesn't make me sleep, it may at least engage my attention with some *trope*.' I picked up the first thing to come to hand, feeling no preference for any particular work, and what should it be but *Kitāb Muwāzanat al-ḥālatayn wa-murāzanat al-ālatayn* (*The Book of Balancing the Two States and Comparing the Two Straits*)[220] by the Honored Shaykh and Productive Scholar of Perfect Virtue, Abū Rushd 'Brains' ibn *Ḥazm*,[221] whose rhetorical skills in both prose and verse have provoked widespread *enthusiasm*. This is a book such as no author before him ever *hatched* nor any writer, however distinguished, ever *matched*, for in it he compares man's two states of wretchedness and *leisure*, of joy and care, of gain and loss, of sorrow and *pleasure*, from childhood till he arrives at *maturity*, then desiccated *senility*, all set out in facing *tables* using a columnar system that comparison *enables*. However, the shaykh (God sanctify his soul and elevate his rank and *worth* to the highest point above the *earth*) living, as it seems to me, a life of goodly *weal*, with abundant fortune and energetic *zeal*, gave undue weight to *pleasure* and failed to treat life's evils in equal *measure*. He even asserts that pleasure is to be had from both deed and *thought*—unlike pain, in which thinking is of no *import*—claiming that were he to picture himself cavorting with a ripe young *wench*, and she with him, he'd be so shaken by ecstasy he'd be entirely carried away, chest and flank, bed and *bench*. However, I doubted his words upon this *point*, thinking to myself, 'Glory be! Every writer, however great, must on occasion be out of *joint*': in my case, when 1.13.3

I pictured the drunkard, the drowser, and the yawner, as I lay there trying to sleep, all that picturing didn't compensate for the actual thing by even a *jot*,[222] and I found no pleasure in it, either a little or *a lot*. I tend to the belief of a certain madman that the pleasure of sleep is not felt by the sleeper, either while, after, or before it *prevails*—a knot those who hold to the humoral theory[223] remain incapable of untying by talking or thinking, or even with their teeth and their *nails*.

1.13.4 "This said, the words of the compiler of these tables are of so full of knowledge and *wisdom* as to bemuse the expert critic, and reduce any maven, in the investigation of either argument, to *confusion*. After, then, I'd turned on them my eye's *gaze*, and it had returned *aglaze*, and I'd applied to them the blade of careful *examination*, only for it to come back full of *indentation*, I determined to throw light on this *problematique* by consulting one known for his skill in debate and insightful *critique*, saying to myself, 'Just as my hand fell upon the nearest *tome*, so let my next choice be the neighbor closest to *home*.' Living near me was a metropolitan whose adornments, worth, and culture by his congregation were lauded and *cheered* at a length equal to his *beard*. I went to see him at midday, all ready to rejoice, and found him wearing a buckle to *amaze*, a habit to set the heart *ablaze*. Setting before him the two tables, I said, 'Rule for me on this *case*, and may you be rewarded by God, Lord of the Human *Race*.' He looked at them, then nodded off and started *blinking*, complaining he was too sleepy to do much *thinking*, and telling me something to the effect that since he wasn't one of those whose ambitions ever *rose* to rhyming in *prose*, he 'hadn't caught their *implication* or grasped their *signification*, though, had they been penned in hackneyed terms, I *vouch*, I'd have got them as easy as sitting on this *couch*!'

1.13.5 "I thought, 'His advancement up the ranks of the clergy has retarded his scholarship and *erudition*, and the longer his beard and sleeves have grown the shorter have become his intellect and *intuition*. Let me enquire *then* of the silliest and least intelligent of *men*, and who other should that *be* but the one who teaches children their *ABC*?' In the *town* was one who, despite his pride and arrogance, had, for these qualities, won *renown*. Off I set, then, to where he was and put to him the *case*, and he stood up, clapped his hands, rolled his eyes, and said, 'Guided by sound judgment, you've arrived at the right *place*. If you wish to know which of the two arguments carries the greater *weight*, is the more correct and *accurate*, place the two columns (minus the binding) in a *scale*. The one that dips will be the weightier; on that all men will agree without *fail*.' I left him, then, in fury and regret, cursing the sleeplessness that had driven me to ask a teacher of young boys, even after I'd read in books on more than one *occasion*, and heard from men of *perspication*, that they were the most feeble of *mind* among God's *creation*, the most to ignorance *inclined*, the furthest from *ratiocination* and most given to foolishness and *hallucination*.

"On that day then I betook myself to a *jurisprudent*, of all that 1.13.6
people the most *resplendent*, who had inflated his turban and coiled it round and *round*, using extra cloth, and decorations on his *gown*, and to him I said, 'Give me a ruling, most virtuous and sagacious man, as to which of the two arguments in your opinion is the closer to the *truth*, which most *sooth*.' Answered he, 'If you've come to me seeking a ruling, by my opinion to be guided and my path to *emulate*, allow me to tell you (due deliberation having been *devoted* to this school of law so *convoluted*) that we—we noble company of jurists, that is—are men of *debate*, makers of the rules that govern the rules that govern the *game*, revealers of fine distinctions among things that might otherwise seem the *same*; likewise that it is our way, to make clear the truth, to analyze in depth and go to great lengths in *argumentation*, since there's no escape, if you'd sniff the aroma of veracity, from *expatiation*, and from seeking the guidance of one of the *schools*, which, by insisting on the impossible and making from the nonexistent something necessarily existent,[224] imposes its *rules*. In my opinion, then, you must add up the words of the two arguments and calculate the number of letters that in each column are

*disposed*, and whichever has more will then be the weightier and better *composed* (though God alone truly *knows*).' So I parted ways with that jurisprudent as I had from his foolish *friend*, telling myself that any who asked him for a ruling had none to blame but himself, in the *end*.

1.13.7 "Next I proceeded to a poet whom I knew to be a great *flatterer*, a mouth-twisting faux-Arabic *patterer*, a would-be master of classical *lays* and spouter of *praise*, a *gusher* and self-*pusher*, and I said to him, 'Here's something off which you can make some money and that may make you *renowned*. Show me which of the two forms is the more brilliant in style, and let the truth *resound*!' Said he, 'Eulogies and poems of love are all I *write*; in the first I express my pain, in the second my *delight*. Be patient while I review my *Collected Works*, leafing through it from cover to *cover*; if I find the panegyrics there more numerous than the sonnets, the good things of this world must be the *fewer*.' I added him then to his friends the jurisprudent and the *teacher*, remarking, 'How many a wound from how many a *speaker*!'

1.13.8 "Then I set off for the scribe of the *emir*, one whose skills of discernment and careful accounting were acknowledged far and *near*, but before putting the question, I praised him to his *face* and said, 'None but you could possibly *suffice*.' Said he, 'Happiness for me lies in being content with my emir and his *contentment*, unhappiness in resenting him and feeling his *resentment*. At this point, given the fighting and all that goes with it that there's *been*, I've forgotten both any anger and any content that I may have *seen*. If you can wait for a month into the *future*, so I may inscribe in my ledger all that I meet with from him that is sweet and all that is sour, all that is gold and all that is *pewter*, I'll inform you of the answer in due *time*; till then, I must *decline*.' I added him then to the three, making him number *four*,[225] and thought, 'I really must consult someone who's still young, for pride of *place* has left of the brains of those who hold high rank and office not a *trace*, and there's nothing left for those who knock at their *door*.'

"To the Fāriyāq then I *went*, to find him o'er his copying *bent*, on his visage the first signs of *transmogrification*, eyes, as I beheld, deeply sunken, hands suffering from *desiccation*, cheekbones as though from the face's surface *hewn*, skin as tight as the shade at *noon*, so that I deplored his *state* and came close to staying silent for pity at his *plight*. When he saw me, though, he rose and came toward me, saying, 'Is there some service you require me to perform, or private word you need to *convey*?' 'Thus and so,' I said, 'have come my *way*, so settle this question, God save you from *harm*,' at which he pulled from inside his tattered coat a scrap of paper and on it wrote without a *qualm*: 1.13.9

You came to me seeking an answer— 1.13.10
    One to mindful men[226] already known—to a question.
Good, compared to evil,
    Is, over a life span, as a drop to an ocean.
See you not how, if one man has the mange,
    To a whole city he spreads his disease,
Yet no one infects his fellows, no matter how close,
    Who's healthy and lives a life of ease?
How many a sickness afflicts the child from the day he cuts his
        teeth,
    And with him to the grave's consigned?
How he, from the first sprouting of his hair and nails,
    No pleasure and no joy can find?
Any limb's more easy broken
    Than it is mended
And that, like the eye, whose corruption will fast destroy you,
    You'll ne'er fix, till time is ended.
Mourning for a child rends his father's heart
    Wears through his every bone,
And in his birth there is no joy
    Equal to the sorrow of his death, by which the greater harm is
        done.

Pleasure cannot come from thinking,
  Nor from recollection; that's naught but an illusion
When you think upon it well—one that may occur
  To the dimwit or victim of delusion.
Can a patient who for the past month's been sick,
  By picturing a cure, his illness treat?
Can one who in winter's depth grows cold
  Feel warm by recalling the days of heat?
This world of ours, to those who know,
  Is naught but loss and tribulation that we must endure.
Man's born enslaved, not free,
  And so he dies, of that you may be sure.

1.13.11 "Thus his words, and as I took the scrap, my gaze upon it *bent*, and started thinking what it *meant*, I realized that these words of his were the most *wise*, those of the others mere drivel and *lies*, and I told him, 'Blessed be the Lord for an age that has brought us the likes of *you*, and guided seekers after knowledge to your good sense and superior *view*, and shame upon the people of this *earth*, should they fail to recognize your *worth*!' Then I departed from where he was, calling blessings down upon his *head*, and heedful of everything he'd *said*."

## Chapter 14

# A Sacrament[227]

Ahahahah! Ahahahah! Thank God! Thank God I'm done with the composition of that *maqāmah*, and with its number too,[228] for it was weighing on my mind. Now all that remains for me to do is to urge the reader to read it. Though more coarsely woven than the finely knit rhymed prose of al-Ḥarīrī and despite its prosodic *irregularities*, it may, for all that, be worn, and commended for its beneficial *verities*. I believe the second will be better than it was, the third better than the second, the fourth better than the third, and the fiftieth better than the forty-ninth. (Don't panic! Don't panic at these attempts to shock and scare! There are in fact, as promised, only four.) 1.14.1

Now I have to squeeze my sconce to extract some more nice thoughts, figures, and choice words, at the same time avoiding chatter, a process that scholars refer to, I believe, as "voiding verbiage." But hang on a moment, and I'll ask them! What do you call words that are so bursting with meaning that they drench the reader, so that I can fetch them for you? If you don't tell me their name right away, don't blame me if I use their opposite. I exist, and it is my custom to look for what exists, not for what doesn't. Given that the term "voiding verbiage" exists and its opposite doesn't, it is perfectly appropriate for me to turn to it in preference to some other term. You may if you wish put your heads together and come up 1.14.2

with a word—but instead of flying at each other's throats and *fighting*, pecking out each other's eyes and *biting*, or striking with *swords* and swiping with *words*, or grabbing each other by your pockets and *skirts*, do so sedately and *soberly*, serenely and *rationally*, for when someone sedate bestows a name on something, it comes out as sedate as he is and cannot thereafter be converted into something different. In fact, the thing named may even acquire dignity from the name given it, even when it is innately insignificant and frivolous. Have you not noticed how the words of a slim poet come out slim, and those of a big poet come out big? As the saying goes, "The words of kings are the kings of words." By the same token, poetry written by a woman is as bewitching to the mind and teasing to the heart as a woman.

1.14.3 An exception to this principle is the donation of the child by the father, meaning the donation by the father of the material used to form the child. By making an exception of this I don't mean to say that the father becomes pregnant and gives birth but that the father may be ugly and the child turn out good-looking. The reason is that, because conception requires the collaboration of two persons, i.e., a man and a woman, it is unclear which contribution is determinative. The father does not have absolute sway to shape the child as he wishes. He may have in mind at that instant a certain form that he finds attractive, while the mother, God protect her, may have another, depending on her preferences and whatever is then uppermost in her mind; as a result the child may come out a bit of this and bit of that. By the way, it cannot be said that the man is incapable of summoning up a familiar form at that moment just because he's all in a tizzy over the business of that formative material. That's not credible in the case of one who's become used to what is always the same old thing where he's concerned, for long acquaintance modifies a person's attitude to a thing, and, as a result, he deals with it with good sense and deliberation. Take for example the well-fed cook, who prepares all the various dishes with perfect skill and mastery, unlike the hungry cook, who hurries his work and botches it.

Know then (after this polished *excursion* and prolonged and stimulating *insertion*) that the Fāriyāq went one day to a priest to make confession to him of all he had done, said, and *thought* that he didn't *ought*. The priest asked, among other questions, "I hear you're fond of poetry and tunes, which are among the worst causes of evil and passion. Has the Recoiler ever put it into your mind to court in verse a woman firm of breast, rosy of cheek, the kohl on her eyes clear to *see*, her buttocks wobbling *free*, slender of *waist*, her teeth widely *spaced*, her legs with thickness and splendor *graced*, her forearms muscled and without *slack*, her hair and nipples *black*, her eyes startling in the contrast of black and *white*, her hands with henna *bright*, her lips *fine*, her eyebrows a thin, arched *line*, her belly-button *round*, her belly folds *unbound*, her smile *sweet*, her figure *svelte*, with saliva like *honey*, sweet enough to turn iron into *candy*?" Said the Fāriyāq, "I have indeed done so, but I see that you are my fellow in this craft, for I note how well you can describe a beautiful woman." 1.14.4

Said the other, "It isn't my job to produce such verbal *fabrication*, just something I've learned by analogy and spontaneous *inspiration*, for all who listen to *verse* find their brains filled with such descriptions *perverse*. But, be that as it may, you must burn your love poems, *each one*, singly and in *sum*, for they incite the heedless to *err* and you'll be punished for them on that day when men are 'seized by their forelocks,'[229] and you hold extrication *dear*." "How," said the Fāriyāq, "can you expect me to burn in a single moment things I stayed up working on for many a night, during which I knew no slumber and on which I worked as hard as a horse in a *race*, or cameleers who, from dusk to dawn, maintain their *pace*? When I finished a line of the poem, it would seem to me as though I'd covered a stage on the road to her whom I was wooing, and, when the poem was done, I'd imagine I'd reached her and all that stood between us was for me to open the door, which made the conclusion in my case an inauguration, in contrast with all other poets. That is why I didn't attempt long poems—lest the time it took to 1.14.5

write them should be as long as the time it took me to cover the distance to my beloved. Does it make sense that all that effort of mine should be thwarted for the sake of the heedless? Not to mention that I don't want them to read what I write anyway, because if they don't understand it, they'll ask the scholars, who will proceed to hold it up to scorn, accusing me of mistakes and pointing out shortcomings. They never see merit in the writings of the young and humble, and even if they do, my only reward will be, 'God shame him! God destroy him! May his mother be bereaved of him! May he have no father and no mother!'" Said the priest, "If on stubbornness you *insist*, and in divergence from the road of right guidance you *persist*, I'll withhold *absolution* and expose your dirty laundry in open church for *ablution*."

1.14.6 "Don't be so hasty," said the Fāriyāq, "for 'haste is of the Devil'! Do you suppose, if I praised you in a long ode, you could take that as expiation for my sin? And if you'd like me to laud therein each monk and nun, each contemplative (male and female), each ascetic (male and female), each recluse (male and female), each person who stands long in prayer (male and female), each hermit (male and female), each ecstastic reciter (male and female), each preacher (male and female), each caller on God's name (male and female), each God-fearer (male and female), each celibate (male and female), each one who arises from sleep to pray (male and female), each one who prostrates him- (or her-)self in prayer, each one who humbles him- (or her-)self before God, and each teller (male or female) of the rosary, I could do so." The priest thought for a moment and apparently discovered that love poetry wasn't such a great sin, for if it described a woman as having huge buttocks, fat arms, and round breasts, and she really did, then it would be just like someone saying "the moon has risen" when it really had, or "the clouds are parting" when they really were. It would be a lie and a sin only if the woman so characterized was in fact flat-chested and flat-buttocked or used stuffing to make people think she had a large backside, and the one who saw her took what she'd done for real and said what he did without exercising due caution.

When the priest had thought the matter through and weighed it in his mind, he said, "It won't do for you to use your praise of me as expiation, for I'm afraid that, once you get hold of me, you'll never let me go, seeing as I do from your rhymes about those who do this and that (male and female) that you're stubborn, leech-like, dogged, and assiduous. You may praise only those close to God and the righteous divines who deny themselves in this world out of desire to see God's face in the next, who wear hair shirts and spend their nights in constant prayer out of obedience to God, and who subject themselves to perpetual mortification out of love for Him, some eating nothing all their lives but lentils and hardtack." 1.14.7

"Followed," said the Fāriyāq, "by the breaking of a tooth and pruritis. Wait! Wait! I forgot to mention something that the lentils have just now brought to mind. Once I was responsible for persuading a young monk to leave his monastery and abandon the path. The reason was the sufferings I'd undergone there, and I did what I did so that I could gloat over the monastery's discomforture." Said the priest, "Your sin in gloating, which is a type of revenge-taking, was greater than your sin in persuading the young monk to leave, for there is no benefit to be had from the residence of most of the monks, or anyone else, in the monastery. In addition, it may be supposed that this young monk will marry and create lots of monks from his children. If, however, you go praising nuns, be careful you don't talk of them as though they had breasts and buttocks, since they know nothing of such things. Their prolonged devotion and seclusion have made them into something different from other women. We, as contemplatives, are the best authorities on them." 1.14.8

The Fāriyāq then asked him, "In the name of Him who's worshipped in Heaven and in Earth, are all priests like you, so witty and funny?" "I have no idea," the other replied. "I do know, though, that I have suffered for what I've learned and would have done better to 1.14.9

remain ignorant like them. Indeed, 'in ignorance lies ease.'" "How can that be?" asked the Fāriyāq. The man replied, "Have you a place well guarded where a secret may be kept?" Said the Fāriyāq, "Secrets to me are like my own blood: I never let them out!" (though I say, he's let it out now). "Would you like me," asked the priest, "to tell you my story?" "It would be an honor," said the other. "Listen well, then," said he.

## Chapter 15

# The Priest's Tale

Without further ado, he spoke. "Know that when I started out in life I was a weaver. However—given that Almighty God had decided, in His sempiternal wisdom, to make me so ugly and short that even my mother, when she looked at me, would thank God that He hadn't made me a girl—I was no good for weaving. The reason for this was that my terrible shortness often caused me to pant and choke in the loom pit, because my whole body would disappear inside it, and I'd find it impossible to breathe, despite which my nostrils, praise God, could take in enough air to fill fifty lungs and fifty bellies. Often I'd faint down there and have to be pulled out at my last gasp. 1.15.1

"When I'd suffered from that craft as much toil and trouble as I could stand, I decided it would be better to set up shop selling a few things that women crave, so I rented me a little store and sat there, and the women would pass by, look at me, and then laugh to one another. Once I heard one of them say, 'If the outside is a true guide to the inside, that shopkeeper's hose will intercede for his body and sell his goods for him.' I put my trust in her words and said, 'Maybe from ugliness will come good fortune, for, as the proverb has it, "from good comes evil."' I went on for a while that way but to no avail, for my nose stood between me and my living, and it grew so monstrous that it left room for nothing but rejection and aversion. 1.15.2

1.15.3 "One day I was sitting thinking about the Almighty's creation of this universe, when I said to myself, 'My, my! What a wise God! How could He make an individual a part of this world and at the same time make a part of that individual an impediment to his earning a living or making his way in it? What use is this huge nose except for having the "buttocks" of "Halt and weep"[230] stuffed up it? And why shouldn't a part of it be cored out and curled about my body? How is it I see that some people have been created as beautiful as angels and others as ugly as the Devil? Are we not all God's creatures? Has not He, glory be to Him, taken them all into His care, on the same footing? Does not the earthly craftsman, when he wants to make something, work on it meticulously and make it as nearly perfect as he can, bringing it to the best state possible? Does a painter paint an ugly picture, unless he wants to make people laugh at the thing portrayed? Could it be that, in a nose of huge size, there is some comeliness, value, or benefit of which we ordinary mortals are unaware?'

1.15.4 "Then I would get up and go to the mirror and contemplate my face and reject it, finding nothing in it to like, and say, returning to my first line of thought, 'If I cannot find anything to like about my face, how can anyone else find it attractive?' People will, however, find good in the faults of others and in their vices virtues. Do you not observe how, to some people's eyes, ugliness is attractive? It is said that blacks find nothing attractive in the fair-complexioned among us, while blackness, being general among them, is something they appreciate. Never do I see anyone carrying around a nose like mine without hoping that he'll find mine attractive. As for color, I belong neither to the blacks nor the whites and am cursed by both their houses. Would that the people of my town were all like me, with big noses; then I could share in their joys and sorrows. From whom did I inherit this boulder, when my father's nose was just like other people's? I wish I knew what my father was thinking about when the idea of bringing me into this universe came knocking at his head, and about what lofty mountain peak, craggy landmark, or minaret my mother was thinking on the night when she collaborated with him in that deed! Would they'd swooned that night and not *awoken*, or gone off the boil and found their appetites *broken*, or been bewitched and lost all *feeling*, or got drunk and and gone about *reeling*!

"I was turning these ideas over in my head and fashioning them into different forms and varying shapes, when behold, a woman with covered face approached, with something that might have been a water pitcher forming a bump beneath her veil; I thought she must have placed a flask of scent by her nose to sniff at when passing the carrion in the city's markets. She asked me about something she wanted to buy, and I told her its price, which she seemed to find high, so she told me, 'Bring it down. Your price is pyretic,' to which I responded 'And your proposal's pruritic.' She laughed and said, 'You did well on the response but you made a mess of the request. Make allowance for the rights of partnership and commonality, for I'm your partner and comrade, which means you should make me a gift for friendship's sake.' 'What partnership can there be between us, God set you to rights,' I asked, 'when this is the first time you have honored me with a visit?' At this she raised her veil, and I beheld that her nose bulged out so far it left almost no room for her face and seemed to stand face to face with mine as though to salute it. It made me think of the story of the lame crow that made friends with a crow with a broken wing, on seeing which a certain poet declared, 'I never knew what people meant by the saying "Birds of a feather flock together" until I saw these two crows.' In the end I sold her what she wanted to buy, trying to get one kiss as a compensation for my loss, but I couldn't because our noses got in the way. Then she departed and I continued for a while as before. 1.15.5

"When I realized that I wasn't cut out for trade (for women buy only from young men who are well-built and supple as a branch, taking the beauty of their faces as a good omen that they will enjoy whatever they buy from them and as as a memento of the happy day on which they made their acquaintance), and that since I'd opened 1.15.6

the store the only thing I'd sold had been to the woman with the bulbous beezer (and that at a loss!), I decided to become a monk. I found my way to a monastery and said to its abbot, 'I come to you disillusioned with this world and eager for the next, for this world can never assume that other's place. The wise man is he who takes this as a metaphor for that, for were this the home that our Creator desired for us, we would live in it for eons, though in fact we see that some people are born into it and live a single day, which is evidence that it's not what we were created for' and similar stuff of the sort that trips off the tongues of contemplatives. The abbot saw virtue in me and accepted me, but the next day he happened to try to climb over the wall to get to the houses of certain partners and the broken end of a tree branch entered his eye and blinded him, so he returned in a fury, saying that my arrival at the monastery had brought bad luck, because for ages before I came he'd climbed that wall all the time and nothing had ever happened to him.

1.15.7 "As a result, he threw me out of the monastery, so I entered another and repeated what I'd said the first time. Its abbot accepted me, and I resided there for a few days, suffering such squalor and dirt as neither God nor man could put up with, in addition to the obduracy of the monks, the divergence of their opinions, their accusations against one another, and their constant complaints to the abbot over matters of no importance, as well as the way the latter lorded it over them, his selfishness over things that he kept for himself alone, allowing them no share in them, and their rivalry over things that women would give them, such as a handkerchief, a purse, or the drawstring from a pair of bloomers.

1.15.8 "To this you have to add the ignorance of them all, for in the whole monastery there wasn't one who could pen an epistle on any topic. Even the abbot himself, God preserve his high degree, was incapable of writing a single line in proper Arabic, using instead the Syriac letters known as *karshūnī*,[231] of his knowledge of which the ignoramus was so inordinately proud that he'd force everyone who entered his cell to say how wonderful they were, and even invite all and sundry to visit him, which the gullible monks thought he did out of noble morals and generosity of character. He had written a line in these letters above his door and another on his wall, and when I looked at it, I'd smile, which he, in his simplemindedness, believed was because I admired them. Other monks who, for all their ignorance, were wily swindlers (and how many a man combines ignorance and dishonesty!) would, in hope of gaining his favor, cozy up to him by telling him, as he sat there with his head lowered in modesty and submissiveness, 'Would you be so generous, Master, as to let me have a sample of your handwriting to use as a model for my own?' and this was one of the best ways for them to get things out of him.

"When, then, their company, and, above all, the awfulness of the food, became too much for me to bear, I took to grumbling and muttering. One day the monastery cook heard me complaining about how little clarified butter there was in the rice he was cooking for a high holiday. He was a ruffian and a knave and he exploded at me in anger, picking me up and putting me over his shoulder as a man might his child, though without the tenderness. Then he carried me through the passageways of the monastery and plunged me into the vat of butter, saying, 'This is the butter with which I cook the rice that you don't like, you schnozzle-*chik*, owl-*chick*, poor man's *portion*, rascal's *scion*, committer of sins great and *small*, emitter of a garlicky *pall*, poisonous wind *anabatic*, blood-sucking tic *parasitic*, *insatiate*, *crapulate*, *indigestate*'—and poured over me many more rhymes of this sort, the dunking in insults received by my good name exceeding the dunking my head got in the butter. After some effort, I contrived to slip out of his clutches and entered my cell to wash, and suddenly there he was again, knocking on the door and bellowing, 'I have to squeeze your nose out, for enough butter's got into it to keep the monks going for days!' Then he reached for my nostrils with hands like iron pincers and set about squeezing them as hard as he could till I thought the soul (*nafs*) was about to about to depart, for the nose alone among the body's orifices (and I say 1.15.9

this in knowing contradiction of the beliefs of a certain school) is the point of entry and exit for the breath (*nafas*), which is why one says that a person *yatanaffas* ('breathes').[232]

1.15.10 "As my sufferings were too much to bear, and I could find no one in the monastery to complain to, because the monks all flattered him and made up to him so that he'd give them enough to eat, even if it were only the *thurtum* (which is the food or condiments left on a dish), I left the monastery, in parlous state, saddened and discouraged, the world in all its expansiveness seeming me a narrow space, and said, 'Where am I to take this nose of mine that has blocked every avenue by which I might make a living, or where is it to take me?' It occurred to me to head for a monastery far away, of which I had heard that its monks were righteous men and that some wrote a good Arabic hand, loved strangers, and honored their guests. So I made my way to it, and when I saluted its abbot and acquainted him with what I had resolved, he praised my opinion highly and welcomed me warmly, though he couldn't prevent himself from gazing at me in surprise and praying for God's protection from any ill consequences that might befall him because of my nose. So I stayed in his monastery for as long as it was God's will that I should stay."

## Chapter 16

# The Priest's Tale Continued

"From the outset and for as long as I was there, I made it my concern to humor the cook, get on his good side, and praise him. He, in return, let me want for nothing that could be had in the monastery. In fact, I spent the greater part of my time in the kitchen. I was also good at cooking dishes he knew nothing of, so I taught him these, and he became exceedingly fond of me. Thus it came to pass that, when the abbot invited someone dear to him to eat with him, or had an urge to eat a certain kind of food on his own, the cook would charge me with preparing it. Because I was as meticulous as possible in doing so, I ended up in his good graces, meaning that I'd sit with him in the evenings and keep him company, acquiring in this way a reputation for righteousness and piety among the monks. I pulled my hood down till it reached the bridge of my nose—and would that custom had allowed it to cover the nose entirely!—and when I walked I kept my head bent toward the ground and cast only brief glances to right and left, and when I ate, drank, slept, walked, or washed my face, I made mention of all of those things, thanking and praising God as I did so. Thus I would say, for example, 'Today I left my cell, praise be to God!' or 'To God be glory!' (the latter being the monks' preferred form), or 'This morning I took a laxative, may this find favor in God's eyes!' and other stuff that those who make a show of piety are known to say. Thus the monks ended up believing 1.16.1

that I was full of righteousness and virtue. I'd also written out a few hymns in bad Arabic for the abbot, who admired and praised me for my hand, promising to promote me to a rank worthy of me, for he believed I was distinguished from the rest of the monks by my learning and excellence of judgment, a faculty he attributed to my being *ghaydār* (meaning 'a suspicious person who ponders a matter and then comes up with a correct interpretation').

1.16.2 "Then God, Lord of Death and Life, decreed that one of those priests who service the laity in certain far-off parts (meaning that they eat and drink in people's houses instead of at the monastery and mingle with their congregants, against the custom of monks, who mix with people only when they have to) should die, causing the abbot to send me to that country to adopt the same position as the deceased (meaning to substitute for him, not to be buried along with him). On my arrival, my congregation received me generously and with open arms, while I demonstrated god-fearingness and chastity to them and my virtues became well known among them. A merchant, one to whom God had denied the pleasure of children, even invited me into his home and asked me to lodge with him, in the hope that, by virtue of my presence, God would 'open his wife's womb,' as it says in the Old Testament,[233] and children be born to him. This wife was beautiful, slender of figure, and well-endowed of *chest*, fond of dissolute pleasure, revelry, and *zest* (God be praised—the mere thought of women produces the urge to write in rhymed prose!), so I stayed with him a *while*, living in the most luxurious *style*.

1.16.3 "Then it occurred to me to flirt with his wife and to *pursue her*, be her close companion and *woo her*. She responded to my enticements, paying no attention to the tip of my *nose*, for it is in women's nature to incline to what's *close*, ignoring what's far away (and I'm sure you're aware of what one woman *said*, concerning 'long converse and closeness in *bed*.')[234] The world now appeared to my eyes at its *best*, I forgot the many hardships that, at the monastery, I'd had to *digest*, and I said to myself, 'So long as my good fortune persists and its currents serve, I shall make up to myself for all the good things of which I saw no *use* when I was a weaver, a cook, and a *recluse*,' and I made it a rule that my pleasures with her be *measured*—taking care that I be *pleasured* once for each day *past* (like any man with his lawful wedded wife) and then once again for the present (which of course didn't *last*), as incitement and impulse might take me—and kept *count*, soon reaching a huge *amount*. The husband, having no ill thoughts and being of a trusting disposition, was quite *unperturbed*, and, with no suspicions to distract him from his work, pleasure's fruits were there for the plucking, the cups of our joy *undisturbed*.

"Now here's an amazing thing that deserves to be recorded in books—she'd pick quarrels with the *maid*, both in her husband's presence and when he was *delayed*, and abuse her in front of him in the nastiest *way*, thus forestalling any suspicions of his that might come into *play*—she fearing no consequences from *this*, nor being concerned at what might happen should she the said maid *dismiss*, for she'd fired many a maid *before*, for good reasons and for *poor*, after subjecting them to every kind of insult, and making them to hatred and anger *inclined*; and this is one of the miracles of women and their strange uniqueness, to the essence of whose extraordinary secret we men are *blind*. In sum, I was entranced by her beauty, just as I marveled at her art, and I dwelt with her in this state in extreme *delight*, like one married without having to pay a bride-price, coddled after calamities, indulging without restraint my every *appetite*.(1) 1.16.4

(1) *afnaqa l-rajul*: 'to live a life of luxury after destitution." [The author's gloss refers to the word *mufniqan* "coddled after calamities." Translator.]

"Then I started another count, longer and more extended than the first, for, as the easy life made me reckless and I felt safe from any blow that fate might *deal*, I couldn't stop thinking I should combine the two *c*s,[235] for 'much prosperity brings much *weal*' and rarely have I seen one truckle with the first who does not also indulge in the second and similar worldly attachments—such as shuffling gaming arrows and twirling bones,[236] cheating at games and accusing others of the same, trading in livestock as yet unborn 1.16.5

and usury, shooting arrows and brandishing spears, arrow-shooting contests and casting lots, flushing game and picking up the dice before a throw, cheating and selling things at arbitrary prices, inciting others to shuffle the gaming arrows and inciting them to lay bets, betting and laying stakes, dealing in grain futures and selling dates while still on the tree, selling seed before it has matured and other fast practice, swapping commodities and making bargains, bartering and defrauding, swindling and misrepresenting, concealing defects and delaying payment of debts, selling grain on the basis of the weight of a single sample and deferring (while at the same time increasing the amount of) a debt, offering blandishments and contracting to buy things on the basis of a description only—at which point [i.e., when he has lost], he wanders, making do with nothing to eat but bread made of sorghum, and he cheats and plots, swindles and lies, jokes around, behaves like a lunatic, and tries to con people, taking his clothes off, stripping naked, and using them as stakes for his bets.(2) So I met with a man of whom I'd heard it said he practiced this *profession* and devoted himself to it seriously and without *digression*, devoting to it great *pains* and expending on it much of his *gains*, while confining his thoughts to that alone. To cut things *short*, and without having to further lengthy rhyme *resort*, I went into the same trade with him." (Here ends the priest's rhymed prose.)

(2) *abahlaṣa* and *tabalhaṣa* both mean "to take off one's clothes," and *bahṣala* means "to remove one's clothes and gamble with them."

1.16.6 "I started funding it from what I gathered from the old women and greenhorns by way of fees for welcoming new souls and seeing off old, as I continued to ply my first profession. Indeed, all the preceding was a stimulus to extra passion from both my side and that of my little cutie, for she now grew greedy for presents and gifts, as women do every time there is some occasion in the lives of their husbands and lovers. The news of my new profession reached my abbot, who sent to demand from me the money that I'd made. I made excuses that he refused and didn't accept, and he found a reason to recall me, seizing the baggage and everything else I had with me, though the loss of all of that didn't upset me as much as the interruption of the first count (the one I'd initiated at the house of the righteous merchant). After a period almost long enough to make me forget the pleasures of those by-gone days, I slipped from that abbot's bonds and set off in search of another, to spite the former. I thus made my way to an abbot who was one of those most hostile to the abbot I'd been with before—for hostility is to be found as much among abbots as among atheists—and the former, fearing that I might come to harm from the latter, sent me off to distant lands in a ship of war.

"Before we'd been at sea for more than a few hours, some of the ship's instruments failed, causing its captain to fear that it would take us down, so he turned back, having decided that I was the cause of his misfortune and telling one of the passengers that what happened had occurred because of my ugly mug. I was greatly amazed to hear his words, for such people[237] are not given to *irtisām*,[238] to *tashā'um*,[239] to *taṭayyur*,[240] to *tafā'ul*,[241] to *taḥattum*,[242] to *tayammun*,[243] to *tasa''ud*,[244] to *tamassuḥ*,[245] or to hanging necklaces of *shubāriq* wood or making use of *ʿaṭaf*; nor do they place any faith in *haqʿah* or *lujām*, *ʿāṭūs* or *ʿāṭis*,[246] *kābiḥ* or *kādis*, *qaʿīd* or *dākis*,[247] *bāriḥ* or *sāniḥ*, *zajr* or *taḥazzī*, *ʿiyāfah* or *ʿaytharah*, *ṭarq* or *ʿirāfah*, *hajīj*, or *kahānah*,[248] *ibnā ʿiyān* or *tanajjī*, *lammah* or *ḥufūf*, *luʿṭah* or *intijā'*,[249] *tashawwuh* or *taʿayyud*, *ṭalāsim*[250] or *tashahhuq* or *ʿazā'im*,[251] *ruqā*[252] or *tamā'im*,[253] *yanjalib* or *tuwalah*, *ḥawṭ* or *ghazz*, *tadsīm al-nūnah* or *shadd al-ḥiqāb*, *rasʿ* or *ṣakhbah*, *qulayb* or *kabdah*, *wajīh* or *sulwānah*, *sulwān* or *ʿuqarah*, *mijwal* or *muhrah*, *ukhdhah* or *ʿūdhah*,[254] *habrah* or *ra'amah*, *kaḥlah* or *hinnamah*, *julbah* or *ṣarrah*, *qablah* or *nushzah*, *qublah* or *nufrah*, *ṣudḥah* or *hamrah*, *zarqah* or *ʿaṭfah*, *faṭsah* or *ṣarfah*, *ghaḍār* or *karār*, *barīm* or *ḥirz*, *khaṣmah* or *ratīmah*, *asḥam* or *ṣihmīm*, *tadha''aba* or *ṣawt al-lūf*, *hāmah* or *ṣafar*, *ukhdhat al-nār* or *tanjīs*, *laḥj* or *inkīs*, *us* or *shaḥīthā*, *ṭibb* or *tawl*, *siḥr*[255] or *māqiṭ*, *ʿāḍih* or *mustanshi'ah*, *naffāthāt fi l-ʿuqad* or *ṣadā*,[256] *shaʿbadhah* or *nīranj*, *shaʿwadhah* or *ḥābil* or *ḥāwī*. 1.16.7

1.16.8 "On that day I learned for sure that a man with a big nose is hated in every country and that half a pound of extra flesh on a man's face will bring him woe and privation, while two pounds on a woman's rump will bring her fortune and success, and my wonder at this world that's built on two-and-a-half pounds of flesh increased, despite which I couldn't bring myself to renounce it. Then I traveled to those lands[257] and found safety in them from the intrigues of my enemies, and rented a house and brought a woman to serve me. It has become customary for priests, in those lands and in the lands of the Franks too, to take a woman to serve them, who comes to him in the morning, while he is still in his comfortable bed, and provides him with whatever he wants from her. Having tasted the sweetness of that life, the Tempter whispered in my ear that I should marry a girl who was poor but beautiful. I wasn't quite certain that her breasts had completely rounded out but had taken a fancy to her all the same. I therefore asked the abbot to increase my stipend, but he refused. I insisted, but he was adamant in saying no, while I was adamant in asking for more. Then, when I argued with him and ended our discussion on an angry note, he decided to send me back to whence I'd come, so I went to an abbot who was friendly with the first abbot, and he was delighted to see me and put me up with him, and I found myself back where I'd begun. Now I'm waiting for an opportunity to exchange this other no-hoper too, for he is very ignorant, and, in my opinion, swapping abbots in these days of oppression brings more benefit than the philosopher's stone." Here ends the priest's tale.

1.16.9 Here are the meanings of the rare words mentioned above:

| | |
|---|---|
| *ibnā ʿiyān,* | [literally, "the Sons of Sight"] "Two birds, or two lines; the augur would draw lines on the ground and say, 'Sons of Sight, tell us quickly what you see!'," etc. |
| *ukhdhat al-nār,* | [literally, "the fire spell"] "Shortly after the sunset prayer; they claim that this is the worst time at which to strike [a flint]." |

| | |
|---|---|
| *ukhdhah*, | "An incantation, like sorcery, or a bead with which spells are made" |
| *irtisām*, | "Saying, 'God is great!' or 'I take refuge with God!' or believing that certain things are inevitable or believing in omens" |
| *asḥam*, | "The blood in which the hands of those swearing oaths are dipped" |
| *us*, | "A word said to the serpent, on hearing which it obeys" |
| *inkīs*, | "A shape made in the sand [by a geomancer]; some call it the *mankūs*"[258] |
| *bāriḥ*, | "Game that passes from one's right to one's left" |
| *barīm*, | "Two separate threads, red and white, tied by a woman around her waist and her forearm . . . and incantation" |
| *taḥazzī*, | *ḥazā*/*ḥazwan*, and *taḥazzā* are synonymous with *zajr* [see below] and *takahhana* ("to divine")[259] 1.16.10 |
| *tadsīm al-nūnah*, | To perform *tadsīm* on a child's chin-dimple is "to blacken it with soot so that 'the eye' does not afflict it" |
| *tadhaʿʿub*, | [One says,] "he suffered *tadhaʿʿub* from the jinn," meaning "they gave him a scare" |
| *tashahhuq*, | [One says,] "the observer's eye performed *tashahhuq* upon him," meaning "it afflicted him with 'the eye'" |
| *tashawwuh*, | One says, "Do not perform *tashawwuh* upon me!" meaning "Do not afflict me with 'the eye'!" |
| *taʿayyud*, | "'The beholder performed *taʿayyud* on the beheld' means he afflicted him with 'the eye' and did so forcefully so as to intensify the injury done to him"; mentioned by al-Fīrūzābādī under *ʿ-w-d* |

| | |
|---|---|
| *tanjīs*, | [literally, "defilement"] "The name given something dirty, or bones from the dead, or a menstrual rag that they used to hang on anyone whom it was feared might have been afflicted with madness by the jinn" |
| *tanajjā*, | "To perform *tanajjī* on (*li-*) someone means to perform *tashahhuq* [q.v.] on him in order to afflict him with 'the eye,' as also *najā*"; *naja'a* with the glottal stop means "to afflict with 'the eye'" |
| *tawl*, | "[The verb] *tāla, yatūlu* means 'to practice sorcery'" |
| 1.16.11 *tuwalah*, | "Sorcery, or anything like it, or beads used to make a woman love her husband"; also *tiwalah* |
| *julbah*, | "An amulet strung on a leather string" |
| *ḥābil*, | "Sorcerer" |
| *ḥirz*, | "Amulet" |
| *ḥufūf*, | "Severe affliction with 'the eye'" |
| *ḥawṭ*, | "Beads and a silver crescent that a woman ties around her waist so that 'the eye' will not afflict her" |
| *khaṣmah*, | "An amulet used by men, worn in battle or when going into the presence of the sultan" |
| *ra'amah*, | "A love bead" |
| *ratīmah*, | "One intending to make a journey would go to a tree[260] and tie two branches together. If he returned and they were still tied, he would say that his wife had not betrayed him; otherwise she had betrayed him. This was called *ratm* or *ratīmah*" |
| *ras'*, | "'He performed *ras'* on the child' means he tied a bead onto his hand or foot against 'the eye'" |

| | | |
|---|---|---|
| *zajr*, | "Divination through *ʿiyāfah* [q.v.] or the taking of auguries" | 1.16.12 |
| *zarqah*, | "A bead for casting spells" | |
| *sāniḥ*, | Opposite of *bāriḥ* [q.v.] | |
| *sulwān*, | [literally, "consolation"] "Something that is drunk to bring consolation, or the taking of dust from the grave of a dead man and making it into something that is given to the lover to drink so that his love-sickness dies, etc." | |
| *sulwānah*, | "A bead used for working magic, and a bead that is buried in the sand and which then turns black, is sought for, [is pulverized], and is drunk by someone, to whom it then brings consolation" | |
| *shadd al-ḥiqāb*, | [literally, "the tying of the *ḥiqāb*"] "The *ḥiqāb* is a thread that is tied around the loins of a child to ward off 'the eye'" | |
| *shaʿbadhah*, | *shaʿwadhah* [q.v.] | |
| *shaʿwadhah*, | "Spells, a form of sorcery: things are seen in a shape different from their original shape as seen by the eye" | |
| *shaḥīthā*, | "A Syriac word by which what is locked may be opened without keys" | |
| *ṣakhbah*, | "A bead used for love and for hatred" | 1.16.13 |
| *ṣadḥah*, | "(also *ṣudḥah* or *ṣadaḥah*) a bead used for casting spells" | |
| *ṣarrah*, | "A bead used for casting spells" | |
| *ṣarfah*, | "A bead used for casting spells" | |
| *ṣihmīm*, | "The sooth-sayer's fee" | |
| *ṣawt al-lūf*, | [literally, "the cry of the loofah"] "A plant with a bulb that is called 'the shrieker' because on the day of the festival it emits a cry which, they claim, causes any who hears it to die within the day" | |

| | | |
|---|---|---|
| | *ṣafar,* | "A serpent in the belly that clings to the ribs and bites them," or etc.[261] |
| | *ṭibb,* | "Also *ṭabb* and *ṭubb*; gentleness, and magic" |
| | *ṭarq,* | "The soothsayer's mixing of cotton with wool when he prognosticates" |
| 1.16.14 | *ʿāḍih,* | "Magician"; *ʿiḍah* means lying, falsehood, and magic |
| | *ʿāṭūs,* | "Something that is sneezed at and a beast from which an evil omen is taken"; the *ʿāṭis* is "a gazelle that approaches head-on" |
| | *ʿirāfah,* | A *ʿarrāf* is a soothsayer, or a physician, and his profession is called *ʿirāfah*; the verb ["to practise soothsaying"] is *ʿarafa*, on the pattern of *kataba*[262] |
| | *ʿaṭaf,* | "A plant some of whose roots are twisted and . . . thrown over a misogynist to make him love his wife" |
| | *ʿatfah,* | "A bead used for casting spells" |
| | *ʿuqarah,* | "A bead worn by women in order not to give birth" |
| | *ʿūd al-shubāriq,* | "[The wood of] a tall tree, necklaces made of which are hung around the necks of horses and other beasts to protect them from 'the eye'" |
| | *ʿiyāfah,* | "[The verb] *ʿiftu* [first person singular perfect], *uʿīfu* [first person singular imperfect], *ʿiyāfatan* [verbal noun]) *al-ṭayr* is synonymous with 'I took an augury from the birds,' meaning that one takes into consideration their names and their descents and ascents and then draws a happy or an unhappy omen" |
| | *ʿaytharah,* | *ʿaythara l-ṭayr* means, he saw the birds flying and took an augury from them |

*ghazz*, "To perform *ghazz* upon camels or a child is to hang colored threads on them against 'the eye'" 1.16.15

*ghaḍār* and *karār*, "The *ghaḍār* is a piece of pottery worn to ward off 'the eye'; a *karār* is a bead for casting spells. The witch says, 'O *karār*, turn him back! O *hamrah* [q.v.], knock him flat! If he come this way, give him joy! If he turn his back, give him pain!'"

*faṭsah*, "Beads they use for casting spells; women say, 'I take him with the sudden death, the yawn, and the sneeze!'"

*qablah*, "A kind of bead used for casting spells"

*qublah*, "What the magician uses to summon up a person's face for his friend"

*qulayb*, "A bead used for casting spells"

*kābiḥ*, "Things [i.e., animals] used for taking auguries that approach one head-on"

*kādis*, "Things used in divining, such as a good omen, a sneeze, or the like; the *qaʿīd*, said of gazelles, is the one that comes up behind you, and from it a bad omen is drawn, and the *dākis* is the same"

*kabdah*, "A bead for love"

*kaḥlah*, "A bead used for casting spells, or against 'the eye'"

*lujām*, "Things from which omens are drawn" 1.16.16

*laḥj*, "'He performed *laḥj* on him with his eye' means 'he afflicted him with it'"

*luʿṭah*, "The noun formed from [the expression] *laʿaṭahu bi-sahm* ('he struck him with an arrow') or *bi-ʿayn* ('with "the eye"'), meaning 'he afflicted him'"

| | |
|---|---|
| *lammah,* | "One says, 'He was afflicted by a *lammah,* or fit, or a touch [of madness] from the jinn' . . . and *al-'ayn al-lāmmah* (literally, 'the gathering eye') is that which afflicts with evil" |
| *māqiṭ,* | "The minor magician who claims powers of divination and knocks small stones together"[263] |
| *mijwal,* | "Cantrip" |
| *mustanshi'ah,* | "The woman soothsayer" |
| *muhrah,* | "A bead women used to attract love" |
| *nushrah,* | "A spell with which the insane or the sick are treated" |
| 1.16.17 *naffāthāt fī l-'uqad,* | "Witches"[264] |
| *nufrah,* | "Something hung on a child for fear of 'the eye'" |
| *nīranj,* | "Charms that look like magic but are not" |
| *hāmah,* | "The *ṣadā*, which is a bird that emerges from the head of a murdered man, according to the Arabs of the Days of Barbarism" |
| *habrah,* | "Beads by which men are bewitched" |
| *hajīj,* | "A line drawn on the ground for purposes of divination" |
| *haq'ah,* | "A ring on a horse that is regarded as ill-omened" |
| *hamrah,* | "A bead used for casting spells" |
| *hinnamah,* | "A bead used for casting spells" |
| 1.16.18 *wajīh,* | "A bead, too well-known to require definition,[265] as is *wajīhah*"; it seems to me they must be [worn] to impress with "high-standing" (*wajāhah*) |
| *yanjalib,* | "A bead for casting spells, or for return after flight" |
| *ḥāwī.* | "The man called a *ḥawwā'* or a *ḥāwī* collects snakes." I declare: This is all that the author of the *Qāmūs* says under the root *ḥ-y-y*, though it |

appears that the root is really *ḥ-w-y*; however, the *Qāmūs* relates the word to the root *ḥ-w-y* when he doubles the *w* and says, "It is claimed that *ḥayyah* ('snake') is from this root because of its coiling upon itself (*taḥawwī*)," etc. His statement that the *ḥāwī* "collects snakes" (*yajmaʿu ḥayyāt*)—as if the word was derived from *ḥawā* ("to gather")—is inconsistent with his definition of the word *ḥinfish*, namely, "[the viper] or a great serpent with a huge head, variegated black and white, given to lying still; if you charm it (*ḥawwaytahā*), its jugular swells." Here he relates it unambiguously to the casting of spells, as I state, along with other things, in a separate book.[266]

## Chapter 17

# Snow

1.17.1 No doubt, some readers will find what I have to say in this chapter hard to warm to as I wrote it on a "frowning day, *inauspicious*,"[267] a day of cold that was *vicious*. Snow at the time o'er the rooftops was *sifting*, had blocked the highways, and into house and palace was *drifting*. It was almost enough to extinguish any *fire*, put an end to any patience, and thoughts of moon and of money-wagering *inspire*.[268]

1.17.2 Be that as it may, no one can deny that anyone who drinks, eats, or plays with snow derives from it a feeling of heat. The same goes for the reader of my words: if he finds himself getting chilly, all he has to do is seek protection with me from the cold, in which case the goal, which is to put his brain through some warm-up exercises, will have been achieved. This will be especially true if the said brain still carries some traces of anger and indignation left over from the preceding chapter, though I meant nothing by telling the tale but to speak the truth, and, had it crossed my mind to lie or fib, I would have done so in a poem concluding with prayers and praise for some miser; if anyone doesn't believe me, let him ask the priest himself. All the same, snow differs from my words in one thing: snow falls on what is black and makes it white, while my words fall on paper and make it black. Both, in my opinion, are a delight to the eye, and the two share the following feature: a few days after the sun rises over the snow, it melts, and the same is true of my words, for almost nothing will remain of them in the reader's head after the passing of one moonlit night or the rising over him of one Shining Orb. And here's a further point of resemblance: the falling of the snow gives rise to a clearing and brightening of the weather; so too the descent of my words from my head brings about a brightening of the weather of my thoughts, a clearing of my mind, and a readiness on its part to delight and please. In any case, I'm sure you'll agree that the comparison is appropriate here and my excuse to the point.

To proceed. I see that the well-off and well-to-do, in their spa- 1.17.3
cious homes, use one set of living quarters for the summer and another for the winter, one nook for passing the night and another for taking a bath. Others, who have only one house, aren't worth the visiting, unless that house happens to be close by at the time for visits or the time for visits happens to coincide with closeness to their houses. It follows that, in emulation of their better-off betters, scholars should assign themselves, in their roomy heads, numerous and varied locations for the cold, tepid, and hot words that come to them. That way, when their blood is hot and their natural tempers are aroused, they'll be able to read something cold and so reduce the underlying causes of the heat that has exercised them, and when things are quiet they'll be able to recite out loud from the hot, or pursue the opposite strategy, in keeping with the school of those who treat things with their like and not with their opposite. Let no one say that the reader will be wasting his time if he spends it distinguishing between the cold and the hot among these chapters, for the only way to thoroughly digest their contents is to read them through to the end, unlike other books, in which the sin of "cold talk"[269] isn't committed and which follow one set curriculum. Every one of these chapters, I declare, has a title that points to its contents as unambiguously as smoke does to fire; anyone who knows what the title is knows what the whole chapter is about. If, for example, you happen to come across some chapter with the word *bālūʿah* or *ballūʿah* or *ballāʿah* ("drain") or *barbakh* ("drainpipe") or *irdabbah*

("sewer") as a heading, you can assume that one of the donkeys at the monastery must have dived into something of the sort looking for help with their Arabizations and translations.

1.17.4 On the other hand, of course, just because the reader has got to know the gist of the chapter from its title doesn't mean he can decide not to read it and then boast to his friends and brethren, "I read *Leg over Leg* and understood it all!" That would be like someone who claims to be of noble origin(1) saying, "Today I saw the emir, God strengthen him, and spoke to him," when all he saw of him was the back of his head, and that from a distance, and it wasn't granted to him to kiss the noble hand; or the same emir asked him about something and he stammered over his reply or had to think about it, so the emir insulted his father and forefathers and cursed him out, threatening to have him crucified or to have his eyes put out with hot irons; or like some *habanqaʿ* (one who puts on airs, is stupid, and loves talking to women) saying, "I saw such and such a woman today, and, when she was face to face with me, she stopped and sighed deeply," when she probably stopped to spit, or she sighed a deeply malodorous sigh. The reader should, preferably, on opening this book, go through it page by page, from the beginning to the end, including the footnotes and page numbers.

(1) *muqnis* ["claiming to be of noble origin"]: *aqnasa l-rajul* means "he laid claim to a *qans sharīf*, i.e., a noble origin, when he was a low-born upstart."

1.17.5 It is believed that each author has his own style and no one can please everybody, for people's likes are diverse, their opinions various. One mystery I've never been able to get to the bottom of is that a certain author will appear slothful, with neither energy or good cheer, ill at ease with anything that might stir up commotion or conflict, tepid in both inaction and action, viewing everything that happens as though it was just what he'd expected—and yet set every vein of the reader's throbbing and every muscle aquiver the moment he takes up the pen; and there are some whom you'll find lively and brisk, always in a hurry and a rush, quick and agile, coming and going, running around and falling over himself, chasing and speeding, ducking and weaving, shoving and jostling—and then, when he composes something, it falls out of his head onto the reader's brain like snow and almost douses the fires of his intelligence.

When I thought about the matter and looked into it in depth, I started to doubt that snow could be created by an excess of cold formed in the air. I decided that, on the contrary, it may well, in fact, be caused by the creation by excessive heat of an irritated patch on the air's breast above the inhabitants of the Earth plus a superabundance of ire inside its guts, followed by the precipation of the latter onto the said inhabitants in the form of snow, to pay them back for the abominations they practice on cold nights, meaning the way that some of them try to turn nature upside down and heat their beds with an instrument containing fire or, in the case of others, one containing piping hot water or, of others, by using an instrument containing drink, or of others, one containing meat.[270] Such meat might even include pork, God save your dignity, and the air would therefore drop accumulations of snow upon them to prevent them from leaving their houses to make use of these instruments, and thus be relieved of their corruption, be it but for a couple of days. 1.17.6

What would have escaped its notice, however, is that many of these same people make use of one instrument to instrumentalize another, or several others. An example of the first would be the rich man who sits cross-legged in his tub, wraps himself in his fur mantle, and says to his servant, "You there! Off with you to such and such a store and bring me an instrument with which to heat my bed tonight!" so that the servant treads the mire and snow while his master's foot stays clean. An example of the second would be if the master is open-handed and liberal and sends his servant in a vehicle either belonging to him or hired off the street, or, if he's a sovereign emir and wants to keep his secret from his servant (it being ever the pleasure of servants to slander their master's good name and pretend that they are worthier to be served than he), in which case the master will make use of another, or a couple of others, or of several others, in place of his servant, he having sent them, ahead of time, via his servant, a gift as a way of showing his generosity or 1.17.7

perhaps having given it to them with his own hand. Whatever the case may be, the falling of snow will have been the cause of heating and warmth, for, if the latter be regarded as due to the action of the master, it would be the cause of his having made use of the instrument, and if it is regarded as being due to the action of the servant or others who might take his place, it would be attributable to envy, which is one of the most effective stimulators of warmth and heat.

1.17.8 Despite the fact that it (the snow, that is) appears to fall everywhere in the city without favoring one house over another, in reality this precipitation (by the sky, of its anger) targets only the heads of certain people, though it would be more proper if its sentence were inclusive and thus felt equally by all, unlike sentences of earthly precipitation, which are applied to some groups and not others. The difference between the two precipitations is that it might have been supposed that the snow, given that its falling, or precipitation, is top down, would be deposited on all heads with equal force and thus include old and young, fat-headed and long-headed. Earthly sentences and laws, on the other hand, given that their precipitation is bottom up, or in other words from the heads of people who are themselves ruled to the heads of those who rule,[271] are unlikely to carry strongly enough to reach those who are possessed of high status and elevated station, whose heads are so high that the clouds pass beneath them.

1.17.9 It is also the case that snow, however much misery and trouble it may bring in reality to those who are familiar with it, often looks delightful to someone who has never seen it before. We have been told that a certain vagabond was once the guest of people who failed to honor and celebrate him[272] because he was inferior to them in terms of acquaintance and social eminence, their country being one in which snow never fell. When he left them and went to another, which he found to be a land of plenty and where he witnessed snow falling with his own eyes, he exclaimed and cheered at the sight and was as pleased as he could be, to the point that he claimed that it was a gift from God that the latter had made specific to that particular spot to distinguish it from all others, just as the Almighty had denied it to the first country in which he'd been a guest.

Of the same type are my words here,[273] for, despite all the digression and padding, the words that have been squeezed into figures of speech and the meanings that have been made knotty with allusions and *insinuations*, transformations and witty *formulations*, someone unused to such minglings may find it appealing; indeed his admiration may even drive him to seek to outdo and emulate it. Too late, though! The door has closed in the face of competitors. While I do not claim to be the first writer in the world to follow this path or thrust a pinch of it up the noses of those who pretend they are dozing, I do notice that all the authors in my bookcase are shackled to a single stylistic chain. I don't know whether they've changed their style now or not: more than five years have passed since I left them. Once you've become familiar with one link of the chain, you feel as though you know all the others, so that each one of them may truly be called a chain-man, given that each has followed in the footsteps of the rest and imitated them closely. This being established, know that I have exited the chain, for I am no chain-man and will not form the rump of the line; nor do I have any desire to be at its front, for the latter is an even more calamitous place to be than the former. I follow what I see to be good, seize what I find appealing by the forelock, reject the impositions of tradition. 1.17.10

## Chapter 18

# Bad Luck

1.18.1 The reason I gave the nib of my pen a little rest from the snapping teeth of the Fāriyāq's name, after leaving him with the self-denying priest, and distracted myself by talking about snow was that I was so angry at the two of them. Where the priest's concerned, I was angry that he'd betrayed his friend who had taken him in and had played fast and loose with his womenfolk; had the Almighty given that merchant a son whom he'd accepted in good conscience as his own—or, in other words, had He "opened his wife's womb," as it says in the Old Testament[274]—four quarters of the child would have been from the priest and the rest, which is his name, from the merchant, the latter thus putting himself in the position of a raiser of bastards, though the first male to open a womb is, as the Old Testament says, "blessed and magnified among the nations."[275] That is why, among the British, the right of inheritance goes to the eldest, or the "opener of the womb."[276] How could the priest have attempted, by doing so, to bring both a curse and a blessing down on the head of any of God's creatures? It's unthinkable.

1.18.2 As to the Fāriyāq, I was angry because he was the cause of the secret's being revealed[277] through the obstinacy and blustering that he demonstrated in hanging on to his verses, in which, I have no doubt, he was guilty of falsity, overstatement, and objectionable exaggeration to no purpose (despite which he thinks he's a great poet). As for the claim that the child's physical resemblance to its father constitutes definitive proof of his being his son, there is no consensus. Some believe it is an insufficient indication because it is possible that the mother, even while fornicating, might be thinking about her husband and picturing him to herself, in which case the fetus would take on the form of that image. Others say that the mother, on her own, has no role in the shaping of the fetus; some children come out looking like their paternal or maternal uncles, or someone their mothers never ever set eyes on.

Now I must resume my tale, presenting it to the reader's *ears* without leading either of us to choke on his *tears*. Thus I declare: as stated earlier in this book, the Fāriyāq was born with the misfortune of having misfortune everywhere in the ascendant, the Scorpion raising its tail to strike at the Kid, or Billy Goat, and the Crab set on a collision course with the horn of the Ox. Here you must know that bad luck is of two kinds—inseparable bad luck and separable bad luck. Inseparable bad luck is the kind that dogs a person in his waking and sleeping, his eating and drinking, in his setting off of a morning and his coming home at night, and in everything that comes his way. Separable bad luck is the contrary, by which I mean that it is the kind that dogs a person under certain conditions and not others, the best-known such conditions being the critical ones, such as marriage, travel, writing a book, and the like. 1.18.3

The specificities of inseparable bad luck are various too. One kind is like a tightly tied knot, another like a noose, another like a nail, another like a peg, another like a clip, and another like a lock without a key; one is like fish glue, another like corn glue, another like flour paste, another like bookbinder's paste, another like birdlime or mistletoe slime, or like arrow-feather glue or shoe-maker's glue or chrysocolla; one is like the skin and another like the blood that courses through the body's every joint and member[278]—the breastbones and polyps, the vertebrae tips and osmotic membranes, the thoraces and collarbones, the rib cartilage and shoulder blades, the gristle and the four long ribs, the upper thighs and lower belly, the 1.18.4

muscles and the sinews of the arm, the veins and the flesh between the shoulder and the neck, the intestines and fatty deposits, the vein that runs on the inner side of the spine and is joined to the aorta and the hemophilic vein, the jugular and aorta, the seminal ducts and the two hidden veins at the cupping-place on the neck, the esophagus and the cephalic vein, the gullet and the backbone nerve, the spinal vein that is cut to cure jaundice and the bone marrow, the jugular veins and the sweaty place behind the ear, the stifle joint and the small bone in the knee that is sometimes displaced, the inner-arm sinews and the arteries, the two veins that supply blood to the brain and the limbs, the spine and the extremities—and it was to this type that the Fāriyāq's bad luck belonged. It shouldn't be understood, however, that he was "bloody" in the sense of having much blood, or being fond of shedding or wallowing in it; he was innocent of all such characteristics. It's just that his bad luck was like blood in being inseparable from him under any circumstances.

1.18.5 He has said—and if he lied the responsibility is his—that one night he saw in his dreams that he drank an iced drink and then, immediately after it, a hot drink and started complaining of a severe pain in his molars and of a hoarseness in his throat. On other occasions, he would dream he was plunging from a mountain top or falling off a camel's back, so that he ended up bent double. If he dreamed that he ate pickles, he would get a stomachache from them that same night, if he drank salty or brackish water, he would vomit, and if he smelled a bad smell, he would faint. And if anyone were to tell him that he'd seen a fair, full-bodied girl in his garden, that night in his dreams he would see himself

| | |
|---|---|
| in Wayl, | "A valley in Hell, or a well or a gateway there" |
| or in al-Mawbiq, | "A valley" there |
| or in al-Falaq, | "Hell, or a pit therein" |
| or in Būlas, | "A prison" there |
| or in Sijjīn, | "A valley" there |
| or in Athām, | "A valley" there |

| | |
|---|---|
| or in al-Ḥuṭama, | "A gateway" there |
| or in Ghayy, | "A valley" there, or "a river" |
| or in al-Ṣaʿūd, | "A mountain" there with, ranged about it, |
| Lubaynā | "Name of the daughter of Iblīs" 1.18.6 |
| or Zalanbūr, | "One of the five sons of Iblīs" |
| or Miswaṭ, | "A son of Iblīs who tempts men to anger" |
| or al-Surḥūb, | "A blind devil that lives in the sea" |
| or Khanzab, | "A devil" |
| or al-Sarfaḥ, | "Name of a devil" |
| or al-Jimm, | "A devil, or a number of devils" |
| or Nuhm, | "A devil" |
| or Hayāh, | "A name used by devils" |
| or al-Ḥubāb, | "Name of a devil" |
| or al-Azabb, | "Name of a devil" 1.18.7 |
| or Azabb al-ʿAqabah, | "Name of a devil" |
| or al-Hirāʾ, | "Name of a devil in charge of nightmares" |
| or al-Walhān, | "A devil who tempts men to use too much water when performing their ritual ablutions" |
| or al-Khubth and al-Khabāʾith, | "Male and female devils" |
| or al-Safīf, | "Iblīs, also called al-Mubṭil ('the Joker')[279] and known by the patronymics Father of Bitterness and Father of Molten Brass" |
| or ʿAmr, | "The name of al-Farazdaq's devil"[280] |
| or al-Qillawṭ, | "One of the children of the jinn and the devils" |

or al-Shayṣabān,[281] al-Balʾaz, al-Qāz, the Corrupter,[282] the Recoiler, the Whisperer, the Seducer, or Cut-nose.

Similarly, if he looked through the window of his house and saw a neat trim little girl, it would seem to him in his dream that he was in 1.18.8

| | |
|---|---|
| an *arḍ khāfiyah* | "a land of the jinn"[283] |
| or *birāṣ*, | "dwellings of the jinn" |
| or in al-Ballūqah, | "A place in the area of Bahrain, above Kāẓimah, that they claim is an abode of the jinn" |

| | | |
|---|---|---|
| | or al-Baqqār, | "A place in the Sands of ʿĀlij where there are many jinn" |
| | or al-ʿĀzif, | [literally, "the Maker of Sounds"] "A place so named because the jinn make sounds there" |
| | or in al-Ḥawsh, | "Lands of the jinn" |
| | or in Wabār, | "Wabār: (of the pattern of *qaṭām*, with or without nunation)[284]—a stretch of land between Yemen and the Sands of Yabrīn, called Wabār ibn Iram.[285] When the Almighty destroyed ʿĀd, He bequeathed their territory to the jinn, and thus no human may stay there" |
| | or in ʿAbqar, | "A place full of jinn" |
| | or in Jayham, | "A place full of jinn" or that he was facing |
| 1.18.9 | the Shayṣabān, | "A tribe of the jinn" |
| | or the Banū Hannām, | "A tribe of the jinn" |
| | or the Banū Ghazwān, | "A clan of the jinn" |
| | or Dahrash, | "The name of the forefather of a tribe of the jinn" |
| | or Aḥqab, | "The name of one of the jinn who gave ear to the Qurʾān"[286] |
| | or Zimzimah, | "A sub-section of the jinn" |
| | or the Shiqq, | "A kind of jinn" |
| | or Shiniqnāq, | "A chief of the jinn" |
| | or the ʿIsl, | "A tribe of the jinn" |
| | or the ʿIsr, | "A tribe of the jinn and also the name of a territory belonging to the jinn" |
| | or the Siʿlāh, or the ʿAysajūr, or the Shahām, | "Witches of the jinn" |
| 1.18.10 | or the Saʿsaliq, | "The mother of the Siʿlāh witches" |
| | or a *ʿaḍrafūṭ*, | "A beast ridden by the jinn" |
| | or the Naẓrah, | "Jinn that roam by night" |

| | |
|---|---|
| or the Zawbaʿah, | [literally, "the Whirlwind"] "A chief of the jinn" |
| or *al-khāfī* or *al-khāfiyah* or *al-khāfiyāʾ*, | [literally, "the Hidden Ones" (male, female, and collective)] "The jinn"; *al-khabal* means the same |
| or *al-tābiʿ* or *al-tābiʿah,* | [literally, "the Followers" (male or female)] "The male or female jinni, because they are among men and follow them wherever they go" |
| or the ʿAkankaʿ or the Kaʿankaʿ, | "Male ghouls" |
| or a *khaydaʿ*, | "A deceitful [female] ghoul" |

or the Siltim, the Ṣaydānah, the Khayʿal, the Khaylaʿ, the Khawlaʿ, the Khaytūr, the Samarmarah, the Summaʿ, the ʿAwlaq, the ʿAlūq, the Hayraʿah, the Hayʿarah, the Mald, and the ʿAfarnāh, (all names of ghouls)

1.18.11

| | |
|---|---|
| or a *ʿitrīs*, | "A male ghoul" |
| or a *timsaḥ*, | "An ignoble *mārid*"[287] |
| or al-Dirqim, | The name of the Antichrist, also known as the Missīḥ (of the pattern of *sikkīn*) |
| or a *ṭughmūs*, | "A rebellious devil or ignoble ghoul" |
| or *zabāniyyah*, | Plural of *zibniyyah*. "Rebellious persons, whether humans or jinn"; synonym *ʿikabb* |
| or a *ḥayzabūn*. | I think our friend must be wrong about this one: |

I can't find it in the *Qāmūs*,[288] and how can the Fāriyāq have seen it in a *vision* when it's nowhere to be found in that paragon of *precision*? On the other hand, the lexicographer,[289] God rest his soul, does use it as the pattern-word for *ḥayzabūr* (synonym of *ḥayzabūn*), *khaytaʿūr* ("fading mirage"),[290] *qaydaḥūr* ("person with an ugly face"), *ʿaylajūf* (the name of the ant mentioned in the Qurʾān),[291] *ʿayṭabūl* ("tall" (of a girl)), *hayjabūs* ("hasty, rough man"), *jayhabūq* ("rat feces"), *zayzafūn* ("fast" (of a she-camel)), *jaythalūṭ* (an insult invented by women, of unclear meaning), and *ʿayḍafūṭ* (synonym of *ʿaḍrafūṭ* (see above)).

1.18.12 and if he were to hear by day a sweet-toned coquettish girl talking in dulcet tones to a man, at night he'd hear the moaning and laughing of the jinn, their twitterings and whisperings, their cheepings and chitterings, their clamorings and their *ziy-ziy* (all of which are sounds made by the jinn); and if he saw a girl hopping(1) on one foot all day long, he'd be assailed in the middle of the night by a bad dream—by the dream that lies prone upon the breast, by the incubus, by the succubus, by the dream that kneels on the chest, by the dream that pollutes, by the dream that humiliates, by the nightmare.

(1) *radat al-jāriyah*: she raised a foot and moved using the other, in play.

1.18.13 One night he saw a bride brought to him in procession, after which a billy goat came to him and started butting him with its horns. He awoke, and, lo and behold, the place on his head where horns would be was bruised. Another night he dreamed that he came across some gold and silver coins on the river bank, so he stretched out his hand and took fifteen silver coins, no more. When he crossed to the other side, he saw an old man who had a ball in his hand that he was twisting, and every time he gave it a twist, the Fāriyāq was taken by a severe pain in his back, like that of the illness known in the Syrian lands as "the jumper,"[292] and when the pain increased so much that he threw the coins from his hand, it went away. And another night he saw a man from the west bestow something on him, at which a man from the east immediately snatched it away and made off with it. "And," he declared, "he still hasn't brought it back, even though I've waited for him all night!" The rest of his dreams were of the same sort.

1.18.14 Among the verses that he composed on dreams are the following:

Meseems at night my cares, from underneath my pillow,
Draw al-Hirā'[293] to me, that him against me they may pit.
They say he spent the day upon me pissing
"So tonight you have to make him shit."

And

At day's end I'm happy
For I have hopes of dreams of pleasure.
But then I dream of strife and toil
And night and day are shrunk to equal measure.

And again

O Lord, you scare me even in my sleep
With dreams confused that torment and distress.
Would I might toil by day and then, when I'm asleep,
Enjoy the sight of my belov'd and there find rest.

One day it occurred to him to write a eulogy to one of those possessed of sovereign felicity. After he'd been permitted the privilege of kissing the latter's noble threshold and of reciting his ode and had retired backward in accordance with the custom of the people of that land, which dictates that a young man must not show the nape of his neck to an older (in acknowledgment of the fact that only older persons have backs to their heads), the chamberlain came to tell him that the emir, might God preserve his rule for ever and a *day* and immortalize his *sway*, make of the sun and moon *shoes* for his horse's *hooves*, make each day of his better than the one *before*, spread his shadow the earth as a protection *o'er*, anoint the eye of the universe with his slipper's *dust*, make the Pleiades his stepping-stone and Capella, through the eyelets of his boots, as laces, *thrust*, make all existence rejoice in his name and make his *portal* the desired gate of every *mortal*, make . . .—but here the Fāriyāq could no longer contain himself and interrupted by saying, "Enough 'makes,' you mayfly! What says the emir?" 1.18.15

The man replied, "The emir—the *magnified*, the important and highly *dignified*, he of the blessings *overflowing* and favors *evergrowing*, he who, when he speaks, passes forthwith into *action*, and who, when asked, is generous in *benefaction*; who, when he clears his throat strikes terror into the hearts of those who are his *foes*, and, when he coughs, makes those who hate him shiver to the tips of their *toes*; whose whole palace quivers at his majestic *pose* when 1.18.16

he blows his *nose* and whose *fart* makes the whole council chamber *start*; whose. . . .” Said the Fāriyāq, “Pew to this vile smell, you villain! Tell me what the emir said and relieve me of these orotund *phrases*—you’ve outdone the poets with your lavish *praises*.” He said, “He says you did a good job on your ode and achieved your ends very well when you likened him to the moon, the sea, a lion, a sharp sword, a firm-set mountain, and a watercourse in spate, all of which he is worthy of being compared to. Except that, in one verse, you called him a pimp.” “How so?” said the Fāriyāq, “may the emir remain far above all pandering!” “It’s true,” said the other. “In one verse you said that he ‘hands out money and gems with open hand, and befriends the virgin.’ Also, in another you said that his name was ‘worthy to be praised (*muḥammad*)’ and that his virtues were ‘praiseworthy (*maḥmūd*)’ but he’s no Muḥammad or Maḥmūd,[294] and because of this appalling mistake he has banished you from his sight.” The Fāriyāq replied, “This is but the way of poets—they keep smacking their lips over ‘unbored pearls’[295] and ‘praiseworthy virtues,’ but that doesn’t mean that they’re accusing the person praised of pimping.” “That’s all I have,” said the other. “Don’t even think of appearing in the presence of our venerable emir again.”

1.18.17 Thence, then, the Fāriyāq returned, deprived of that happy source of profit, and his anger grew so fierce that it diverted him from the straight path, and he walked another road, reaching home only after many a mishap. He started thinking how ill-omened was the star under which he’d been born and how much bad luck his pen had brought him, and in his folly it seemed to him that the pen was the unluckiest thing any man could adopt as the instrument of his livelihood, that the cobbler’s awl was more profitable, that the letter *nūn*, when preceding the words of the Almighty “*Nūn*. By the pen, and what they inscribe . . .” had been put there to indicate “bad luck,”[296] and that what the astrologer had said of his birth stars was correct. He interpreted the woman who was brought to him in a wedding procession in his dream as being the Scorpion, the billy goat that had butted him as the Kid, and himself, as he retreated from the emir's presence, as the Crab, for he would have tripped over the rugs of his sublime council chamber had he not grabbed onto its noble supporting poles. Likewise he interpreted the Ox as being the emir who was the object of his praise.

However, the earlier statement—namely, the astrologer's words concerning "the misfortune of having misfortune everywhere"—were not limited to one incident; rather, they encompassed every condition and event, as shall be explained. Thus, when the Fāriyāq heard from his confidant with whom he'd exchanged confessions that trading in polemics was a profitable *affair*, with prospects *fair*, he was taken by the idea of trying his hand at making money out of the paltry supply he had of such goods. He did not, however, display them right away to some ecclesiastical bigwig[297] in the hope that he might buy them, as his friend had done, but took, on the one hand, to turning them upside down and removing the *nits*, combing through them and picking them to *bits*, and, on the other, to holding them up to the light to check for defects, at which they appeared to him so old and worn that hardly anyone could be expected to want them. 1.18.18

Now, it so happened that, at this time, a roving peddler had arrived, crying that he would buy, mend, exchange, or dye old goods, claiming he could restore them to their original color, that nothing was impossible for him, and that the owner himself would be so amazed on seeing them after dyeing and mending that he wouldn't recognize them. He (the peddler, that is) also claimed that, when he'd heard back in his hometown of the dire state of the goods in these parts, he'd hot-footed it over, bringing with him a large saddlebag[298] full of dyes and containing the tools to darn any tear and restore any faded color. The Fāriyāq therefore hurried off to do some bartering and came to an arrangement by which he would exchange all his old goods for others that were new and pleasing to his eye, for, as they say, "All things new have appeal." Then he returned home, pleased with his bargain. 1.18.19

When, however, his family and neighbors found out, they erupted in rage against him, saying, "By the Lord of Hosts, it is not 1.18.20

our custom in these lands to change, barter, mend, or dye goods" and soon thereafter the news reached the bishop of the district, one of the big-time fast-talking market traders.[299] You would have thought a knife had fallen on his windpipe or mustard got up his nostrils, for he fumed and frothed, thundered and lightninged, surged and thrashed, roared and bawled, conspired and plotted, jabbered and prattled, wheeled and dealed, remonstrated and reproached, and jumped up and down, braiding his beard, in his fury, into a whip, and trying to inveigle every other bilious beard-plucker like himself to rise up with him as he cried, "God's horsemen against the *infidel*![300] They shall *roast in Hell*![301] How dare this accursed rascal, this raving *lunatic*, choose a path other than that laid down for him by his masters *ecclesiastic*, that followed by his very own patriarch? How dare he, in his impertinence, brazenness, and *infamy*, have dealings with that miserable traveling peddler and barter away to him what's been passed down to him from his ancient *ancestry*? Are there in our land no *roods*, no stocks, no leathern *hoods*? Bring him to us in *disgrace*! Flog him in the nude! Throw him in the *fireplace*! Feed him to the *fishes*! Make him eat *ashes*! Cut out his tongue and make him drink camel *snot*! Bring him to me while the iron's *hot*!" At this, one of those present leaped forth and said, "I shall bring you the little squit 'before ever thy glance is returned to thee.'"[302] Then he hot-footed it over to the Fāriyāq, whom he found poring over the ledger in which were written the prices of the goods, and set upon him with his sword and injured his scalp, after which the Fāriyāq was handed over to the aforementioned butcher.

1.18.21 When the latter set eyes upon him, his jugulars swelled, his nostrils flared, his brow knotted, and his lips turned *blue*, his mustaches quivered, his eyes turned red, and from his teeth smoke *flew*, and they proceeded to engage in the following dialog:

The Trader: Woe unto you, you sucker! What made you barter away your goods?

The Fāriyāq: If they're my goods, as you have just admitted, what's to stop me?

The Trader: Misguided man! They're your goods in the sense that you inherited them from your forefathers, not in the sense that they're yours to do with as you please.

The Fāriyāq: This is against custom and truth, for a man may do whatever he likes with his inheritance.

The Trader: Liar! You inherited them precisely so you could preserve them, not so you could squander them or exchange them for something else.

The Fāriyāq: It's my inheritance and I shall do with it as I wish.

The Trader: Accursed one! I am the warden of the inheritance and its preserver from all that might sully it.

The Fāriyāq: That's the first time we've heard of someone being put in charge of someone else's inheritance, unless the heir's incompetent.

The Trader: Dupe! You *are* incompetent and I am your guardian, your trustee, your sponsor, your agent, and the one who will hold you to account.

The Fāriyāq: What proof is there that I'm not competent, and who made you a trustee and a guardian?

The Trader: Deviant! The proof of your gullibility and error is precisely that you traded in your inheritance for other goods. As to my being a trustee, everyone else in my position attests to that fact, just as I attest that they are the trustees of others. 1.18.22

The Fāriyāq: Exchanging one thing for another isn't evidence of error and deviation if the thing exchanged and the thing it is exchanged for are of the same kind, especially since I'd observed that the color of the old had almost completely faded and that the material was worn through. That is why I exchanged it for something more attractive and stronger.

| | |
|---|---|
| The Trader: | Blasphemer! He blinded you so that you couldn't distinguish among the colors. |
| The Fāriyāq: | How can that be, when I have two eyes to see with and two hands to touch with? |
| The Trader: | Blind man! The senses can be deceived, especially sight. |
| The Fāriyāq: | If my senses were deceived, how come you've been able to preserve yours from being deceived too when you're a human being just like me? |
| The Trader: | May you perish! Though I was once a human being just like you, I am now an authorized agent of the Market Boss, who has let me in on the amazing powers that God has bestowed on him, which include my being able to see through any false claims or dishonesty that may come my way, because he himself could never cheat. |

1.18.23 Said the Fāriyāq (who had a speech defect involving the letter *f*): And where is this "Boff of the Market Difgwace"[303] (then he corrected himself and said) "I mean 'the Marketplace'? Shouldn't the addition of these eighty require the eighty-lash penalty?"[304]

| | |
|---|---|
| The Trader: | Curse you! He is far away and between us lie seas and mountains. But his holy spirit courses within us. |
| The Fāriyāq: | What happens if he falls sick or goes mad, or is touched by some wandering jinni or afflicted with pleurisy? In such a state, how can he distinguish low-quality goods from high? |
| The Trader: | May you perish! He is never afflicted by such attacks, for he is the keeper of a mighty gate, and he has in his hand two mighty keys to close the door tight, one from in front and one from behind. |
| The Fāriyāq: | That's no proof, for any person in the world could become a doorkeeper with two keys. |

The Trader: Depraved sinner! He alone has sole charge of this plot of land, for it was entrusted to him by its All-commanding Owner.

The Fāriyāq: When was that?

The Trader: May you be crucified! About two thousand years ago.

The Fāriyāq: You mean to tell me that this "boss" has been around for two thousand years?

The Trader: Atheist! It came to him by inheritance.

The Fāriyāq: From whom did he inherit it? From his father and grandfather?

The Trader: You should be punished as a warning to others! From a person not considered to be a member of his family.

The Fāriyāq: That's odd! How can a person inherit anything from a stranger? If a stranger dies without leaving an heir, his money goes to the public treasury, which has a better right to it than any individual. 1.18.24

The Trader: May you be tortured! It's a sacrament that you have no right to discuss.

The Fāriyāq: And what proof is there that it's a sacrament?

The Trader: Now you've gone too far! Here's the proof (and he got up in a hurry, fetched a book, and started leafing through it from beginning to end, looking for what he wanted—for he hadn't studied it at any great length—until he found a passage that said, in summary, that the Owner had once loved a man, so he'd given him a number of gifts, among which were a cup, a basin, a stick with a carving of two snakes on the end, a robe, a pair of shorts, a pair of sandals, and a door with two keys, and had said to him, "All these things I give unto you. Use them and enjoy them.")

| | |
|---|---|
| The Fāriyāq: | I swear there's nothing in such a donation to prove it's a sacrament, not to mention that both the benefactor and the beneficiary have died and the whole gift has been lost. How can just the keys be left, when the door's gone and they're useless without it? |
| The Trader: | May you be shown up for the liar you are! The keys are all we need now. |
| The Fāriyāq: | By the power of these two keys over you, My Lord, if you can show me just once in my lifetime the cup—that's all—you can have complete authority over me from that day on. |

1.18.25 Faced by this resolute attitude, the trader burned with ire and was on the point of bringing the Fāriyāq the door and the cup when someone called him to table. Rising energetically, he appointed a few of his knaves to see to the Fāriyāq, for at that moment he was so convulsed with hunger that he believed the sight of the bottom of the pots in the kitchen would be more appetizing to him that that of the Fāriyāq's face, and he pretended to forget about him. The Fāriyāq thus escaped from that sticky situation and set off at a run to the Bag-man and told him, "I lost by my trade with you, for the goods almost landed me under the scalpel, so I want to revoke the deal—or if you will not, and you have in your bag a head that will fit my body when the latter's deprived of this one, show it to me now and calm my nerves, for I cannot live without a head. If all you have in the bag is the tongue, it is of no use to me. Here's your property. Take it."

1.18.26 Said the Bag-man, "This is no way to do business. You have to endure patiently the consequences of the deal, according to the way of all those where we come from who agree on terms, this being one of the distinguishing features of this trade. But do not fear: another of its features is that it protects those who protect it and preserves those who preserve it. He who engages in it will need no head if the top of his is lopped off, or eyes if his are put out, or tongue if his is pulled out, or legs if his are clamped in the stocks, or hands if his are shackled in irons, or neck if his is *snapped*, or liver if his is *popped*." The Fāriyāq replied, "I don't see things the way you do: being sorry doesn't revive the *dead*, regret doesn't bring back what's *fled*. If you have a storeroom in which I can keep my goods safe from the enemy, lodge me there. If not, this is the parting of the ways between us." The Bag-man hung his head for a while, then took him into a little room and closed the door, and he set about putting the Fāriyāq to the test, as will be explained in the following chapter.

## Chapter 19

# Emotion and Motion[305]

1.19.1 It is the custom of people everywhere to say when they love or long for something, "My heart loves" that thing or it "feels drawn to" it or "desires" it. I don't know the underlying reason for this usage, for the heart is only one of the many organs of the body, and it's not possible that the sensory capacities of all the organs should be gathered together in just that one. The proof is that if someone loves a certain kind of food, for example, the cause is to be sought in the gustatory organs that give rise to his desire for it, and if someone loves a woman, the cause is to be sought in the organ that gives rise to his desire for her. Natural inclinations that do not call for the employment of any visible organ—such as love of leadership, good fortune, or religion—must be attributed to the head, these being abstractions that have nothing to do with that lump of flesh called the heart. By the same token, as the spleen, which is the Vizier of the Right-hand Side, has nothing to do with these matters, so the heart, which is the Vizier of the Left-hand Side,[306] can have none either. However, given that the motion of the heart is more rapid than that of other organs because of its greater proximity to the lungs, where breathing originates, people think that the heart must be a primary source for all a person's affections and desires. It is also their custom, to avoid having to search for numerous reasons and causes and of having to be certain of their facts, to reduce everything to one cause among the many. In the same way, poets, for example, attribute the proximate causes of bad luck to fate and of ill-fortune and separation to crows.

Based on this belief (namely, that all affections are attributable to the heart), the Bag-man wanted to test the Fāriyāq's in order to find out whether or not love for the new goods beat strongly within it. He started off by asking him, "Do you feel in your heart that the new goods are better than the old, and does it pound with joy and pleasure when you hear them mentioned? Does it feel happy, expansive, and care-free when the thought of them occurs to your mind and does it clench itself, shrink, and recoil at the mention of the other? When you read the price list, do you feel that every single letter in it has been imprinted on it (meaning, on your heart), so that, even if it weren't there, those same letters could take its place? Does it sometimes ignite and burn, and then at others go out, only to return more strongly, like the celebrated phoenix? Do you feel too that it's being prodded by a prodder, pricked by a pricker, squeezed by a squeezer, constricted by a constrictor, ripped by a ripper, and pressed by a presser?" 1.19.2

The Fāriyāq told him, "As for the pounding and the choking, my heart's always that way, being subject to such sensations in both joy and sadness, for the least thing affects it. As far as igniting and melting are concerned, though, I don't know what you mean." "What is meant by 'burning' here," replied the Bag-man, "and by 'prodding' and 'squeezing,' is ardor, enthusiasm, and obsessive interest, and imagining that what isn't there is present and what is a fantasy is real. An example would be someone walking in a waterless desert who becomes so thirsty that he thinks the mirage is water and the sun's rays, too, are pure, sweet water, and keeps on going in the hope of finding water until he's crossed the waste, because intense imagining and obsessive interest help a person put up with trials and tribulations, and, though he be sinking under their weight, he will imagine that he's reclining at ease on a couch. Thus the figurative and the real, the tangible and the intangible, all come to be 1.19.3

on the same plane to him, to the point that he reckons hunger a dining table, the bier a throne, the impaling stake or cross a pulpit. He may have a wife and children and use them as though they were no more valuable than china plates and go running off through distant lands to promote his goods, giving up family, friends, and companions in favor of the contents of his saddlebag. This he carries on his shoulder, gladly and with high hopes, trudging high and low over the earth, offering to make any mortal who crosses his path his partner and co-financer. He goes on this way until his time is up, and nothing pleases him better than to die thus engaged. The bag! The bag! No other trade or work have we than it. The goods! The goods! No other reward have we than they." At this point he broke down, weeping and sobbing.

1.19.4 When, after a while, he'd recovered his composure, the Fāriyāq asked him, "Do you Bag-men have a marketplace and a boss to take charge of it?" He said, "No." "Who, then," said the Fāriyāq, "checks the quality of the goods?" He replied, "Each of us does so himself and we don't need anyone else." The Fāriyāq was amazed and said to himself, "Now here's a wonder! We have a group of undercapitalized parasites who have a market boss but no saddlebags, and a similar group who have saddlebags but no boss. But perhaps my friend is in the right: if it were otherwise, he would not have undertaken to bring his bag from such distant lands or braved the dangers of the journey and all the rest." Now, however, the Recoiler poisoned his mind with the thought that perhaps the Bag-man hadn't found anywhere to set up shop in his own country, so he'd brought what he had in stock to get rid of here. If a merchant stocked up on, say, silk-wool, or cotton goods, and brought them to another country, he couldn't be regarded as doing so out of love for its inhabitants; it had, after all, become commonplace for those in search of work to roam the world. Next, though, it occurred to him that the Bag-man's perseverance and his equanimity and patience must inevitably be complemented by good sense and resolve, in contrast to rashness and flightiness, whose only complements are conceit and error, and he concluded that, in view of his said perseverance and mild manners, the Bag-man must be following the right path and that the metropolitan, with his vehemence and eagerness to do evil, must be among the misguided.

He said, therefore, to the Bag-man, "Sir, I have heeded everything with which you've filled my ears and believe the truth to lie with you alone. I am your partisan, your follower, and the co-carrier of your bag. Just protect me from these undercapitalized parasites, for they are like ravening lions that feel no mercy or pity for God's creatures. They think that destroying a soul out of zeal for religion will earn them a place close to Him. They hold tight to such exterior meanings of the words of the gospel as they believe are in keeping with their aims and will increase their standing and authority. They say, for instance, that Christ's words 'I came not to send peace, but a sword'[307] license them to apply the said instrument to people's necks to make them return to the true path. They have cast behind them the essence, substance, and consequence of religion, which are friendship among all men, affection, assistance, and a proper certitude as to the existence of God Almighty. Those who have gone astray and are blind to the truth find no difficulty in extracting from any book, divinely inspired or not, whatever may suit their purpose and corrupt creed, for the door of exegesis is a wide one. Should the Emir of the Mountain, once he's grown old and wrapping himself up in his clothes is no longer enough to keep him warm, be permitted to cozy up to a beautiful virgin girl, i.e., warm himself with her and heat himself with the warmth of her body, like King David? When he makes war on the Druze and God grants him victory over them, is he permitted to slay their married women and their children and leave their virgins alive for the stud bulls among his troops to debauch, the way that Moses did to the people of Midian, as stated in Numbers, chapter 33? Is he permitted to marry a thousand women, queens and concubines, as Solomon did? Is a priest permitted to have intercourse with an adulteress and beget bastards, as did the prophet Hosea? Or to tolerate one of his governors slaying 1.19.5

every man, woman, and suckling child among his enemies, as Saul did at the Lord's command with the Amalekites, the Lord even being angry with him that he hadn't killed along with them the best of their sheep and oxen and had spared Agag, King of Amalek, and repenting that he had made Saul king over the Children of Israel, so that Samuel arose and hewed Agag in pieces before the Lord in Gilgal? Moreover, I have read in the index to the Old Testament printed in Rome, under the letter *h*, the following: 'We (i.e., the adherents of the Church of Rome) are obligated to destroy the heretics (i.e., innovators and schismatics)'; in justification, they cite the fighting, bloodshed, and assassination that occurred between the Jews and their enemies, as outlined above. Thus, if the religion of the Christians makes lawful the slaying of men, women, and children and the debauching of virgins, and allows the seizing of other people's property without first inviting the victims to join the true religion but out of mere ferocity and tyranny, as does the religion of the Jews, why did the first abrogate the second and declare its laws null and void? In fact, though, the Christian religion is built on high moral values and its aim from beginning to end is to maintain peace among men and urge them to what is righteous and good. Otherwise, we might as well go back to being Jews."

1.19.6 When the Bag-man heard this, he decided that behind the words was a sly dog, so he exerted himself to save the Fāriyāq from the hands of the arrogant,[308] thinking it best to send him to an island known as the Island of Scoundrels,[309] believing it would make a safe haven for him. The Faryāq thus embarked on a small ship going to Alexandria, but before they had gone far, the sea rose and threw the ship about, and our friend became so dizzy he had to stick to his bunk, where he set to complaining of the dolors of the sea and to lamenting, as follows:

### The Faryāq's Lament and Plaint

1.19.7 "Alas for my traveling and alack for my *travail*! Why do I endure this painful distress to *no avail*? What good this bargain when this mighty affliction is all it *earns*? What tempted me to take on the traders when such low meddling could bring me no *returns*? I was born into this world and lived there many a year *before*, without giving a thought to the squabbles of every dolt and *boor*. Why did I enter these *straits* and get embroiled in these sterile *debates*? Why should the shouting matches engaged in by people west and *east*, with their corrupt thinking and low characters, concern me in the *least*? Ah how I miss the pen, however hard over its nib-notch I've *toiled* and even if the page onto which it spits its ink with fly shit's *soiled*! Ah how I miss the donkey that brayed and kicked—who will bring me back that *beast*? He may be better off than me these days—he may be living a life of *ease*, while I, today, am cut off from all I once held *dear*. Who will bring me back the inn and brethren—each one a gracious and companionable *peer*? All I had to do then was sing, warble, and *quaff*—would that I'd gone along with all the rest and worshipped the *golden calf*!"[310] (I seek refuge with God—our friend has blasphemed!). "Not every second has to be given over to wrangling and trying to grab your opponent by the *collar*. The metropolitan gave me sound advice when he said the senses deceive mighty and meek, stupid and wise, ignoramus and *scholar*. He knows the truth but says something different, fearing all who are 'ignoble and, beside that, basely *born*,'[311] for nothing pleases the ignorant more than to distract and *suborn*. Did he not tell me, 'You cannot renew the old, or straighten what is *bent*?' True, the senses deceive and alike in this are the murderer and the man of mercy, the vile and the *benevolent*."

After pausing for a moment to marshal examples of the preced- 1.19.8
ing, he resumed, "When an ugly, misshapen (*shawhā'*) woman looks at her face in the mirror, she says, 'I may be ugly and misshapen to some but to others I am handsome,' which is why the author of the *Qāmūs* says, '*Shawhā'* means both "a woman who frowns" and "a beautiful woman"; a word with two opposite meanings.' When a man with a big nose looks at that crag on his face, he says, 'It may well be that some good-looking women will desire it and see in it no

crookedness or curve.' Painters portray our ugly overlords, kings, queens, and any others on whom fortune has smiled as though they were comely and they, in their years of spinster- and bachelorhood, see themselves exactly as the painters have portrayed them. We see the sun as though it had risen, when according to the scientists it hasn't yet done so, and we see a stick in water as though it were crooked, though 'there is no therein no crookedness.'[312] A mirage shows a person as though double and certain colors appear in two different forms. Magicians make observers think they are walking on water or going through fire without being burned. To a person in a ship plowing along opposite houses and property, the part of the land closest to him appears to be moving and mobile, when it is unmoving and fixed. A person who sits at a window opposite another at the same level sees the latter as though it were higher than his own. Maybe, then, the Bag-man's tears were not for his goods but for some other cause, for I hear that the players in theaters weep and laugh at will. Maybe weeping is one of those arts that the Bag-men are instructed in when young. What benefit to me is the saddlebag now? I call on it, and it abandons me? I love it, and it hates me? I pick it up, and it spurns me?"

1.19.9 When he started in on this foolishness—which the Bag-men regard as blasphemy, the Market-men as glorification of the Lord, and those in between as generated by fear (for to this day people can agree only to disagree)—the ship gave him a violent shove, such as the Bag-men would consider to be the Lord's revenge and the Market-men entirely incidental, and he began yelling, "Forgive me, Market Boss! By your beard, which is at the barber's, save me! Bag! Goods! Price list! Traders! Undercapitalized parasites! You who weave the goods and you who dye them, you who warp and you who weft them, you who hem and you who embroider them, you who ornament and you who stripe them, you who darn and you who stitch them, you who sew and you who edge them, you who baste and you who unroll them, you who fold and you who crease them,(1) you who wrap and you who sew them edge to edge, catch me, by your lives, or I am done for!" This cry had barely left his lips before the ship gave a list to one side that sent his little head rolling like a watermelon, so he started yelling and calling for help, saying, "I'll never cry goods for sale again! If this is what's in store for us at the start of the road, where will it all lead?" Then he fainted and started raving, saying, "Sh . . . ! Sh . . . !" which made a passenger who overheard him repeating it again and again think he must be complaining that there was one of "the two impure things" in his bed.[313] Finding nothing, though, he said to himself, "He must be raving with pain" and left him.

(1) The "creaser" (*al-qasāmī*) is "the person who gives clothes their first folding, so that they take their creases according to the way he makes them."

Then God decreed that the sea grow calm and the weather turn fair, and after some hours the Alexandrine shore appeared, and the same man came and gave him the good news that land was in sight, so he arose stoically, washed his face, and changed his clothes. When they left the ship, the Fāriyāq was ahead of them all, and no sooner had he set foot on the ground than he picked up some pebbles from its surface and swallowed them, declaring, "This is my mother and to it I return. On it I was born and on it I shall die." Then he made his way to a Bag-man who was in the city and presented him with his letter of recommendation from the other Bag-man, and he stayed with him while waiting for a ship leaving for the island. Let us then congratulate him for arriving safe and sound, and let us present a memorandum to the Princely See and Royal Presence, His Excellency the Patriarch of the Maronite Sect, whoever he may be, after which we shall turn our attention for a short while to the Market-men and the Bag-men and set out the differences between them. 1.19.10

## A Memorandum from the Writer of These Characters

The Fāriyāq now has escaped your *lands* and slipped through your *hands*. He's blown a raspberry in all your *faces*, and at your threats his pulse no longer *races*. All that remains is for me to remind you of 1.19.11

the injustice, tyranny, oppression, and aggression that you carried to such great lengths against my brother, the late Asʿad,[314] to wit, that you held him in your prison at your official abode at Qannūbīn[315] for around six years and that, after you had forced him to taste every form of humiliation, degradation, misery, and distress in the small cell that was his sole abode—for he never left it for a place where he could see the light or breathe the air that the Creator has bestowed on the innocent and guilty alike among his creatures,—he gave up the ghost. Your only reason for imprisoning him was that he was at odds with you over matters that call for neither punishment nor reproach. You had no authority over him, either religious or civil. As for the religious aspect, Christ and his apostles never ordered the imprisonment of those who disagreed with what they had to say; they merely held themselves aloof from them. If the Christian religion had adopted from its beginnings the same vicious cruelty that characterizes you now—you, the shepherds of the lost and guides of the erring—no one would have believed in it, for no one converts unless he believes that the religion he is adopting is better than the one he is abandoning. Everyone in the world knows that there is nothing good to be said for imprisoning, starving, humiliating, threatening, discomforting, and reviling people, not to mention that Christ and his apostles acknowledged the authority and government of the sovereign and never themselves did more than urge on people the noble virtues and command them to piety, modesty, peace, endurance of suffering, and mildness of behavior, which are the goals of every religion known to man.

1.19.12 And as for the civil aspect, given that my brother Asʿad did nothing reprehensible and committed no crime against his neighbor or his emir, or against the state—which, if he had done so, would have required that he be tried before the legal authorities—the patriarch's maltreatment of him is no less than maltreatment of the person of Our Lord the Sultan, whose slaves we all are and to whose safekeeping and rule we all appeal. All of us are equal in rights, for the patriarch has no right to take a single silver coin from my house by force; how much less then is his right to take a life by force! Even if we concede that my brother debated and argued over religion and said that you were misguided, it was not yours to kill him for that reason. If you acknowledged his status as a scholar and feared the consequences of his activities, you ought to have pulled apart his evidence and refuted his arguments orally or in writing; if not, you should have banished him from the country, as he asked you to do. Instead, though, you persisted in your ferocious punishment in order to make an example of him and claimed that the fact that he once escaped from your abode in an attempt to save himself exacerbated his crime and increased his guilt, meaning that your own tyranny and injustice toward him should also be increased.

Do I hear you, you confederacy of cretins, claiming that to destroy 1.19.13
one soul for the salvation of many is a praiseworthy act that should be encouraged? If you had any insight or good sense you would know that persecution and compulsion only increase the persecuted in his love of that for which he is persecuted, especially if he is convinced in his heart that he is right and his tormentor wrong, or that he is blessed with knowledge and virtue while the other is innocent of them. The fact is, you are without either religious or political understanding and have exposed your honor to defamation and blackening and your reputation to revulsion and condemnation for as long as sky is sky and earth earth, and that my brother's reputation, God have mercy upon him, though he be dead, will never die. Whenever anyone of good sense and insight mentions him, he will mention along with him your misdeeds, your atrocities, your excesses, your ignorance, and your ugliness. I swear, he drove more of your blood-thirsty community out of their allegiance to you by his death than he would have done if he had remained alive—suffice it to mention the Most Honorable Khawājā Mikhā'īl Mishāqah[316] and other persons of wealth and capability.

Did you feel no compassion, you bull-necked thugs, for his 1.19.14
youth and beauty? Were your hard hearts not affected by the pallor of his face when you kept him from the light and air, when

his firm and tender body withered and nothing was left of his well-turned physique but skin and bones (and even then you were too stingy to release him with just those)? Did you take no pity on him when you saw that his fingertips had been worn away for want of those very things to which the al-Aṣmaʿī in your monastery had unfettered access? How many a time, by God, did they take up the pen only to use it to write out what kings wished to hear and how many a time, by God, did he ascend the pulpit and preach to you extemporaneously, the sweat pouring from that shining brow, and how hard did his listeners weep as they remembered their sins and determined to renounce them! How many a time did he write and translate insipid books for you and instruct your stupid monks and bring them out from the shadows of their ignorance! Did not the modest decency that shone from his face put your own impudent countenances to shame—he who was more bashful than the most demure of women? Or his dearness to his family, the honor paid him by emirs, the love shown him by lords and commoners? His unblemished purity and honorable morals? The elegance of his language, the good cheer he brought to those he was with? Is one such as him to be imprisoned for six years, humiliated, punished, and to die (and God alone knows of what he died)?

1.19.15 How do you explain that neither the French churches nor the Austrian nor the English nor the Muscovite nor the Greek Orthodox nor the Greek Catholic nor the Coptic nor the Jacobite nor the Nestorian nor the Druze nor the Mutawālīs[317] nor the Anṣārīs[318] nor the Jews perform such abominable and vile acts as are performed by the Maronite church? Or is it alone possessed of the truth, while all others are in error? Do you not claim that the King of France is the protector and defender of religion? Yet at the same time, the Catholic citizens of his kingdom continue to print books condemning the vices, shameful deeds, stupidity, obscenity, lustfulness, and atheism of the leaders of their church. Some of them, indeed, have written histories devoted to the immorality, depravity, and bad conduct of the popes, as of their denial of the truth of the immortality of the soul, of divine inspiration, and of the divinity of Christ.[319]

One has said that Pope Amadeus VIII, known as the Duke of Savoy,[320] was elevated to the papacy when he was a layman. Another that the Council of Basel was convened specifically to depose Pope Eugene[321] and found him guilty of sedition, bribery, sowing discord, and betraying his vows. Another that Pope Nicolas I excommunicated Bishop Günther of Cologne because of a disagreement with him at the council that was convened in Metz in 864 and that the aforementioned bishop sent letters to all his churches in which he said, "Although Vicar Nicholas, who has taken the title of pope and considers himself to be simultaneously pope and secular leader, has excommunicated us, we have dismissed his folly."[322] And another that Ambrose, governor of Milan, obtained the rank of bishop, even though his belief in the Christian religion was unsound.[323] Another has said that Pope John VIII sent delegates to Constantinople, where they convened a synod at which four hundred bishops met and that all of them found Photius innocent and declared him to be worthy of the rank of bishop.[324] Another that Pope Stephen VI ordered that the body of Formosus, Bishop of Porto, be exhumed from its grave because he had incited strife against his predecessor John VIII, and then sentenced him, dead as he was, to have his head and three of his fingers cut off, after which his body was thrown into the Tiber.[325] 1.19.16

And that Pope Sergius[326] appointed Theodora, the mother of Marozia,[327] who was married to the Count of Tuscany, a senator[328] and that he, that is, the pope, fathered a boy[329] on the said Marozia and had him raised inside his palace far from the eyes of the people of Rome, after which Marozia married Hugh, King of Arles,[330] and intrigued to have Pope John X[331] killed because he was in love with her sister, smothering him between two pieces of bedding and assuming absolute power. Next, she schemed to appoint Leo[332] to the same position, and then, a few months later, murdered him in prison; after him, she appointed another man whose name has 1.19.17

now fallen into oblivion[333] and he ruled for a few years, after which she deposed him, placing John XI—her son by Sergius III—on the throne when he was only twenty-four years old, imposing on him the condition that he should implement no decision that did not directly derive from his rank as pope. She also poisoned her husband[334] and married her brother-in-law the king of Lombardy,[335] to whom she delegated the rule of the Papal States. One of her sons by her first husband[336] rose up and incited the people of Rome against her, imprisoning her and her son, the pope, in Sant'Angelo. After him, Stephen VIII[337] held office but he was hated by the Romans because he was from Germany, and they so disfigured his face that he could not show himself among the people.[338] Then Marozia's grandson Octavianus was elected pope at the age of eighteen, being known thereafter as John XII.[339] He was licentious, indecent, depraved, a scoffer at religion, entirely given over to the satisfaction of sensual pleasures and his appetites, infatuated with horse-riding and chivalry—a situation that failed to disturb the church only because most other churches and nations were in the same state.

1.19.18 When Otto, the emperor,[340] learned that this pope was secretly in revolt against him, and the people of Italy called on him to come and set their affairs to rights, he made his way from Pavia to Rome and, after settling the affairs of the city, convened a synod that the pope himself attended along with many princes of Germany and Rome, forty bishops, and seventeen cardinals, in the church of Saint Paul. There, in the presence of all, the emperor made a complaint against the pope that the latter had fornicated with a number of women, and specifically with Étiennette, who died in childbirth, that he had ordained as bishop of Todi a boy who was only fourteen years old, that he used to sell church titles and offices for money, that he had put out the eyes of his godson at his baptism, that he had "snipped" (i.e., castrated) a cardinal and then murdered him, and that he did not believe in Christ, along with other charges, the emperor thus being obliged to depose him and install Leo VIII[341] in his place. Barely, however, had the emperor left Rome before the pope (John XII) whipped up the people of the city, convened a synod at which Leo VIII was deposed, and ordered the amputation of the hand of the cardinal who had recorded the complaint against him. He also had the tongue of the clerk who had recorded these events cut off, as well as his nose and two of his fingers. John XII was later murdered while embracing a woman—the murderer being, according to some, the woman's husband.

Next, Consul Crescentius,[342] son of Pope John X by Marozia, mobilized the people of Rome against Otto II and imprisoned Benedict,[343] who was of the emperor's party, and he died in prison. When this reached Otto's ears he appointed John XIV,[344] but Boniface VII,[345] who had been appointed to the top position by the consul, rose up against him and killed him, leaving the consul a free hand in the running of affairs and execution of decisions until Gregory,[346] the emperor's sister's son, was installed and Otto III[347] deposed Crescentius; the emperor then played a trick on him, cut off his head, and ordered that his body be hung up by the feet.[348] Pope John XV, who had been elected by the Romans, had both eyes put out and his nose cut off,[349] and was then thrown from the top of the castle of Sant'Angelo. After this, the papacy was put up for sale, to be bought successively by Benedict VIII[350] and John XIX,[351] who were brothers to the Count of Tuscany. Then it was bought for a boy aged ten, Benedict IX.[352] Then two further popes were elected, each of whom excommunicated the other,[353] only to reconcile later on the basis that they divide the wealth of the church between them, each living with his concubine.[354] 1.19.19

Others have stated that the Church of Rome once issued an edict by which it ruled that one of the kings of France should divorce his wife and perform acts of penance for seven years[355] and that, when the edict was published in the kingdom, the king lost his sanctity in the eyes of the people, who, lords and commoners alike, ostracized him to the point that he was left eventually with no one but two servants. Some say that Pope Gregory VII[356] convened a synod against Henry IV,[357] king of Germany, in Rome, where he declared, 1.19.20

"I hereby depose Henry as ruler of Austria and Italy and absolve all Christians from obedience to him, and I will permit no one to serve him as a sovereign king." When Henry IV could stand it no longer, he was forced to go to Rome. When he went to the pope, he found him alone with Countess(1) Matilda[358] at Canossa,[359] and the emperor stood at the gate, with no guard of his own, asking for permission to enter. When he entered the first courtyard, his way was barred by some of the pope's servants, who stripped him of his royal mantle and dressed him in a hair shirt, and again he stood and waited for permission, barefoot in the castle courtyard, in the middle of winter. Then he was told he had to fast for three days before he could kiss the pope's foot. When the three days were over, he was brought into the pope's council chamber, where the pope promised to pardon him provided he should wait to see what sentence the Diet of Augsburg might pass on him. The writer goes on to say that the aforementioned pope died and was succeeded by the abbot of a monastery, under the name Urbanus II,[360] who was as arrogant and tyrannical as his predecessors and, as such, set about inciting the two sons of Henry IV[361] to fight their father, which was the second time the pope had set the sons against their father. They rose up against him and put him in prison but he escaped and died at Liège, pitiful and humiliated. Some say that Henry VI,[362] son of Frederick II, went to Rome to have himself crowned by Pope Celestine[363] and that when the emperor, crown on head, bent over to kiss the pope's foot, the pope lifted his leg and kicked off the crown, which fell on the ground; the pope was eighty-six at the time.

(1) "Countess" is the feminine of "Count," a title of nobility among the Franks.

1.19.21 Someone else says that one of the popes, Innocent III[364] I think, excommunicated King Louis and his father but that the French bishops abrogated the sentence and ordered him to cancel it, and that Pope Innocent IV[365] convened the thirteenth synod against the emperor Frederick II[366] in 1245 and there found him guilty of unbelief and of taking Muslim girls as concubines. The emperor's preachers and the members of his party stood up for him and responded by accusing the pope of having deflowered a virgin and of taking bribes on more than one occasion. Another has said that the aforementioned pope seduced the aforementioned emperor's physician into slipping poison into his food, and that Pope Lucius II[367] on one occasion took command in person of besieging Rome and died as the result of a stone striking him in the head; that Pope Clement XV[368] used to roam about in Vienne[369] and Lyons collecting money with his mistress, that a Dominican monk poisoned Emperor Henry on the orders of the pope (and at communion too!), that in 1200 two popes jostled for the throne, each gathering his party in readiness for a fight, on the banner of each the image of the keys, that one of these seized the liturgical vessels of the church of Saint Peter and sold them in preparation for the war, and that Pope Urban[370] used to torture any cardinal who disagreed with him. At this time also, the French state refused to acknowledge the pope and its bishops ruled tyrannically over the people. Some say that Pope John XXIII[371] was accused of poisoning his predecessor, selling church offices, murdering a number of innocents, and being both an unbeliever and a sodomite, as a result of which he was deposed by the emperor.[372] And so it continues, beyond the scope of this book, for it has not been my intention to belittle religion; I simply provide the foregoing by way of a digression.

However, if what these French authors say is true, then my 1.19.22 brother was far more pious and godly than these leaders of the church, for no one ever accused him of practicing sodomy or adultery or poisoning anyone or inciting sons to kill their fathers, or of making off with the church plate or behaving unjustly or rebelling against his sovereign or taking bribes. The whole matter comes down to no more than arguments between him and a patriarch over things that have no fixed measure or number or weight or volume. *You* might say that the steps from Qannūbīn to Sijjīn[373] are three in number; *he* might say three hundred; *I* might say three thousand—what role do prison and torment have to play in such matters? If, on the other hand, what these writers say is lies and slanders, that would call for them to be punished and for retribution to be exacted upon them for slandering God's priests and successors with libels so vile no fetish-worshipper could come up with anything more appalling. In fact, however, we are not aware of any of them having been tortured or banished or scared out of their houses or summarily removed from their abodes—quite the opposite, as their books have been printed time and time again and are priced in the market as scholarly works.

1.19.23 Someone may say, "This memorandum of yours is addressed to the present patriarch, who is a man of virtuous and noble qualities and not the one who imprisoned and killed your brother, who was his predecessor." I reply, "I am aware of that, but so long as he believes that what his predecessor did was right he is his partner and sooner or later will mete out the same treatment to those who have followed in my brother's footsteps. By the same token, all metropolitans, bishops, priests, and monks are equally blameworthy if they condone what the deceased patriarch did. I would have preferred to conclude this memorandum with a word of censure addressed to His Excellency Metropolitan Būlus Musʿad, our maternal uncle and confidential secretary to the patriarch. But I see that I'm in danger of going on too long, and what I've said above should be enough for the wise."

## Chapter 20

# The Difference between Market-men and Bag-men

You must know that the Market-men are famous everywhere, for they have, since ancient times, held a monopoly over the goods, which they keep in warehouses of theirs, declaring, "We shall exact revenge on anyone who does not buy from our warehouses." They have also hidden the price list from the buyers and jacked up the prices of the various items to an exorbitant degree, demanding from the buyer several times the original price. More recently they opened workshops and warehouses in all the cities, and they have kept these dark, with no apertures or openings for the light, and they sell from them without showing the true colors of the goods or the kind of cloth. They keep the items they sell wrapped and packaged, and the buyer takes them and goes off without having set eyes on them. They have innumerable weavers, tailors, darners, and dyers, and these make them whatever they ask for. 1.20.1

One year it happened that a devastating die-off of cattle occurred, and the land was laid waste. Their stocks of wool and silk were thus reduced, and the looms and workshops were close to falling idle. One among them, a man of sound judgment and perspicuity, decided to use hair and certain kinds of plant in place of the silk and other stuffs that they could not find, and the work that he did with such materials was so well and cleverly made that most people were taken in. Then a company of those hard-pressed 1.20.2

types who have been driven by their poverty-stricken situations to broaden the scope of their thinking and to look into and compare and contrast things—for the majority of scholars and original thinkers are vagabonds—went to one of the warehouses to buy what they needed and took what they'd bought to their homes, wrapped and untouched, as usual.

1.20.3 Now one of them was in love with and wanted to marry a woman, and he'd bought her a handkerchief. When he presented it to her in the presence of the others—it being noted that she was, like all women, skilled at examination and inspection and the uncovering of what is hidden—she took the handkerchief and, before thanking him for his kindness, brought it close to the light of the lamp (for she was visiting him at night), only to find in it a large hole, even though the light was weak and on the point of going out. Before them all, she cried, "Woe to him who sold you this! He cheated you. It's got a hole in it as big as the one that holds you in thrall!" When they heard this, they were put on their guard, some picking apart what they'd bought, others measuring their clothes against their bodies, and so on, until it became plain to them that the wares were not what they'd asked for. He who had gone to buy something red found it was black, he who had wanted a long robe found it was short, and he who had wanted silk found it was cotton.

1.20.4 The next day, they returned to the salesmen and told them, "You sold us things we didn't ask for" and gave them reasons and justifications for returning the goods. Said the owner of the handkerchief, "You almost blackened my face in front of my white-skinned beloved, and she would have quarreled with me over the low quality of what I gave her, had she not been anxious to get something better." The salesmen, however, told them, "We sold you what you requested but 'over your eyes there is a covering'[374] that stops you from seeing the colors or kinds of cloth and from recognizing either quantities or measurements." "How," asked the one who had bought a robe, "can a person be ignorant of his height and another know it?" And the man who had the black but had wanted red said, "Look! The robe you sold me is black, and these two companions of mine will bear witness to what I say. See! It's clear to anyone with eyes." "You are blind and cannot distinguish colors," said the salesman. Then he went to fetch some eye-wash with which to treat the man's eyes, but the other refused, saying, "On the contrary, it's you who are blind, and stupid, too." The one who'd bought cotton instead of silk now said, "Suppose the eyes can deceive. Can touch also mislead the blind man?" Thus debate and intransigence did battle between them, and they filled the place with shouting and uproar.

While they were so engaged, a man came up at a run, panting 1.20.5
and gasping. His tongue was hanging out, and he was holding his midriff with his hands. He had barely entered the store before he fell to the ground and could move no more, and he started moaning and saying, "Ah my wife! Ah my wife!" Then he passed out for a time. When he revived, he cast looks right and left, caught sight of his foe, and could not restrain himself from leaping up from where he lay and saying, "You wicked people! You pushers of goods that have exhausted their *life*! You stirrers-up of conflict twixt a man and his *wife*! You drivers of wedges between father, son, and *daughter*! You veilers of the eyes of those who can see and cheaters of gullible buyers without *quarter*! How can you think that it is allowable in God's sight to cheat me and sell me something of which I have no need? Yesterday I came to you and asked you to sell me meat so that I could make broth for my wife who has been sick for some days, and you sold me crusts of bread and told me they were tender flesh. When I lit the fire to cook them, I found they were bread, and my wife went the whole night without tasting food and when morning came nothing of her moved, except her tongue, which never ceased cursing the wretched hour in which she set eyes on me before we married and abusing the priest who was the cause of our doing so, and she swears that, if she recovers from this sickness, she will

give orders to all women to be to their husbands contrarians, excuse-makers, and bed-deniers."(1) As he said this, the blood in his brains apparently boiled, and he leaped up from where he lay and would have beaten the salesman had not some of the workers in the store grabbed hold of him.

(1) "contrarians, excuse-makers, and bed-deniers": *ḍuju'* is the plural of *ḍajū'*, meaning "a woman who is at odds with her husband" (I hold the form to be strange, for it derives from *ḍaja'a* ("to lie down") so it ought to imply obedience); *mufassilah* means "a woman who tells her husband when he wants to sleep with her, to keep him away, 'I am having my period'"; and *manāshīṣ* is the plural of *minshāṣ*, meaning "a woman who keeps her husband from her bed."

1.20.6 When the salesman had wriggled from his grasp, he mounted a pulpit and declared, "Listen, all you adversaries, and do not rush to criticize. Typically, as critics, your eyes have become so clouded you see black as *red*, your taste buds so corrupted you think meat toasted *bread*, your minds so enfeebled and *jaded* you believe jewels to be colored pompoms that have *faded*. Only the Market Boss can judge fairly between us, so off with us to *him*, otherwise you must be counted people of unbelief and *sin*!" When the others heard the man's words and realized that for him to have them tried before the Shaykh of the Market would be fast practice because the latter, by reason of his extreme old age, was weaker both in sight and judgment than they, they erupted in anger and started overturning the goods, jumbling them, and scattering them, ripping to pieces everything they could lay hands on, stamping on everything they could stamp on, and smashing every implement, box, glass, and cup they could reach. Then they left, heads held high. Next, they agreed among themselves to convene a council that night to arrange matters.

1.20.7 When it was evening, they met and said, "It's become clear to us that these salesmen are oppressors and cheats and that our senses perceived everything the way it really is. Thanks then to God and to the Lady of the Handkerchief, who guided us to this. Come, let us be independent in our *affairs* and set up our own warehouses and workshops as they did *theirs*," and they found themselves partisans and confidants, friends and assistants, and brought prices down so much that many became well disposed toward them. To these they said, "Our covenant with you is that we will sell you the goods in such a way that your eyes can see them, your hands touch them, and your tongues taste them, and if anyone's unhappy with what he's bought, we'll exchange it for something better." Then they looked for the price list and published it in all the lands, using a variety of means to that end, and they said to the people, "Behold the clearest of *ledgers*, the most extensive of *registers*. Buy from us nothing that isn't according to the price *sheet*. Don't go to the Market Boss; he is beyond redemption in his *conceit*." The people, pleased with the conditions these men had set themselves, split off from the aforementioned Market Boss and his party, and each of the two parties took to accusing their opposite numbers of lying, and calumny, calling them stupid, excoriating them, rebutting their claims, accusing them of feeble-mindedness, cursing them out, calling them unbelievers, and charging them with sin and *fornication*—glory be to Him who makes each of man's days succeed the one that went before, in never-ending *fluctuation*.

END OF BOOK ONE

# Book Two

## Chapter 1

# Rolling a Boulder

I have cast from me, thank God, Book One, and relieved my pate of its burden. I scarcely believed I'd ever get to the second book, the first made me feel so dizzy, especially when I set out upon the waves to pay the Fāriyāq a respectful and honorable farewell. Anyway, I'm under no obligation to follow him wherever he *goes*, and for a while, after he reached Alexandria and swallowed the pebbles off its ground, my pen just sat there smacking its lips, my inkwell *closed*. 2.1.1

Then my energy returned and I started writing again, thinking it best that I commence Book Two with something weighty, so that it should be given greater *consideration* and remain for longer a matter of *cogitation*, and, just as I commenced Book One with something to demonstrate my thorough knowledge of certain high matters—and I'm assuming you haven't already forgotten what you read earlier—I thought it would be a good idea now to start with certain low matters, to keep things symmetrical. In addition, given that plain rock must be counted among the precious stones that are both hard to obtain and beneficial, it occurred to me that I should roll a boulder of that material down from the topmost peak of my thoughts to the lowest bottoms of men's ears. Now, then, if you stand and watch its progress without getting in its way or trying to stop it, it will pass you by just as happiness has me, which is to say, without touching you. Otherwise (if you think it a simple matter to bar its descent), 2.1.2

it will pass over you and thrust you under it, and God protect us from the consequences of such a thrust! Observe: here it is, shifting in preparation for its fall, and now it's on its way. Beware then, and beware! Stand at a distance and hear the message in its thunder: "Who looks on this world with the eye of reason—on the diversity and convergence of its states and *conditions*, of what's *essential* and what *incidental*, of objects and *ambitions*, of customs and schools of thought, of ranks and *dispositions*—will find that the quintessence of all that passes before him is beyond his comprehension and moves too fast for his discernment and that, while our senses may have become familiar with certain things, that very familiarity leaves us no room for wonder. Those same things never cease, all the same, to be amazing and puzzling and any who subjects even the least of them to proper scrutiny will realize that his failure to pay them due attention is equivalent to the omission of the performance of a religious obligation.

2.1.3 "Observe, for example, the different types of plants there are on Earth—how many flowers of which we cannot say, brilliantly constructed and amazingly formed though they be, that they serve a specific purpose. And look at the different types of animals—reptiles, vermin, insects, and others: some are beautiful to look at but have no use and some are ugly to look at but are most urgently needed. And look at the heavens, at all their stars—

| | |
|---|---|
| their *darāriʾ*, | a star that is *dirrīʾ* or *durrīʾ* is "a star that burns and flashes" |
| their *khunnas*, | "the *khunnas* are all stars, or the planets, or 'the Five Stars,'"[375] etc. |
| their *bayāniyyāt*, | "those stars that neither the sun nor the moon takes down with them at their setting" |
| their *tawāʾim* | [literally, "twins"] "with reference to either pearls or stars, those that are conjoined" |
| their *burūj* | [literally, "the Houses" (of the zodiac)] "too well known to require definition" |

| | |
|---|---|
| their *Tinnīn*, | [literally, "the Dragon," i.e., Draco]; "the Dragon is an obscure whiteness in the sky whose body lies in six constellations of the zodiac while its tail is in the seventh," etc. |
| their *Mijarrah*, | ["the Milky Way"] "the gateway of the sky or its anus"[376] |
| their *rujum*, | ["shooting stars"] "the stars used for stoning"[377] |
| their *aʿlāṭ*, | "the *aʿlāṭ* stars are the bright ones (*al-darārī'*) that have no names" |
| their *ināth*, | [literally, "the females"] "the *ināth* are small stars" |
| their *khussān*, | "the stars that never set, such as Capricorn, the Pole Star, Ursa Minor and Ursa Major, and the Two Calves"[378] |
| and their *anwā'* | "a *naw'* [singular] is a star that inclines toward its setting point or sets in the west at dawn while, at the same time, another rises opposite it in the east" |

—stars so dazzling that the eye turns from them in exhaustion.

"Observe too the differences among people's countenances 2.1.4
and heads, for you see scarcely one human face that resembles another or find among their heads, meaning their minds, one that is like another. There are mortals who have chosen propinquity and mixing, jostling and crowding, pressing together and colliding, vying with and trying one another, pushing and shoving, battling and butting, competing and blackening each other's names, bargaining and chaffering, and so on, according to their different persuasions; examples are traders and women. Others provide a contrary model, having chosen isolation and withdrawal; examples are ascetics and hermits. Yet others have made it their business to fall over one another to tell lies and *blather*, exaggerate and *flatter*, such as poets and the hirelings who sing the praises of kings in all those gazettes that they print,[379] while yet others again confront the latter with the opposite, preferring truth-telling and investigation,

enquiry and careful consideration, definitive decisions and the comparison of past, present, and future; examples are the great philosophers, physicians, and scientists.

2.1.5 "Some work all day long, toiling with both hands and both feet, quite possibly without uttering a single word; examples are those involved in arduous industries. Others move neither hand nor foot nor shoulder nor head and pronounce only a few words on certain days of the week, the rest of which they spend coddled in comfort, lolling in luxury's lap; examples are preachers, homilists, and religious guides. Some murder, batter, wound, and kill, such as soldiers, while others treat, medicate, cure, and revive, like nurses and the Friends of God Almighty, men of extraordinary spiritual feats and miracles.[380] One man is hired to bring about divorces,[381] another as a 'legitimizer,'[382] one for impregnation and another for inhumation, one to put asunder and another to make peace between persons. Some lurk in their houses and hardly ever leave them unless obliged to do so, while others climb mountains and lateen yards, trees, and *pulpits* or descend into valleys, drains, and *cesspits*. Some stay up all night writing books, while others can't sleep a wink till they've burned one. Some rule and others are ruled. Some lead and others are led. And yet, for all that contradiction and contrast, all their efforts and actions bring them to the same end, which is that, when a person gets up each morning, he sticks his nostrils into a foul smell before sniffing the scent of *flowers* and enjoying the pleasures of the daylight *hours*."

2.1.6 Stranger, though, than any of the situations you have just passed in review is that of our friends the Market-men and the Bag-men. Given that their trade depends on the employment of just two tools, namely surmise and assertion, and has no need of any others, and that the wellspring of their statements and source of any *tirade*, the basis of their claims and greater part of their *stock-in-trade* is to say,[383] "It is likely that this thing to which you refer falls under the rubric either of the trope attributive or the trope lexical, or the trope tropical or the expression periphrastic, or it may be that it belongs to the category of referring like to like, or opposite to opposite, or under that of 'expressing the intrinsic while intending the extrinsic' (or the reverse), or belongs to the type known as 'mentioning the part while intending the whole' (or the reverse), or to the category known as 'the method of the sage,'[384] or is to be approached via the door of irony, or the aperture of allusion, or the peephole of person-switching,[385] or the rent of redundancy, or the casement of carefully crafted composition, or the inlet of implication, or the tear in 'tight weaving,'[386] or the spiracle of the quasi-paradoxical simile, or the knot-hole of the substitution of what is known for what is not, or the toe rings of the generalization of the attribute, or the eyelet of the appositional aside, or the portholes of punning," it is inappropriate for them to mix in among all these "ors" and "ifs" any of the following:

| | | |
|---|---|---|
| *ʿarrādāt,* | "*ʿarrādah* [singular] is a thing smaller than a *manjanīq*" | 2.1.7 |
| or *dabbābāt,* | "the *dabbābah* [singular] is an engine of war that is pushed to the base of the [besieged] fortress, after which the men inside make a breach" | |
| or *darrājāt,* | "a *dabbābah* made for siege warfare, which men get underneath" | |
| or *manjīqāt,* | "the *manjanīq* is a machine with which stones are thrown; also spelled *manjanūq*—an Arabized word[387]—and *manjalīq*" | |
| or *naffāṭāt,* | "the *naffāṭah* [singular] is a copper device with which bitumen is thrown" | |
| or the *khaṭṭār,* | "the *khaṭṭār* is the [same as the] *manjanīq*"; it also means "a man who thrusts much with his spear" | |
| or *sabaṭānāt,* | "the *sabaṭānah* [singular] is a hollow reed through which projectiles are blown" | |

| | | |
|---|---|---|
| | or the *ḍabr*, | "the *ḍabr* is a leather-covered wooden structure containing men who approach fortresses in order to fight" |
| | or the *qafʿ*, | "protective structures made of wood beneath which men get and which they move up to fortresses in war" |
| | or *julāhiq*, | "balls that are thrown"; similar are *barāqīl* and *banādiq* |
| 2.1.8 | or *ḥasak*, | "devices of iron or reed for use in war that are thrown down around the soldiers and that work like common caltrops"[388] |
| | or the *qurdumānī*, | "a padded outer garment used in war; also a weapon the Caesars kept in their storehouses; also thick shields"[389] |
| | or the *tijfāf*, | "a device for war worn by horse and man alike"[390] |
| | or *yalab*, | "shields and coats of armor made of leather" |
| | or *sard*, | "a general term for armor" |
| | or *daraq*, | "shields made of leather without wood or sinews; similar are *ḥajaf*" |
| | or *ḥarshaf*, | "foot soldiers; ornaments for weapons" |
| | or *ʿatalāt*, | "the *ʿatalah* [singular] is an enormous iron pole with a blunt head with which walls are demolished" |
| | or *minsafāt*, | "the *minsafah* [singular] is an instrument for uprooting built structures" |
| | or the *falaq*, | "the jailor's pillory, consisting of a length of wood with holes the size of the shanks" |
| 2.1.9 | or *khanāzir*, | "the *khanzarah* [singular] is a large axe used for breaking stones" |
| | or the *ʿadhrāʾ*, | "a thing made of iron with which people are tortured to make them confess, etc."[391] |
| | or *maqāṭir*, | "the *miqṭarah* [singular] is a piece of wood with holes the size of the prisoners' legs" |

| | |
|---|---|
| or *marādīs,* | "the *mirdās* [singular] is an instrument with which a wall, or the ground, is pummeled" |
| or the *dahaq,* | "two pieces of wood with which the shanks are squeezed" |
| or the *ṣāqūr,* | "a large axe" |
| or *malāṭis,* | "the *milṭas* [singular] is a large *miʿwal*" |
| or *maqārīṣ,* | "the *miqrāṣ* [singular] is a knife with a curved blade" |
| or *malāwiẓ,* | "the *milwaẓ* [singular] is a stick for beating" |
| or *maqāmiʿ,* | "the *miqmaʿah* [singular] is a piece of wood with which people are beaten on their heads" 2.1.10 |
| or *maqāfiʿ,* | "the *miqfaʿah* [singular] is a piece of wood with which the fingers are beaten" |
| or the *ḥadaʾah,* | "a double-headed axe" |
| or the *minqār,* | "the metal blade of the axe" |
| or *mahāmiz,* | "the *mihmazah* [singular] is the same as the whip (*miqraʿah*) or the stick (*ʿaṣā*)" |
| or *ʿarāfīṣ,* | "the *ʿirfāṣ* [singular] is the whip with which the secular power metes out punishment" |
| or *makhāfiq* | "the *mikhfaqah* [singular] is the whip, or a lash made of wood" |

or lacerating lances or severing swords or shooting shafts or bloodletting blades or stinging sticks or weakening whips or crucifying crosses or impaling posts or chinking chains or flaming fires or invasions or raids or murderous onslaughts or surprise attacks or looting or rapine or the bereavement of mothers or feuds or grudges or, last but not least, the rough treatment of women during intercourse.

Dear God, how much blood they have shed! How many a sol- 2.1.11
dier they have destroyed! How many a virgin's honor they have defiled! How many a time they have violated the sanctity of the home, thrown men into confusion before their families, tormented bachelors, made wives into widows and sons into orphans, reduced houses to ruins, pillaged wealth, ripped veils from the faces of decent women, made off with treasure chests, ravished that which

was protected, and violated sanctuaries! Were such things done by those who, before them, were custodians of

| | |
|---|---|
| al-Anṣāb, | "al-Anṣāb were stones that formerly stood around the Kaaba [of Mecca] at which they used to celebrate and make sacrifice to other than God Almighty" |
| or al-Kaʿabāt, | "al-Kaʿabāt, or Dhū al-Kaʿabāt, was a holy house that belonged to the tribe of Rabīʿah which they used to circumambulate" |
| or al-Rabbah, | "a kaaba belonging to the tribe of Madhḥij" |
| or Buss, | "a holy house belonging to the tribe of Ghaṭafān built by Ẓālim ibn Asʿad when he saw Quraysh circumambulating the Kaaba of Mecca and running between al-Ṣafā and al-Marwah: he measured the holy house [of the Kaaba], took a stone from al-Ṣafā and a stone from al-Marwah, and then returned to his people, built a holy house of the same size as the house [of Mecca], set down the two stones, and said, 'These are al-Ṣafā and al-Marwah' and he set up his own pilgrimage to rival that of Mecca. Then Zuhayr ibn Janāb al-Kalbī raided [Ghaṭafān] and killed Ẓālim and demolished his house" |
| or ʿAbdat Marḥab, | "an idol that used to be in Haḍramawt" |
| or al-ʿAbʿab, | "an idol" |
| or al-Ghabghab, | "an idol" |
| or Yaghūth, | "an idol belonging to the tribe of Madhḥij" |
| or al-Bajjah and al-Sajjah, | "two idols" |
| or Saʿd, | "an idol belonging to the Banū Milkān" |
| 2.1.12 or Wadd, | "an idol; also spelled Wudd" |
| or Āzar, | "an idol" |

| | |
|---|---|
| or Bājar, | “an idol worshipped by the tribe of al-Azd; also pronounced Bājir” |
| or Jihār, | “an idol of the tribe of Hawāzin” |
| or al-Dawwār, | “an idol; also pronounced al-Duwwār” |
| or al-Dār, | “an idol, after whom ʿAbd al-Dār, the founder of a clan [of the tribe of Quraysh], was named” |
| or Suʿayr, | “an idol” |
| or al-Uqayṣir, | “an idol” |
| or Kathrā, | “an idol belonging to Jadīs and Ṭasm[392] that was broken to pieces by Nahshal ibn al-Raʾīs, who then attached himself to the Prophet, may God bless him and grant him peace” |
| or al-Ḍimār, | “an idol worshipped by al-ʿAbbās ibn Mirdās[393] and his company” |
| or Nasr, | “an idol of the Dhū l-Kilāʿ tribe in the land of Himyar” 2.1.13 |
| or Shams, | “an ancient idol” |
| or ʿUmyānis, | “an idol belonging to the tribe of Khawlān by whom they would swear against their flocks and their crops” |
| or al-Fils, | “an idol belonging to the tribe of Ṭayyiʾ” |
| or Juraysh, | “an idol of the Days of Barbarism” |
| or al-Khalaṣah, | “an idol that was in a holy house called ‘the Yemeni Kaaba’ belonging to the tribe of Khathʿam” |
| or ʿAwḍ, | “an idol belonging to the tribe of Bakr ibn Wāʾil” |
| or Isāf, | “an idol set up by ʿAmr ibn Luḥayy[394] at al-Ṣafā” |
| or Nāʾilah, | “another idol that he set up at al-Marwah; sacrifices were made both to it and the preceding” (according to one definition) |
| or al-Muḥarriqah, | “an idol belonging to the tribe of Bakr ibn Wāʾil” |

| | | |
|---|---|---|
| 2.1.14 | or al-Shāriq, | "an idol of the Days of Barbarism" |
| | or al-Baʿl, | "an idol that belonged to the people of Ilyās, peace be upon him"[395] |
| | or Suwāʿ, | "an idol worshipped in the days of Nūḥ, peace be upon him; it was submerged by the Flood, then Satan made it reappear, and it was worshipped and came to belong to the tribe of Hudhayl and pilgrimage was made to it" |
| | or al-Kusʿah, | "an idol" |
| | or al-ʿAwf, | "an idol" |
| | or Dhū al-Kaffayn, | "an idol belonging to the tribe of Daws" |
| | or Manāf, | "an idol" |
| | or Yaʿūq, | "an idol belonging to the people of Nūḥ, or a righteous man of his time who died, and when they mourned for him, Satan came to them in the shape of a person and told them, 'I shall make you a representation of him in your sanctum so that you shall see him whenever you pray'; so they did that with him and with seven of their righteous men after him, and in the end things reached a point at which they took these representations as idols and worshipped them" |
| | or al-Ashhal, | "an idol who gave his name to the tribe of Banū ʿAbd al-Ashhal Luḥayy, of the Arabs" |
| | or Hubal, | "an idol that was in the Kaaba" |
| 2.1.15 | or Yālīl, | "an idol" |
| | or al-Baʿīm, | "an idol; also a statue made of wood and a doll made of condiment" |
| | or al-Asḥam, | "an idol" |
| | or Nuhm, | "an idol belonging to the tribe of Muzaynah, whence the name ʿAbd Nuhm" |
| | or ʿĀʾim, | "an idol" |
| | or al-Ḍayzan, | "an idol" |

| | |
|---|---|
| or al-Madān, | "an idol" |
| or al-Jabhah, | "an idol" |
| or al-Lāt, | "an idol" belonging to the tribe of Thaqīf "named after a man in whose house parched barley meal used to be moistened (*yulattu*) with clarified butter; then the word was shortened"; it is to be found in ʿUrwah's hadith "al-Rabbah"[396] |
| or Dhū al-Sharā, | "an idol belonging to the tribe of Daws" |
| or al-ʿUzzā, | "an idol, or a gum-acacia tree, that was worshipped by [the tribe of] Ghaṭafān, the first to adopt it as an idol being Ẓālim ibn Asʿad; at the top of Dhāt ʿIrq,[397] nine miles from al-Bustān. He built a holy house over it and called it Buss, and they used to hear a voice inside. The Prophet (God grant him blessings and peace) sent Khālid ibn al-Walīd, and he knocked down the house and burned the tree" 2.1.16 |
| or Manāh, | "an idol" |
| or al-Ilāhah, | [literally, "the Goddess," means] "the serpent, or idols, or the crescent moon, or the sun; also pronounced al-Alāhah, al-Ulāhah, al-Ilayhah, al-Alayhah, and al-Ulayhah" |
| or al-Ṭāghūt, | "the idols al-Lāt and al-ʿUzzā, or a soothsayer, or Satan, or any leader in error, or any idol, or anything that is worshipped to the exclusion of God" |
| or a *zūn*, | "any idol or anything that is taken as an object of worship; also a place in which idols are gathered, erected, and adorned" |
| or a *jibt*, | "any idol, or a soothsayer or magician, or magic, or anything in which there is no good, or anything that is worshipped to the exclusion of God Almighty" |

or by those who worshipped the sun or the moon or Saturn or Jupiter or Venus or Mars or Mercury or *Furdūd*,[398] Pherkad, Edasich, *al-Katad*, *al-ʿAwāʾidh*, Hadar, *al-Aḥwal*, *al-Zubrah*, *al-Aẓhār*, Aludra, *al-Maʿarrah*, *al-Aʿyār*, *al-Nathrah*, Gemini, *al-Birjīs*, *al-Tiyāsān*, Almeissan, *al-Sunnayq*, Sheratan, *al-Fāriṭān*, Alsafi, *al-ʿAyyūq*, *al-ʿAwhaqān*, *al-Ṣarfah*, Alterf, *al-Abyaḍ*, *al-Ḍibāʿ*, Heka, Alhena, *al-Ridf*, *al-Maʿlaf*, *al-Nāqah*, Nusakan, *al-Simākān*, *Shuhayl*, Shaula, *al-ʿAwkalān*, *al-Mirzamān*, *al-Sullam*, Botein, *al-Qadr*, *al-Ḥayyah*, *al-Taḥāyā*, *al-Kharatān*, Alchibah, *Suhā*, *al-Shāh*, Auva, and *Kuwayy*?

2.1.17 They would have done better to have reached a consensus and said, "Given that our trade requires, thank God, neither measuring nor counting—unlike that of practitioners of the natural sciences, engineers, and mathematicians, who, whenever asked for proof by an opponent in debate, immediately set about providing it through the use of quantities, areas, and arithmetic, exhausting themselves and their questioners alike—we should pursue a more restful path that will bring us and those with whom we deal closer to the desired end, which is to facilitate the learning of this trade by any who is obliged to practice it. Thereafter, anyone who wishes to wear an outer garment or robe, with drawers underneath or with wrestlers' breeches, can make them himself of any color he pleases and of any shape he likes, for it makes no sense for one person to raise objections to how another, just like him, may dress or to his taste or to how he sleeps."

2.1.18 From the day of his first cry till he reaches his fourteenth year, the human lives quite independently of us and without any need for what we plan for him. Instinct guides him to what is appropriate to and good for him. Do you not see how a child, if left to his own devices and nature, will not wear thin linen in winter even if it be embroidered, or furs in the heat of summer even if they be edged with brocade? How, when he feels hunger, he asks for food and, when he gets sleepy, sleeps, even if you seek to distract him with all the music and songs known to man? How, when he gets thirsty, he drinks and, when he gets tired, he rests? In other words, he is in no need of us because of his natural inborn disposition. He could even live, through the strength of the Almighty, for a hundred and twenty years, plus a month, without looking on the face of any one of us or setting eyes on our crowns and gorgeous robes, our signet rings of precious metal, our silvered sticks.

Let us then leave people, unmolested, to their humble pursuits 2.1.19
and to their work and not stick our noses into their business or charge them with tasks beyond their ability to perform. If God had wanted to make the child dependent on us, he would have inspired him to ask his parents, from the moment that he started to grow and flourish, their names and station and about the matters over which we wrangle and debate—all the back and forth, the mutual wretchedness and recrimination, the sniping and snippiness, the vilification and reviling, the contradicting and cutting. Better than letting him go down that path, we should concern ourselves with teaching him manners and morality, with refining him and teaching him skills that will help him to earn a living and provide for himself and his parents—such as reading, penmanship, arithmetic, letters, medicine, and painting—and in advising him to exert himself for his own good and that of his parents, his acquaintances, his community, and everyone to whom the term "human" may be applied, without regard for the styles of people's dress or differences of color or country. The wise and well-guided man sees in others only their common humanity, and any who pays attention to incidental matters such as colors, food, and costume distances himself greatly from what is central to humanity. And all that we do in this regard will be good only if we do it for the sake of God Almighty, not as seekers after rewards or gifts, offerings and donations, but like those many physicians who treat the hard-up for free and whom you'll see leaving their food and beds and going to a patient with a fever, or leprosy, or the plague, in anticipation of only heavenly reward. All people are God's children, and the person God loves best is he who is of greatest benefit to His children.

2.1.20 This is what they should have said and is what I say now. Take a Bag-man. He has undertaken to make the circuit of the world's seas and *metropolises,* to roam its mountains and *wildernesses,* to expose himself and his allies to insult and abuse, hostility and hatred, all so that he can tell people that he knows better than they do what they are about. If you ask him for medication for a rheumy eye or an ulcerated *leg,* a swollen scrotal hernia or a finger that's *bled,* or if he's asked, "What say you to one whose litter has *grown* while his wealth has *flown,* whom Fortune has put to the *test* and whom by his government's been *oppressed,* so that he's afflicted with *hunger* and condemned to *insomnia* and now, wherever he walks, people, seeing his podex is *bare,* refuse to acknowledge that he's *there,* and will not do business with him or employ him, thinking in their minds that a poor man cannot do a job well; to one whose children have started to weep and wince with *pain* and whose wife has begun to ask for mercy and *complain,* though none spare a thought for the youth she's lost in raising her children?" or if someone says to him, "Have you any refuge for a guest who's a *stranger* and has none to take his side against *danger*?" he'll say, "I didn't come to you to provide such things. I came only to inspect the looms on which you weave your goods, and their colors, which cannot rival the brilliant colors that I have in my saddlebag. It is no concern of mine to look into what might bring you ease; my ease lies in your troubles. If all your workshops fall idle because you're incapable of producing these colors of mine that I have displayed to you in the shape of samples and specimens and you thus earn the reproof of your merchants, plowmen, and physicians, that is of no importance to me."

2.1.21 And here's your Market-man, one eye trained on his neighbor's mouth, the other on his eyes, who then binds him hand and foot and tells him, "Today you have to be 'distressed'(1) for the Market Boss awoke with indigestion, complaining of pains—in other words, 'distress'—in his stomach, guts, and molars. We must therefore be as he is and abstain along

(1) "To be distressed" (*tatanaḥḥas*) means here "to abstain from eating meat."

with him"; or "Today you aren't allowed to use your eyes because staying up late last night with his boon companions (male and female) has laid the aforesaid boss low, and he woke up with pus or rheum in one of his noble peepers"; or "Today you aren't allowed to work with your hands or to move your feet, and you mustn't listen with your ears or breathe with your nostrils because no market was held today, and no sales were made." If someone then says to him, "Can you not make peace between Zayd and his wife, for yesterday she wouldn't do his bidding after she came back from your most honored store, and they fell to tugging at each other's hair, and the wife swore she'd make him wish she were an old hag, or would complain of him to one of her friends among the big-time traders?" or "The merchant ʿAmr has been in prison these last two days because he lent money to one of the emirs and couldn't obtain a judgment against him or recover what he is owed, and the judge bankrupted him and had him mounted on a donkey and paraded through the marketplaces, facing the donkey's rump," or "So and so has fallen ill and taken to his bed because he got into an argument with one of the emir's servants, so the emir punished him by beating him with sticks on his feet and slapping him with slippers on the back of his neck, and the next day he couldn't move, and his feet swelled up, and his nape was all puffy," all he'll say is, "So long as the market and its boss are safe and sound, the rest of the world is too. Business is going well, and the market's up and *running*, bellies are full, mouths are *munching*, stomachs are digesting, molars are *crunching*, hands are *snatching*, joys are *everlasting*, fortunes are *accumulating*, bosses are *prohibiting*, Providence is *protecting*, women bearing ex-votos in droves are *arriving*, pious bequests are all-*encompassing*, the mouths of the Fates are smiling, and all's well that ends well. To market! To market! There's the box of delights, there the trove of truths! Into the chest! Into the *chest*! Morning and evening, the *chest* is *best*!"

Many a time, I swear, has that chest been filled with gold and precious stones, only to be emptied again on confrontations, 2.1.22

confabulations, pointless investigations, and foolish matters. We have been informed that one of the market traders spent a vast amount of money over a period of six years on study and debate concerning the shape of a certain hat. To be specific, he looked at himself one day in the mirror and, being somewhat acquainted with the principles of engineering and construction, noticed that his head was round, like a watermelon. It therefore seemed appropriate to him that he should adopt the use of a round hat of the same shape as his head, for round goes best with round, as good taste has long determined. One of his colleagues from another market, who was of higher standing and dignity and more learned than he, saw him and made mock of him, asking, "Who whispered in your ear, you featherbrain (*Ibn Quba'ah*),(1) that you should wear that bird's nest of a bonnet (*qubba'ah*) when your head in fact is conical?" "You are misled," he replied. "My head is, on the contrary, rounder than yours, as the Market Boss will testify." "You lie," said the other. "It truly is conical, as you should know since you keep looking at it in the mirror, and I am better guided and walk a straighter path than your boss." "You blaspheme," said the first, "and are blind to your own self; how then can you know others?" "And you," said the second, "are a godless innovator; nay, you are confounded and confused and have become stupid and silly in refusing to accept my advice. People today can tell the rounded from the *turned*, the con-man from the *burned*."

(1) *Ibn Quba'ah* [literally, "Son of a (certain) bird (smaller than a sparrow)"] and *Qābi'ā'* are epithets used to describe stupidity.

2.1.23 At this, obduracy seized them in its relentless grip, and they grabbed each other by their collars, their pockets, and their shepherd's sacks, and then by their long hair, and then by their reputations, each man tearing apart that of his friend, meaning his enemy. Next they screamed, appealed for help, and complained of each other before the ruler, each calling the other a fool and reviling him. When it became clear to the ruler that they were both acting like lunatics (*shabāziqah*),(2) he decided it would make better sense to cure them with

(2) ["like lunatics":] a *shabzaq* [plural *shabāziqah*] is one whom the Devil has afflicted with insanity.

a heavy fine than to confine them in the pokey. Each then departed, after paying a fine of such and such a number of purses. Afterwards, the first trader adopted a hat that was half and half, that is, half round and half conical, and none but the most learned of scholars and most expert of examiners could tell which it really was, and he returned to his store like a conquering hero or one who'd captured a *diḥyah* (that's an army *general*), or even a prize-winning *cockerel*. The first thing he did when he reached the edge of the marketplace was to command all the hatters to come out and receive him—with entertainment and salaams (*taqlīs*), not with reproaches and slams (*talqīs*).(1) So they went forth accordingly, making noise and saying, "Today is the Feast of the *Hat*! Today the day of the firecracker! What a *twat*! What a *twat*!" and the ruler's henchmen, beholding them as they crowed, supposed them to have thrown off the yoke of *obedience* and abandoned their *allegiance*, so they set upon them with instruments that[399] hit, strike, smite, knock, belt, bat, clout, bang, slam, dash, bash, punch, jab, thwack, smack, clap, crack, swipe, whack, wham, whop, clump, bonk, clip, cut, swat, sock, slog, thump, pound, beat, maul, drub, thresh, spank, thrash, whip, slap, club, kick, stamp, stomp, push, shove, and fling, until they had made of them a warning for all who have eyes to see.

(1) *Taqlīs* is receiving rulers on their arrival with various sorts of entertainment, and also a man's placing his hands on his breast and bowing. *Talqīs* is reproaching someone in an exaggerated fashion, i.e., denouncing him and calling him names.

The market trader then fled with his hat, having landed his people in ignominy and disgrace, which afflicted the men with grievous loss and brought the women even greater, despite all of which the Market Boss, who was so taken with him, thought the matter of no importance. In fact, he continued to devote himself to the taking of opium because of his endless insomnia and nightly brooding; he had stuffed his ears with pages from the market ledgers so that he wouldn't hear the screams of those who called on him for help and none should wake him from his stupor, and he's 2.1.24

stayed flat on his back to this very day, which is to say, up to the day of the recording of this incident. If he awakes, it will be up to the reader to enter that fact at the end of this chapter, and I have left him space to do that. Here ends the rolling of the boulder, praise be to the Prime Mover.

# Chapter 2

## A Salutation and a Conversation

"Good morning, Fāriyāq! How are you and how do you find Alexandria? Have you learned to tell its women from its men (for the women in your country do not veil their faces)? And how do you find its food and drink, its clothes, its air and water, its parks, and how its people honor strangers? Is your head still *swimming*, your tongue with disparagement of travel still *brimming*?" Replied he, "So far as the city's situation is concerned, it's elegant because it's on the sea, and the number of foreigners it contains adds to its brio: in it you see some people whose heads are covered with tall pointed hats and others with tarbushes, some with round caps and others with *maqāʿiṭ* turbans, some with burnooses and others with ordinary turbans, some with *aṣnāʿ* turbans and others with fillets, some with headgear of a generic nature[400] and others with *madāmīj* turbans, some with sailors' caps and others with hoods, some with caps and others with bonnets, some with further turbans and others with watermelon-shaped(1) and cantaloupe-shaped caps,[401] and others with head scarves large and small, some with judges' tun-caps[402] and others with antimacassars,[403] some with undercloths for turbans and others with head rags, some with the turban under the name *mishmadh* and others with the turban under the name *mishwadh*, and some with Frankish hats shaped like earthenware jars, or carp, or the creases between 2.2.1

(1) The *arṣūṣah* (plural *arāṣīṣ*) is a cap like a watermelon.

the cheek, nose, and eye, or the crevices between the same, or the children of the jinn, or armpit sinews, or white varan lizards, or disreputable demons, or babies' clouts.

2.2.2 "Some of them have long saggy drawers that sweep the ground behind and before them and some have no drawers at all, so that their anuses are on display and the people pass their hands over what is in front of the latter.[404] Some of them have short breaches and some drawers without legs, some of them have drawstrings and some have belts, some have leggings (drawers made of one piece of material) and others have *underwear*,[405] some have boxers and others briefs. Some ride mules and *asses*, others dromedaries and *horses*. Camels are on every *side*, people *collide*. One moving among them must never slacken in his pious exclamations,[406] saying, 'God protect! God preserve! God be kind! I have put my trust in God! I seek God's help! I seek refuge with God!'

2.2.3 "As for women's face veils, if they conceal the beauty of some, at least they relieve the eye of the ugliness of the rest. It is, however, the ugly ones who most often cover their faces, for the pretty ones think it a pity, when they leave their cages, to fly through the markets without the onlookers being able to see their charms' *array*, behold their comeliness, and make much ado over the beauty on *display*, saying, 'As God wills![407] God be blessed! How mighty is God! O God, O God!' When such a one returns to her house, she believes that all the inhabitants of the city have fallen passionately in love with her and sits there expecting them to send her gifts and tokens of *esteem*, verses and sonnets with an amatory *theme*. Whenever anyone raises his voice in song, she cocks an attentive ear and believes she hears him rhapsodizing over her name, and if, then, she sets off early the following day to the marketplace and finds everyone busy with their work, she's amazed that they're still conscious and capable of effort and action.

2.2.4 "She therefore shows off more of her hidden charms, her elegance, and her forbidden fruits. She bewitches them with her gestures and nods, her eye-rolling and her gestures behind her back, her expressive looks and glances, her come-hither winks and cow eyes, her billings and cooings, her haughtiness and conceit, her vanity and coquetry, her playfulness and her turning aside of her cheek in pride, her comings and goings and goings and comings, her demurrals and her mincing walk, her glances to the side and her glances askance, her looks of surprise and swivelings of her eyes, her backward glances of spite or surprise and her angry looks, her peepings through her fingers against the sun to see[408] and her turnings to observe what lies behind her, her shading of her eyes against the sun to see and her peering through her fingers against the sun to see, her wantonness and her conceitedness, her staggering and swaying, her tottering and strutting, her bending and bowing, her coyness and bough-like curvaceousness, the trailing of her skirts over the ground as she walks and her sweeping by, her turning of her face aside as she proceeds and her walking with a swinging gait, her stepping out manfully and her walking proudly in her clothes, her ambling and her rambling, her stepping like a pouting pigeon and her rolling gait, the swinging of her mighty buttocks and her sashaying, the insinuating wriggling of her shoulders, her pretty waddling and the way she walks as though she were short, her shaking of her shoulders, her sprinting and her haughtiness (especially in walking), her taking short steps and her sinuosity, her ponderousness and her modesty of deportment, her hastening and her willowiness, her slowness of motion and her looseness of motion, her slow stepping and her skipping from foot to foot, her stretching out her hands as she paces and her walking with short steps, her swaying and her slowness, her walking proudly like a high priest of the Parsees and her sudden startings off the road, her sprightly running and her bending as she walks, her languishing gait and her strutting, her galloping and her striding out, her stalking and her swaying from side to side, her nonchalant sauntering and her walking with the limbs held close to the body, her swaggering, her walking finely and loosely and her staggering as though intoxicated, her walking with her thighs far apart kicking up her feet and her walking with a swing, her striding fast and her rushing, her skelping and her stepping quick, her tripping quickly along with short steps and three other ways of walking, each with a difference of one letter, and her walking nicely, her limping and a fourth way of walking with yet another letter changed[409] and her walking making her steps close together, her gliding and her walking slowly, her shambling and a fifth way of walking, with further letters changed,[410] her walking with tiny steps[411] and her shuffling, her walking with conceit and her walking as though too weak to take long strides, her running with short steps and her walking fast, her disjointed walking and the moving of her buttocks and sides as she walks, the looseness of her joints as she walks and her walking with close steps, her walking with a rolling gait and her slowness and turning in walking, her walking fast with close steps and her close stepping, her walking with steps as close as closely written letters and her walking with steps as close as rapidly uttered words, her hopping like a shackled camel and her rolling walk, her walking with small hurried steps and her moving like a fast, well-gaited donkey, her easy pacing and her twisting and turning, her marching proudly (spelled two ways),[412] her walking arrogantly and her tottering, her walking so fast that her shoulders shake and her cleavage rises and her moving like a wave, her walking as though falling onto a bed and her walking proudly like a horse, her walking like an effeminate man and her fast, agitated walking, her handsome way of walking and the same said another way,[413] the beauty of her walk and her walking like a dove dragging its wings and tail on the ground, her walking like a pouting pigeon and her floppy walking, her walking with close, fast steps, moving her shoulders, her swashbuckling and stepping like a crow, her nubile grace, her hastening as she sways and her running with close steps, her lion-like pacing and her hurrying, her swaying as she walks and her walking slowly with long steps, her walking finely and the way she drags her skirts behind her, her active way of walking and her racing, her nimbleness and her knock-kneed running, her starting like a scared gazelle and and her leaping, and her jumping up and down in place and her facing forward and facing backward—and all the time her appetite for presents grows. I have composed two lines[414] on the face veil that are, I believe, without precedent:

Only a fool would think to keep a girl
From love's pursuit with nothing but a veil:
Not till the cloth's been set to the wind
Is the ship in a state to sail.

"As for the city's men, the Turks boss the Arabs around like tyrants. 2.2.5
The Arab is as much forbidden to look into the face of a Turk as he is into that of another man's wife. If by some quirk of fate a Turk and an Arab should walk together, the Arab will follow the custom that has been imposed, namely of walking on the Turk's left-hand side out of modesty and submission, head bent in self-derision, making himself as small and as thin as possible, shriveling, shrunken, unextended, drawing into himself, shrinking, cowering, tightly compressed, withered, making himself as short as possible, walking slowly and curled over himself, puckered, suckered, snookered, desiccated, tight as a miser, crouching, hugging himself to himself, making himself as small as possible, sucking in his sides and holding his buttocks tight, retracting and contracting, quaking and frozen in place, depressed, head and elbows pulled in, head bowed, aloof, dispirited, humiliated, regimented, intimidated, terrified, petrified, eyes downcast, recoiling and regressing, cringing, curled into a ball like a spider, debased [?],[415] twisted, coiled upon himself like an old snake, bent over in abjection, drawing back, cleaving, constricting himself and restricting himself, pulling back, holding back, compressing, repressing, and constringeing himself. If the Turk sneezes, the Arab tells him, 'God have mercy on you!' If he clears his throat, he tells him, 'God protect you!' If he blows his nose, he tells him, 'God guard you!' And if he trips, the other trips along with him out of respect and says, 'May God right you and not us!'

2.2.6 “I have heard that once the Turks here held a consultative assembly at which, upon deliberation, they decided that they would use the backs of the Arabs as a comfortable conveyance, for they had tried horse saddles and camel saddles (both *bardhaʿah*s and *ikāf*s, as well as *qitbah*s and *bāṣar*s[416]) and their riding mats, and all other kinds of carrying devices, namely,

the *kifl*, [a kind of saddlecloth] “a thing for men to ride on”

or the *shijār*, “a conveyance for an old man or anyone whom illness prevents from moving”

or the *ḥidj*, “a conveyance for women resembling the *miḥaffah*”

or the *ajlaḥ*, “a camel litter that does not have a high peak”

or the *ḥawf*, “something that resembles a litter but is not one”

or the *qarr*, “a conveyance for men, or a *hawdaj*”

or the *miḥaffah*, “a conveyance for women”

or the *farfār*, “a conveyance for women”

or the *ḥaml* or *ḥiml*, “a camel litter”

or the *ḥilāl*, “a conveyance for women”

2.2.7 or the *kadn*, “a conveyance for women”

or the *qaʿsh*, “a conveyance like a camel litter”

or the *maḥārah*, “something like a camel litter”

or the *qaʿadah*, “a conveyance for women”

or the *katr*, “a small camel litter”

or the *mītharah*, “plural *mawāthir*: things that people ride on made of silk or brocade”

or the *rijāzah*, “a conveyance smaller than a camel litter”

or the *ʿarīsh*, “something like a camel litter”

or the *ʿabīṭ*, “a conveyance”

or the *ḥizq*, “a thing people ride on resembling the *bāṣar*”

or the *bulbulah*, “a camel litter for noble people”

or the *ḥiql*, “a camel litter”

or the *tawʾamah*, “a conveyance for women; plural *tawʾamāt*”

or the *fawdaj*, "a camel litter; a conveyance for a bride"
or saddles, wheels, thrones, dead men's stretchers, bridal litters, podiums, beds, and biers, and found that none were good enough for them.

"Once I saw a Turk leading a band of Arabs with a thread of paper[417] while all of them were 'leading' him. . . . Whatever am I saying? I meant 'were being led *by* him.'[418] I have never been able to work out the reason for the sense of superiority felt by these Turks here with regard to the Arabs, when the Prophet (peace be upon him) was an Arab, the Qur'an was revealed in Arabic, and the imams, Rightly-guided Caliphs, and scholars of Islam were all Arabs. I think, though, that most Turks are unaware of these facts and believe that the Prophet (peace be upon him) used to say *şöyle böyle* ('thus and so') and *bakalım kapalım* ('let's see-bee')[419] and 2.2.8

*Ghaṭālıq*[420] *chāp khay dilhā*
*Ṭughālıq pāq yakh balhā*
*Ṣafālıq pāh khusht wa-kurd*
*Faṣālıq hāp daraklahā*
*Dakhā zāwusht geldi nang*
*Khudā shawizt qardlahā*
*Eshekler hem gibi va-llāh*
*Qalāqiluhā balābiluhā*

"Never, I swear, was the language of the Prophet so, nor that of the Companions or the generation that followed them or the Rightly-guided Imams, God be pleased with them all unto the Day of Resurrection, amen and again amen!

"As for the city's waters, what a fine and wholesome head is theirs! Though, on the other hand, what a filthy tail![421] All the animals of the earth and every fowl of the sky pollutes it; even the fish of the sea, when they catch a summer cholera, leap on top of this tail and vomit onto it whatever it is that's making them sick. 2.2.9

"The food they eat there is fava beans, lentils, chickpeas, darnel seed and darnel weed, water clover, *kharfā* vetch, *julbān* vetch, 2.2.10

broad beans, the fruit of the *ghāf* tree, the black-eyed pea called *dajr*, *khullar* vetch, *buls* lentils, bitter vetch, lupine, the black-eyed peas called *khurram*, *shubrum*-lentils, black-eyed peas *tout court*, and everything else that makes the belly distend. This is because its people find nothing good in an empty stomach. It has even been reported to me that the women use a paste made of dung-beetles, eating some every morning so that they may grow fat and develop overlapping belly folds.

2.2.11 "The most noxious thing I came across there was Qayʿar Qayʿār.[422] He came to the city from the Himyaritic lands[423] and made the acquaintance of a group of Christians there, to whose houses he would repair, spending the evenings with them. Finding that they had no scribes among them, he appointed himself their scholar and said that he knew the science of 'subjects' and 'objects'[424] and of chronograms.[425] He got hold of a few books, some of which were missing their beginnings and some their ends, some of which were worm-eaten and some so faint as to be illegible, and if anyone asked him about anything, he'd turn to one of these, open it, gaze upon it, and then say, 'As I thought. This is one of those things over which scholars differ. Thus some of our shaykhs in the Himyaritic lands interpret it this way and some of them in the Damascene territories that, and they have yet to reach a consensus. When they do, they will certainly let me know.'

2.2.12 "Once," the Fāriyāq continued, "I heard someone who was bothered about some urgent business ask him the time, and the man told him, 'Such-and-such an hour and five minutes. Now, as to the word *sāʿah* ("hour"), from it are derived the words *sāʿī* ("errand boy"; literally "one who strives" or "makes effort") and *ʿĪsā*.[426] *Sāʿī* is so derived because all effort depends on the hours, for no-one can undertake any work outside the confines of time. All acts and motions are confined within time, just as . . .' and he looked about him for something to use as a comparison and caught sight of a tin mug belonging to some child and said, '. . . water is confined within this p'tch'r.'[427] Then he saw a palm-leaf basket belonging to some other child and said, 'Or like this child's lunch in this b'sk't. As for *'Īsā,* it is so derived because 'Īsā contained within himself all knowledge and branches of learning as completely as the hour contains the minutes. Note too that, when I say "five," the real meaning is "four plus one" or "two plus three" or vice versa. They say *khams daqā'iq* ("five minutes") and not *khamsah daqā'iq* in pursuit of a more concise form and faster speech,[428] for the longer the words you use the more time you waste. The word *daqā'iq* ("minutes") that I just employed is the plural of *daqīqah,* which derives from the *daqīq* ("flour") that is milled, for they resemble and correspond to one another in that each is a "congregator of fineness" (*jāmiʿ al-nuʿūmah*).[429] There are many words that refer to time, namely *masā'* ("evening"), *layl* ("night"), *ṣubḥ* ("morning"), *ḍuḥā* ("forenoon"), *ẓuhr* ("noon"), *'aṣr* ("late afternoon"), *dahr* ("epoch"), *abad* ("eternity"), *ḥīn* ("point of time"), *awān* ("right time, season"), and *zaman* ("period"). The first six have "partings,"[430] the others do not.' Here, one of the important men who were present raised an objection, saying, 'I am confused, dear professor, by what you say. Both my slave girl and her mistress have partings!' The shaykh laughed at the man's foolishness and told him, 'My words here relate to the domain of time, not that of place.' Then another asked him, 'Where's this Nuʿūmah Mosque that you said has the flour in it?'[431] The man laughed again and said, 'To us scholars, the word *jāmiʿ* is known as an "active participle," meaning that it assumes the doing of something, whatever it might be (albeit for a long time I've had it in mind to discuss this terminology with them because someone who dies, or falls asleep, for example, cannot correctly be said to be "doing death" or "doing sleep"); when I used *jāmiʿ*, then, it was in accordance with the rule as recognized by us, namely as a noun descriptive of that which congregates a thing. It would be perfectly correct to apply the word *jāmiʿ* even to a church, because it congregates (*yajmaʿu*) the people.' When he said this, the faces of his listeners turned dark." The Fāriyāq resumed, "I then heard one of them muttering, 'I do not believe the shaykh holds a correct Christian belief.

Our bishops were right to forbid people to delve deeply into the sciences, and especially this science of logic that our shaykh refers to. How rightly is it said, "He who practices logic practices unbelief!"' Then they all left him, muttering under their breath.

2.2.13 "And once a priest asked him about the etymology of the word *ṣalāh* ('prayer') and he said, 'It derives from the word *iṣlā'* ("burning") because the one who prays "burns" the Devil with his prayers.' The priest asked him, 'If the Devil has dwelt in hell fire these thousands of years without being burned up, how can prayer burn him?' so the man picked up one of the books to extract from it an answer and declared, 'A certain learned monk has said, "Burning is of two kinds: physical burning, as when someone is burned by fire, and figurative burning, as when someone is 'burned' by love as practiced by the tribe of 'Udhrah."' Then he paused and sighed, saying, 'Our Lord the monk was in error, because *'adhrā'* has to be stretched out at the end.'[432] The priest, enraged by the thought that the Virgin could be stretched out if she did not so desire, declared, 'Woe unto you! You're another who doesn't know the rules for the use of long and short vowels at the end of words, when the very children playing in the alleys in our country know them! Truly, it's a good idea to keep to a minimum one's conversations with those who accuse monks of error.' Then he turned and left him, muttering under his breath."

2.2.14 The Fāriyāq went on, "And once he told me, 'My studies have shown me that the proper way to use the verb *da'ā*, if one intends the meaning of "to pray," is to follow it with the preposition *'alā*. Thus one should say *da'awtu 'alayh,* just as one says *ṣallaytu 'alayh.*'[433] I told him, 'Just because two verbs have the same sense doesn't mean they should be followed by the same preposition,' but this was too much for him; he couldn't get his head around it. And once a man he knew complained to him that a bout of diarrhea was causing him pain, and he said to him—either to correct him or to amuse him—'Thank God for it! I wish I were like you.' 'How can that be?' said the first. 'If it goes on too long, it is fatal and carries the whole body off with it.' He replied, 'It is a blessing from God. Do you not hear how everyone who has a worry says, "Lord, make it pass easily"?' The merchant replied, 'I'm not worried about things passing easily, I'm worried about things passing through my bowels *too* easily.' 'It comes to the same thing,' the first told him, 'because verbs of the pattern *afʿala* and those of the pattern *faʿʿala* both lend transitivity—one says either *anzaltuhu* ("I sent it down") or *nazzaltuhu* (ditto)—and because both *tashīl* and *ishāl* contain the sense of "ease."'"[434]

"And once he wrote to one of the great metropolitans, 'My request, Your Grace, after kissing your noble buttocks and raising your elevated, sophisticated, delectated, de-germinated, etiolated, uncontaminated, well-soled, much extolled, and often resoled slippers is . . .'—at which point I asked him, 'What do you mean here by "buttocks?"' and he replied, 'In the usage of the metropolitans, it means "hand."' In no time at all, the same metropolitan had sent him back his blessings and a letter praising him hugely for his learning and virtues, of which the following is an excerpt:[435] 'Your sodomitical missive reached me when I was outside the church, and I could read it only after I'd entered my cell and penetrated it. When I came to the shittiest part of it, I realized that you were possessed of *excrements*, a creator of *pestilence*, a "congregator" of both the branches of knowledge and its roots, long of *tongue* and with 'ands too short (to do any *wrong*), with a broad little brow, deeply in *debt*, wide of waistcoat, of ideas *bereft*.' At the end of it he wrote, 'May God prolong your life and livery, grant you happiness, and awaken your hopes! In conclusion, our greetings, and a greeting for our conclusion. May the grace of the apostles embrace you, once, twice, and all the way up to ten!' The man made a habit of showing this letter off to all his acquaintances and especially those who had left him in anger over his interpretation of the word *jāmiʿ*. In view of the metropolitan's words, these were thenceforth relieved of all confusion and doubt as to the correctness of how to use it, and the man increased in dignity and venerability in their eyes. 2.2.15

2.2.16 "Turning now to your question concerning the hospitability of this town, in the days of their first forefathers they were exceedingly liberal and generous. However, when they started to excel in the world of commerce and to mix with the people of those Frankish hats that you wot of, they caught from them their reticence, miserliness, bad faith, and avarice; indeed, they've come to surpass their teachers. When they find themselves gathered together, the only talk they make is of buying and selling. One will say, 'Today, a Turkish trooper came to me in the morning to buy something, which I took as an evil omen for the morning and for the start of business, for, as you well know, troopers incur debts but don't pay them, and if they're gracious enough to provide the price in cash, they give the merchant only half. So I told him, "I don't have what you're looking for, effendi" (showing him the deference of this title solely in the hope that he would treat me politely). No sooner did he hear my words than he entered the store and threw the goods everywhere, taking what he wanted and what he didn't. Then he left, shouting insults.' Another will say, 'I too had a run-in with a Turkish lady. She sailed in early today, wallowing under the weight of her jewelry, approached me smiling, and said, "Have you, sir, any brocaded silk?" Taking a happy omen from her coming, I said, "I have." "Show me the goods," she said, so I showed them to her. Then she leaned forward and gave me a slap with her slipper, saying, "Is one such as I to be shown such stuff? Show me something else," so I showed her something that she liked, and she took it, saying, "Send someone with me to collect the money," so I sent my young servant, who followed her till she entered a large house, where she ordered her steward to give the boy a sound drubbing. The steward, however, being a Turk and seeing that the lad was comely and smooth, couldn't find it in his heart to beat the boy, but implemented his mistress's command in a different way that nevertheless brought him both injury and pain.' Thus they pass their days in evil ways and their nights in going over them. I think merchants go into ecstasies simply at the mention of buying and selling, even if they aren't making a profit.

"As to what befell me after my arrival, I put up at the home of a Bag-man who was the friend of my previous friend. I occupied a room close to his and each night would hear him beating his wife with some implement, while she produced moans and groans, sighs and nasal cries. His acts roused the desire in me to give him a hiding, and I often thought of getting out of bed but was afraid that it would be for me as it was for the Persian who practiced medicine and lived next door to a community of Copts: one night he heard one of his neighbor-women screaming. There being so many scorpions in the houses of Egypt, he thought one must have stung her, and, fetching a flask of medicine, placed it under his arm and set off in her direction at a run. When he opened the door, though, he found a man lying on top of the woman and treating her with his finger, after the custom of that people. When the doctor saw this, he was amazed, and the flask fell from his hand and was broken. 2.2.17

"This Bag-man had white skin and blue eyes that were both small and round. His nose had a finely molded tip and went crooked at the bridge, and his lips were thick. I tell you these details only so that they can remain with you as a prototype against which to measure any other Bag-men or others you may see. On the roof of his house he had made a small, pyramid-shaped stack of empty bottles of alcohol, the roof being higher than those of his neighbors. One day it occurred to him to set me the task of composing a sermon in praise of saddlebags that I was to deliver at a small oratory he had hired. When I finished, I submitted it to him, and he took it to Qayʿar Qayʿār. 'What do you intend to do with this baggish rigmarole?' the latter asked him. 'I intend the one who composed it to deliver it to the people. What do you think of it?' 'It's good,' he said, 'but it does have one drawback, which is that nobody will understand it except him and me, and we've both already read it, so there's no call to have it read out again.' Consequently the man gave up the idea. 2.2.18

"It also happened that one delightful summer's evening when I was staying with him, I went out to take a walk on my own, a copy of the ledger in my hand. My head being filled with thoughts of how I 2.2.19

was separated from my family and friends and with memories of my homeland and of how I had been exiled from it not for any reason linked to ordinary affairs but because of a feud between Market-man and Bag-man over polemical matters, I kept on walking until I ended up on the outskirts of the city, to which I had been followed by a man who, having seen the copy of the ledger and recognized it, had privately decided to bring a disaster down on my head. Now he approached me, spoke to me, and led me left and right, distracting me with talk, until we arrived at an empty wasteland, where he left me, telling me that he had to see to some business. I tried to return to where I was staying but suddenly found myself face to face with a huge pack of dogs that had run up, barking at me, and were closing in. I tried to scare them off with the book, but they attacked me like a Market-man attacking a Bag-man and divided my body, my clothes, and the book between them, as creditors might a debtor's possessions, some biting, some drawing blood, some dragging me, and some threatening to come back for more. I managed, barely, to escape their clutches, though my clothes and skin were torn to shreds, and the ledger too was ripped to pieces, both pages and binding. When I returned home and the Bag-man saw me in this state, he paid no attention to me or maybe didn't even see me, so preoccupied was he with the bag. When he discovered, however, that I had returned without the ledger, he imagined I must have given it away to someone, and this gave him such immense joy that he wanted to keep me with him in Alexandria for Bag-man business. However, he decided that he should consult his friend first and therefore wrote to him about me. The friend rejected his idea and said he had to send me on to the island, because this was what had been previously decided (though how sweet it can be when decisions are changed!). My host therefore decided to put the plan into action, and here I now am, awaiting the ship."

## Chapter 3

# The Extraction of the Fāriyāq from Alexandria, by Sail[436]

A typical example of our friend's bad luck was that, at the time of his leaving for the island, the Franks had yet to discover the special properties of steam. Travel by sea was dependent on the wind, which blew if it felt like it and didn't if it didn't. As al-Ṣāḥib ibn ʿAbbād has said,[437] 2.3.1

> 'Tis but a wind you cannot control,
> For you're not Sulaymān, son of Dā'ūd.

It follows that the Fāriyāq departed on a wind-propelled ship of that ilk.

In the course of his voyage, he learned some words of the language of the people of the ship related to greetings and salutes. One of these was a prayer that they utter when drinking wine at table, namely, "Good health to you!" Their word *health*, however, resembles their word *hell*, so he used to say, "Good hell to you!" and they'd laugh at him while he cursed them in his heart, saying, "God destroy these louts! They live in our country for years and still can't pronounce our language properly. They pronounce *s* with a vowel before it as *z*, and the palatal letters and others are a lost cause for them, despite which we don't laugh at them. 2.3.2

2.3.3 "I have heard that a priest who had lived in our country for years decided one day to preach to the people. When he ascended the pulpit, he stood there shaking for an hour before finally saying,[438] 'Good yolk, my lime is up but I shall peach to you next Fun Day, God willing.' Then he went to see an expert and learned acquaintance of his and implored him to write him a sermon that he could commit to memory or read out loud. The people came in great numbers to hear him, and, when the church was full to overflowing, he mounted the pulpit and declared, 'In the Name of God the Immersible!' Then it seems he noticed his mistake and realized that this wouldn't please the Christians and that the writer had written it according to his own tenets, so he corrected himself and said,

"'No, no! I ain't mean to say me Muslim man. Islam he say "In the Name of God the Immersible, the Inflatable." Contrarily, Kitchen People he say "In the Name of the Father, the Son, and the Holy Boast."

"'Blessed children lathered here today to spear my peach and listen to my insides, if you have lathered here while your farts are still fizzy with the Pleasures of This Knife, inform me, that I may submit you to my denture, and let none complain of its length or how it hurts. If not, then today's my inopportunity, as one who bears no importunity, to urge both women and men to bedrink themselves and to warn you of the Day of Insurrection and Beckoning—a day when neither honey nor blends will avail, nor indigestion nor regurgitation. Know, may God inflate you, that This World is ephemeral, its temptresses virginal, its mates undependable, its towering sights despicable. Stand on lard against it and let not its pleasures and temptations lead you into terror. Keep your lances from it averted. Hang not your ropes upon it. Examine your farts concerning it before you lay down your heads upon your holsters and sleep. Spray regularly when distressed or undressed. Coffer the churches your contributions, be they but spittle. Spray God's paints that they may help you and shave you from all piles and infibulations. Be of good fart if you would be freed from the cabbages of fate. (1) Respect your monsters and piss-offs, venerealize them,

(1) "'Cabbages' (*al-kurunb*) is a misspelling for 'ravages' (*al-karb*).

and wallow in their footsteps. Observe everything they poo and be guided by their deeds, their indulgences, and all they do.

"'Good Kitchen People, our religion is the Roof! Its premises are the best licensed! Its dressings are the most humorous! Its market has the best rices! Have no intercourse with the fag-men, who have recently inserted themselves into you, pricking you into leaving the straight bath with the dignified and mild feces that they put on for you. They are naught but ravening poofs in clams' clothing cruising in every land and strand, accusing us of aberration and of spreading flies, when they are the most fly-blown of any who took a bath and the flightiest of any who ever cheated on a friend or led a companion down the primrose path.'

"Then he said,

"'O you who are clowning in a sea of pecker-dildoes, stay clear of all that may feed you to them, for the result will be disasters and calamities. Don't let them get up to their old tricks, but cut them off at the ass. Resist their fins resolutely. Pull them out by their boots directly. Strip off any ironing of theirs that makes you perspire and you will be granted retribution. The pricks! The pricks! Cut off your pricks, that you be saved on the Day of Beckoning from any stunts or tricks!'

"Despite all this, none of his listeners boxed his ears. On the contrary, they sat quietly until the end of the sermon as given above. Then, however, a quick-witted woman who had just married, on hearing the last passage, grew angry and said, 'God curse the day we first set eyes on these non-Arabs. They have monopolized our resources and wealth and corrupted our lands and they compete with our own people in obtaining their sustenance from our own soil. They have taught those of us who have come to know them miserliness, stinginess, fickleness, and shamelessness. Never, I swear, would they have obtained these abundant riches were it not for their greed and avarice, for we hear that when one of their menfolk sits down at the table with his children, he eats the meat and throws them the bones to suck on, and because they are thieves 2.3.4

and cheats, and swindle when they sell, and I've been told that their brethren in their own countries are even more disgusting and depraved than they. Now this wretch is inciting our husbands to commit an abomination so as to leave the field open to him to do as he wishes, for I know, without any doubt, that what these pulpiteers say with their mouths is not what is in the hearts. They teach people abstinence and emasculation in this world, while there isn't a human or a jinni who cares more about intercourse than they or is greedier for it. Let his reward now be to have his tongue cut off, so that he can know how much it hurts. Sometimes, I swear, one finds it hard to cut one's fingernails because they're a part of one, which is why our sisters, the women of the Franks, grow their nails and show them off. Those, though, are quick to grow back. How then can it be permitted to cut off the means by which life is generated?'" (Well said, you who are so new to marriage and so experienced in the criticism of such oafs! Would that all women might be like you and I might kiss your lips!)

2.3.5 "When the priest left the church, everyone rushed to kiss his hand and the hem of his garment, and all thanked him for the elegant figures of speech he had vouchsafed them, not to mention all the other wonderful things, for it had become an established fact to them that the books of the Christian religion should be written in as feeble and corrupt a style as possible, because 'the power of the religion requires it, so that everything be of one piece,' as stated by the Arabic-language-challenged,[439] Feed-sack-carrying, Sweetmeat-chasing, Marrow-slurping, Rag-sucking, Bone-gnawing, Finger-licking, Half-a-morsel-biting, Cauldron-watching, Drippings-drinking, Bottom-of-the-pot-scraping, Scourings-scarfing, Leftovers-off-polishing, Dinner-sponging Aleppine Metropolitan Atanāsiyūs al-Tutūnjī[440] in a work of his called *Al-Ḥakākah fī l-rakākah* (*The Leavings Pile Concerning Lame Style*)."[441] Said the Fāriyāq, "Since God had seen fit to afflict me with the company of such wretches, I had no choice but to compliment them and be cordial to them until such time as He grant that I be rescued from them."

I declare: since what the Fāriyāq had to say about his first voyage has already come and gone, there's no need to repeat here his complaints concerning the dolors of the sea. However, we will note that during his sufferings and afflictions, he did swear that he would never embark thereafter on any of the following sea-going vessels: 2.3.6

| | | |
|---|---|---|
| the *jufā'*, | "the empty hulk of a ship"; mentioned by the author of the *Qāmūs* under *j-f-'* | |
| the *mirzāb*, | "any great, or tall, ship" | |
| the *zabzab*, | "a sort of ship" | |
| the *bārijah*, | "any large ship for fighting" | |
| the *khalīj*, | "a small ship of less size than the *'adawlī*" | |
| the *ṭarrād*, | "any small, fast ship" | |
| the *mu'abbadah*, | "any tarred ship" | |
| the *ghāmid*, | "any loaded ship; also *āmid*" | |
| the *dasrā'*, | "any ship that plows through the water with its prow; plural *dusur*" | |
| the *zurzūr*, | "any narrow ship" | |
| the *zanbarī*, | "any huge ship" | 2.3.7 |
| the *qurqūr*, | "any long, or very large, ship" | |
| *kār*, | "ships on the down run containing food" | |
| the *hurhūr*, | "a kind of ship" | |
| the *qādis*, | "any very large ship" | |
| the *būṣī*, | "a kind of ship" | |
| the *ṣalghah*, | "any big ship" | |
| the *nuhbūgh*, | "any fast-moving ocean-going ship; also called *dūnīj*, a non-Arabic word" | |
| *dhāt al-rafīf*, | [literally, "the planked," i.e., "boat bridges"] "ships used to cross over on, consisting of two or three ships set side by side, for the king" | |
| the *shuqduf*, | "a boat; also a place in the Hejaz" | |
| the *ḥarrāqah*, | "plural *ḥarrāqāt*; ships containing flame-throwers" | 2.3.8 |
| the *zawraq*, | "any small ship" | |
| the *burrāqiyyah*, | "a kind of ship" | |

| | |
|---|---|
| *ʿadawliyyah,* | "ships named after ʿAdawlā, a village in Bahrain; or . . . ."[442] |
| the *jarm,* | "a small Yemeni ship" |
| the *khinn,* | "the empty hulk of a ship" |
| the *shawnah,* | "any boat equipped for battle at sea" |
| the *talawwā,* | "a kind of ship (small)"; mentioned [by the author of the *Qāmūs*] under *t-l-w* |
| the *jufāyah,* | "any empty hulk"; mentioned [in the *Qāmūs*] under *j-f-y* |
| the *khaliyyah,* | "any great ship, or one that sails without needing a navigator to sail it, or which is followed by a small boat" |
| the *shadhā,* | "a kind of ship" |
| and all the way down to | |
| the *rikwah,* | "any small boat" |
| the *qārib,* | "any small ship" |
| the *ramath,* | "pieces of wood fastened together on which one rides at sea" |
| the *ṭawf,* | "inflated water skins that are tied together to form a platform on which one rides on the water and on which loads are carried" |
| and the *ʿāmah.* | "tied sticks on which one rides at sea or crosses a river; also called *ghāmmah*" |

2.3.9 On arriving at the island's harbor, fine quarters were made available to him in which to "purify his breath" for a period of forty days, for it has become the custom among them to distribute around the harbor, before they enter the country, anyone who comes to them from the lands of the Levant and has inhaled their airs. He stayed there then, eating and drinking with two English notables who had been on the ship, and found life with them pleasant, for they had traveled widely in the Levant and absorbed the habit of generosity from its inhabitants.

2.3.10 When the period was over, the Bag-man came and took him to his house in the city. This man had lost his wife on the very day that the Fāriyāq had made his decision to go to him and had given himself over to mourning and *squalor*, living in the clutches of melancholy and *dolor*. All he ate was pork (God elevate you above any pollution from the very notion!) and he had ordered his cook to produce it in every variety. One day the man would cook its head, another its feet, a third its liver, a fourth its spleen, and so on until he had covered all its parts; then he'd start over again with the head. You are well aware that the Christians of the Levant imitate the Muslims in all things other than those pertaining to religion, from which it follows that pork is an abomination to them. Thus, when the Fāriyāq sat down to table and the cook brought out some part of that hated animal, he thought that the Bag-man was trying to trick him by producing for him something he was unfamiliar with, and he refused to take a bite, in the hope that he would be given something else. But the Bag-man kept right on going, finished his lunch, and launched immediately into prayer and thanks to the Almighty Creator for what He had provided. To himself, the Fāriyāq said, "I swear our friend is making a mistake. His thanks are misdirected, for to give thanks to the Creator, glory be to Him, for something immoral or for eating something forbidden is not allowed." The following day, the cook brought him another limb, and the man gobbled it up and thanked him once more. The Fāriyāq said to the cook, "Why does our friend thank God for eating pig?" and he replied, "Why not, when he has made it his duty to thank Him 'for every condition and every thing,' as it says in some book of religion? He even used to carry out the same rite each time he spent the night with his wife." "And did he thank Him for her death?" he asked. "Yes," the man replied, "for he believes she's now in the bosom of Ibrāhīm." "For my part," said the Fāriyāq, "if I had a wife, I wouldn't want to see her in any man's bosom."

Thereafter, the reign of the pig grew mightier and yet greater, and 2.3.11
the Fāriyāq's intestines grew lean and shriveled up, and he'd go the whole day on bread and cheese. Then he heard that the city's bread was kneaded by foot, but by the feet of men, not of women, so he took

to eating as little of it as he could, until emaciation reduced him to a pitiful *state,* his molars become rusty so little he *ate,* and two of them fell out, one on each side—which was hunger's first act of evenhandedness on the face of this earth, since if both of them had fallen from the same side, one would have become heavier and the other lighter, and the movements of his body would have become unbalanced.

2.3.12 As to the city, one coming to it from the lands of the east will find it handsome and *mighty* and one coming to it from the lands of the Franks will disdain it and regard it as *paltry*. Two classes of things most moved the Fāriyāq to wonder: the priests and the women. As for the priests, there are so many of them that you find the markets and parks swarming with them. They wear three-cornered hats on their heads that do not look like the hats of the Market-men of the Levant, and they wear drawers that are more like breeches, for they reach only to the knee, while their shanks are clothed with black hose. It seems that the island is a mighty place, for all the priests on it are well-fed and fat. It is also the custom there for the priests and other great men and good to shave their mustaches and beards. The priests specifically however have to wear short, form-fitting drawers, and the beholder can make out what is beneath them.

2.3.13 As to their women, what surprised the Fāriyāq was the difference of their dress from that of the rest of the women of the Levantine and Frankish lands, and the fact that many have mustaches and short beards, which they neither shave nor pluck, and I have heard that many Franks are attracted to mannish women, so perhaps this strange fact may have reached their ears too (and how could it not, when men's fancies are no secret to women?). Beauty is extremely rare among them, and their docility toward their priests is strange. A woman will sometimes favor her priest over her husband, her children, and the rest of her family. It is inconceivable for her to partake of some special dish until she has given him the first taste, and she will eat only after he has eaten.

2.3.14 I was told about a married Market-woman, meaning one belonging to the party of the Market Boss, who saw a handsome Bag-man, and, deciding it was a pity he should be theirs, said, "If that man enters our church, it will grow in sparkle and allure." She therefore sent an old woman to him to invite him to visit her, and the young man obeyed her invitation, for the enmity between the Market-men and the Bag-men is limited to the market traders, the people who connive to drive up prices, and the professionals, and has no impact on ordinary men and women. She talked to him at length and eventually told him, "If you follow our path, I will give you the freedom of my body and forbid you nothing." The young man replied, "As to going to your church, nothing could be easier for me, for it is close to my house, and as to your creed, leave that to my conscience, for I reject that 'confession' that the priests of your church force on you. Lying and cheating are not in my nature that I should confess to the priest my peccadilloes and suppress my major transgressions, as do many Market-men, or tell him what I haven't done and hide from him what I have." At this the woman sighed and bowed her head, pondering and nodding. Then she said, "So be it. It will be enough for us if you conform outwardly, or so my priest informs me." Then they embraced and made love, and he started paying visits to her and the church together. Even wantons on this island are obsessed with religion, and you'll see in their houses numerous statues and pictures of the saints, male and female, whom they worship, and when some lecher goes in to see one of them and perform debauchery with her, she turns the faces of the statuettes toward the wall so they can't see what she's doing and testify against her on the Day of Resurrection that she was a debauchee.

It is a curious fact about the people of this island that they hate 2.3.15
strangers but love their money, which is odd, for a person's money is an expression of his life, his blood, and his very self, to the extent that the British, when asking how much money a person possesses, say, "How much is the man worth?" to which the response may be, for example, "He's worth a thousand in gold." How can it occur to anyone to hate another and yet love his life? They contend with one another, too, over every stranger who comes their way. Thus, one

will take his right hand to show him the women, another his other hand to show him the churches, and the winner takes all.

2.3.16 Another curious thing about them is that they speak a language so filthy, dirty, and rotten that the speaker's mouth gives off a bad smell as soon as he opens it. The men and the women are alike in this. If you sniff at a beautiful woman who is silent, you'll find yourself intoxicated by a delicious scent, but if she utters a word, it's transformed into halitosis. Another is that if one of the women is afflicted with a disease in one of her limbs, she will go to a jeweler and tell him to make her a likeness of that limb out of silver or gold and give it to the church; a woman who is not well-off will make it of wax or the like. Another: the shaving of beards and mustaches is deplored and the shaving of everything else is forbidden, to the degree that the priests ask the women insistently during confession about the two issues of hair plucking and shaving and urge them to guard against committing any such acts. Also: the people of the church have a custom of taking, on certain specified days, the figures and statues, heavy and bulky as they are, from the churches and lifting them onto the shoulders of religious zealots who run through the streets with them making a lot of noise. Stranger still, they light candles before them, at a time when anyone else would want to take refuge in a cave under the ground from the excessive heat of the sun.

2.3.17 There are many other customs, too, that caused the Fāriyāq to wonder, since the people of his country, even though they are Market-men and excessively hostile to the Bag-men, do not practice them. At this point he became convinced that the Bag-men were on the right path (except in eating pork) and that the Market-men were in error (except for their women's preference for young and good-looking Bag-men). However, there is no path in the world that does not have praiseworthy and blameworthy aspects, and one finds that individuals are rational and discerning at times and ignorant and misguided at others. Glory then to the One who alone may be described as perfect, and let the fair-minded critic look to the more beneficial aspects of each system and compare it with those of others. If he finds its positive qualities outweigh its negative qualities, he may judge it to be meritorious. He should not indulge in dreams of discovering perfection. As the poet says:[443]

And where is the man whose every feature pleases?
Sufficient nobility in a man it is that his vices be few enough to count.

Furthermore, just as hunger had caused two molars to fall from the mouth of our ravenous and insatiable friend, so his witnessing such matters drove from his mind all respect for both the Market-men and their cousins,[444] where either religion and rationality were concerned, for it seemed to him that their acts were better considered those of madmen. Thus he felt oppressed in their country, and his patience was exhausted, not to mention that he felt in need of the delicious food that he had been accustomed to in the Levant, as well as of clothes that suited him, for the Bag-man had informed him that those who sold the Bag-men's wares should pay no attention to what they wore, the sole point of the bag being to carry it (even though the Market-men believe that Bag-men attract their salesmen by giving them money and gifts). 2.3.18

For these reasons, the Fāriyāq was always mournful and sad, and he was unable, at that time, to master the language of the Bag-men, learning from them just a few words related to the promotion of the goods. In addition, there was in the house of the aforementioned Bag-man an evil junior Bag-man of spiteful ways with a yellow complexion, blue eyes, a thin tip to his nose, and big teeth. One day he noticed the Fāriyāq looking though a window in his room at the neighbors' roof, and the Devil prompted him to nail the window closed. When the Fāriyāq saw that the window had been boarded up, he took it as a good omen that his bad luck could get no worse, and so it was, for within a few days he had fallen ill, the doctor had advised the Bag-man to send him to Egypt, and off he had set, carrying a letter of recommendation to yet another Bag-man. 2.3.19

## Chapter 4

# A Throne to Gain Which Man Must Make Moan

2.4.1 As long as sea's *sea* and wind's not ceased to *be*, the Fāriyāq's ascendant star will never cease to *slip*, his tongue to *trip*. When he reached Alexandria, he found a new Bag-man in the place of the old, one who had been through times so rough even Shaykh Khalīl ibn Aybak al-Ṣafadī[445] would have refused to put up with them. As a result, he had failed to advance, and his name was mud among his peers. He had been brought to this pass by his belief that the air in these lands was too warm for him, as a consequence of which he'd decided to make use of a pair of pyramids that he'd scale whenever the weather turned hot, just as his predecessor had made use of a pyramid of wine barrels. After he'd spent enough silver on the pair to fill a valley, the news of his extravagance got out and his friends became upset with him.

2.4.2 The Fāriyāq left Alexandria for Cairo and gave the letter of recommendation to the Bag-man, who put him up in the house of a colleague of his that was next door to the house of a Levantine, at whose home a group of singers and musicians used to gather each night. From his room the Fāriyāq would hear the *singing*, be moved by passion and *longing*, and, recalling his days in the Levant, yearn and ache to be ensconced amongst friends *again*, imagining he'd been transported from the world of jinn to that of *men*, that life had unveiled for him pleasures novel and lusts long in *abeyance*, joys untrammeled and hopes now in *abundance*.

Thus he forgot the miseries of dizziness and the deathly gasps he'd suffered at the *ocean's hand*, the hunger and boarding up of his window he'd suffered on *land*, the sore throat he'd contracted on his salesman's *mission*, the grief induced by blind *tradition*, and found in Egypt, as a state, sparkle and *self-confidence*, and, as a place to live, bounty and *opulence*, for all its people are like members of a never-ending wedding *celebration*, or jousters for ever engaged in competition and self-*acclamation*, while their women display their wit and *sophistication*, beauty, refinement, grace, and *coquetry*, pride and *vanity*, as they move through the streets like galleons in full sail in silk and velvet *wrapper*, causing the cares that cluster about the heart to *scatter*. I am not the first to describe them as seducers of the *mind*, conquerors of every virile male they *find*: thus has described them every master of prose and of the poetic *arts*, and any, old or young, who's sought to deceive them has mentioned their *smarts*. As the proverb that's going around would have it, "Cairo's dust is *gold*, its maidens are the best of playthings, and its spoils go to the *bold*." 2.4.3

The most amazing thing they do on slipping their hobbles and leaving their bridal *recesses* is straightway to mount tall, imposing *asses*, sitting upright atop them on a throne with galia moschata *daubed*, their scent thus being by every nostril *absorbed*, while the blacks of their irises and the whites of their *eyes* make men to think of the maidens of the gardens of *Paradise*. All who behold a houri of this type exclaim, "How great is *God*!" and see the world, beside the beauty of her visage, as but a paltry *sod*. One calls out to catch her *eye* and, having done so, "Praise the Lord!" goes up his *cry*. Another expresses his wish to hold her stirrup or her dress to *touch*, to carry her slippers or her train to *clutch*, to be a lining to her *shawl* or the porter at her *hall*, to be a go-between between her and her *lover* or her companions' follower's *follower*, to be a tire-woman dressing her *hair* or her tailor sewing up a *tear*, to be a jeweler fashioning for her wrist a *band* or a blacksmith forging her a nail by *hand*, to be a bathhouse attendant massaging her to release a *knot* or any other 2.4.4

inconsequential thing that might bring him closer to her you-know-*what*, while she, from on top of that throne, *revels* and *repulses*, *glares* and *stares*, casting at this a glance that makes him *bleed*, at that a wink that steals his heart, never to be *freed*, bringing commerce to an *end* and sending the unemployed right round the *bend*. Even the jackass beneath her seems to know the worth of what he *bears* and understand what drives her halleluiah-shouting fans as they let fly their *cheers*, for he doesn't bray, is never heard to snort, and never sniffs (unlike the others) she-donkeys' *rears*. On the contrary, he lords it over every *horse* and struts in pride and glory as he pursues his *course*. As for the the donkey's driver, he thinks he's in a *class* outranking the army's topmost *brass*, and that the people are in need of his *ministrations*, for which he requires presents and *oblations* (and how could it not be so, when he derives his very name from his "stable management (of affairs)," his "leadership qualities," and his "horse sense"?)[446]

2.4.5 And here's a matter to which I forgot to draw *attention* and so must enter here and *mention*: hearts are more easily set *alight* by women whose faces are fully veiled than those whose faces are in plain *sight*. This is because, if the eye beholds a beautiful *face* (even the most charming and intriguing that could be), the imagination rests and ceases to *race*. If, however, one gazes upon one that's got a veil on *top* (assuming that the heart believes its owner to belong to the beloved sex and especially if evidence of this is provided by the prettiness of eye, length of lash, and penciling of eyebrow), the imagination comes flying, freighted with thoughts, and finds no barrier at which to *stop*.

2.4.6 Then (and here the rhymed prose can end, because it's filled a page) the mind declares, "This face could be

| | |
|---|---|
| *uthʿubānī*, | *uthʿubān* or *uthʿubānī* refers to "a face that is magnificent in its comeliness and whiteness" |
| or 'possessed of *insibāt*,' | "one says, 'There is in his face *insibāt*,' i.e., 'length and extension'" |
| or is *muṣfaḥ*, | "a *muṣfaḥ* face is smooth and handsome" |

| | |
|---|---|
| or *mutham'idd*, | "a *mutham'idd* face is full and comely" |
| or *mudannar*, | "one says, 'his face shone like a dinar' meaning 'it gleamed'" |
| or *mulawwaz*, | "a *mulawwaz* face is handsome and comely" |
| or *makhrūṭ*, | "a *makhrūṭ* face is one that has length" |
| or *sāji'*, | "a *sāji'* face is regular and comely of appearance" |
| or *'anmī*,[447] | "a handsome ruddy face" |
| or *fadgham*, | "a full handsome face" |
| or possessed of *kalthamah*, | "*kalthamah* is seamlessness of the flesh of the face without bloatedness" |
| or *masnūn*; | "one says, 'A man whose face is *masnūn*,' [meaning] his face is smooth, handsome, even" |

or could bring together all the components of good looks to embrace smooth, lean, and wide, or compact and rounded, cheeks, with, in each cheek, when she laughs, a crinkle or a *dimple*, or a speckle or a *pimple*, a [?][448] or chin cleft, 2.4.7

or those cheeks might have on them

a *'ulṭah*, the *'ulṭah*, or *lu'ṭah*, is 'a black mark that a woman draws on her face for adornment'

or each might have a *mole* that adds beauty to the *whole*, and reinforces the charm of it *overall*;

or both, or one, might have a *khidād* (a brand upon the cheek) or a *tarkh* (a light incision);

or a *waḥṣ* or a *'udd* or a *ẓibẓāb* (the *waḥṣ* is 'the eruption that comes out on a pretty girl's face' and *ẓibẓāb* are 'eruptions on the faces of pretty girls; synonym *'udd*');

and this face might include also front teeth that are *munaṣṣab*, with *shanab*, *ratal*, and *ḥabab* (front teeth that are *munaṣṣab* are those that 'grow straight'; *shanab* is 'a fluid, or a softness, or a coolness, or a sweetness, on the teeth,' or 'spots of whiteness thereon,' or 'the canines being so sharp that they look like a saw' (synonym *gharb*); *ratal* is 'whiteness of the teeth and their extreme moistness' and *ḥabab* is 'even spacing of the teeth, and the fluid that passes over them making them look like pieces of glass),'

or a gap between the incisors caused by the milk, with *ushur* and *washr* (the *ushur* of teeth, or of a woman, are 'the file-marks on them that are either caused by nature or deliberately—one says, "the woman filed (*asharat* or *ash-sharat*) her teeth"'; *washr* is 'a woman's sharpening and pointing her teeth'),

or the owner of this face might have a *ʿitrah* in love with which has fallen a *ʿitrah* (the first *ʿitrah* is 'the file-marks on the teeth and the precision with which they are sharpened,' and 'purity,' and 'a fluid that runs over [the teeth],' and 'sweet saliva'; the second is 'a man's offspring and his people and clan, consisting of his closer relations, both the living and the dead,'

or on her chin there might be a cleft that seeks protection in Sūrat Nūn,[449]

or her lip might be 'moist,' or 'red shading into black,' or *nakiʿah*, or have 'a blackness of gum and lip' or a 'dryness' or honey might ooze from it copiously, or she might have a *thurmulah* that heals love-sickness (a *thurmulah* is 'the depression that is on the outer part of the upper lip'; lips that are *nakiʿah* are 'bright red'),

or her *ṭurmah* might contain *ṭirm* (a *ṭurmah* is 'a swelling in the middle of the upper lip' and *ṭirm* is 'honeycomb, butter, or honey'),

2.4.8 or she might have a *turfah* more appetizing than any *turfah* (a *turfah* is 'a raised thing in the middle part of the upper lip (a congenital feature),' and it also means 'tasty food' and 'something nice that you give only to your friend'),

or she might have a *ʿurʿurah* besides which would pale the blaze on a horse's face (the *ʿurʿurah* is what is between the nostrils), or a *khawramah* that would make the scent of the *khurramah* yet sweeter (the *khawramah* is 'the most forward part of the nose, or what is between the nostrils,' and *khurramah* is the unit noun from *khurram,* which is 'a plant like the black-eyed pea, violet in color, to smell and behold which brings such great joy that any who sees a person holding it falls in love with him; an ointment is made from its flowers that is good for the ailments mentioned'),

or a *nathrah* before which vast sums might be scattered (*tunthar*) (the *nathrah* is 'the nostril and the parts close to it, or the parting between the two wings of the mustache, in front of the septum'),

or her *marāʿif* have a *ghafr* that would repulse the most courageous (the *marāʿif* are 'the nose and its surroundings' and the *ghafr* is 'the nap on a garment'),

or she might have a *khunʿubah* that would stiffen rotten bones (the *khunʿubah* is the 'philtrum, or thing that is suspended in the middle of the upper lip, or the interstice between the two wings of the mustache, in front of the septum; also occurs as *khubnuʿah*'),

or a *ʿartabah* fit to cure the stricken heart (the *ʿartabah* is 'the nose, or the soft parts thereof, or the circle in the middle of the lip, or the end of the septum'),

or a *ʿartamah* that is an expression of beauty (the *ʿartamah* is 'the foremost part of the nose, or what is between the latter and the septum, or the circle in the middle of the upper lip' (synonym *harthamah*),

or she might have on her *malāmiẓ* and her *malāghim* a *lagham* fit to expel *grief* and bring to sorrow *relief* (the *malāmiẓ* are 'the parts around the two lips' and the *malāghim* are 'the parts around the mouth' (synonym *malāmij*) and *lagham* is 'a little perfume'), or it might be that she has a *nabrah* that is the acme of *naḍrah* (the *nabrah* is 'the central part of the depression in the visible part of the lip' and *naḍrah* is 'beauty'),

or a *tufrah* to bend his head over which is to prolong his moans (the *tufrah*, or *tafrah*, or *tifrah*, is 'the depression in the middle of the upper lip'),

2.4.9 or a *ḥithrimah* that leaves hearts infatuated (the *ḥithrimah* is 'the circle that is beneath the nose in the center of the upper lip' or 'the tip of the nose or its end'),

or a *watīrah* worthy to be ransomed for a thousand buxom and willing lasses (the *watīrah* is 'the partition between the two nostrils'),

or a *khayshūm* that would cure blindness or cool *wamah* (the *khayshūm* is 'the part of the nose above its front end starting from the bony part and the nasal gristle that lies beneath it' and *wamah* means 'extreme heat'),

or a *qasāmah* on which the lover swears his oaths (*qasāmah* is 'beauty, and the face . . . or the nose and its two sides, or the middle of the nose' etc.),

or a *dhalaf* that would cure illness (*dhalaf* is 'smallness of the nose and straightness of the tip of the nose, or its being small and fine, or a thickness of the nose and a straightness at its end without a thick edge'),

or a *khanas* before which the *khunnas* set (*khanas* is 'having a *retroussé* nose with a slight upward tilt to its tip, a woman with such a nose being called *khansā'*,' and the *khunnas* are 'all stars, or the planets'),

or her nose might be *muṣfaḥ* (a *muṣfaḥ* nose is one that has a straight bridge);

or *ashamm* (being *ashamm* means 'having the bridge of the nose elevated and handsome with a straight upper part and erectness of the tip'),

or it might be possessed of *qanā* (*qanā* of the nose is 'elevation of its upper part, crookedness of its middle, and length and fullness of its end, or prominence of the middle of the bridge and narrowness of the nostrils; a male with these characteristics is said to be *aqnā*, a female *qanyā*"),

or it might have two *ghurḍ*s fit to distract one from *taghrīḍ* and silver (the *ghurḍ* of the nose is the part that slopes down from the bridge on either side,' and *taghrīḍ* is 'eating fresh (*gharīḍ*) meat, and making merry');

or this girl might have *nāẓir*s for which we would give our eyes in ransom (the *nāẓir*s are 'two veins on either side of the nose'), 2.4.10

or *nāḥirah*s for which we would trample upon our upper chests and eyes (the *nāḥirah*s are 'two veins in the jawbone and two of the ribs of the chest, or they are the two short ribs, or the collar bones'),

or a *ḥāfizah* fit to relieve a heart that's oppressed and over which the poet's mouth would *yatalaḥḥaz* (the *ḥāfizah* is 'the fold in the corner of the mouth' and *yatalaḥḥaz* means 'to drool (of the mouth) from eating a sour pomegranate or the like because you find it so delicious (synonym *yatalazzaḥ*))';

or it might be that hearts would hover over her *khinnābah*s (the *khinnābah*s are 'the sides of the nose');

or that this girl would have *ṣāmigh*s to delight the heart and quench the *ghayn* (the *ṣāmigh*s, or *ṣamāgh*s, or *ṣamgh*s, are 'the sides of the mouth, meaning the place where the lips meet next to the corner of the mouth' (variant: the *sāmigh*s)); *ghayn* means 'thirst.'" (I would love to know whether they are so called because honeycomb forms at them, and whether they are pressed close together or parted, and whether the poor poet drools over the thought of them as he drooled over the *ḥāfizah*s, but God alone knows.)

Then the mind continues, saying, 2.4.11

"Or she might have a *ḥutrah* his love for which is prolonged by his *ḥatr* (the *ḥutrah* is 'the place where the corners of the mouth meet' and *ḥatr* is 'fixing of the gaze'" (and wouldn't he just be drooling?!),

or *māḍighs* with which one might take refuge against 'the eye' (the *māḍighs* are 'the points at which the jawbones start, at the place where the molars sprout'),

or a *ghunbah* that would *tuhannid* the fancy-free for a *sanbah* (*ghunbah*, according to the *Qāmūs*, is the singular of *ghunab*, which are 'circles in the center of the corners of the mouths of pretty boys,' though I have decided that our veiled lady has the better claim to them, so let there be no *protestation* or *negotiation* over this *appropriation*; *tuhannid* means 'entice' or 'cause to yearn' and a *sanbah* is 'an age');

and perhaps her *ʿāriḍ* will send her lover insane with desire (the *ʿāriḍ* is 'the flat of the cheek' or 'the side of the face'),

or it may be that she has a *ʿilāṭ* to bewitch the *niyāṭ* of any who see her (the *ʿilāṭ* is 'the flat of the neck' and the *niyāṭ* is 'the heart'),

or a *buldah* that would enchant the people of a *baldah* (a *buldah* is a 'freedom from hair of the space between the eyebrows' or 'the pit between the two collar-bones, with the part around it, or the middle thereof' [and a *baldah* is 'a town']),

or *maḥājir* for which *maḥājir* might be sold (the *miḥjar* of the eye is 'that part of the face, below the eye, that may be seen through the type of veil called the *niqāb*' and the other *maḥājir* are 'the tracts surrounding a town or village'),

or *asārīr* to which one seated upon the bed (*sarīr*) is subservient (the *asārīr* are 'the beautiful features of the face' or 'the cheeks');

or it may be that her *ṭulyah* would cure a *ṭalyāʾ* (the *ṭulyah* is 'the neck, or the place from which it arises' and the *ṭalyāʾ* is 'an ulceration like a bubo'), her *ladīd*s a *ladūd* (the *ladīd*s are 'the sides of the neck below the ears,' and the *ladūd* is 'a pain that affects the mouth and throat'),

and her *lazīz*s a *lazz* (the *lazīz* is 'the point where the flesh comes together above the throat' and *lazz* is 'a piercing'); 2.4.12

or that her *mafāhir* are dearer to the mail-clad knight than *fahīrah* (the *mafāhir* are 'the flesh of the breast' and *fahīrah* is 'pure milk into which heated stones are put; when it boils, flour is sprinkled over it and it is mixed' [and eaten]),

her *sālifah*s remove the need for even the best of *sulāf* (the *sālifah* is 'the side of the forepart of the neck, from the place of the suspension of the earring to the hollow of the collarbone' [and *sulāf* means 'wine']),

her *naḥr* ('throat') puts that of the day to shame (the *naḥr* of the day, or the month, is its beginning);

and her *tarā'ib*s are more to be valued than one's *atrāb* (the *tarā'ib* are 'the bones of the chest' or 'the part immediately following the two collarbones' and the *atrāb* (singular *tirb*) are one's 'coetaneans'; or the latter might also correctly be read as *itrāb*, a verbal noun, in the sense 'the man experienced *itrāb*,' meaning 'his wealth increased,' in which case the speaker would have to be asked which meaning he intended),"

and so on, to include other possibilities that the man of insight and sound judgment will agree are necessary; I have prolonged my words here simply because I am copying them from one who looked deep into every veiled face(t)[450] and found himself, to his surprise, so stricken, that his mouth flowed with ropy saliva.

In the end, the point I'm trying to make is that a man who has slept with a woman wrapped up with her in a single undergarment but hasn't seen her as did Our Master Ya'qūb,[451] peace be upon him, has suffered the same fate as our friend with all his maybes and ifs and buts.

2.4.13 Someone ought now to say, "The matter is the opposite of what's been *proposed* when we speak of a woman fully *clothed*, for if a man's glance falls upon her when she's decently covered, his imagination will take him no further than a certain point. It's different, however, if she is naked. Then the imagination and the heart, on beholding her, will fly toward her, stopping at nothing, for the imagination will picture certain things, while the heart will desire yet others." Then the defender of the original proposition should respond by saying, "This is simply a result of the face-body *differential*, for the body, being larger, brings the imagination flying to it and holds the heart hovering over it by a process *consequential*."

2.4.14 One party, among them Professors Amorato, Gropius, Randinski, and Copulatius,[452] have asserted that it is not the body's size per se that is responsible in such cases for any flying or hovering, for even if only one part of it were visible it would be enough and the issue therefore remains unresolved. To this the response should be that their argument consists simply of stating that a body is a body and a face a face, which shows that the assertion is ridiculous because it is a tautology. Others have claimed that the reason that the face is more arousing than the body is that the face is a locus for most of the senses, for it contains the repositories of smell, taste, and sight, with that of hearing close by. A second party, among them Professors Killjoy, Ejaculatio-Prematore, and Impotenza, has accepted this, but rejoinder has been made that these senses have no bearing here, for what is meant by "essence of woman" doesn't depend upon them anyway, so she is in no need of them.

2.4.15 It has also been claimed that the body is *more* arousing than the face because the body contains many different shapes. Thus, there is what is pear-shaped-with-a-long-neck, what is pomegranate-shaped, what is euphorbia-fruit-shaped, what is hoop-shaped, what is ring-shaped, what is dome-shaped, what is pillar-shaped, what is in the shape of a prominent rock, what in is the shape of the letter *ṣād* and what is in the shape of the letter *mīm*,[453] what is in the shape of a set of steps, what is in the shape of a cone, what is in the shape of a crescent, and what is obtusely angled. To this, rejoinder has been made that it is the same argument as that made by those who claim that the body is more attractive because it is larger and may be refuted on the same grounds. It has also been claimed that the body is more exciting precisely because the face, under normal conditions, is revealed, while the body is concealed, and, should a person see anything that violates this norm, his thoughts will be plunged into commotion and his ideas fly in all directions. Other arguments have been made too and God alone knows the truth. It is also quite possible that this rule that I have advanced and retracted so often is incorrect, in which case, I wish I'd ignored it, for by mentioning it I have obliged us to engage in an academic discussion.

In sum, when this veil-passion was laid and hatched in the Fāriyāq's head, the little birdies therein twittered to him that he should get himself a musical instrument, and, in no time at all, he had returned from the market with, under his arm, a small tambour, which he began playing at a window of his room that overlooked the house of a Copt. Now, the Bag-man had a Muslim servant, who had fallen in love with the Copt's daughter, and the tambour made him jealous, so he denounced the Fāriyāq to his master and said, "If the passers by in the street hear the sound of the tambour coming from your house, they will think it's a tavern or an inn or a *thuknah* ('headquarters and gathering place of soldiers under the banner of their commander,' etc.), not a Bag-men's abode, because this instrument is used only by the Turks." The Bag-man thanked him for this, accepted that what he said was true, and instructed the Fāriyāq to get rid of the instrument, which he did, while at the same time starting to think of how he could escape the hands of this band whose bane never ceased to get at him through every window, on island and on mainland. A few days later the servant fled with the girl and he married her, after she had converted to Islam, praise be to God, Lord of the Worlds. 2.4.16

## Chapter 5

# A Description of Cairo[454]

2.5.1 Many an ancient historian toward Cairo has bent his *gaze* and on it hosts of poets past have lavished *praise*, and here now stand I, to describe it and to praise it as did no scholar in former *days*. Thus I declare: Cairo is one metropolis among metropoli, one city among cities, one settlement among settlements, one borough among boroughs, one seat among seats, one town among towns, one citadel among citadels, one village among villages, one urban center among urban centers, one capital among capitals, one locality among localities, one territory among territories, one land among lands, one township among townships, one region among regions, one thing among many things. Its people, though, would say, "It is *the* metropolis among metropoli, *the* city among cities, *the* capital among capitals, *the* thing among all other things" and so on, and I do not know how to account for the difference. However that may be, it is indeed a city replete with permissible pleasures, bursting with boundless appetites, answering to the needs of hot-humored men (contrary to what ʿAbd al-Laṭīf al-Baghdādī has said).[455] There the stranger finds amusement and *accommodation*, in it he forgets family and *nation*.

2.5.2 Among its curiosities[456] is that what leaves the bodies of its men enters the bodies of its women, and the women are therefore as fat as cottage cheese and clarified butter eaten on an empty stomach, while its men are like dry bread with sesame oil eaten on a full. Another is that its markets in no way resemble its men, for its inhabitants are full of refinement, sophistication, literary culture, and wit, qualities pleasing and morals pure, while its markets are utterly without such things. Another is that its water in no way resembles its bread, which they call *ʿaysh*, for the first is sweet while the second is worthless. Another is that its scholars are scholars, its jurisprudents jurisprudents, its poets poets, its profligates profligates, its lechers lechers. Another is that its women walk sometimes on the ground like other women and sometimes on the ceiling or the walls.[457]

Another is the treatment of the feminine as masculine and of 2.5.3
the masculine as feminine,[458] even though its people are masters of scholarship (and what masters too!). Another is that, in their bathhouses, they constantly recite a sura or two of the Qur'an that mention "glasses" and "those who pass around with them," so that one emerges in a state of simultaneous ritual purity and impurity.[459] More amazing still, many of the city's men have no hearts, such men substituting for them two pairs of shoulders, two backs, four hands, and four legs.[460] And further, many of the girls who launder their shifts in the channels of the Nile, make them, once washed, into turbans, which they place on top of their heads; then they walk about stark naked. Another is that a tribe of them once heard that women in China use—or, more accurately, have used upon them—iron forms to reduce the size of their feet to below that of the norm, so they took to lopping off their fingers in the belief that if the hand has only four fingers, it will work more dexterously and be more useful to its owner.[461] This was despite the fact that they have no custom of covering their fingers and palms that would impose additional expense on them, unlike Franks, who leave no limb uncovered, either out of a desire to magnify the glory of those and show them off, or to guard against infection.

In addition to these (to these curiosities, that is, not these limbs), 2.5.4
girls employed in public works to carry bricks, plaster, dirt, mud, stones, lumber, and so on, do so on their heads, and do so joyfully,

energetically, gallopingly, canteringly, cantabulatingly, celebratorily, and merrily, not sighingly, dejectedly, stumblingly, sinkingly, frowningly, or weepily. She to whose lot fall bricks will compose for them a brickish *mawwāl* or, if plaster, will sing to it a plastery song, as though walking in a bridal procession. And further, there are there two great offices, each called the Domestic Services Office. The first is presided over by a man and provides men with whatever they need to cool their beds by way of hes, the second, of lower standing and status, is presided over by a woman and provides them with whatever they need to warm them up by way of shes. The founder of the first is of Persian origin and has now became so well-known and respected among the Arabs that you hear him mentioned with praise everywhere, and hardly a social, musical, or literary gathering is without his presence.

2.5.5 And further, the Frankish bonnet grows there and expands, gets thicker and huger, widens and lengthens and broadens and deepens to the point that, when you see one on its wearer's head, you think it must be a grain silo. Said the Fāriyāq, "I often used to wonder at this and say, 'How came it to be considered right and proper, or seem acceptable to the eye, that heads so misshapen, meager, and *miserable*, so vile and *contemptible*, so ignominious and meet to be *condemned*, so strange and so *ill-omened*, so evocative of filth and so *emetic*, so ugly to look at and so *pathetic*, so disgusting and *repulsive*, despicable and *convulsive*, should bear these most noble bonnets? And how could the air of Cairo have made them develop so and grow, when as long as they were in their own countries they weren't worth a bottle of bubbles or a fountain of frittilaries? And how can it be that there they were like dust, and here they've been metathesized into diamonds? O air, fire, water, dust of Cairo, turn this tarbush of mine into a Frankish bonnet (even if the former be better and of greater *élan* in the sight of God and *man*, more imposing and *correct*, to the eye more brilliant and *perfect*, to the head better *fitted*, to the body better *suited*, not equipped with horns that truckle for *tucker* and that the birds have to shit on if you're to find *succor*)!' But my cry helped not at all—the tarbush was on my head to *stay*, fate had turned to look the other *way*."

2.5.6 And further, a tribe of craving catamites there dress and talk like women and "veil their beards"[462] to keep them out of *sight*, jostling at the watering hole of femininity those who wear such veils by *right*, plucking out their facial hair, making eyes at men, dressing to the *nines*, mincing, tittupping, and speaking in sugary *whines*, though they are the ugliest of God's creatures. And further, the city's police chief is so solicitous of its people's welfare that it amounts almost to tyranny, for he commands everyone who walks its highways by night to have with him a lantern, even if the night is moonlit, out of fear lest they trip over something in one of the city's marketplaces and fall into a hole or a pit and their legs be broken or their necks crushed. If anyone, other than someone wearing a Frankish hat, be found roaming around at night without a lantern in his hand, his foot is shackled to his hand, his hand to his neck, his neck to a rope, the rope to a peg, the peg to a wall, and the wall to Nākir and *Nakīr*, to the roasting of *hellfire*. And further, the Sons of Ḥannā[463] there have a way of writing that is known to none but themselves[464] and have letters like our own but which can be read only if one holds them within an inch of one's face, as I have seen them do. Another is that, when one of them dies, his family wails and keens over him in the hope that he will return to them, his milkskin filled with cured fish fry.[465] A further curiosity of the place is that ignoble birds there may pretend to be mighty eagles,[466] flies hawks, cow-camels bull-camels, donkey foals oryxes, and cats tigers—provided only that these animals have been imported from distant lands.

2.5.7 Further, many of its inhabitants believe that many thoughts in the head lead to many worries and vexations and vice versa, that the mind that ponders at length grasps the distant matter in the same manner that the tall man grasps the distant fruit, etc., that such abundance is a cause of destitution and such prolonged cogitation results in a shorter life. They adduce many pertinent proofs for this, saying that the mind is to the head as the light to the wick: if the light is left burning, the wick will be used up, and the latter can be preserved only if the former is extinguished; or that it's like the water in a water course: if the water keeps flowing, it must inevitably either soak into the ground or empty into the sea, but when it's contained it remains; or like money in a purse: so long as the exiguously monied one (meaning the owner of the money)[467] keeps putting his hand into the purse and spending, what he has will disappear (unless he tie down his hand so it can't reach the purse, or the purse so it can't reach his hand); or like a leaping billy goat: if he keeps on leaping, his vital juices will leak out and he will perish, so that a thong must be tied from his willy to his belly to prevent him from mounting the female.

2.5.8 Consequently, they have agreed among themselves on a method of halting the flow of the mind through the open arena of the brain at certain times so that it will be available to them at others, the method in question being to smoke, chew, contemplate, or talk about, hashish, for when they consume it, care takes off and pleasure *advances*, grief turns its back and the whole place *dances*. Any who sees them in this state longs to be registered among their *company* and entered among their *constituency*, be he even the chief judge. And further, its roads are ever packed with loaded camels, and, if anyone walking them sees one coming, he has to make way; if he doesn't, there's no guarantee he won't lose an eye. This crowding may bring with it good things, as in the case of the woman who went with her mother to attend her sister's wedding: the rise in her fortunes came from her setting herself down.[468]

## Chapter 6

# Nothing

I had thought that, if I abandoned the Fāriyāq and set about describing Cairo, I'd find rest, but the second turned out to be just like the first, or, to put it differently, the *vice* was the same as the *versa*. I must now therefore sit myself down a while in the shade of this short chapter to brush off the dust of my labors. Then I shall arise once more, should the Almighty so allow. 2.6.1

## Chapter 7

# A Description of Cairo

2.7.1 I am risen to my feet once more, praising and thanking God. Now, where are my pen and inkwell, that I may describe this happy city, which deserves the eulogies of all who behold it, for it is the home of good things, the mother-lode of bounty and magnanimity? Its people are refined, cultured, and kind to the *stranger*, and there's such amiability in their speech that the grief-struck of getting any sadder need never be in *danger*. When they *hail* you, they *regale* you. When they *salute* you, they *save* you. After they've visited you, you can't wait to see them once *more*, and when you visit them, they open to you their hearts, to say nothing of their *door*. As for their scholars, praise of them has spread to every *quarter*, leaving the rest dead in the *water*. In fact, their geniality, natural delicacy, modesty, and welcoming mien cannot be over-extolled, while, for every condition of men among them, there is an appropriate respectful salute, be they Christians or others. The latter address the former as "My Master," and have no aversion to visiting them, mixing with them, or keeping company with them, in contrast with the custom of the Muslims of the Levant, and this a virtue to be credited to their account as against others.

2.7.2 It seems that these traits, of high moral character and natural delicacy, are things ingrained in all the people of Cairo, for their common folk too are good-natured and courteous. All of them are eloquent and articulate, quick-thinking and good at pleasant joking and joshing. Most have a liking for the kind of jokes they call *anqāṭ*, which are something like *mujārazah*, which is "a kind of joking back and forth that resembles mutual abuse,"[469] and are almost a kind of puzzle, for anyone not trained in them will find it impossible to understand the slightest thing about them, even if he's a poet.

All of them love music, amusements, and license, and their singing is the most tuneful possible; anyone who gets used to it finds that no other can move him. Similarly, their instruments seem almost to give tongue to the one who plays them, the most important being the lute, while they pay scant attention to the reed flute. They have methods and styles of playing the lute that seem almost to belong to the world of the divine mysteries. I would criticize their singing for one thing only, which is that they repeat a single word of a line of verse or a *mawwāl* so many times that the listener loses the pleasure of the meaning. However, this is mostly to be found among those who merely sponge off the art. At the opposite pole you have the method of the people of Tunis, whose singing is closer to chant; they claim that this was the way of the Arabs of al-Andalus. 2.7.3

It has to be stated here that the Christians native to the Islamic lands, who follow the Muslims in their customs and morality, are always inferior to them in the chasteness of their language, in literature, in aesthetics, in intelligence, in sophistication, and in cleanliness. They are, however, more active than them in travel, trading, and manufacturing, and bolder and more steadfast in taking on difficult tasks. This is because Muslims are a nation of self-denial and *abnegation* while Christians have an insatiable appetite for territorial *expansion*, not to mention the acquisition of pure-bred horses, precious gems, and luxury goods. If you enter the house of a wealthy Christian in Cairo, you'll find he has both serving women and serving men, around twenty tobacco pipes of the most expensive kind (half of them valuable waterpipes), three rooms upholstered in the best materials, silver vessels for eating and drinking, along with smooth, high beds, luxurious clothes, and so forth, and yet, for all 2.7.4

that, not a single book. Also, if someone wants to buy something from a Muslim trader, he'll find it costs him twenty-five percent less than the Christian's goods. This avarice is, however, found, for the most part, only among foreign Christians. The Copts are more like the Muslims, and few of them practice trade.

2.7.5 As far as the Egyptian state is concerned, it had reached in those days a peak of splendor, strength, magnificence, munificence, and glory. Those inducted into its service enjoyed a huge salary in the form of money, clothing, and provisions, more than was customary in any other state. Its viceroy[470] awarded high rank and tokens of imperial favor to Muslim and Christian alike, though not to Jews, in which Egypt differed from the Tunisian state, whose honors fell on all men equally.[471] Despite the large amounts earned by both merchants and craftsmen and the generous livings obtained by the servants of the state, prices in Cairo were exceedingly low, and, as a result, one might observe everyone, members of the elite and commoners, engaging together in work and play. The gardens overflowed with pleasure-seekers and revelers. The cafés were meeting places for friends. At the weddings, singing and musical instruments of every kind might be heard. The men swaggered in silk-wool and brocade, the women staggered under the weight of their jewelry. The horses, mules, and donkeys wore saddles and saddle-coths of embroidered silk. Any land blessed by fortune, however—if our friend the Fāriyāq ever entered it—inevitably changed for the worse before he exited it. Return, then, with me now so that we can release him from the hands of the Bag-men, for I left him a while ago engaged in trying to do just that.

## Chapter 8

# Notice that the Description of Cairo is Ended

We—that is, all my good friends and I—had left the Fāriyāq trying to shake the Bag-men's bag off his back. Now I, to the exclusion of the others, have come to know that he spent a night pondering the fact that everything that skill may set firmly in place external factors will shake to the core, and, this being the case, he decided to take the shaking business into his own hands. When morning came, he left the place where he'd been playing and started to wander through the markets, shaking his shoulders with every step and saying, "I shall turn him upside down! I shall give him the *push*! I shall send him back to where he came from! I shall beat him to *mush*! He has broken, meaning galled, meaning chafed, my back. Am I become today no better than one *ass* owned by another? A pretty *pass*!" 2.8.1

A man of some sophistication observed him shaking his shoulders and said to himself, "There is something afoot with this man" and approached him and spoke politely to him, finally extracting his secret from his *navel*, and learning his condition and the reason for his *travel*. "Never mind," he told him. "Cairo—God protect it!—is the mother-lode of good things and *benefaction*, though to win them you will have to take *action*." "What greater action can I undertake than what you observe?" he asked. "There's no call for such things," the other replied. "Have you a ready ear, a clever *mind*, 2.8.2

a foot to effort *inclined*?" "I have," he said. "Then listen while I tell you," said the other.

2.8.3 "In this metropolis is a poet of great skill,[472] a Christian, who has influence and standing with the whole elite." Said the other, "These aren't the characteristics of a poet, and to me your words appear an oxymoron. How can this riddle be solved, this puzzle explained?" The other replied, "There is no contradiction: he's a poet by nature, not by trade, the difference being that the poet by trade is one who depends on his verse to make his living; thus he eulogizes this one and flatters that in order to get something from them. The poet by nature, on the other hand, speaks poetry because he cannot help himself—without having to force himself or in expectation of reward." "That's not the difference mentioned by al-Āmidī,"[473] said the Fāriyāq. "Then scoot al-Āmidī back to Āmid[474] and listen to me," said the other. "Voilà! I've *a-i-m-(e)-d* him and scooted him," he said, "so what's the scoop?" "I advise you to write a letter to this scholarly man and beg him, through the deployment of your praise, for an audience. If he is kind enough to grant this, use the occasion to tell him of your sufferings and seek his help. He is certain to say yes, for he is known for his noble morals and loves the titillation of high self-esteem. Your chances are especially good, because he loves to keep company with literary types and make their lives more comfortable. Speak to him courteously, and I guarantee you'll realize your hopes through him." The Fāriyāq thanked the man for his advice and returned to his lodging comforted and expecting the best.

2.8.4 When night came, he took his pen and paper and wrote the following:

> A greeting I send that, if 'twere carried on the breeze, the horizon with perfume would *freight* and if 'twere made a halo for the moon, would save the latter from its monthly *fate*; if 'twere added to the tawny wine, would cause no headache to follow its *potation* and if 'twere swallowed or licked by a sick man, would cause him

no fever or *excruciation*; if 'twere hung upon a tree, though the season were autumn, would make its leaves straightway burst *out* and if 'twere used to water gardens, would make each charming and delightful flower *sprout*; if 'twere laid o'er the strings of a lute, would have them induce ecstasy without need of any agent *instrumental* and if at a gathering 'twere sung, would render all sweet-smelling plants and instruments purely *incidental*; if 'twere hung in the ear as a *pendant*, it would be one of those that, being from its upper rim *dependent*, are the more clearly *seen* and, if 'twere used to whet the dulled sword's edge, would make it *keen*; if 'twere portrayed, would be as blooming gardens and meadows of that *ilk* and soothing liquids and purest *milk* and if 'twere suspended from one's *head-dress*, would render amulets *superfl'ous*; if 'twere worn as a ring by one by passion *misled*, would serve him in oblivion's *stead* and if 'twere written on a *tombstone*, would distract the grieving mother from making *moan*, or on the waist of a slender *lass*, would take the place of a *sash*, or on the nose of one with a *rheum*, for nose drops would leave no *room*, or on a cripple's *feet*, would make him hop ahead and all others in the race to the wellhead *beat*, or on a dumb man's *tongue*, would cause the knot therein to come *undone*, or on a miser's *hand*, would make it easier for him his gold and silver to *spend*, or on brackish water, would make it sweet at just one *go*, or on sand, would cause it to make even basil *grow*; plus salutations *ornamented*, sweet-smelling and *scented*, softer than the *breeze*, sweeter than heaven's *mead*, than good health for the sick a more sought-after *goal*, more brightening for the eye than *kohl*, dearer to the assayer than purest *gold*, clearer than sweetest water fresh and *cold*, dearer to the heart than hope of the beloved's *arms*, more distracting than a coquette's *charms*, brighter than the light of *morn*, more brilliant than the anemone's *bloom*, more fragrant than wine's *aromas*, more closely guarded than *tiaras*, dearer to al-Bustī than *paronomasias*,[475] to Abū l-ʿAtāhiyah[476] than ascetic *verse*, to Abū Nuwās[477] than poems about wine (and *worse*), to al-Farazdaq[478] than *panegyrics*, to Jarīr[479] than *lyrics*, to Abū Tammām[480] than *sagacity*, to al-Mutanabbī[481] than poems demonstrating rhetorical *capacity*— to be presented to that honored *person* of respected *station* who is the resort of the *depressed*, object of the entreaties of the *oppressed*, protector of those who've suffered *wrong*, refuge of the victims of the *strong*, watering hole of those who aspire to his *attention*, wellspring of those who seek his *intervention*, may God preserve his good fortune for ever and a *day*, and never let his glory fade *away*!

2.8.5 To proceed: Master, I am come to these territories bearing a bag that has broken my *back* and in my patience made a *crack*, and I have found none to relieve me of even a little of the *encumbrance* and can see no way to rid myself of it without *assistance*. In the midst of this inky darkness I have been guided to your kindly *light*, informed that you alone, to the exclusion of any other *wight*, can free me from my *plight*. Will you then permit me to visit your noble circle and to you myself *unburden* of that from which I endlessly suffer, and of my dolorous hurt, in *person*? On you alone can I *rely* to take the hand of one without *ally*, knowing that, should you but look on him with favor, you'll make his wishes come *true* and help him obtain all he has in *view*, and should you take him to yourself, he will thenceforth owe you a debt of *gratitude* and of thankfulness for your pious *attitude*. Such a one thus asks this of you as a petitioner in the forecourt of your *dignity*, and your willingness to oblige will be but further token of your kindness and far-reaching *benignity*. Farewell.

For the address he wrote:

To be honored by the fingertips of my most generous, most nobly descended, most imposing, most unique, most bountiful, most fortunate, most exemplary, most well-guided, most complete, most glorious, most sublime master, Khawājā So-and-so, may God preserve him for ever in splendor and ease!

2.8.6 When this message reached the *khawājā* in question and the latter perused the affected similes employed in the elaboration of the greeting, he couldn't contain his laughter and guffaws and said to one of those seated with him in his salon, a man of culture, "Glory be! I find that most of our writers abandon themselves in their presentation of greetings and salutations to the addressee as unrestrainedly as if they were presenting him with the throne of Bilqīs or Our Master Sulaymān's ring,[482] comparing him to things he doesn't resemble, drowning him in immoderate praise, and boiling him over the fires of excess, with the result that he ends up soaked and singed. Sometimes they come up with two phrases that are identical in meaning, such as when the writer of this epistle here says 'object of the entreaties of the oppressed, protector of those who've suffered wrong.' Then, as soon as they move from salutation to content, they write excellently. I don't know why the writers of compositions have thought good to waste their time on such hackneyed metaphors and similes and on composing phrases of identical sense, when the scholar can, with ease, demonstrate his erudition in a single phrase if it's well worded and effective at conveying the meaning. Twelve hundred years have passed, and we still find Zayd chewing over what ʿAmr[483] uttered and ʿAmr masticating what Zayd said. This vice has entered the veins of every writer.

"When it comes to eulogizing the addressee in the address with 'the most sublime,' 'the most glorious,' 'the most fortunate,' 'the most exemplary,' and the like, there is a particular issue. The custom of delivering the mail via the postal service is not observed in our country; it is sent with persons who have no knowledge of the roads or the neighborhoods, which, as you will be aware, are innocent of any written signs. If the letter is borne by a man who doesn't know how to read, he will ask everyone he meets on the road about the addressee by name. If the address doesn't give a clue as to who he is, any who read it will be confused, for many share the same name, though they may differ in fine qualities and morals. In addition, it may happen that the one who is to deliver the letter, after asking more one than one person the name of the addressee and finding all of them to be illiterate and having wasted half his day searching for the way and and after failing in the end to be guided to it, finds a servant in the street watching him. As soon as he sees him, then, he seizes hold of him and sends him off in some direction he thinks 2.8.7

correct. The letter stays with the new messenger for a while, and then he passes it on to someone else, and that someone else may face the same problems he did and so pass it on to another, etc., etc. One should therefore go into great detail when describing the addressee in the address."

2.8.8 His companion then said, "In that case, dear sir, all the addressee's characteristics should be mentioned in the address. If the addressee is, for instance, beautiful, intelligent, rich, shapely, of large turban, and broadly cummerbunded, he must be referred to as 'the beautiful, the intelligent, the rich,' etc." Responded the other, "As far as describing someone as beautiful, rich, and so on is concerned, to do so is a grave offense against him,[484] and as far as the rest, such as the size of his turban and the breadth of his cummerbund, is concerned, these are non-specific characteristics, for everyone's on the same footing in such matters. How much more appropriate it is to employ other forms of address, as you will soon see, God willing. Such other forms may on occasion make one laugh—as when one describes a man as being characterized, for example, by hypertrichotism, or hirsutism, or triticoidism, or hypermetacarpalism, or superrhysism, or partial hirsutism, or pyknism, or ectomorphism, or mesomorphism, or endomorphism, or somatomegalism, or exophthalmism, or planirostrism, or glabrotism, or acromegalism, or macrocephalism, or macrolabialism—but are better than others that create confusion over the addressee's distinguishing features. I'm told that many letters containing important messages that don't spell out the address explicitly and don't have directions have been opened so as to discover for whom they're intended, and this has been a cause of injury to both sender and recipient." Here ends their dialogue.

2.8.9 Be informed here that, when the the *khawājā* in question received the Fāriyāq's epistle, he was sick and so did not answer immediately. As a result, the Fāriyāq was left waiting days for his reply and finally came to believe, being unaware, as he was, of the reason, that all his rhyming had gone for nought, and during this time he was prey to constant worry and anxiety. I shall leave him now in that state, waiting for an answer, and leave too the one who is to send it to take his medicine and get better, and turn aside for a little to the ranks of titles and titles of rank then recognized, on condition that you allow me to move on to a new chapter, namely . . .

## Chapter 9

# That to Which I Have Alluded

2.9.1 The definition of a title in the minds of Orientals is that it is an insignificant fleshy protuberance or a flap of skin,[485] or an extra bag hung onto an already loaded camel, that dangles from a man's essential being. The author of the *Qāmūs* has said, "'*alāqā* means 'titles,' because they are hung onto people (*li-annahā tuʿallaqu ʿalā l-nās*)." To Occidentals, which is to say Franks, it is a second skin that wraps itself around the body. Our commentary on this is that an insignificant protuberance may be cut off and totally excised with ease, and the same goes for the skin tag and the extra bag, which may be overturned or inverted; the second skin, however, cannot be removed from the body without harm to its owner. Our super-commentary—for every commentary must have a super-commentary, however incomprehensible—is that the skin flap is not hereditary among the people of the East, or only rarely so (and every rule must have its exceptions). Among Franks, on the other hand, the second skin is passed from older to younger by inheritance. Examples of the former are the titles *Bāshā* ("Pasha"), *Bēh* ("Bey"), *Afandī* ("Effendi"), and *Aghā* ("Agha"). Even *Malik* ("King") is limited in its application to the person so titled and is not extrapolated from him to his son, for the son of a minister or a king may be a clerk or a sailor. Among Franks, however, it is incorrect to refer to the son of a marquis as a "marquisito" or as being "marquisate."[486] Regardless of the fact that the former is finite and the latter infinite, the essential meanings of "skin flap" and "second skin" may converge at a certain point, in that both generally have their origin in an itch that affects the bodies of those in positions of power because of the aggravation caused them by their blood. Such aggravation cannot be quieted, and such itches cannot be scratched, without creating either a flap or a second skin.

The archetype of this would be a king getting angry, for example, with some man or other for an offense he had committed, that man sending him a naked intercessor to placate him, this intercession soothing the eruption of the king's anger, the aggravational modality then combining with the gymnological quiddity, these two forming a second skin around the one who'd been in fear of losing his first skin through flaying, and he thenceforth flaunting this among his peers as a permanent adornment, never again to fear that fate might one day turn on him and gore him. In general, such second skins require two bodies—a body with which someone is angry and a body interceding on the former's behalf—while, in general, the insignificant protuberance requires just one. 2.9.2

One kind of insignificant protuberance is the ecclesiastical, which is of two sorts, the earth-bound and the air-borne. The earth-bound is that which has an abode or place of origin in the earth where it grows and bears fruit; such would be the case, for example, of some "catholicos" abiding in a house or a monastery who has authority over the people, who send him tithes and the like and whom he therefore commands, forbids, rules, and judges according to the requirements of the law, or whim. He is bound to have a secretary to keep his secrets off the *books*, to stiffen his backbone one or more *cooks*, a treasurer to hoard his golden *dinars*, a jail to hold anyone who differs from him in opinion or his ambitions *bars*, and so forth. The air-borne is the opposite of the preceding, an example being the protuberance borne by Metropolitan Atanāsiyūs al-Tutūnjī, 2.9.3

author of *The Leavings Pile Concerning Lame Style*,[487] whose master has invested him with it so that he can use it to rule over Levantine Tripoli, even though there are none of his sect in that city to send him his tithes, make him his food, or write a letter for him; he has been invested with it, it follows, simply for decorative purposes, in keeping with the custom of certain ancients, who would give the protuberance of "emir" to one who raised donkeys and "king" to the shaykh of some benighted village. The object of all this is to set one individual apart from the rest by the use of some distinguishing mark.

2.9.4 Now that you have become aware of this, know too that the titles *Khawājā*, *Muʿallim*, and *Shaykh* are not to be considered either protuberances or second skins, because obtaining them calls neither for intercession nor for any pruritic combining with gymnological quiddities.[488] They are merely rags to cover the shame of the naked name that has been given its bearer and are neither stitched, tacked, buttoned onto, or wrapped around it. In fact, they are more like a ticket tied onto the one wearing it to show his value. Frequently, however, the mistake is made of attaching them to persons to whom they have no connection. Thus in Egypt, for example, they apply the word *Muʿallim* to Coptic Christians, who are neither *muʿallim* nor *muʿallam*, if we are to derive the word from *ʿilm* ("knowledge"),[489] though if we are to derive it from *ʿalāmah* ("mark"), there can be no objection. They apply the term *Khawājā* to others too,[490] and as its original meaning is the same as that of *Muʿallim*, the same objection holds true. The word *shaykh* appertained originally to one who had reached old age; then it was applied to someone who had advanced in learning and other things, as a figurative extension of advancement in years, for the minds of the elderly are discriminating and their judgment is sound, even if women will have no more to do with them. This distinguishing characteristic was then transferred to those who engage in scholarly pursuits.

After pondering the matter, it seems to me that these protuberances and skin flaps do great injury both to those whom they adorn and those who are devoid of them. The first argument in support of this is that a person who bears one believes, in the depths of his heart, that he is better than others, physically and morally. Thus, he looks at the other as a ram with horns does at one without and contents himself with this external feature instead of seeking to attain praiseworthy qualities and meritorious inner traits, and this allows it to lead him in the direction of moral torpor and vicious pleasure. The second is that, should Saturn's noose get caught round his neck one day and drag him into the orbit of its adversities, if he fails to find a woman with a second skin like his, he'll be unable to withstand those adversities with any other; and it may happen that he fall in love with a beautiful serving girl who works in his house, in the kitchen or the stable, and his father, or his father-in-law, or his other relatives, or his emir, may tell him to have nothing to do with her, in which case beautiful girls will be left high and dry, which is regarded by Islamic law as reprehensible—nay, the scholars have all asserted authoritatively that it is absolutely forbidden. 2.9.5

The third is that it might happen that he marry a woman with a second skin who is as badly off as he and not well-heeled. Then, if she bears him children, he will lack the means to bring them a shaykh to teach them at home and he'll be too embarrassed to send them to the local school to learn along with everyone else's. Should this be the case, his children will grow up unlettered, and the process will repeat itself with their offspring for as long as God wills. The fourth is that both protuberance and second skin impose upon those who bear them devastating expenses and catastrophic costs, driving their owner to excessive outlay and *profligacy*, to collapse and imminent *bankruptcy*, which may even lead him, in the end, to the noose of a palm-fiber rope. The fifth is that humans in their native state have neither protuberance nor second skin and to add 2.9.6

them at a later stage is contrary to nature, or at least a form of meddling or recklessness. Other arguments exist, but I have decided not to mention them here for fear of going on too long. At least it must be clear to you by now that the Khawājā in question was possessed of neither protuberance nor second skin, though perhaps, had it not been for his natural inclination toward poetry, he might have acquired one or the other. But everything has its drawbacks.

## Chapter 10

# A Doctor

May God relieve you—or shrive you or deceive you,[491] following those who read *ṣirāṭ* or *sirāṭ* or *zirāṭ* or those who say "Demand the choicest of camels as your ransom!" and read the last word as either *buṣāq* or *busāq* or *buzāq*—of your sickness, Khawājā Yanṣur! You left the Fāriyāq in a state of unease and *apprehension,* waiting for an answer from you, morning and evening, in a state of *tension.* Replied the poet, "It grieves me greatly that your friend's letter should have reached me while I was feverish and had a headache, thus preventing me from responding quickly. I would have liked to do so, despite my sufferings, had not the doctor, envoy of 'Azrā'īl,[492] forbidden me to move. But you must hear the story of what happened to me with that cuckold. 2.10.1

"One day, I got indigestion from eating bulgur that I'd bolted down, lock, stock, and barrel, so that the next day I was ill and nauseous. It so happened that I was visited that morning by one of those emirs to whom, when they insist that something is thus and so, you have to say 'Yes' instead of 'No' and when they insist that it isn't, you have to say 'No' instead of 'Yes.' Seeing me in that state, he asked, 'What ails you?' so I told him what had happened. 'You must let my doctor see you right away,' said he. 'He is the most skillful of all doctors because he just arrived from Paris a few days ago. Were it not so, I wouldn't have taken him on as a physician for me and my family.' 'It is my custom,' I said, 'to endure minor illnesses for a 2.10.2

few days, and seek to cure them through dieting and precaution, for this may render medicines unnecessary. I find that doctors treat illnesses by conjecture and guesswork, and, by the time they arrive at cause and effect, one's soul is almost coming out of one's gullet, for they try one medication this time and another the next.'

2.10.3 "'If the disease hadn't already got to you,' he replied, 'you wouldn't be talking this way. We must bring him now,' and he kept on at me until, shame-faced and embarrassed, I sent my servant to him. Then it occurred to me that, among us, a host, from an excessive sense of hospitality, may force a guest to eat and even sometimes feed him with his own hand something the other cannot stomach but that I'd never heard of anyone doing the honors by forcing another to take medical treatment, so I couldn't stop myself from laughing. 'What's making you laugh?' he asked. 'Nothing,' I responded. 'No one laughs at nothing,' he said. 'There must be something going on.' I said, 'I thought of the doctor who visited a sick man and said to his family, "God recompense you for your loss!" "He isn't dead yet," they replied. "He will be soon, God willing," said the doctor, so I laughed.' 'Don't worry about it,' said the emir. 'This doctor isn't like that one, and anyway you're a bachelor and don't have any family he could say that to.'

2.10.4 "Presently, the servant came back with the doctor, who was sicker and thinner than me, for it seems he had no work that would take him out of the house. When he entered, he felt my pulse and looked at my tongue. Then he furrowed his brows and looked down at the ground, soliloquizing (which means 'talking to himself'). Next he raised his head and told my servant, 'Bring the basin.' 'What do you want to do?' I asked. 'It's my body. Shouldn't you consult me?' 'Either I bleed you or it's the tomb,' he said. 'God guide you aright, old man!' I said. 'All I did was eat bulgur with meat—what people call *kubaybah*.' 'I know that,' he said, 'I know. You Levantines—you all die of eating that *kubbah* stuff.[493] I must have buried a hundred cases when I was in your country. It's definitely the *kubbah*.' 'A *kubbah* up your patootie, God willing!' I said. 'There's no *kubbah* whatsoever in my patties!' he replied.[494] I turned to the emir and laughed, but, as far as I could tell, he didn't get it either.

"To keep it brief, he and the emir kept on finding fault with my opinion until I surrendered myself to destruction and put out my hand, and he worked away at it with his scalpel like someone cutting a watermelon with a knife and out came the blood, spurting everywhere, some of it even getting into his eyes, which made him let go of my hand and go off to wash his face. When he returned after a short while, I had fainted, so my servant ministered to me with orange-blossom water and other things, while the emir gazed at the smoke made by his tobacco and the doctor whispered in his ear. When I revived, he bandaged my hand and left with the emir, the two of them telling me to look after myself and that they'd come and visit me soon, while I said, under my breath, 'May God never bring you back!' 2.10.5

"Next day, the doctor returned with an armful of medicinal plants. 'What are those plants for?' I asked. 'An enema,' he replied. 'One will be enough for me,' I said. He replied, 'The emir says you have to take enemas, if not for your sake, then to do him honor.' 'There's no harm in honoring him with an enema,' I thought to myself, 'but once again he's going against custom, which is that the person visited should adjure the visitor by the name of God and the names of His angels, His apostles, His books, and the Last Day and the Resurrection, to take something to eat or drink for his sake, but here it's the visitor, and he's insisting on flushing me out!' Then I took the enema. The next day, he showed up again, carrying a small pot. 'What's that in your hand?' I asked. 'A laxative,' he replied, 'of the kind I make specially for the emir.' So I swallowed it down. 2.10.6

"Then the following day he came to me carrying nothing, so I rejoiced and told him, 'The laxative was so powerful it's drained me of all my strength.' 'Today,' he replied, 'you have to take the hottest bath possible, so that you sweat. I have tried it before on the emir's family and found it to be most beneficial.' He undertook to heat the water himself and made me get into a bathing tub that I'd bought. When 2.10.7

I got in, the heat struck me with such force that I fainted, though it had time to scald my skin first. I was pulled out at my last gasp, and my servant ministered to me with pungent herbs until I recovered.

2.10.8 "The day after that he came to me carrying nothing, and I was again delighted and thought, 'Maybe he's exhausted his box of tricks and the bath was the last thing he had up his sleeve.' He asked me how I was. 'As you see,' I responded. 'Sick?' he said. 'Sick indeed,' I answered. 'You have to be bled,' he said, his words falling on my ears like 'a rugged boulder hurled from on high by the torrent'[495] and I said, 'It seems you're going back to what you began with. When will this cycle end?' He replied, 'One of these *giaours* (plural of *cure*)[496] is bound to get rid of what you have.' 'That's true,' I said. 'As for the first named, that's you, and as for the second, that's my blood or living spirit,' and I stood firm and refused, saying, 'Tell the emir that I am, thank God, a bachelor, so why is he trying to send me away from here so quickly?' but he didn't get it.[497] 'I want to bleed you,' he said to me, 'not be your messenger.' 'But I don't want you to,' I said, 'so grant me rest, may God grant you the same.'

2.10.9 "At this he showed me his back and departed, sending me soon after his bill, in which he demanded of me five hundred piasters, for he claimed to have people in the countryside among the peasants who collected those medicinal plants for him, even though they were the same that sprout from the walls of Cairo's houses. Not content with this, he threatened that, if I was as reluctant to pay as I had been to get bled the second time, he'd bring a case against me in his consul's office.[498] I paid him, therefore, the aforementioned sum in full, saying to myself, 'God damn the hour that showed us foreigners' faces, and their backsides!'

2.10.10 "Now here I am today, feeling much better, and I'd like to meet with your friend. Before the visit, though, I must do him some honor"—and he ordered his servant to select a trunkful of fine clothes and take it to the Fāriyāq, who at the time was dressing as a Frank. Then he wrote him a short message with a few lines of verse inviting him to his salon the following day, details to come in the following chapter.

## Chapter 11

# The Fulfillment of What He Promised Us

The Fāriyāq had a friend from the Damascene lands who used to visit him, and he was with him when the servant arrived with the letter and the set of clothes. He told the Fāriyāq, "I shall go with you to see Khawājā Yanṣur, for I have often heard him mentioned and would love to meet him." "But," the Fāryaq said, "turning up with another (*al-izwā'*)(1) may be considered a discourtesy to the person visited, for it is inappropriate for an invitee to bring a companion with him." "Forget about that," said his friend, "for it's the Frankish way. In Egypt, on the other hand, a guest may bring anyone he wishes, and his companion too, should he come across any acquaintance on the way, has the right to bring him along with him, and the latter too has the right to bring along another, and that other another, till they turn into a chain of friends, the only condition being that none of the links be female; all of them, without exception, talk to the person being visited, are treated to his hospitality, and are welcomed by him. He can't question one of them and say, 'You! What do you want, what letter of introduction do you have, and what are the names of your wife and your sister, and how old are they, and on what street do they live?' like your Frankish friends. Have no fear that the man will receive us harshly. And anyway, we have literature to commend us to him, and that will relieve us of the need to invoke pedigree." 2.11.1

(1) *al-izwā'* is "a man's coming accompanied by another."

2.11.2 So the Fāriyāq agreed to his request, and they set off to see the man together, the Fāriyāq strutting along in his new clothes; he had also got himself a large turban that made him think of his turban in Lebanon and his ill-fated fall.[499] When they'd settled down in the aforementioned salon and been greeted and received with warmth and welcoming faces, and once "We've been looking forward to meeting you" had been followed up with "You bring us good cheer," and "You bring us good cheer" had fallen fast on the heels of "We've been looking forward to meeting you," and after the salutations of kindly men had followed hard on the kindliest of salutations, as is the custom among both elite and commoners, the Khawājā said to the Fāriyāq, "I am delighted with your arrival in these lands and that God, Glorious and Almighty, has granted me His blessing in allowing me to make you my partner here, for as the poet has said,

Sexual congress, they claimed, is the most desirable thing
But that, I replied, is clearly misguided.
A favor done to one in need
Is more gratifying, of more lasting effect, and easily provided

"—which doesn't mean I'm saying that you're in need of me, though I did infer from your complaint that you require a doughty friend to keep you in good cheer, or shore up your spirits, or share your sorrows; and the duty of keeping your spirits up so long as you are preoccupied, whether by providing consolation or offering advice, has fallen to me, especially as it's clear to me that you are new to the pursuit of knowledge and interested in rhyming. Notwithstanding this, there are things in your writing that I might criticize you for, though this is not the time for criticism or the listing of faults. I would like to ask you, however, what books of literature you have read."

2.11.3 Here his friend took the lead in anwering in his stead and said, "He's read the *Baḥth al-maṭālib* (*The Discussion of Issues*)."[500] "You were too quick with your answer!" the Khawājā replied. "That's a book on grammar, not literature, though you students from the

Mountain reckon that any who's read it has effectively imbibed all that the Arabic language has to offer and feel no need to complement it with any of the books on the lexicon or literature, or the commentaries. When one of you students wants to pen a book or a speech in high-flown style, he uses a few hackneyed rhyme words with no vowel on the rhyme consonant, for fear of getting confused between *-u* and *-a*.[501] They strain to produce a few mediocre metaphors and rigid similes that they've stuffed with feeble phrases and faltering figures without any knowledge of which verbs, triliteral or qadriliteral, should be used, or which should be used with a preposition to make them transitive." When the man said this, the Fāriyāq remembered how the metropolitan had written to Qay'ar Qay'ār "*wa-awlajtu fī-hā*"[502] and he mentioned this to the aforementioned Khawājā, who laughed so hard he scuffed the ground with his foot.

"Indeed," he said, "all church books are full of horrible mistakes of that sort. I once read in one, of a certain monk, that he was 'endowed with great humility, to the extent that, whenever the head of his monastery passed him, he stood up *to him* (*'alayh*)' (meaning *for him* (*lahu*)), and of another that 'he was told, of a nun, that she was a wonder-worker and a seer of visions, and he constantly *wanked* to see her' (for he *wanted* to see her), and, of another, that he left his monastery and was absent for a long period; then he returned and found that its former abbot had died and one of his friends had taken over his position, and, after they'd consulted and congratulated one another, the abbot appointed him 'to smut up the monks at night,' meaning 'to wake them up' (from *habba* meaning 'to rise'),[503] and, of a certain metropolitan, that 'when he preached a homily in the church, everyone who heard him stood erected,' meaning 'stood corrected,' and so on and so forth, with too many examples to count. Indeed, even in the New Testament and the words of the apostles there is language whose meaning has been corrupted, the source of such corruption lying, I believe, in the 2.11.4

ignorance of those who translated them into Arabic. For example, in the gospel according to St. Matthew, there is an oration handed down from Christ, peace be upon him, in which he says, 'Take heed that no man deceive you. For many shall come in my name, saying, I am Christ; so do not believe them,' but what is meant is that 'many shall adopt my name, and each shall claim that he is the Messiah'—and what a difference there is between the two versions![504] And in St. Paul's epistle to Timothy it is written, 'Let the deacons be the husbands of one wife,'[505] when what is meant is that the deacons should jointly pay one dowry. God forbid that these words of mine should be taken as showing contempt for religion; I cite them only as testimony to the ignorance of those of our community who worked as translators into Arabic and composers of prose. True, some metropolitans have composed useful works excellently expressed and with well turned figures, but the mass of the clergy are stupid ignoramuses who like only poor, lame language.

2.11.5 "This aside has diverted us from our goal. Let us return to what we were about, which was how to help you, my dear friend, relieve yourself of the burden of the bag. Would you be interested in being a scribe in the establishment of a certain rich prince who wishes to set up a Panegyricon[506] in which to record in writing, in different languages, his mighty deeds and noble virtues? Your work there would be to compose each day two or more lines of verse, as needed."

2.11.6 The Fāriyāq went on, "I told him, 'I am not, Sir, a scholar senior enough to qualify for such a rank. Here we are in the land of scholarship and literature, and I fear some group may obstruct my path, claiming that what I say is spurious and erroneous, after which I'll be too ashamed to look any man in the face, for I'm a man who prefers obscurity, and what I have to offer in this respect is but meager.' 'Don't worry about that,' he told me. 'The people of Egypt, though they may have reached the limits of learning and surpass all others in merit and culture, would not pick a quarrel with a writer, be it of poetry or prose, who made a hash of a word *unintentionally* or trashed a trope *inadvertently*. They are a tolerant and easy-going people. At the same time, though, if one who wants to make a name for himself in poetry finds no one on one occasion to critique his work and on another to find fault with it, he will never reach the rank of the truly celebrated poets, and, if he keeps composing verses and trusting to his ear alone, he will never learn to distinguish the incorrect from the correct. Almost no one succeeds without first making mistakes.

"'Also, it has become the custom for some poets to condemn 2.11.7
the rhetorical figures and words that others commend, so that the poet or prose writer is always caught between two—between a critic and a commender, a fault-finder and an excuser, an accuser and a defender, an opponent and an ally, a render and a mender, a ripper and a darner, a perforator and a patcher, a forbidder and a permitter, a narrower and a widener, one who asks, "Why?" and one who answers, "Because!"—until, in the end, his good qualities come to outweigh his bad, and everyone circulates his verses. How often people have tried to attain fame through compositions that deserve to be *rejected* and *not accepted*. Some wrote verses using only unpointed letters, meaning those that are devoid of dots, and these were *neglected*;[507] some in their verses cleaved to "binding," by which they make the first letter of each line of the poem one of the letters of the name of the person being eulogized, and these were disregarded and *disrespected*; and some took paronomasia and far-fetched punning as their path, and these were refused and condemned as too *affected*. All that such poets sought from such things was celebrity among their fellows, and they cared nothing for blame or rebuttal, and I pray God that you are not to be counted among their number, for I saw in your composition hints of refined ideas that point to an excellent *intuition*, and a lively inborn *disposition*. But, to get back to our original discussion, who has never done wrong?'"

Said the Fāriyāq, "I told him, 'By God, now you have two great 2.11.8
claims on my gratitude! The first is your concern for my welfare, the

second your galvanizing me to write verse, for I had resolved to do so only far from people's eyes. Behold now, My Master, my *gratitude* and hear me broadcast, like a lion roaring, your generous *attitude*!'" Then he left his house, calling down blessings on the other's name, having decided that he would part company with the Bag-man the following day.

# Chapter 12

## Poems for Princes

Our friend the Fāriyāq had no heavy baggage at the Bag-man's house other than his own body, so he took his tambour under his arm, put his pen-box in his belt, and told the man, "God has come to my aid and shown me a path different from that laid down for me by you and your company of Bag-men. Today I shall leave you and nothing shall dissuade me." "How can you leave me, when I've done you no injury?" asked the other. "This tambour," replied the Fāriyāq, "bears witness against you that you did." "If the tambour-player isn't acceptable as a witness, how can the witness of the instrument itself—the reason for the discounting of its owner's witness—be valid?"[508] "On the contrary," said the Fāriyāq "it's as valid as your father's mare's, can announce your sins as loudly as your grandfather's she-ass, and can demolish the castles where you store your peddlers' goods as well as any kingly trumpet!"[509] Said he, "What am I to make of such a *peroration*?" "That it's revelation and *inspiration*!" he replied. "It doesn't matter if you play your tambour," the Bag-man said, "for I've discovered that the servant only brought the complaint against you out of envy." "Never!" said the Fāriyāq. "I'm going to play it to people who tell me, 'More!' and 'Encore!' and 'Well done!' and '*Allāh*!'[510] not to foreigners who only say God's name when praying." "You're a trouble-maker and have gone too *far*!" said the man. "And you've let me down and haven't treated 2.12.1

me *fair*!" the Fāriyāq retorted. "You're *untrue*!" he said. "And you're a *Jew*!" he responded. Then he turned his back on him, head held high, eyes bulging with fury, and set off, and he rented a room, where he stowed his tambour and made his way to the Panegyricon.

2.12.2 He had barely had time to take his seat before a messenger appeared before him with a piece of paper in his hand, on which were two lines of verse that were to be translated, for after they had been presented to those translating into languages other than Arabic and delivered by them to the Grand Panjandrum of the Panegyricon, it was finally the Fāriyāq's turn. He took up his pen and wrote,

The prince this day rode the best of his steeds
  But would that he'd taken his seat on our backs!
Among us there's none that bucks or kicks (*rāmiḥ aw rāfis*)—
  Nay, through him, all of us are turned into hacks.

When the Grand Panjandrum compared these verses to the original, he found that they encapsulated the meaning as the belly does the fetus or the intestines the duodenum, without at the same time stuffing it with the words that poets usually use to fill in the weak spots in their poems. Delighted, he said, "These verses are preferable to the translations made by the foreigners, in which I find only repetition. But maybe such is their way, so let us leave them to their own devices."

2.12.3 However, when the verses became known to the critics, some objected that *rāmih* and *rāfis* were synonymous, so either the first or the second had to be considered an error, and it would have been better if he'd written *jāmiḥ* ("bolts") *aw rāmiḥ*, which, in addition, form a doublet. To this response was made that the word *rāmiḥ* has many meanings, among them "a bull with two horns," and it may be used as the verbal adjective of *ramaḥa* meaning "to thrust with the lance (*rumḥ*)" or in the sense "he became armed with a lance"; there's also *ramaḥa l-barq* meaning "the lightning flashed." To this the riposte would be that there's no way for a bull to get in there with his horns because people don't ride bulls, even if al-Mutanabbī raises such a possibility in the ode of his known as *Al-Ghabab* (*The Wattle*),[511] and that the verbal adjective from "to thrust" is inappropriate since a "mount" cannot "thrust."

The following day a second messenger appeared bringing a piece of paper on which were two more verses, and the Fāriyāq wrote, 2.12.4

The prince arose betimes—all earth shaking
At that early rising—to partake of his matitudinal potation.
Or could it be that the sun reached out to him with its rays,
Through his window, on beholding his elation?

Objection was made that the second verse is poorly tacked on to the first, to which the response is that it follows naturally from it and is linked to it because when the earth shook, it scared mankind with its brutal power, and then along came the sun and reassured it with its rays. The riposte to this was that the sun's reassurance would have been feeble compared to the shaking of the earth and so would have done no good, to which the response is that such reassurance is an inescapable fact, as the sun cannot rise before sunrise. Certain persons made fun of this explanation.

The third day, another messenger appeared, and the Fāriyāq wrote, 2.12.5

The prince slept soundly last night
With nary a care in his noble head.
When he sleeps, the nation of men-and-jinn sleeps too.
When he rises, it rises, and then it's a crime to be a-bed.

Objection was made to the word "men-and-jinn" (*al-thaqalayn*) on the grounds that it was "heavy" (*thaqīlah*), and that "nation" ought to have been put in the dual.[512] The response is that the word is light and its derivation from *thiqal* ("heaviness") has no bearing.[513]

The fourth day, another messenger appeared, and he wrote, 2.12.6

The prince drank, thus rend'ring the consumption of wine
permitted—
He dispensed with the lawyer's rule that says it's not admitted.
Should any who say it's a sin insist,
The aid of your sharpest sword enlist!

Objection was made to the ugly exaggeration amounting to blasphemy and disregard for the Revelation, to which the response is that it just follows the original.

2.12.7 The fifth day, another messenger appeared, and he wrote,

The prince repaired with his squadron on foot (*māshiyan*)
To the bathhouse in the pre-dawn dark, there to luxuriate.
The pair of hands that has scrubbed their two bodies but once
Are thenceforth something one cannot but osculate.

Objection was made on the grounds that it would have been more proper to say "on their two sets of feet" (*māshiyayn*), to which the riposte would be that there's nothing wrong with "on foot" because appeal to the rule of *taghlīb* as applied to *māshiyayn* implicitly admits that the prince may stand for both.[514] Further objection was made that it would have been chaster to say "the body (singular) of each of the two" or "the bodies (plural) of each of the two,"[515] to which the response would be that chaster does not invalidate chaste. Then it was claimed that he had committed the fault of bending the rules of grammar under pressure from the exigencies of verse by omitting the preposition in the last hemistich, since correct diction would require *bi-an* in place of *an*, not to mention that the use of the dual here in reference to "hands" is meaningless, for the scrubber doesn't use both hands. To this the response would be that one is allowed to omit the preposition with *an*, while the dual is there to announce that the scrubber's every limb was created to serve the object of the panegyric.

2.12.8 On the sixth day, another messenger appeared, and he wrote,

To a eulogist extreme in his praise this day
The prince, they say, gave his shoes away.
Rejoice, ye band of poets, at one so free with both wealth (*yumn*)
And pelf (*sunḥ*)!

Objection was made that *yumn* and *sunḥ* mean the same, to which the response would be that it's the same as when the poet[516] says, "And I find her words to be both falsehood and ballyhooing."

On the seventh day, another messenger appeared and he wrote, **2.12.9**

The prince this day scratched his nether parts
With nails (*aẓāfir*) that had nailed down (*ẓafirat*) his every aspiration,
So everyone either whistled or chanted
Or beat the tambourine or blew the pipes or drummed, in jubilation.

Objection was made that that *aẓāfir* should not be treated as though it were inflected, to which the response would be that it is not forbidden to treat it as such, especially given that it is followed by the word *ẓafirat*.[517]

On the eighth day, another messenger appeared, and he wrote, **2.12.10**

Blessed is he who shaves of a morn
The piebald (*aḥlas*) clean-licked (*malḥūs*) princely pate!
May it remain bordered with God's grace as long as razor
Can find upon it one noble hair to abbreviate!

Objection was made that "clean-licked" isn't a quality associated with heads, to which the response would be that it was allowable there for the sake of the paronomasia.[518] Then it was claimed that "bordered" in association with "head" was "heavy," to which the response would be that in the prince's case the border was quite light. In my opinion, they would have done better to criticize him for writing "Blessed is he who . . . ," because the phrase is absolute and doesn't indicate that the prince was shaved on a particular day, though the paronomasia in the second hemistich puts in a good word for the line as a whole.

2.12.11 On the ninth day, another messenger appeared, and he wrote,

Time's lips parted to reveal a radiant fate,
The day our prince took a bath and was rendered depilate.
His noble nether parts thus appeared less hoary
And poetry, through his pubes, gained in glory.

These two verses were very well received because of the antithesis and the perfect paronomasia and so on that they contain. Except for the words "in glory."[519]

2.12.12 On the tenth day, another messenger appeared, and he wrote,

The prince coughed (*qaḥaba*), and what glorious and gallant gentleman
Of his ilk, among the human race, has never had a cough?
It's a habit imposed upon all mankind,
And any who hasn't should be hung on a cross!

Fault was found with the word *qaḥaba*, to which the response was made that it is a chaste word meaning "he coughed."[520]

2.12.13 On the eleventh day, another messenger appeared, and he wrote,

The prince sneezed, so tears of blood we wept, one and all,
While both globe and celestial sphere recoiled in horror.
God protect his brains from another such sneeze
Lest it so scare the angels that they die of terror!

2.12.14 On the twelfth day, another messenger appeared, and he wrote,

The prince let off a string of silent farts, and what heady odor
Within the universe was spread, what musk unpent!
Would that the limbs of all mankind
Into noses might turn, to inhale that scent!

Fault was found with the word *fassā* ("let off a string of silent farts"), since the repetitive form[521] has no meaning here, to which the response would be that even what is little becomes much when attributed to a prince; a similar logic applies to the words *ẓallām li-l-ʿabīd* ("a (repeated) oppressor of mankind"),[522] since the least degree of outrage (*ẓulm*) against what is due to the Almighty Creator in terms of the ruler's dealing justly with His creation is too much.

On the thirteenth day, two messengers appeared, and he wrote, **2.12.15**

The prince at mid-morn this day let off an audible fart,
The sky being dark, no hint of sun revealed,
And all parts of our land with its perfume were scented
For t'was a fart (*ḥabq*) that the scent of basil (*ḥabaq*) concealed.

These lines were well received because of the paronomasia that they contained.

On the fourteenth day, two other messengers appeared, and he wrote, **2.12.16**

The prince's bowels this day were loosened (*ushila*) and as one
Did all rejoice, for his looseness (*ishālihi*) brought him ease (*tashīl*).
They purchased some silk-wool for him, embroidered,
And rushed to claim that constipation's a fatal disease.

The first verse was well received because of the paronomasia but fault was found with "embroidered" because there's no call for embroidery in this context, indeed, it would cause pain; to which the response was that it follows the original and a good translation neither adds to nor subtracts from the original from which it is taken, especially where important and significant matters are involved. Fault should have been found with the words "as one did all rejoice" (albeit he does go on to explain what he means, by saying "for his looseness brought him ease"), for the hearer's natural first reaction is that the looseness of the bowels will lead to the death of the object of the panegyric; the paronomasia, however, may be considered to draw a veil over this solecism.

2.12.17 With this redolent episode behind him, the Fāriyāq decided it was his duty to visit his friend and let him know how things had gone. After he had been honorably received and seated in the man's salon, the Khawājā asked how he was, to which the Fāriyāq replied, "I would have wished, sir, to visit you sooner but was afraid that some trace of the smell that was all over me would fill this gathering of yours." "It would have done no harm," the other returned, "for I am used to it, and not a day goes by in this salon without similar smells filling it from the visits of the Prince and his like, which is an insalubrious calamity. But how are you doing in your everyday life?" "I've rented a small place," said the Fāriyāq, "bought a donkey, acquired a maid to take care of the first, hired a manservant to take care of the second, and am now, thanks to your patronage and bounty, doing very well." Then he left him, calling down blessings upon his head.

2.12.18 (A Secret between Me and the Reader)

The doctor on the island advised the Fāriyāq to set women to one side—meaning to keep his distance from them, not stick to their sides—for proximity to them would be his *undoing*. He dismissed his words as "both falsehood and *ballyhooing*."[523]

## Chapter 13

# A *Maqāmah* to Make You Sit

I shall not sleep well tonight unless I compose a *maqāmah* first. I have made it the custom of my pen at this point[524] to do nothing but *rhyme*, producing elegant periods that charm the *mind* and are appetizing and pleasing to the ear. I thus declare: 2.13.1

Faid al-Hāwif ibn Hifām in lifping tones, "Once, as I walked through Cairo's markets, my eyes o'er their attractions wandering *aglaze*, the beauty of their sideways-glancing girls absorbing my *gaze*, overtaken by camels from its every *zone*, so that now I was against this wall crushed, now at the foot of that one *thrown*, at one moment placing my hand over my eye, at another over something that might smaller or larger be, a young man signaled to me from a store he seemed to *own*—a youth bearing every sign of prestige and high-standing—with an agitation that pierced one's *chest* and settled there to *rest*. 2.13.2

"'If you like,' said *he*, 'climb up here with *me*, till this crush of camels has *dispersed* and the hideous climax of these distressing straits has passed its *worst*, for you are to us as a close *friend* and to do you honor I *intend*.' I found his invitation as compelling as 'Hie ye to security!'[525] so said, 'None refuses the offers of the *kind* but he who's devoid of righteousness and to the path of prosperity is *blind*. How can I say no, when my limbs are once more about to be injured and the loads on your camels' *backs* leave no place in this 2.13.3

land, broad as it is, on which to make *tracks*?' He smiled, indicating a wit quick to *answer*, a nature ever alert to render a *favor*.

2.13.4 "Having climbed up to where he was, I found with him a party of men each wearing a turban of a different *fashion*,[526] their faces full of good-natured *compassion*. After I'd uttered a friendly salutation them to greet and found among them a seat, I was asked by the owner of the store, 'In a debate that since the middle of the morning has kept us busy, would you care to take your *turn* (a debate for which we've made our ears like the cloth that's spread to catch the crumbs beneath the *quern*)? From each to each the turn's *relayed*, each one's opening words amplifying, in sequence, what the last one *said*, there being no punishment or consequences to be *paid*, for it's not a matter here of calling religion into *question*; it's an issue into which any may make *investigation*.'

2.13.5 "'You ask of me a terrible thing,' said I, 'and go too far by including me among your ranks, if your appeal be to the *mind*, for I'm no book-worm, but rather one to roaming and travel *inclined*. If, though, your appeal is to natural *intuition*, then mine, naturally, is sound, just as upright is my *disposition*.' 'The second,' said he, 'is the point round which it all revolves, the factor in our discussion that will lead to a *decision*.' 'Fill, then,' said I, 'my ears with your *debate* and throw upon my back the matched loads of argument between which you *hesitate*.' 'Know,' said he, God save you all *grief*, 'that I, to God be thanks, am a Muslim who to God and His messenger, His inspiration and His revelation, owes *belief*. My dear friend here (and he pointed to one of the seated) is a Christian, the other a *Jew*, the next a man with no ideas of his own, who to neither belief nor unbelief will *hew*. Know too that the debate whose cup we've wrested from each other in *turn*, and in which we've taken as many separate ways as pilgrims leaving 'Arafāt,[527] has matrimony as its *concern*.

2.13.6 "'Now, the Christian claims that to divorce a woman is a very grave *sin*, an occasion for regret bringing its initiator naught but trouble and *chagrin*. The proof of its evil, according to his claim and in keeping with his degree of comprehension, is that, once a wife finds she's no more to her husband than a disposable chattel or worn-out bit of *kit*, her presence hostage to any chance mistake or trivial *slip*, she'll never again honestly share with him her *introspection* or grant to him her sincere *affection*. On the contrary, as long as she's with him she'll be depressed and full of *misapprehension*, lonely, sad, bad-tempered, and prone to *desperation*, practicing deceit and *falsification*. If she thinks of him as someone by whom she's been *bought*, believes his belongings aren't hers and that soon enough sworn allegations of adultery will be *brought*, or that he'll leave her, or strip her of her clothes, dress her in those of a *divorcée*, and tell her, "Back to your *family*!" or "Good luck on your own!" or "You are to me as my mother's back!"[528] or "Your nose-rope's on top of your hump!"[529] or "Return to your covert,[530] among your kith and kin, for you're no family to *me* and I'm no husband to *thee*!" she'll never be solicitous of his secrets or what he may *need* and to whatever evils may befall him she'll pay no *heed*.

"'She may betray him with regard to his honor or his *monies* and lay traps to make him an object of scandal before his peers and *cronies*. And there's another danger too, more calamitous still and leading to greater *sorrow*, more injurious and harmful, yet more painful and harder to *swallow*, which is that, if a wife hates her husband because of what she's suffered at his hands and fears what havoc he may *wreak*, she'll not bother to care for his children or the welfare of his household *seek*, for if a woman doesn't love her husband, she'll not love his offspring and his *seed*; she'll love her husband only if he maintains their union and fulfills her *need*. Any man who has a wife to whom he does not give his heart and devote his entire *affection* will be taken by her as a deadly foe, not a friendly *companion*, in which case he's to be pitied even by those who observe his misfortunes with *glee* and those who inveigh against him should leave him *be*, for when things reach this point his breast becomes a wellspring of sorrow, his head a place for horns to grow, his home a camping-ground for *ire*, and, in short, his condition that of Those Who Dwell in *Fire*. 2.13.7

2.13.8 "'I, on the other hand, object to those who'd forbid *divorce* and the obligations of their wives *enforce*, on the grounds that, if a wife knows her husband's body with hers is *one*, that his secrets are on her *tongue*, making them like a single person, not a *pair*, whether they plumb the depths or rise to great heights in the *air*, that naught but the file of death this solder can *fray*, naught untie the knots of this condition but the dissolution of their earthly *clay*—so that, should she sicken, he too falls *ill* and, if she takes a stand, he must (un)buckle to her *will*, her every demand *fulfil*[531]—then she'll rebel and *disobey*, play tyrant and insist she have her *way*. One time she'll force him to buy jewelry and *clothes*, another insist on his swallowing some other bitter *dose*; then woe unto him if he *concurs*, and double woe if he *demurs*! If he spends one night away from home, all her guile on him she'll *vent*, and if some profitable business of his distracts him from her, she'll do anything she can to his *detriment*. Thus he makes it his habit to placate and *flatter her*, to play up to and *humor her*, to pay her compliments when she gives him the cold shoulder and be nice to her if she leads him a *dance*, to play the woman with her when she plays the man, and cower when she looks at him *askance*. Can life be sweet when one knows he's a pawn to the whims of *another* and at his hands condemned to *suffer*?

2.13.9 "'As for the children (the reason for putting up with this pain in the liver), if a couple are in a state of aversion and *contumely*, conflict and *contumacy*, the way they bring them up will be simply an invitation to *imitation*, a training, through their agency, in *abomination*, and how much better it would be to divorce the *mother* and leave them sans upbringing, concord being a factor more important than any *other*. In addition we know—from experience gained since the day the Almighty decreed that marriage be the law and saw that it was *good*—if a woman knows her husband can divorce her and slip from her clutches, she'll treat him lovingly and as she *should*, indulge him and be a good *friend*, go along with his whims and help him *unbend*, put right anything that's wrong and agree with his *views*, compliment him and use language that *soothes*, fearing lest her life become unbearable should he leave her or she be deprived of what he owes her of this world's *joy*, for if there's no concord between them, "Divorce! Divorce!" will be his *cry*. This Jewish friend of ours doesn't differ in his opinion *much*, for he disagrees with me only over the conditions for divorce (which, for him, are such and *such*).

"'As for our wishy-washy *friend*, he's at sea as to where this 2.13.10
thorny issue will *end*. Sometimes he says divorce leads to ease, at others that it must disturb life's *calm* and be nasty as a slap with the *palm*. On occasion he claims that a set period for legal dalliance[532] or marriage is more likely to lead to a successful *conclusion*, for even when that ends the contract may be renewed, with official *collusion*, until the two part without any *grudge* and settle it all mutually without recourse to a *judge*, this being less likely to create inconvenience and expose the purse to *ravages* (albeit it's also the practice of certain *savages*). On others he says that, on the contrary, keeping a concubine is more comfortable, pleasant, and restorative for the *listless*, and there is no substitute for keeping a *mistress*. At moments, he decides to make do with a plump little serving girl as wife, at others with the bachelor's solitary *life* (taking any, much-anticipated, opportunities as may be on offer), at yet others to cut off his tackle *completely* (supposing, if we may, that one can slice through such snares so *neatly*).'

"The speaker now declared, 'We're discussing all this because 2.13.11
I've descended the staircase of this business from top to *bottom* and suffered each of the kinds of danger and perdition with which it's *rotten*, for at every step I found a chasm into which discernment *vanished* and where reason was *banished*, where strength waned and bankruptcy was to be *relished*, a chasm beside which all other disasters seemed *diminished*, to the point that I became convinced that it plays no useful *role* and benefits not one living *soul*. It's a sickness none can cure, a smart but poisoned garment that pleasure to those both who see and those who wear it *brings* but ulcerates their joints and *limbs*. With the exception of this *curse*, any matter in the world may be sized up by the astute and dealt with for better or for

*worse*, for it all goes back to the individual's *disposition* and neither good sense helps, nor resolute *decision*.'

2.13.12 "Then said he, moaning like a mourning mother, 'To the words of the wishy-washy man I would add what *follows* (and I fear not the censure of my *fellows*): How many a heart has been tied to the *rack*[533] by reason of that *crack*, by reason of that *cleft* how many of all tranquility *bereft*! How many a head for its sake has been softened and *contused*, how many a mind weakened and *abused*, how many a neck *chopped* and eye *popped*, how many a tooth *split* and nose *slit*, how many a head of hair shaved smooth and beard plucked out, how many a hand cut off and lineage *lost*, how many a brigade raised and tome *off tossed*' (a category to which this tome belongs) 'or horse galloped or sword *flashed* or lance flourished or band into battle *dashed* or mountain crumbled and *shattered* or house abandoned, its stones *scattered*, or possession plundered, or king by adversity *crushed*, or land reduced to *dust*—nay, how many a nation has disappeared and been *dismembered*, how many a generation receded and ceased to be *remembered*!' And then he sighed and added, 'Or goods *depleted* and gold coins *deleted*.'"

2.13.13 Said al-Hāwif, "Then I realized that 'the crack' had cracked him in his *pocket*, and its 'uvula' bitten him, once well inserted in its *socket*. That was why he'd gone on at such length in his discourse and waded so *far out*: to discover if any other had suffered as had he and knew of aught that might bring a cure *about*. Now he turned to me, his eyes full to the *brink*, and said, 'And you, what do you *think*?' 'Verily,' I replied, 'it is a very great *woe*,[534] a dilemma fit to make tears *flow*. For long the greatest scholars have been confounded as to the *affair*, and of ever understanding it the wisest of sages are in *despair*. Let there be no misapprehension, knowing each celestial sphere and every *star*, diving where lie Earth's metals and wonders *bizarre*, or comprehending its secrets and things *exotic*, would be easier by far for me than giving a yes or no on such *a topic*. So it seems to me I'd better say nothing.' Then, while they all argued to and fro, at length and in brief, who but the Fāriyāq should come riding briskly *by* on a trotting donkey that bowled along, its head held *high*. Catching sight of him, I called, 'Get down, get down, and hie thee to this locus of *indecision*, for none but you, we think, is capable of ridding us of its reek and presenting the facts with some *precision*!' He asked, 'Into what muddled matter have you *waded* and regarding what muddy miasma do you seek to be *persuaded*?' We told him, 'Matrimony. Now give us your remedy *instantaneously*!' at which he launched into the following, quite *spontaneously*:

The question of marriage has e'er a thorny matter been
    And so for ay it will remain.
If divorce should e'er to the husband
    Be permitted, at the drop of a hat his rights he'll claim.
I don't think it right then that his wife be stopped
    From divorcing him too or from wedding again.
If they can't agree on a friendly way out,
    Let them do what's moderate:
Whenever they want, get a divorce and separate.

"We laughed at his adoption of a position not found in the books in any shape, form, or *way* and told him, 'Back to your donkey without *delay*! We think your opinion's quite *absurd*, and ill you answered though well you *heard*!'[535] Then we split up just as we'd *congregated*, each marveling at what he'd heard *debated*."

# Chapter 14

## An Explanation of the Obscure Words in the Preceding *Maqāmah* and Their Meanings[536]

2.14.1 There is no word in this noble tongue of ours, or in that of any other nation, for an active subject or a passive object, or two actives, who, having participated in one and the same act for their own pleasure and advantage, are in need of someone to burst in upon them to inform himself as to what kind of "raising" and "erecting" they are engaged in.[537] This may be demonstrated by the fact that our word *zawāj* ("marriage") means the joining of one thing to another in such a way that each forms a conjunct (*zawj*) with its companion without, however, specification of time or place. Thus, if Zayd enters into conjunction (*tazawwaja*) with Hind on a plain or on a mountain top or in a cave, or on a Sunday or a Monday or a Saturday, and provided there is mutual consent to the man's writing the woman a document publicly proclaiming that he has formed a conjunction with her, or he brings two men to bear witness to the same, then all is as it should be. This was the way of the earliest prophets and others, as recorded in their histories; in fact, they didn't even tie themselves down with documents or witnesses.

2.14.2 As to the word *nikāḥ* ("copulation"), it means having a woman, however that may come about. This is because the Arabs of the Days of Barbarism had no conventions governing intercourse, or eating, or anything else. Then the Revelation came and classified the categories of intercourse and distinguished the permitted from the forbidden. Abū l-Baqāʾ states in *al-Kulliyyāt* (*The Universals*)[538]—well, I can't find it in the chapter on the letter *nūn* but if I come across it in someone else's work, I promise to get you the reference.

I'd hoped to cite what he has to say, namely that the noun *nikāḥ*[539] remains in use until now and occurs in books of jurisprudence innumerable times, which is an argument against those Christians who deny this and anyone who throws up his hands in horror when it's employed. Scholars of religion used it without embarrassment for several reasons. The first is that it was used anciently in the Days of Barbarism and that same usage was then confirmed in the Era of Rationality. The second is that it occurs in the Qur'an. The third is that it is composed of four letters and thus accords with the humors, the elements, and the directions. The fourth is that the letters of which it is composed occur among the "mysterious letters"[540] of the chapters of the Qur'an; thus the *nūn* occurs in "*Nūn*. By the Pen and what they inscribe,"[541] the *kāf* in *kāf-hāʾ-yāʾ-ṣād*,[542] the *alif* in *alif-lām-fāʾ*,[543] and the *ḥ* in *ḥāʾ-mīm*.[544] The fifth is that if you write the word backward, you will find two noble meanings, the first being an active participle of the verb *ḥ-y-y*, the second an imperative verb formed from *kāna*;[545] thus God's creation is *revealed*, the essential truths made manifest to those whose eyes can pierce the veil to arrive at what's *concealed*. The sixth is the lightness of the word on the tongue and its sweetness to the taste. The seventh is that its beginning signifies its end and its end its beginning, this kind of word play being called by some "the signifying of the end by the beginning and vice versa." The advantage this bestows lies in the fact that, if a judge calls on someone to bear witness against the commissioner of such an act and the witness utters the letter *nūn* followed by the letter *kāf*[546] and then swoons, or the judge swoons, from lasciviousness, those left standing in the judge's chambers will understand what the speaker was trying to say. Similarly, should he be overcome in the course of his testimony by such longing and dread that he can no longer speak and all that can be heard from him 2.14.3

is the *alif* and the *ḥā'*,[547] this last part of the word, though consisting of only a small number of letters, will provide all the signification that could be asked for.

2.14.4 I declare, "This analysis is indeed elegant. It is not, however, to be found in the books of the rhetoricians and the stylists. Personally, I'm not fond of long words, so the best thing would be to create a new, shorter, one from that assemblage of letters by keeping only the end.[548] If it be said, 'But you used very long words when you described a bonnet as being *mustaqbiḥah* and *mustafẓi'ah*[549] even though you could just as well have described it with short words,' I reply, 'That falls under the rubric of "maintenance of consistency," for it is required by the height of the bonnet, whereas what is signified by the word in question doesn't take long.'"

2.14.5 I started to say something at the beginning of this chapter and didn't finish it, the pen, as usual, having drawn me unawares into another topic, and I doubt that Your Elevated Honor or Sublime Presence understood it. I now therefore declare: "If the ideal of marriage be that each of the two spouses take his companion for his own sake and not for that of his countrymen, acquaintances, or friends, the way that 'Ulayyān ate Umm 'Alī's chicken's thigh,[550] it would be unreasonable for someone wearing a bonnet to intrude upon them and tell the woman, 'Don't marry so-and-so because he wasn't given the name Buṭrus' and then to the man, 'Don't marry so-and-so because she wasn't given the name Maryam' or 'Today's Sunday, and marriage is not allowed' or 'This room isn't licensed for the contraction of marriages.' Nor would it be proper for him to say to them, 'I want to see the kohl-stick stuck in the pot.' Such things, I swear, are not fit to be spoken or written of by any.

2.14.6 "Then again, the woman is one of those things that, like the sun or the moon, are so much looked at that the mind doesn't pay them the attention they deserve. This may be demonstrated by the fact that God, Mighty and Powerful, created woman from man to be a helpmeet to him in his daily *affairs* and a comfort to him in the midst of his anguish and *cares*. It seems to us, though, that this underlying intention is so frequently distorted that man's calamities, care, loneliness, ill fortune, wretchedness, and deprivation, nay even his perdition, come from woman, thus turning that *collaboration* into a cause of *aggravation*. In brief, one is born into this world in need of many things required for one's survival (such as food, drink, sleep, and warmth) and others that are not but that exist rather to rectify one's nature so that it does not become imbalanced (such as laughter, speech, recreation, listening to songs, and having women). This last, however, while originally created for the rectification of nature (as evidenced by the fact that a man can live for a while without it), has gained the upper hand over all other mundane requirements of life which cannot be foregone. Observe that a man who dreams of a woman gets from her in his dream what he would have had were he awake, while this is not true of one who dreams of eating honey or drinking the best wine, which is anyway something that very rarely happens, even to one who is hungry or thirsty. How often have our friends the poets been content to see the image of the beloved in their dreams! None, however, was ever content to have the object of his eulogies send him a glass of wine or a pot of porridge in a dream. Likewise, if a person partakes of some tasty food, be it of one kind or two, he will remain satisfied with what he's eaten for a number of hours and give no thought to the cooking pot and its potential contents. Then, when revisited by hunger, he will start thinking again of having another meal. Never, however, has it been heard that one in a state of hunger or thirst, on seeing a bird, would wish for it to fall onto the spit in his house so that he could gulp it down or keep ogling the cooks', grocers', and oil chandlers' shops or peering through their keyholes, the chinks in their doors, or the cracks in their walls at the different kinds of food inside.

"True, in our country 'the hungry man thinks that everything 2.14.7
round is a loaf,' as the saying goes, and it may be that in some Frankish countries, where they have so many different kinds of food, they harbor similar thoughts about everything round, oblong, or cloven like a sheep's hoof, but one who is hungry for women has no one

shape to fix on. The same goes for drink, for a thirsty man, having once quenched his longing with water, will feel aversion to drinking more, even if a glass filled with the nectar of paradise is brought him. Similarly, one who is cold and needs warmth, once he has put on some clothes to warm himself and cut himself a fine figure in public, will not thereafter stand on tiptoes to peer at every garment he sees displayed for sale in the merchants' stores. Were he to see, for example, a rainbow or a meadow brocaded with gay flowers, he wouldn't want the same colors to be on his drawers or his shirt; he would see it and simply find it beautiful without exercising his mind and heart over it or dreaming that same night of an elegant garden or imagining as he lay on his bed that, if it were next to his pillow, he'd feel more comfortable or live longer. The same goes for the sleeper: if he gets enough sleep on his hard bed, the subsequent sight of a luxuriously comfortable bed will be of no interest to him. In sum, everyone has a brain in his cranium that guides him to what will benefit him and what will hurt him and to what will do him harm and what will bring him pleasure, and, in both his stomach and his gullet, there is an accurate set of scales that measures what food and drink he needs and that enables him to grasp the meaning of the saying, 'One meal precludes many another.'

2.14.8 "Where women are concerned, though, the self-denying ascetic becomes a lustful lecher, the reasonable man a slave to his passions, the clement ruler a tyrant, the well-guided person a lost soul, the wise man an idiot, the scholar an ignoramus, the eloquent a stutterer (and vice versa), the patient man a prey to his impulses (but not vice versa), the young man old (but not vice versa), the rich man a pauper (and vice versa), the lout a sophisticate (but not vice versa), the fat thin (and vice versa), the healthy an invalid (but not vice versa), the steady-going reckless (and vice versa), the miser generous (but not vice versa), the immobile mobile (and vice versa), and all things their opposites (and vice versa, and so on, and so forth). If a man finds a woman who hates him, how often will he fall in love with her, if one who ignores him devote himself to her, if one who avoids him throw himself in her path, if one who flatters him and offers him false hopes become infatuated by her, if one who throws him her bag,[551] however heavy, go mad for her—unless he attend a gathering where there's

| | |
|---|---|
| a *waḍī'ah,* | "a woman who is comely and clean" |
| or a *hayyi'ah,* | "a female who is comely of form" |
| or a *mukhba'ah,* | "a secluded girl who has not yet married" |
| or a *dhab'ah,* | "a thin, cute, jolly girl" |
| or a *jarbā',* | "a cute girl" |
| or a *khidabbah,* | a female who is "huge" |
| or a *khur'ūb,* | "a supple, shapely young woman or a fine-boned, fleshy, stout, soft, white young woman" |
| or a *khanibah,* | "a coquettish girl of thrilling voice" |
| or a *raṭbah,* | too well known to require definition[552] |
| or a *sarhabah,* | "a tall, stout woman" |
| or a *shaṭbah,* | "a shapely girl" 2.14.9 |
| or a *shiṭbah,* | "a tall, blooming, shapely girl" |
| or a *shanbā',* | "having lustrous teeth" (of a female); mentioned under *burqu'*[553] |
| or a *ṣaqbah,* | a female who is "tall and full-bodied" |
| or a *ṣahbā',* | ["a red-headed woman"] "*ṣahab* is redness or blondness of the hair; synonyms *ṣuhbah* and *ṣuhūbah*" |
| or a *'ajbā',* | "a woman whose beauty is to be wondered at" |
| or a *qabbā',* | a female who is "slim-waisted and slender-bellied" |
| or a *kabkābah,* | "a fat woman" |
| or a *makdūbah,* | "a pure white woman" |
| or a *kā'ib,* | a woman whose breasts stand up |
| or a *la'ūb,* | a female "with a nice way of flirting" 2.14.10 |
| or a *waṭbā',* | a female who is "large breasted"; a *waṭb* is "a large breast" |
| or a *hadbā',* | a female "having thick eyelashes" |

| | | |
|---|---|---|
| | or a *dhāt ṣulūtah*, | [“having a clear, or prominent and straight, brow”] “*ṣalt* means ‘a clear brow’; *ṣaluta* means ‘to develop such a brow’” |
| | or a *ṣamūt al-khulkhālayn*, | “having legs so thick that her anklets make no sound” |
| | or a *khawthāʾ*, | a female who is “young and smooth” |
| | or a *baljāʾ*, | *buljah* is having “a space between the eyebrows”; masculine adjective *ablaj*, feminine *baljāʾ* |
| | or a *mibhāj*, | a female who is “shapely” |
| | or a *jāʾiʿat al-wishāḥ*, | a female who is “slender-bellied”; synonym *gharthāʾ al-wishāḥ* |
| | or a *khadallajah*, | “a woman with plump arms and legs” |
| 2.14.11 | or a *daʿjāʾ*, | [“a dark- and wide-eyed woman”] “*daʿaj* is . . . blackness of the eye combined with wideness” |
| | or a *rajrājah*, | a woman whose flesh quivers upon her |
| | or a *zajjāʾ*, | “*zajaj* is the delicate lengthening of the eyebrows, and the delineating [thereof]”; masculine adjective *azajj*, feminine *zajjāʾ* |
| | or a *muʿadhlajah*, | “a plump, smooth, shapely woman” |
| | or a *mufallajat al-asnān*, | [“a gap-toothed woman”] “*falaj* is having a distance between the teeth” |
| | or a *baydaḥ*, | a female who is “corpulent”; similarly, *baldaḥ* |
| | or a *daḥūḥ*, | a female who is “large” |
| | or a *dhāt sajāḥah*, | [“a smooth-cheeked woman”] “*sajiḥa*, of the cheek, means that it became smooth, soft, and moderately long” |
| | or a *dumluḥah*, | a female who is “huge and full-bodied” |
| | or a *ṣaldaḥah*, | a female who is “broad”; similarly, *salṭaḥah* and *ṣalṭaḥah* |
| 2.14.12 | or a *fuqqāḥ*, | “a shapely woman” |
| | or a *waḍḍāḥah*, | a female who is “of a pleasing white color” |
| | or a *baydakhah*, | a female who is “full-bodied” |

| | |
|---|---|
| or a *bulākhiyyah*, | a female who is “large or noble” |
| or a *ṣamikhah*, | “ a blooming woman” |
| or a *ṭubākhiyyah*, | “a sturdily-built young woman” |
| or a *fatkhā’ al-akhlāf*, | [“a high-breasted woman”] “a she-camel whose *akhlāf* (‘teats’) are *fatkhā’* has them raised (toward the belly) (a blameworthy quality in she-camels, but praiseworthy in women and women’s udders)” |
| or a *firḍākhah*, | a female who is “huge and broad” or “tall and with large breasts” |
| or a *qufākh*, | “a fat woman of comely physique” |
| or a *lubākhiyyah*, | “a female who is fleshy” |
| or a *habayyakhah*, | a female who is “smooth and full-bodied” |
| or a *bakhandāh*, | “a woman with a perfectly developed figure”; also *bakhandā* 2.14.13 |
| or a *burakhdāh*, | “a smooth, full-bodied girl” |
| or a *mubarnadah*, | a female who is “well-fleshed” |
| or a *tha’dah*, | a sturdily-built “well-fleshed woman” |
| or a *thawhadah*, | “a fat, shapely woman”; also *thahwadah* and *fawhadah* |
| or a *thahmad*, | a female who is “fat and large” |
| or a *jaddā’*, | a female who is “small-breasted” |
| or a *jaydā’*, | a female “having a long, finely formed neck” |
| or a *baḍḍat al-mujarrad*, | “revealing tender skin on undressing” |
| or a *khabandāh*, | “a girl described as *khabandāh* has a perfectly formed figure, or is stoutly built, or has heavy haunches; a leg so described is rounded and full” |
| or a *kharīd*, | “a *kharīd* is an untouched virgin, or a bashful woman who maintains long silences, speaks in a low voice and conceals herself from public view”; also, *kharīdah* and *kharūd* |

(Note: women who are nanoid, endomorphic, adipose, fubsy, hebetudinous, impulchritudinous, chamaephytic, and troglodytic are more coquettish and sensual than any of the above.)

| | | |
|---|---|---|
| 2.14.14 | or a *rikhwaddah*, | a female who is "soft-boned and fat" |
| | or a *riʿdīd*, | a female who is "soft to the touch" |
| | or a *rahīdah*, | "a smooth, soft, young woman" |
| | or a *ʿubrud*, | "a girl who is white and smooth and quivers with good living" |
| | or a *ʿaḍād*, | "a woman thick of upper arm (*ʿaḍud*)" |
| | or a *ʿumuddah*, | "a young woman bursting with youthfulness; synonym *ʿumudāniyyah*" |
| | or a *ghādah*, | "a smooth, pliant woman of patent pliability" |
| | or a *ghaydāʾ*, | "a woman who walks with an affected swaying, out of pliability" |
| | or a *maqṣadah*, | "the large, perfect woman who pleases all men and tends to shortness" |
| | or a *maʾdah*, | "a smooth girl" |
| 2.14.15 | or a *mamsūdah*, | a female who is trimly built |
| | or a *umlūd*, | "a soft, pliable woman" |
| | or a *nāhid*, | a female who is "full-breasted" |
| | or a *bahīrah*, | "a noble lady, of small stature and weak"; synonym *bahīlah* |
| | or a *bashīrah*, | a female who is "beautiful" |
| | or a *mabshūrah*, | a female who is "comely of face and body" |
| | or a *tārrah*, | a female who is "full-bodied" |
| | or a *turrah*, | a female "comely and frivolous" |
| | or a *juḥāshirah*, | "a huge woman, of beautiful physique and large joints, and well built" |
| | or a *jahrāʾ*, | feminine of *ajhar*, which means "a male of comely, perfectly formed appearance and body, or a male with an attractive squint" |
| 2.14.16 | or a *ḥādirah*, | "a fat, or comely and beautiful, woman" |
| | or an *aḥwariyyah*, | a female who is "white and smooth" |

| | | |
|---|---|---|
| or a *ḥawāriyyah*, | “the *ḥawāriyyāt* [plural] are the women of the great cities” | |
| or a *ḥawrā’*, | [“having *ḥawar*”] “*ḥawar* is when the white of the eye is extremely white and the black extremely black and the pupil is rounded, the eyelids delicate and surrounded by white,” etc. | |
| or a *dhāt tadahkur*, | a female “whose body shakes” | |
| or a *mudahmarah*, | a compact, well-knit woman | |
| or a *muzannarah*, | a female who is “tall, large-bodied” | |
| or a *zahrā’*, | “a woman of radiant face” | |
| or a *masbūrah*, | a female “of comely form” | |
| or a *masmūrah*, | “a girl with a sinewy body and no loose flesh” | |
| or a *shaghfar*, | “a comely woman” | |
| or a *ṣayyirah*, | a female “of comely appearance” | 2.14.17 |
| or a *‘abqarah*, | a female who is “full-bodied and beautiful” | |
| or a *‘abharah*, | a female “with delicate, shining white skin or who is fat and full-bodied, synonym *‘abhar*; also a female who brings together all beautiful qualities of body and physique” | |
| or a *‘ajanjarah*, | a female “of compact physique and a light spirit” | |
| or a *mu‘ṣir*, | “a girl who has completed her girlhood and attained or entered into the menses, or who is approaching twenty” | |
| or *gharrā’*, | “white”; synonym *farrā’* | |
| or a *dhāt iftirār*, | [a woman “with a pleasant laugh”] “*iftarra* means ‘he laughed a pleasant laugh’” | |
| or a *fazrā’*, | a female who is “fleshy and fat-laden, or approaching the onset of the menses” | |
| or a *qufākhiriyyah*, | “a large, noble woman” | |
| or a *murmūrah*, | “a *murmūrah*, synonym *mirmārah*, is a girl whose skin is smooth and whose flesh quivers” | |

| | | |
|---|---|---|
| | or a *mashrat al-aʿḍāʾ*, | "a fragrant woman" |
| 2.14.18 | or a *maṭirah*, | a female who "constantly uses the teeth-cleaning stick, or cleans herself, or washes" |
| | or a *dhāt makrah*, | [a woman "possessed of a *makrah*"] "a *makrah* is a comely, thick calf" |
| | or a *mamkūrah*, | "a woman with a curvaceous physique and rounded calves, or one who is of slender waist and corpulent" |
| | or a *māriyyah*, | a female who is "of a brilliant white"; from [the verb] *māra* |
| | or a *dhāt naḍrah*, | [a woman "possessed of *naḍrah*"] "i.e., of comeliness and good looks" |
| | or a *wathīrah*, | "the woman who is *wathīrah* has much flesh, or is ready to be bedded" |

(Note: women who are dirty crockadillapigs, shorties, runts, trolls, long-necked pinheads, midgets, wide-wooed woofers, waddlers, bitty-butted beasts, scrawnies, and spindle-legs are more coquettish and sensual than any of the above.)

| | | |
|---|---|---|
| 2.14.19 | or a *hudakir*, | "a woman who brings her flesh and her bones into play when she walks" |
| | or a *haydakūr*, | a female "with a lot of flesh on her" and "a huge young woman who is attractively coquettish"; synonym *hadkūr* |
| | or a *biliz*, | "a huge, or a light, woman" |
| | or a *ʿukmūzah*, | a female who is "thick and full-fleshed" |
| | or a *ghammāzah*, | "a girl skilled at massage" |
| | or a *kināz*, | a female "with much flesh, and solid" |
| | or a *ānisah*, | "a cheerful girl" |
| | or a *bayhas*, | a female who "walks well" |
| | or a *kharūs*, | "a girl who has not yet brought forth, in the first period of her pregnancy" |
| | or a *khansāʾ*, | ["snub-nosed"] already mentioned under *burquʿ* |

| | | |
|---|---|---|
| or a *murkis,* | "a girl whose breasts are emerging; when they become compact and large, they are said to have 'become full' (*nahada*)" | 2.14.20 |
| or a *ʿayṭamūs,* | "a beautiful woman, or a comely, tall, full-bodied woman"; synonym *ʿuṭmūs* | |
| or a *ʿalṭamīs,* | "a full-bodied girl of attractive physique" | |
| or a *ʿānis,* | "a female who has remained so long with her family after having reached puberty that she is no longer counted among the virgins" | |
| or a *qudmūsah,* | a female who is "huge and big" | |
| or a *qirṭās ,* | "a white girl of lanky physique" | |
| or a *kanīsah,* | "a comely woman" | |
| or a *laʿsāʾ,* | "one who has the slightest hint of blackness to her complexion" | |
| or a *lamīs,* | a female "soft to the touch" | |
| or a *ʿashshah,* | "a tall woman with little flesh, or one with fine-boned hands and feet" | |
| or a *kharbaṣah,* | "a young, full-bodied woman" | 2.14.21 |
| or a *dakhūṣ,* | "a girl full of fat" | |
| or a *rakhṣah,* | ["soft"] "too well known to require definition" | |
| or a *baḍbāḍah* | a female who is "soft-bodied, delicate-skinned, | |
| *baḍḍah,* | full-fleshed" | |
| or a *kharīḍah,* | "a full-fleshed, white, comely, youthful girl" | |
| or a *raḍrāḍah,* | synonym of *rajrājah* | |
| or a *ghaḍḍah ghaḍīḍat al-ṭaraf,* | ["a blooming girl with a drowsy eye"] "*ghaḍḍah* is 'blooming' (*nāḍirah*); an eye that is *ghaḍīḍ* is 'drowsy'(*fātir*)" | |
| or a *fāriḍ,* | a female who is "huge" | |
| or a *faḍfāḍah,* | "a tall, well-built, fleshy girl" | |
| or a *mufāḍah,* | a female who is "huge-bellied" | |
| or a *khūṭānah,* | "a girl who is *khūṭānah*, or *khūṭāniyyah*, is smooth and tall as a tree branch" | 2.14.22 |

| | | |
|---|---|---|
| | or a *sabṭat al-jism*, | a female "of pleasing figure" |
| | or a *shaṭṭah*, | a female "of pleasing physique and tall" |
| | or a *shināṭ*, | "a woman of pleasing color and physique" |
| | or a *dhāt ʿanaṭ wa-ʿayaṭ*,[554] | a female "having a long and attractive neck" |
| | or a *dhāt shināṭ*, | a female "fully and copiously fleshed" |
| | or a *mulaʿʿaẓah*, | "a well-built, tall, fat girl" |
| | or a *batʿāʾ*, | a female "having strong joints and sinews to her body" |
| | or a *barīʿah*, | a female "outstanding in beauty and brains" |
| | or a *bazīʿah*, | a female who is "quick-witted, witty, and charming" |
| 2.14.23 | or a *mutliʿ*, | a female who is "attractive because she stretches out her neck (*tutliʿu ʿunuqahā*) when addressing those who look upon her" |
| | or a *sanīʿah*, | a female who "has beautiful, soft joints and fine bones" |
| | or a *shabʿā l-khulkhāl wa-l-siwār*, | a female who is "huge and fills her anklets and bracelets with fat" |
| | or a *shamūʿ*, | a female who is "merry and playful" |
| | or a *ṣamʿāʾ*, | "a female with small ears, or a small, fine ear that is flattened against the head" |
| | or a *ḍarʿāʾ*, | a female who is "large-uddered" |
| | or a *farʿāʾ*, | a female "with perfect hair" |
| | or a *laʿʿah*, | a female who is "chaste and cute" |
| | or a *lāʿah*, | a female who "flirts with you but doesn't let you"(because, I believe, she torments (*talūʿu*) her suitor by so doing) |
| | or a *anūf*, | "a female with a sweet-smelling nose" |
| 2.14.24 | or a *khanḍarif*, | "a huge, fleshy woman with large breasts" |
| | or a *dhalfāʾ*, | ["smallness and straightness of the nose"] *dhalaf* has been mentioned above under *burquʿ* |

| | |
|---|---|
| or a *dhāt sajaf,* | [possessed of] "*sajaf,* which is narrowness of the waist and lankness of the belly" |
| or a *surʿūf,* | "a smooth, tall woman" |
| or a *sayfānah,* | a female who is "thin, svelte, and tall" |
| or a *ẓarīfah,* | "*ẓarf* [the quality of being *ẓarīfah* ('charming, witty, sophisticated')] may be used only of the tongue, or of comeliness of face and appearance, or of both tongue and face, or of graciousness and quickness of both sensibility and wits, or it may be that only lively young men and women may be described as having it, not old men or lords" |
| or a *qirṣāfah,* | "a *qirṣāfah* is a woman who rolls like a ball" |
| or a *qiṣāf,* | "a huge woman" |
| or a *laffāʾ,* | singular of *luff* meaning "tall, fat girls" |
| or a *ḥasanat al-maʿārif wa-l-mawqifayn,* | ["a female comely of those parts that may be seen"] the *maʿārif* are "the face and those parts of a woman that show" and the *mawqifān* are "the face and the feet, or the eyes and the hands and whatever has to be shown" |
| or a *muhafhafah,* | a female "lank-bellied and small-waisted" |
| or a *hayfāʾ,* | ["slender-waisted"] *hayaf* [the quality of being *hayfāʾ*] is "lankness of the belly and delicacy of the haunches" 2.14.25 |
| or a *barrāqah,* | "a beautiful female possessed of brio and brilliance"; synonym *abārīq*[555] |
| or a *buhluq,* | "a very ruddy woman" |
| or a *ḥārūq,* | "having a certain quality welcomed in a woman during copulation"[556] |
| or a *khirbāq,* | a female who is "tall and large, or a fast walker" |
| or a *rashīqah,* | a female who is "comely and refined of figure" |

| | |
|---|---|
| or a *raqrāqah,* | a female who "looks as though water were running over her face" |
| or a *rūqah,* | a female who is "comely and admired" |
| or a *sawqā',* | a female "with long, or comely, legs" |
| or a *'abiqah,* | "a woman who continues to give off a pleasant smell for days though she applies to herself the smallest amount of perfume" |
| 2.14.26 or a *'ātiq,* | "a girl who has just reached the start of puberty" |
| or a *'ashannaqah,* | a female who is "tall without being huge or ponderous" |
| or a *ghubruqat al-'aynayn,* | a female "having wide eyes with intensely black pupils" |
| or a *ghurāniq,* | "a woman who is *ghurāniq*, or *ghurāniqah*, is young and full-bodied" |
| or a *dhāt gharnaqah,* | [a female "possessed of *gharnaqah*," which means] "flirtatiousness of the eyes" |
| or a *dhāt limmah ghurāniqah,* | [a female "possessed of a lock of hair that is"] "smooth and played with by the wind" |
| or a *funuq,* | "a girl who is *funuq* or *mifnāq* is pampered" |
| or a *labiqah,* | a female "pleasing in her coquetry and way of dressing" |
| or a *mulṣaqah,* | a female who is "small and well-knit" |
| or a *lahiqah,* | a female who is "extremely white" |

(Note: women who have dilated dugs or deflated bellies, who are blubber-lipped, gross, flighty and gangly, fleshy, hippo-haunched, ill-starred and vile, gross-bodied, and flabby-fleshed, with pendulous pendentives, are more coquettish and sensual than any of the above.)

| | |
|---|---|
| 2.14.27 or a *mamshūqah,* | a female who is "lightly fleshed" |
| or a *rawdakah,* | a female who is "comely, in the bloom of youth" |
| or a *ḍibrik,* | "a woman with huge thighs" |
| or a *ḍakḍākah,* | a female who is "short and plump" |

| | |
|---|---|
| or a *ḍunʾakah,* | a female who is "solid and sparely fleshed" |
| or a *muʿrawrikah,* | a female who is "well-knit" |
| or a *ʿakawwakah,* | a female who is "short and compact, or fat" |
| or a *ʿaḍannak,* | "a tall, fat (*laffāʾ*) female, the point of convergence of whose thighs has been narrowed by plumpness" |
| or a *ʿātikah,* | a female who is "stained red with perfume" |
| or a *mufallik,* | "a girl whose breasts have rounded out" |
| or a *makmākah,* | a *makmākah* and a *kamkāmah* are females who are "short and compactly built" 2.14.28 |
| or a *habrakah,* | "a smooth girl" |
| or a *asīlat al-khaddayn,* | ["smooth and even, or long, of cheek"] "a cheek that is *asīl* is long and even" |
| or a *mubattalah,* | "a female so beautiful it is as though her comeliness had been cut up (*buttila,* i.e., *quṭṭiʿa*) and distributed to all of her limbs and who does not have parts of her flesh riding on top of other parts, and in whose limbs there is looseness" |
| or a *bahlakah,* | "a smooth, blooming woman" |
| or a *jamūlun jamlāʾ,* | "a *jamūl* is a female who is fat and a *jamlāʾ* is a female who is beautiful and comely of form, whether human or non-human" |
| or a *khadlah,* | "a woman with thick, rounded legs, or whose limbs are full-fleshed with fine bones"; synonym *khadlāʾ,* |
| or a *khallah,* | "a light woman" |
| or a *daḥmalah,* | a female who is "huge and full-bodied" |
| or a *dumaḥilah,* | a female who is "fat and comely of physique" |
| or a *miksāl,* | [literally, "sluggish"] "epithet for a coddled girl who can scarcely get up from her seat (a compliment)" 2.14.29 |
| or a *rakhīmah,* | ["a woman with a thrilling voice"] "one says *rakhumat al-jāriyah,* meaning 'the girl |

| | |
|---|---|
| | acquired a thrilling voice'; adjective *rakhīmah* and *rakhīm*" |
| or a *raqīmah*, | "a noted, intelligent woman"; and under *b-r-z* "a 'noted woman' (*imra'ah barzah*) is one whose good qualities are conspicuous (*bārizah*), or 'a bold, mature, magnificent' female, etc." |
| or a *mīsānat al-ḍuḥā*, | "a compliment: a female who slumbers deeply in the forenoon"; similar is "*[imra'atun] na'ūmu l-ḍuḥā* ('a woman who sleeps in the forenoon')" |
| or a *ḥasanat al-khafiyyayn*, | [literally "comely of the two that appear"] meaning her voice and her footprint; one says, "if the two things that appear of a woman are comely, the rest of her will be comely" |
| or a *ghāniyah*." | "a woman who is pursued and does not herself need to pursue, or whose beauty is such that she may dispense with adornment" |

(Note: women who are brevo-turpicular, magno-pinguicular, vasto-oricular, ignobilar, exiguo-deformicular, flaccido-ventricular, obesar, rancidular, nigero-malo-incultular, and hyper-rustico-rapacular are more sensual and bolder than any of the above.)

2.14.30 The continuation of this description of feminine charms will come in Chapter 16 of Book Four, as I have no strength or energy left and imagine my reader doesn't either. I merely declare: Indeed, were all these charms in all their variety present at such a happy gathering, he would want to string them all on a single thread and put them round his neck, like prayer beads round the necks of God's Chosen Friends, and I refer any who challenge me on this to the story of Our Master Sulaymān, peace be upon him, whose thread, for all that he was given wisdom—and what wisdom!—had on it a thousand women, three hundred of whom were concubines, the rest great ladies, which means that each day he had two-and-half-plus-a-bit women.

Why, were any man to see the sun rising, the full moon coming out, and the stars shining, the first thing it would occur to him to say would be, "Now that the sky has been adorned with these glorious heavenly bodies, when will my chamber be adorned with one of their sisters, or two, or three, or ten, or an entire string of prayer beads?" Likewise, if he beheld a dip or a mound, two hills standing next to one another or a perky little bump, a large dome or a high mountain, a hollow or a rounded dune, a little sand hill or the stern of a ship, a branch bending or a sea surging, a trough between waves, a peacock, apples, pomegranates, a necklace of strung pearls, or anything else that pleases the eye, he would immediately fantasize about a woman; indeed, he might imagine one whom he'd never even seen and on whom he'd never clapped eye. And if he beheld a ship plowing the high seas, its sail set, he would liken it to a woman strutting the highways in her fine clothes, as a certain venerable Bag-man used to do. If he beheld two doves feeding each other with their mouths and cooing to each other, he'd say, "Would there were with me now one whom I might feed and who might feed me too, to whom I might coo and who might coo to me, whom I might peck and who might give me a peck!" If he beheld a rooster among his hens, feeding them morsels of his own food, flapping his wings at them, bristling and puffing up his feathers, and then stalking among them, he would want to be like him. 2.14.31

Enough, though, of such low-mindedness and abuse of that human form which is said to have been shaped in the image of the Creator (too sublime though He be to have like or peer)—despite which, should you come across him down Our Master Yūsuf's well even, or on board Our Master Nūḥ's ark, or in the belly of Our Master Yūnus's whale, or on the back of Our Master Ṣāliḥ's[557] camel, or with the People of the Cave, he'd be shrieking, "A woman! A woman! Who will get me a woman!", and if you set him down in a 2.14.32

| | | |
|---|---|---|
| | *bunānah,* | "a verdant meadow" |
| | or a *raqmah,* | "a meadow, or the side of a watercourse, or the confluence of its waters" |
| | or a *daqīrah,* | "a beautiful meadow covered in vegetation" |
| | or a *radīfah,* | "a green meadow" |
| | or a *ghalbā',* | "a dense garden" |
| | or a *'uljūm,* | "a grove of many palms" |
| | or a *makhrafah,* | "a grove" |
| | or a *ḥadīqah,* | "a meadow with trees" |

or in a chamber or an upper room or a compartment or a ladies' bower or an alcove or on a dais,

| | | |
|---|---|---|
| 2.14.33 | or a *sidār,* | "something like a ladies' chamber (*khidr*)"; the *khidr* is also called a *muwaṣṣad* |
| | or a *ḥushshah,* | "a large dome" |
| | or a *junbudhah,* | "[a thing] like a dome" |
| | or a *'arsh,* | "a tent, or a housing used for shade like a trellis" |
| | or a *kirḥ,* | "a monk's abode"; synonym *rukḥ* |
| | or a *kūkh,* | "a hump-shaped house of reeds" |
| | or a *ṣawma'ah,* | [a monk's cell] "an abode of the Christians" |
| | or a *rī',* | "a *ṣawma'ah*" |
| | or a *fanzar,* | "a chamber placed on top of a piece of wood of some sixty spans as a watch-tower" |
| | or a *bahw,* | [a hallway or antechamber] "a chamber advanced in front of other chambers" |
| 2.14.34 | or a *ḥillah,* | "a group of residential dwellings, or a hundred dwellings, or a place for sitting, or a gathering place" |
| | or a *fusṭāṭ,* | "the structure called a *surādiq* ('an enclosure around a tent'), similar to a *miḍrab*" |
| | or a *kibs,* | "a dwelling of mud" |
| | or a *ḥifsh,* | "a very small dwelling" |
| | or a *janz,* | "a small dwelling of mud" |
| | or a *khuṣṣ,* | "a dwelling of reeds, or . . . ."[558] |

| | | |
|---|---|---|
| or a *radhah,* | "the largest kind of chamber" | |
| or a *majlūh,* | "a dwelling that has no door or anything to preserve its privacy" | |
| or a *wa'm,* | "a warm dwelling" | |
| or a *uqnah,* | "a dwelling of stone" | |
| or a *ṭirāf,* | "a dwelling of hide" | |
| or a *wasūṭ,* | "a dwelling like the hair tent, or smaller" | 2.14.35 |
| or a *ṭanaf,* | "the projecting roof over the door of a house" | |
| or a *nuzul,* | "a place prepared for guests to stay in" | |
| or a *maghnā,* | "an abode whose people had no need of it and so departed, or [a house] generally" | |
| or a *maʿhad,* | "an abode dedicated to a specific purpose" | |
| or a *maʿān,* | "a home or an abode" | |
| or a *nadī,* | "a place where people gather and sit by day, or . . ."[559] | |
| or a *murtabaʿ,* | "a location where they[560] reside at the time of the autumn rains" | |
| or a *maṣīf* or *mashtā,* | ["a summering or a wintering spot"] "too well known to require definition" | |
| or a *daskarah,* | "a building like a palace with houses around it, or . . ."[561] | |
| or a *mashraqah,* | "a place to sit in the sun in winter" | 2.14.36 |
| or a *maḍḥāh,* | ["a land of sunshine"] "a land that is *maḍḥāh* is one that is sunny almost all the time" | |
| or a *ẓullah,* | "something like a portico in which one finds shelter from the heat and the cold" | |
| or a *mashrabah,* | "a chamber, or upper chamber, or portico" | |
| or a *suʿnah,* | "a rooftop shelter from the heat and humidity, or any shelter whatsoever" | |
| or a *miẓallah,* | "the larger kind of tent" | |
| or a *sābāṭ,* | "a roofing between two houses with a street beneath it" | |
| or a *ʿirzāl,* | "a small house used for the king when he is at war, or . . ."[562] | |

| | | |
|---|---|---|
| | or a *kinn*, | "a house" |
| | or a *qayṭūn*, | "a closet" |
| 2.14.37 | or a *sarab*, | "a subterranean excavation" |
| | or a *dīmās*, | "a *kinn*, or a *sarab*, or a bathing chamber" |
| | or a *burj*, | [tower] "too well known to require definition" |
| | or a *ṣahwah*, | "a tower on top of a hill" |
| | or a *ṣarḥ*, | "a palace, or any tall building" |
| | or a *ʿaqr*, | "a high building" |
| | or a *ṭirbāl*, | "any tall building" |
| | or a *azaj*, | "a kind of building"[563] |
| | or a *īwān*, | "a large portico, like the *azaj*" |
| | or a *riwāq*, | "a house like a *fusṭāṭ*, or a roof at the front of a house [i.e., an arcade]" |
| 2.14.38 | or a *ajam*, | "any square, roofed house; spelled *ujum* it means 'a fortress'" |
| | or a *kaʿbah*, | "a room, or any square house" |
| | or a *uṭum*, | "a palace, or any fortress built of stone, or any square, roofed house" |
| | or a *washīʿ*, | "a trelliswork structure constructed for the chief in a camp" |
| | or a *sunnayq*, | "a house plastered with gypsum" |
| | or a *jawsaq*, | "a palace" |
| | or a *dawshaq*, | "a house that is neither large nor small, or a huge house" |
| | or a *quhqūr*, | "a tall stone structure" |
| | or a *bughbūr*, | "a stone on which an offering is sacrificed to an idol" |
| | or a *zūr*, | "a gathering place for singing" |
| 2.14.39 | or a *budd*, | "the house of an idol" |
| | or a *zūn*, | "a place where idols are gathered, erected, and adorned" |

| | |
|---|---|
| or a *masjid*, | ["mosque"] "too well known to require definition" |
| or a *kanīsah*, | ["church" or "synagogue"] "too well known to require definition" |
| or a *fuhr*, | "the *midrās* ('midrash') of the Jews in which they gather on their festival, or . . ."[564] |
| or a *midrās*, | "a place in which the Qur'an is recited; origin of the *midrās* of the Jews" |
| or Kawkabān, | "a castle in Yemen whose inside was studded with rubies so that it shone like a star" |
| or al-Jawsaq, | "a house built for al-Muqtadir[565] inside the caliph's house in which was a pool of lead[566] thirty cubits by twenty" |
| or Qaṣr al-Nuʿmān, | [the Palace of al-Nuʿmān][567] that was built for him by al-Sinimmār; the latter was an artisan who built a palace for al-Nuʿmān, son of Imru' al-Qays; when he finished it, the latter threw him from its highest point so that he could never build another like it; or he was a slave of Uḥayḥah[568] who built a castle; when he finished, Uḥayḥah asked him, "Have you made it strong?" and he responded, "I know a stone in it which, if pulled out, will lead to its utter collapse" and Uḥayḥah asked him which stone it was, so he showed it to him, and then Uḥayḥah pushed him off the castle and he was killed |
| or al-Jaʿfarī, | "a palace of al-Mutawakkil's[569] close to Surra Man Ra'ā" |
| or al-Mārid, | ["the Defiant"] "a castle at Dawmat al-Jandal"[570] 2.14.40 |
| or al-Ablaq, | ["the Piebald"] "a castle at Taymā', one of two that al-Zabbā' tried and failed to take, leading |

| | | |
|---|---|---|
| | | her to say, ʻal-Mārid defied me, and al-Ablaq was too strong'” |
| | or Ṣirwāḥ, | “a castle built by the jinn for Bilqīs” |
| | or Dār al-Khayzurān, | “at Mecca, built by Khayzurān,[571] the caliph's slave girl” |
| | or Qaṣr Bahrām Jūr, | “made from a single rock, near Hamadhān” |
| | or Qaṣr Ghafrāʾ, | “in Syria” |
| | or al-Badīʿ, | “a large building of al-Mutawakkil's, at Surra Man Raʾā” |
| | or Zuʿayrah, | “a castle close to al-Karak” |
| | or Qaṣr ʿIsl, | “at Baṣrah” |
| | or al-Nadd, | “a castle in Yemen” |
| 2.14.41 | or al-Ghufr, | another castle there |
| | or Samadān, | another castle there, large |
| | or al-Shakhab, | another castle there |
| | or Tharabān, | another castle there |
| | or Hirrān, | another castle there |
| | or Shuwāḥiṭ, | another castle there |
| | or al-Mawhabah, | another castle there |
| | or al-Ẓafīr, | a castle east of Ṣanʿāʾ |
| | or Lasīs, | “a castle in Yemen” |
| | or al-Nujayr, | “a castle close to Haḍramawt” |
| | or Ghumdān, | “a palace in Yemen built by Yashrukh, with four faces, one red, one white, one yellow, and one green, inside of which he built another palace with seven roofs, each roof forty cubits distant from the next” |

he still wouldn't stop yelling, “A woman! A woman! Who will get me a woman?” and “No life without a woman!” and if you set him down in

| | | |
|---|---|---|
| 2.14.42 | Shiʿb Bawwān, | “one of the four paradises” |
| | or Ṣanʿāʾ, | “a town in Yemen with many trees and much water resembling Damascus” |

| | |
|---|---|
| or al-Sughd, | "pleasure gardens and places filled with fruiting trees, in Samarqand" |
| or al-Shaʿrān, | "a mountain close to Mosul, one of the mountains most overflowing with fruits and birds" |
| or al-Wahṭ, | "an orchard, or a property belonging to ʿAmr ibn al-ʿĀṣ,[572] three miles from Wajj,[573] that took a million pieces of wood to trellis, each piece costing one dirham" |
| or Balansiyyah, | [Valencia] "A town in eastern al-Andalus, surrounded by gardens where all one can hear is water gushing and birds caroling" |
| or Mursiyyah, | [Murcia] "An Islamic town in the Maghreb, with many parks and orchards" |
| or Thamānīn, | [literally, "Eighty"] "A town built by Nūḥ, peace be upon him, when he left the ark with eighty souls" |
| or Jābalaṣ, | "a town in the Maghreb, beyond which nothing human lives" |
| or al-Rāhūn, | "a mountain in India, on which Adam, peace be upon him, fell"[574] |
| or al-Jūdī, | "a mountain in al-Jazīrah,[575] on which the ark of Nūḥ came to rest" |
| or Qāf, | "a mountain that surrounds the earth, or one made of emeralds, a vein of which is present in every town and on which is an angel to whom God, should He wish to destroy a people, gives an order, which the angel carries out, causing them to be swallowed up by the earth" |
| or Qīq, | "a mountain that surrounds the world, also called Fīq" |
| or al-Sāhirah, | "a land that God will strip bare on the Day of Resurrection" |

he wouldn't stop yelling, "A woman! A woman! Who will get me a woman?" and "No life without a woman!" In fact, even if he ascended to

| | |
|---|---|
| 2.14.43 al-Mishrīq, | "a gate for repentance, in Heaven" |
| or Ṭūbā, | "a tree in Heaven" |
| or ʿIlliyyīn, | "in the Seventh Heaven, to which the souls of the Believers ascend; plural of *ʿIllī*" |
| or al-Ḍurāḥ, | "the Prosperous House in the Seventh Heaven" |
| or Burquʿ, | "a name for the Seventh, Fourth, or First Heaven" |
| or al-Ḥāqūrah, | "a name for the Fourth Heaven" |
| or al-Ṣāqūrah, | "a name for the Third Heaven" |
| or al-Ghurfah, | "the Seventh Heaven, also called ʿArūbā; it contains the lote tree beyond which none may pass"[576] |
| or ʿIqyawn, | "a sea of wind beneath the Throne in which there are angels of wind with spears of wind gazing at the Throne whose Magnificat is 'Glory to Our Lord Most High!'" |
| or the Aʿrāf, | "a wall between Paradise and the Fire" |

he would set about yelling with all the force his throat could muster, "A woman! A woman! So long as I am human, I must have a woman!" and if you were to show him such wonders as

| | |
|---|---|
| 2.14.44 the Sakīnah, | "a thing that had a head like a cat's, made of chrysolite and ruby and with two wings" |
| or the Kilwādh, | "the Ark of the Torah" |
| or Māriyyah's Earrings, | "she was Māriyyah, daughter of Arqam, or Ẓālim, who had two hundred dinars in her earrings, or jewels valued at forty thousand dinars, or two pearls like pigeon's eggs the like of which had never been seen before, so she gave them to the Kaaba" |

| | |
|---|---|
| or the Bridge of Khurradhādh, the mother of Ardashīr, | "in Samarqand, between Aydaj and the fort, one of the wonders of the world, one thousand cubits in length and one hundred and fifty in height, mostly constructed of lead and iron" |
| the Sepulcher of Tāḥah, | "Tāḥah was the daughter of Dhī l-Shufr; Ibn Hishām[577] says that a flash flood washed away the earth from a grave in Yemen in which was a woman around whose neck were seven ropes of pearls and on whose hands and feet were seven times seven bracelets, anklets, and armlets and on each of whose fingers was a precious stone and at whose head was a chest full of money and a tablet on which was written 'In Your Name, O God, God of Ḥimyar![578] I am Tāḥah, daughter of Dhī Shufr [sic]. I sent our purveyor to Yūsuf, but he made no haste to help us, so I sent my trusted lady-in-waiting with a bushel of silver that she might bring us a bushel of flour, but she could find none, so I sent a bushel of gold, and still she could find none, so I sent a bushel of fine pearls, and still she could find none, so I ordered the pearls brought and had them ground up, but I benefited nothing and had no food to give out, so let any who hears my plight be merciful to me, and let no woman who dons one piece of my finery die any death other than mine.'" |
| or Dhū l-Faqār, | "the sword of Sayf ibn Munabbih who was killed at the battle of Badr;[579] he was an unbeliever, so his sword became the property of the Prophet (peace and blessings upon him) and of 'Alī"[580] |

| | | |
|---|---|---|
| | or the Kashūḥ, | “one of the seven swords that Bilqīs presented to Sulaymān, peace be upon him” |
| | or the Ḥinn, | “a tribe of the jinn to which jet-black dogs belong, or the meanest and weakest of the jinn and their dogs, or creatures between men and jinn” |
| | or Awram al-Jawz, | “a village near Aleppo in which is a wonder, to wit, that at night the neighboring villages see firelight there in a tabernacle, but when they go to it they find nothing” |
| | or the Ra’iyy, | “a jinni who, once seen, is loved” |
| | or Qāyin’s horse, called Hijdam, | “it is said that, when Adam’s son, the murderer, first mounted him, he charged his brother, but the horse held back, so he said, ‘Bestir thy blood! (*hij al-dam*),’ so it surged forward” |
| 2.14.45 | or the ʿAṣāfīr, | “a kind of tree called ‘Who Has Seen My Like?’ which has the shape of birds (*ʿaṣāfīr*), plentiful in Persia” |
| | or the Nasnās, | “a species of creature that jumps on one foot; in the hadith it says that a tribe of ʿĀd[581] rebelled against their prophet, so God turned them into Nasnās, each one of whom had a hand and a foot on one side of the body and who hopped like birds and grazed like beasts; it is also said that those have become extinct and that what currently exists of that form are a separate species, or that they are of three kinds—*nās*, *nasnās*, and *nasānis*;[582] or that the *nasānis* are the females, or that they are a higher form than the *nasnās*, or that they are Yājūj and Mājūj,[583] or that they are a group of humans, or creatures that are in the shape of people but differ from them in certain things and are not of them” |

| | |
|---|---|
| or Daʿmūṣā, | "an adulterer whom God turned into a *daʿmūṣā*, meaning a certain creeping thing, or a black worm such as is found in rain pools when they dry up" |
| or ʿAbbūdā, | "a black slave, the first person to enter Paradise" |
| or ʿĀmir ibn Jadarah, | "the first person to write using our script" |
| or Murāmirā, | "the inventor of the Arabic script" |
| or Abū ʿUrwah, | "a man who shouted, 'Lions!' and then died, and when his belly was cut open, his heart was found to have moved from one place in his body to another" |
| or Ṭakhmūrath, | "one of the great kings of the Persians, who reigned for seven hundred years" |
| or al-Waḍḍāḥ, | "a man who ruled the earth; his mother was of the jinn, so he returned to them" |
| or the Rābiḍah, | "angels" who descended "with Adam, or the remainder of the bearers of the Proof, which no part of the earth is without"[584] |
| or the *yabrūḥ*, | "the mandrake root, which resembles a human" |
| or Sukaynah, | "the name of the bedbug that got up Numrūdh's nose" 2.14.46 |
| or Ṭākhiyah, | "an ant who spoke to Sulaymān,[585] peace be upon him" |
| or ʿAyjalūf, | "the name of the ant mentioned in the Qurʾan"[586] |
| or the *tukhas*, | "a sea beast that rescues drowning men by offering them its back to save them from having to swim; also called the *dulfīn* ('dolphin')" |
| or the *jassāsah*, | "a beast to be found on islands that seeks out news and passes it on to the Antichrist" |
| or the *rukhkh*, | "a large bird that can lift a rhinoceros" |

or the *karkadan*, ["rhinoceros"] "a beast that can lift an elephant on its horn"

or the *zabaʿrā*, "a beast that can carry an elephant on its horn"

or the *ʿaqām*, "a fish, or a snake that lives in the sea—the lion comes from the land and whistles on the shore, the *ʿaqām* comes out to it, and they intertwine; then they part and each returns to its dwelling"

or *bint ṭabaq*, [literally, "daughter of a plate"] "the tortoise, which lays ninety-nine eggs, all of which are tortoises, and one more, which hatches to reveal a snake"

2.14.47 or the *falatān*, "a bird that hunts apes"

or the *bulat*, "a bird with burning feathers which, should they fall on other birds, burn them"

or the *samandal*, "a bird in India that cannot be burned by fire"

or the *tihibbiṭ*, "a grayish bird that clings on with its feet and makes a sound as though it were saying *anā amūt anā amūt* ("I am dying, I am dying")

or the *unan*, "a bird like a dove whose sound is a moan—'ouhi-ouhi'"

or the *zummāḥ*, "a bird that takes children from their cradles"

or the *hadīl*, "a chick in the days of Nūḥ, peace be upon him, that died of thirst or was caught by some bird of prey, so that every dove now weeps for it"

or the *qarqafannah*, "a bird that wipes the eyes of the complacent wittol with its wings, making him yet more pliant"

or the *faqannas*, "a large bird with forty holes in its beak that sings every exhilarating, wonderful tune and air; it comes to the top of a mountain and collects as much firewood as it wants and sits and mourns for itself for forty days, during which everyone gathers to listen to it and take pleasure; then it climbs atop the firewood and claps its wings, and fire is struck from them, and the firewood and the bird catch fire, and it turns to ashes; then a new bird just like it is formed from them; Ibn Sīnā mentions it in the *Shifāʾ* (*The Cure*)"[587]

he would crane his neck and cup his ears with his hands[588] and cry to all the world, "Hey! Hey! A woman! A woman! Show me a woman! Nothing can take the place of a woman for me," and if you were to seek to divert him with

| | | |
|---|---|---|
| a *junābā*, | "a child's game" | 2.14.48 |
| or a *ḥadabdabā*, | "a game of the Nabataeans" | |
| or a *ṭabṭābah*, | "a broad stick used when playing ball" | |
| or *qarṭibbā*, | "a way of playing, or a kind of wrestling" | |
| or *kibkib*, | "a game" | |
| or *kūbah*, | "backgammon, or chess" | |
| or *habhāb*, | "a children's game" | |
| or *kutkutā*, | "a game" | |
| or *buḥḥaythā*, | "a game using *buḥāthah* (i.e., 'soil')" | |
| or *kuthkuthā*, | "a game using soil" | |
| or *ṭathth*, | "a children's game, in which they throw a round piece of wood called a *miṭaththah*" | 2.14.49 |
| or a *lūthah*, | "a piece of cloth, picked up and played with" | |
| or *unbūthah*, | "a game in which they bury something in a hole they make and the one who gets it out wins" | |
| or *shiṭranj*, | ["chess"] "too well known to require definition" | |
| or *kharīj*, | "a game also called *kharāji kharāji*" | |
| or *fanzaj*, | "a non-Arab dance" | |
| or *qajqajah*, | "a game, also called 'Waḍḍāḥ's Bone'"[589] | |

| | | |
|---|---|---|
| | or *kujjah,* | "a game in which the child takes a piece of cloth and twists it until it takes the shape of a ball" |
| | or *kajkajah,* | "a game also called *ist al-kalbah* ('bitch's butt')" |
| | or a *jummāḥ,* | "a date placed on the end of a stick that children play with" |
| 2.14.50 | or *jamḥ,* | "a child's kicking the heel of another child with his own in order to dislodge it from its place" |
| | or *diḥindiḥ,* | "a children's game, in which they gather and then say this word, and any who mispronounces it has to stand on one leg and hop seven times" |
| | or *dāḥ,* | "gewgaws that one waves at children and by which they are pacified; from it derives the saying *al-dunyā dāḥah* ('the world is a gaudy toy')" |
| | or a *rujjāḥah,* | "a rope that is suspended and that children climb" |
| | or *dubbākh,* | "a game" |
| | or *dumākh,* | "a game played by the Arabs of the desert" |
| | or a *miṭakhkhah,* | "a piece of wood that children play with" |
| | or a *ṭarīdah,* | "a game, called by the common people *al-massah wa-l-ḍabṭah* ('touch and grab'); if a player's hand falls onto another's trunk, head, or shoulder, it is called *massah,* and if it falls onto his leg it is called *asn*" |
| | or *nard,* | ["backgammon"] "too well known to require definition" |
| | or *muwāghadah,* | "a game, in which you do the same as your companion does" |
| 2.14.51 | or *baqqār,* | "a game" |
| | or *buqqayrā,* | "a game" |

| | | |
|---|---|---|
| or *jiʿirrā*, | "a children's game in which the child is carried between two others on their hands" | |
| or *ḥājūrah*, | "a game in which children draw a circle and a child stands inside it and they surround him to try to grab him" | |
| or *dikr*, | "a game of the negroes and Ethiopians" | |
| or *saḥḥārah*, | "something children play with" | |
| or *suddar*, | "a children's game" | |
| or *ʿarʿarah*, | "a children's game" | |
| or *shaʿārīr*, | "a game" | |
| or *minjār*, | "a children's game; the correct form may be *mījār*" | |
| or a *tūz*, | "a piece of wood with which they play at *kujjah*" | 2.14.52 |
| or *ʿarz*, | "when someone plays at *ʿarz*, he takes something in his hand and closes his fingers over it and shows a part of it for another to see but doesn't show him all of it" | |
| or *quffayzā*, | "a children's game in which they erect a piece of wood and compete at jumping over it" | |
| or *nuffāz*, | "a game of theirs in which they compete at bounding, or leaping" | |
| or a *buksah*, | "[the *buksah* is] the *kujjah*" | |
| or *ḥawālis*, | "a children's game" | |
| or *dussah*, | "a game" | |
| or *daʿkasah*, | "a pastime of the Magians, similar to dancing" | |
| or *fisfisā*, | "a game they play" | |
| or *fāʿūs*, | "a game they play" | |
| or *bawṣāʾ*, | "a game they play, in which they take a stick with fire at its end and pass it around on their heads" | 2.14.53 |
| or *raqqāṣah*, | "a game" | |
| or *ḥūṭah*, | "a game that they also call *dārah*" | |
| or *khuṭṭah*, | "a game played by the Arabs of the desert" | |

| | | |
|---|---|---|
| | or *ḍabṭah*, | “a game they play” |
| | or *taḍarfuṭ*, | “this is when you climb onto someone’s back and stick your legs out from under his armpits and put them around his neck” |
| | or *ḍurayfiṭiyyah*, | “a game they play” |
| | or *maqṭ*, | “to play *maqṭ* with the ball is to cast it onto the ground and then catch it” |
| | or a *mirṣāʿ*, | “a child’s spinning top or any piece of wood that is thrown down to hit a mark in a game” |
| | or a *yarmaʿ*, | “the same as a *khudhrūf*” |
| | or *qalawbaʿ*, | “a game they play” |
| 2.14.54 | or *jaḥfah*, | “playing ball” |
| | or a *khudhrūf*, | “a thing that a child turns with a string in his hands and that produces a humming sound; also called a *khudhrah* or a *qirfāṣah*; *khudhrūf* is also clay that is kneaded until it is made into something like sugar that children play with” |
| | or *zuḥlūfah*, | “the sliding of children from the top of a mound to its bottom” |
| | or *ʿayāf*, | “*ʿayāf* and *ṭarīdah* are two games they play” |
| | or *qāṣṣah qirfāṣah*, | “a game they play” |
| | or *ḥuzuqqah*, | “a kind of pastime” |
| | or *dabbūq*, | “a game” |
| | or a *zuḥlūqah*, | “a swing” |
| | or *shafalaqqah*, | “a game consisting of striking a person from behind and then throwing him to the ground” |
| | or *ʿafqah*, | “a game” |
| 2.14.55 | or a *ʿuqqah*, | “such as children play with”[590] |
| | or *qirq*, | “a pastime of the frivolous” |
| | or *kurrak*, | “a game they play” |
| | or *dibbā ḥajal*, | “a game” |
| | or *dukhayliyāʾ*, | “a game they play” |
| | or *diraqlah*, | “a children’s game” |

| | | |
|---|---|---|
| or *diraklah,* | "a game played by non-Arabs, or a kind of dance; or it may be Ethiopian" | |
| or *fi'āl,* | "a children's game consisting of hiding something in the dirt and then dividing the dirt into parts and saying, 'Which part is it in?'" | |
| or *fiyāl,* | "a game played by Arab youths" | |
| or *dummah,* | "a game" | |
| or a *duwwāmah,* | [the "spinning top"] "that children play with, making it revolve; also called *mirṣāʿ*" | |
| or *marghamah,* | "a game they play" | 2.14.56 |
| or *shaḥmah,* | "a game they play" | |
| or *ʿaẓm Waḍḍāḥ,* | "a game they play" | |
| or *mihzām,* | "a stick on top of which fire is placed and which they play with" | |
| or *barṭanah,* | "a kind of diversion, also pronounced *barṭamah*" | |
| or a *tūn,* | "a piece of cloth that they play with, like the *kujjah*" | |
| or *ṭuban,* | "a game they play" | |
| or *qinnīn,* | "a game played by the Greeks on which they gamble" | |
| or *kubnah,* | "a game" | |
| or *damah,* | "a children's game" | |
| or a *mijdhā',* | "a round piece of wood with which the Arabs of the desert play" | |
| or *mikhāsāh,* | "to play *mikhāsāh* with someone is to play with him at walnuts, saying 'Odd or even?'" | |
| or *quzzah,* | "a game" | |
| or *qullah,* | "two sticks that children play with" | |

he would open wide his mouth in a rictus and yell yet louder and more noisily, saying "A woman! A woman! Give me a woman to play with!" and if you charmed his ear with

| | | |
|---|---|---|
| a *rabāb,* | ["rebec, spike-fiddle"] "too well known to require definition" | 2.14.57 |

| | |
|---|---|
| or a *ʿarṭabah*, | "a lute, or a tambour, or drums, or the drums of the Ethiopians" |
| or a *kūbah*, | "a lute, or a small goblet drum" |
| or a *dirrīj*, | "a thing like a tambour that is played" |
| or *ṣanj*, | "a thing made out of brass, one piece of which is struck against the other, or a stringed instrument that is played (an Arabized non-Arab word); the sound made by the *ṣanj* is referred to as *ṣiyār*" |
| or *wanaj*, | "playing on strings or a lute or any musical instrument" |
| or *ʿūd*, | ["lute"] "too well known to require definition" |
| or *mizmār*, | "what is blown on as though it were a reed; also called *zamkhar* or *zanbaq* or *ṣulbūb* or *naqīb* or *qaṣṣābah* or *hubnūqah*" |
| or a *mizhar*, | "the *ʿūd* ('lute') on which one plays"[591] |
| or a *shabbūr*, | "a trumpet, also called *qabʿ* or *quthʿ* or *qunʿ* or *ṣūr*" |
| 2.14.58 or a *ṭunbūr*, | ["tambour"] "too well known to require definition" |
| or *kannārāt*, | "lutes, or large tambourines, or drums, or the tambour" |
| or a *kūs*, | "a drum" |
| or a *barbaṭ*, | "a lute" |
| or a *shiyāʿ*, | "a shepherd's pipe" |
| or a *hayraʿah*, | "a reed on which a shepherd blows" |
| or a *duff*, | ["large tambourine"] "too well known to require definition" |
| or a *mustuqah*, | "an instrument with which cymbals and the like are struck" |
| or a *ʿarkal*, | "a drum or a tambourine" |
| or a *ṣaghānah*, | "a musical instrument (Arabized)" |
| or a *ṭubn*, | "a tambour or a lute" |
| or a *qinnīn*, | "a tambour" |

or a *kirān*, “a lute or the *ṣanj*”
or *wann*, “the *ṣanj*”
he would remain open-mouthed, crying out and saying, “A woman! A woman! Will you not charm me with a woman?” and if you were to feed him with
*jūdhāb*, “a dish made of sugar, rice, and meat” 2.14.59
or *qabīb*, “moist and dry curds mixed together”
or *kabāb*, [“kebabs”] “too well known to require definition”
or *sannūt*, “butter, or cheese, or honey,[592] or a kind of date”
or *lafītah*, “thickened wheat gruel, or a broth resembling *ḥays*”[593]
or *nafītah*, “a dish thicker than *sakhīnah*”
or *ʿulāthah*, “clarified butter and curds mixed together”
or *ghabīthah*, “curds kneaded with clarified butter; synonym *ʿabīthah*”
or *sikbāj*, [“meat cooked in vinegar”] “too well known to require definition”
or *ṭubāhajah*, “sliced meat”
or *nābijah*, “a dish of the Days of Barbarism” 2.14.60
or *akhīkhah*, “flour made with clarified butter or oil”
or *qafīkhah*, “a dish made with dates and drippings”
or *kāmikh*, “pickles”
or *tharīd*, [“crumbled bread moistened with broth”] “too well known to require definition”
or *rashīdiyyah*, “a well-known dish; in Persian *rishtah* (‘noodles’)”
or *rahīdah*, “pounded wheat over which milk is poured”
or *shahīdah*, “grilled lamb”
or *qadīd*, “jerked, sun-dried meat”
or *ḥanīdh*, “*ḥanadha l-shāh* means ‘he grilled the ewe by placing on top of it heated stones to cook it’; the result is called *ḥanīdh*”

| | | |
|---|---|---|
| 2.14.61 | or *zumāward*, | "a dish of eggs and meat, also called *muyassar*" |
| | or *barābīr*, | "a dish made of parched ears of wheat and fresh milk" |
| | or *būrāniyyah*, | "a dish attributed to Būrān, daughter of al-Ḥasan ibn Sahl, the wife of al-Maʾmūn"[594] |
| | or *jāshiriyyah*, | "a dish" |
| | or *jaʿājir*, | "whatever is made of dough, such as figurines, that they then place in inspissated fruit juice and cook" |
| | or *ḥarīrah*, | "flour cooked with milk or fat" |
| | or *ḥakr*, | "clarified butter with honey that children lick" |
| | or *makhbūr*, | fatty dishes or[595] "*khubrah*, or *tharīdah ḍakhmah* ('great *tharīdah*') . . . or food generally, or meat, or the part of a thing that is offered, or food that a traveler takes with him on his journey, or a large wooden bowl containing bread and meat for between four and five persons" |
| | or *khazīrah*, | "something resembling *ʿaṣīdah* ('a paste of flour and clarified butter') with meat" |
| | or *ṣaḥīrah*, | "fresh milk that is boiled and onto which clarified butter is poured" |
| 2.14.62 | or *ghadhīrah*, | "flour to which fresh milk is added and which is then heated with hot stones" |
| | or *furfūr*, | "mush made of thorny carob fruit" |
| | or *murrī*, | "pickles as condiments" |
| | or *maḍīrah*, | "broth cooked with sour milk" |
| | or *najīrah*, | "milk mixed with meal or clarified butter" |
| | or *waghīr*, | "boiled or cooked milk" |
| | or *khāmīz*, | "broth made of *sikbāj* ('meat cooked in vinegar')" |
| | or *khanīz*, | "*tharīdah* ('crumbled bread with broth') made from flaky pastry" |

| | | |
|---|---|---|
| or *murazzaz*, | "food made with rice" | |
| or *basīsah*, | "milled curds pounded with clarified butter" | |
| or *ḥamīsah*, | "synonym of *qaliyyah* ('broth made of camel meat')" | 2.14.63 |
| or *ḥays*, | "dates mixed with clarified butter or curds and then well kneaded" | |
| or *kasīs*, | "meat dried on stones and beaten when dry until it becomes like *sawīq* ('parched barley meal')" | |
| or *harīsah*, | ["a condiment made with chili peppers" or "a sweet confection made with flour, butter, and sugar"] "too well known to require definition" | |
| or *bawsh*, | "in Egypt, a dish of wheat and lentils washed together in a sieve, placed in a jar, sealed with mud, and put in a clay oven" | |
| or *jashīsh*, | "mush and finely milled wheat placed in a pot into which meat or dates are tossed and which is then cooked" | |
| or *rashrash*, | "the drippings from the grill" | |
| or *qamīshah*, | "a dish of milk and colocynth or similar seeds" | |
| or *mukarrashah*, | "a dish made of meat and fat wrapped in camel tripes" | |
| or *kawshān*, | "a dish of rice and fish" | |
| or *āmiṣ*, | "*āmiṣ*, or *amīṣ*, is a dish made of calf meat with the skin, or *sikbāj* broth cooled and with the fat strained off" | 2.14.64 |
| or *khabīṣ*, | "a dish of dates and clarified butter, also called *barūk*" | |
| or *'amṣ*, | "a kind of food" | |
| or *karīṣ*, | "sorrel cooked in milk and then dried; eaten in hot weather" | |
| or *maṣūṣ*, | "a dish of meat cooked and marinated in vinegar, or especially of fowl meat" | |

or *aqiṭ*, “something made from buttermilk of sheep and goats”

or *mubarqaṭ*, “a dish into which a large amount of oil is worked”

or *bahaṭṭ*, “rice cooked with milk (an Arabized word)”

or *khalīṭ*, “kid, skinned and grilled”

or *samīṭ*, “kid, stripped of the hair and grilled”

2.14.65 or *suraytā’*, “a soup, synonym *ḥarīrah*”

or *suwayṭā’*, “a broth with a lot of water and trimmings, meaning onions, chickpeas, and grains of any kind”

or *tashyīṭ*, “meat grilled for the whole group”

or *khadī‘ah*, “a dish of theirs”

or *khadhī‘ah*, “a dish, in the Levant, of meat, the word deriving from *khadha‘a* meaning ‘to shear’ or ‘cut’; *mukhadhdha‘* means ‘grilled meat’”

or *khal‘*, “meat cooked with spices, or in a container made of hide, or jerked meat grilled in a container with its drippings”

or *raṣī‘ah*, “wheat pounded with a stone pestle, moistened, and cooked with clarified butter”

or *waḍī‘ah*, “pounded wheat onto which clarified butter is poured before eating”

or *thamīghah*, “soft food mixed with fat”

or *khaṭīfah*, “flour sprinkled with milk and cooked”

2.14.66 or *ṣafṣafah*, synonym of *sikbājah*[596]

or *ṭiḥrif*, “a thin soup thinner than *‘aṣīdah* (‘thick gruel of flour and clarified butter’)”

or *mūkhif*, “a dish of ground curds sprinkled onto water onto which clarified butter is then poured”

or *alūqah*, “delicious food, or butter with *ruṭab* dates”[597]

or *ḥarūqah*, “a dish thicker than *ḥasā’* (‘soup’)”

or *mudaqqaqah*, “a kind of food (a post-classical word)”

| | |
|---|---|
| or *rawdhaq*, | "lamb roasted with the wool removed, or any meat cooked and mixed together" |
| or *zurayqā'*, | "crumbled bread with broth to which milk or oil is added" |
| or *salīqah*, | "millet bruised and dressed, or curds mixed with legumes, or boiled pulses and the like" |
| or *sawīq*, | ["parched barley meal"] "too well known to require definition" |
| or *shubāriq*, | "meat cut into small pieces and grilled" 2.14.67 |
| or *washīq*, | "meat cut into strips and dried or well boiled and then cut into strips and taken on journeys" |
| or *walīqah*, | "a dish made of flour, milk, and clarified butter" |
| or *dalīk*, | "a dish made of butter and milk, or of butter and dates, or a plant to which red rose hips may be admixed, in which case it becomes as sweet as moist fresh dates," etc. |
| or *rabīkah*, | "curds with dates and clarified butter" |
| or *sahīkah*, | "a dish" |
| or *farīk*, | "a food that is rubbed and pounded with clarified butter and other things" |
| or *labīkah*, | "curds mixed with flour or dates and clarified butter" |
| or *wadīkah*, | "meal parched with clarified butter" |
| or *bakīlah*, | "flour with inspissated fruit juice or clarified butter and dates" |
| or *ḥadhal*, | "the seeds of a tree that are baked" 2.14.68 |
| or *ṭafayshal*, | "a kind of broth" |
| or *'awkal*, | "a kind of condiment" |
| or *zawm*, | "a dish of the people of Yemen, made of milk and delicious" |
| or *abū 'āṣim*, | "either *sawīq* or *sikbāj*" |

| | |
|---|---|
| or *hulām,* | "a dish of calf's flesh with the skin, or *sikbāj* broth cooled and with the fat strained off" |
| or *sakhīnah,* | "a soft dish made of flour" |
| or *kubān,* | "a millet dish of the Yemenis" |
| or *talbīnah,* | "a soup made with bran, milk, and honey" |
| or *jalīhah,* | "dates worked with milk" |
| or *irah,* | "jerked meat, or meat well boiled with vinegar, and taken on journeys" |
| or *āṣiyah,* | "a soup-like dish with dates" |
| or *iṭriyyah,* | "a dish like threads, made of flour" |
| or *kadā,* | "milk in which dates are steeped and which is used to fatten girls" |

2.14.69 and if you were to feed him with all the different kinds of fungi, such as *dhubaḥ* truffles or *farḥānah* truffles or *qurḥān* truffles or *ghard* truffles or the little earth-colored truffles they call "Daughters of Awbar" or *jamāmīs* truffles or soft white *faqʿ* truffles or long red (or short black) *birnīq* truffles or *dhuʿlūq* truffles or *qaʿbal* truffles or the *ʿurjūn* mushrooms that look like *faqʿ* truffles or *ʿurhūn* mushrooms (which are a kind of truffle), or with all the different kinds of fish, such as the *qubāb* (which resembles the *kanʿad*) or the *hāzibā* (one of which is called a *huffah*) or the *kanʿat* (which is the same as the *kanʿad*) or the *kanʿad* (which is a sea fish) or the *khubbāṭ* (the young of the *kanʿad*) or the *baynīth* (a sea fish) or the *muddaj* or the *abdaḥ* or the *qudd* (a sea fish) or the *ghawbar* or the *zimmīr* or the *zunjūr* or the *ushbūr* or the *ṭanz* or the *anqalīs* (which looks like a snake) or the *jūfā* or the *lukhm* (a sea fish) or the *abū marīnā* or

| | |
|---|---|
| 2.14.70 the *ṣilinbāḥ,* | "a species of long, slim fish" |
| or the *ḥāffīrah,* | "a black fish" |
| or the *jirrī,* | "a species of long, smooth fish not eaten by the Jews and having no scales" |
| or the *ṣarṣarān,* | "a smooth species of fish" |
| or the *ghārrah,* | "a long fish" |
| or the *qayṣānah,* | "a round, yellow fish" |

| | | |
|---|---|---|
| or the *shabbūṭ*, | "a species of fish with a slim tail and broad middle, soft to the touch and with a small head, as though it were a lute" | |
| or the *jinnīs*, | "a fish halfway in color between white and yellow" | |
| or the *ḍilaʿah*, | "a small, green fish with short bones" | |
| or the *ḥaffah*, | "a bony white fish" | |
| or the *ʿuffah*, | "a white scale-less fish that tastes like rice when cooked" | 2.14.71 |
| or the *khudhdhāq*, | "a fish with thread-like feces" | |
| or the *ḥāqūl*, | "a long, green fish" | |
| or the *qatan*, | "a fish as broad as the palm of the hand" | |
| or the *ghalāʾ*, | "a short fish" | |
| or *hiff*, | "small fry that flee" | |
| or *balam*, | "small fry" | |
| or *ṣaḥnāh*, | "a condiment made from small fry" | |
| or *ṣīr*, | "*ṣaḥnāh* or something resembling it, or the salted fish from which *ṣaḥnāh* is made" | |
| or *ḥarīd*, | "sun-dried fish" | |
| or *qarīb*, | "salted fish when still moist" | 2.14.72 |
| or *ṭirrīkh*, | "small fish treated with salt" | |
| or *ḥusās*, | "small fish that are dried" | |
| or *nashūṭ*, | "fish that are macerated in water and salt" | |
| or the *irbiyān*, | "a species of fish like worms" | |
| or *ṣuʿqur*, | "fish eggs" | |
| or the *sikl*, | "a huge, black fish" | |
| or *zajr*, | "large fish" | |
| or the *bāl*, | "the mighty whale" | |
| or the *aṭūm*, | "a thick sea fish" | |
| or the *jaydharah*, | "a fish like a huge black negro" | 2.14.73 |
| or the *bunbuk*, | "a beast like a dolphin" | |
| or the *jamal*, | "a fish thirty cubits long" | |
| or the *liyyāʾ*, | "a fish from which high-quality shields are made; also something like chickpeas, | |

| | |
|---|---|
| | extremely white, to which women are compared" |
| or *tukhas*, | previously mentioned under "the wonders" |
| or of shellfish, such as | |
| *sulaj*, | "seashells containing something edible" |
| or the *dullāʿ*, | "a kind of shell found in the sea" |
| or the *qarthaʿ*, | "a small sea creature with a shell" |
| or *jummaḥl*, | "flesh found in the interior of the shell" |
| or of the various kinds of bread, such as | |
| 2.14.74 *ṭurmūth*, | "bread made in the ashes, similar to *mufta'ad*, *muḍbāh*, *ṭurmūs*, *iṣṭakmah*, and *uṣṭukmah*" (an oddity here is that the author of the *Qāmūs* puts the form with *i* after the entry for the root *'-sh-m* and that with *u* after *ṣ-ṭ-m*) |
| or *zalaḥlaḥah*, | "a thin bread, synonym *ṣarīqah*" |
| or *luḥūḥ*, | "bread resembling *qaṭā'if* ('small triangular doughnuts fried in butter and served with honey')" |
| or *anbakhānī*, | "a huge puffed-up loaf of fermented dough" |
| or *khubrah*, | "a huge mess of crumbled bread moistened with broth" |
| or *mashṭūr*, | "bread wiped with sour condiments" |
| or *sillajn*, | "cake" |
| or *khanīz*, | "crumbled unleavened bread moistened with broth" |
| or *rashrash*, | "floppy dry bread; synonym *rashrāsh*" |
| or *hashāsh*, | "soft floppy bread" |
| or *murabbaqah*, | "a bread made with fat; *murawwalah* is similar" |
| or *ruqāq*, | "flaky bread" |
| or *ḍaghīghah*, | "layered rice bread" |
| or *mullā*, | "a well-cooked bread" |
| or of the different kinds of milk, such as | |
| 2.14.75 *samʿaj*, | "sweet, fatty milk; similar are *samlaj*, *samhaj*, and *samhajīj*" |

or *quṭabiyyah*, "goat and sheep milk mixed, or camel and sheep milk mixed"

or *shamīṭ*, "milk that is so tasty that it is impossible to tell if it is curdled or fresh milk mixed with curdled"

or *julaʿṭīṭ*, "thick buttermilk; other terms with the same meaning are *ʿujaliṭ*, *ʿuthaliṭ*, *ʿudhaliṭ*, *ʿukaliṭ*, and *ʿulabiṭ*";

once an insufferable grammarian, who insisted on speaking literary Arabic, went up to a milkman and said, "Milkman, hast thou any milk that is *ʿuthaliṭ*, *ʿulabiṭ*, or *ʿujaliṭ*?" to which the milkman replied, "Be off before I give you a slap on the back of your neck!"

or *kafkhah*, "a white blended butter"

or *liyākhah*, "butter melted with milk"

or *qishdah*, "a runny butter"

or *qildah*, "*qishdah*, dates, and parched barley meal made with pure clarified butter"

or *nahīd*, "runny butter"

or *ʿakīs*, "fresh milk onto which drippings have been poured"

or *thamīrah*, "milk whose butter has appeared"

or *nakhīsah*, "goat or ewe milk mixed together"

or *imkhāḍ*, "fresh milk while still in the churn"

or *ḥālūm*, "a kind of curds or milk thickened until it turns into something like moist cheese"

or of sweet things, such as

*waṭīʾah*, "pitted dates kneaded with milk, or curds with sugar and cake" 2.14.76

or *ʿabībah*, "a food and a drink made from mimosa (sweet)"

or *burt*, "sugar"

or *ḍayḥ*, "honey, or ripe doum fruit"

| | | |
|---|---|---|
| | or *malakh*, | "honey from wild pomegranate blossoms" |
| | or *yaʿqīd*, | "a dish thickened with honey" |
| | or *fārid*, | "the whitest, best sugar" |
| | or *qand*, | "sugar-cane molasses" |
| | or *fānīd*, | "a kind of sweetmeat" |
| | or *ṣaqr*, | "molasses of fresh moist dates, or inspissated fruit juice" |
| | or *ikbir*, | "something like dry *khabīṣ* ('dates mixed with clarified butter') that is not extremely sweet and is brought by bees" |
| | or *fālūdh*, | ["blancmange"] "too well known to require definition; also called *riʿdīd*, *muzaʿzaʿ*, *zalīl*, *kamṣ*, and *muzaʿfar*" |
| | or *mādhī*, | "white, or new, honey, or the purest and best honey" |
| | or *muyassar*, | "a sweet dish" |
| | or *lawzinj*, | [dish made with almonds (*lawz*)] "too well known to require definition; an Arabized word" |
| 2.14.77 | or *wakhīz*, | "moistened crumbled bread made with honey" |
| | or *lawāṣ*, | "blancmange with honey" |
| | or *siriṭrāṭ*, | "blancmange, or *khabīṣ* ('dates mixed with clarified butter')" |
| | or *majīʿ*, | "dates kneaded with milk" |
| | or *qaṭāʾif*, | [small triangular doughnuts fried in butter and served with honey] "too well known to require definition" |
| | or *kursufī*, | "a kind of honey" |
| | or *ṭirm*, | "honeycomb, or butter, or honey" |
| | or *mann*, | "any dew that falls from the sky onto trees or rocks and is sweet and coagulates to form honey and dries like gum" |

| | | |
|---|---|---|
| or *zalābiya*, | ["fritters"] "a sweet dish, too well known to require definition" | |
| or of fruit, such as | | |
| *ṣarabah*, | "something like a cat's head with something like inspissated juice on it that is sucked or eaten" | 2.14.78 |
| or *ʿutrub*, | "a tree, like the pomegranate, whose fruit is eaten" | |
| or *būt*, | "a tree whose foliage is like that of the azarole" | |
| or *raʿthāʾ*, | "grapes with a long fruit" | |
| or *jawḥ*, | "Levantine watermelons" | |
| or *ṣadaḥ*, | "a fruit redder than the jujube" | |
| or *mulāḥī*, | "long white grapes, or a kind of fig" | |
| or *ʿanjad*, | "raisins, or a particular kind thereof" | |
| or *firṣād*, | "the mulberry, or its fruit, or such of its fruit as is red" | |
| or *qathad*, | "a plant resembling squirting cucumber, or cucumbers" | |
| or *kashd*, | "an edible berry" | |
| or *marīd*, | "dates steeped in milk" | 2.14.79 |
| or *maghd*, | "fruits resembling cucumbers" | |
| or *ḥanādh*, | "apricots" | |
| or *ṣufriyyah*, | "Yemeni dates dried before ripening and used in place of sugar when making parched barley meal" | |
| or *ḍamīr*, | "withered grapes" | |
| or *zinbār*, | "figs from Ḥulwān" | |
| or *sukkar*, | "the best grapes" [literally, "sugar"] | |
| or *zaʿrāʾ*, | "a kind of peach" | |
| or *shaʿrāʾ*, | "another kind [of peach]" | |
| or *mighthar*, | "something honey-like exuded by panic grass, milkweed, and the dwarf tamarisk; synonym *mighfar*" | |

| | | |
|---|---|---|
| 2.14.80 | or *ghawfar*, | "rainy-season watermelons, or a kind thereof" |
| | or *qubbaz*, | "long, white grapes" |
| | or *marmār*, | "pomegranates with much juice and little pulp" |
| | or *nahir*, | "white grapes; *kulāfī* are white grapes with a touch of green" |
| | or *jawzah*, | "a kind of grape" |
| | or *mishlawz*, | "sweet apricots" |
| | or *balas*, | "fruits resembling figs" |
| | or *ḍaghābīṣ*, | "small squirting cucumbers, or a plant resembling asparagus" |
| | or *mays*, | "a kind of raisin" |
| | or *kishmish*, | "small, seedless grapes softer than [regular] grapes" |
| 2.14.81 | or *ḍurūʿ*, | "white grapes with a large berry" |
| | or *aqmāʿī*, | "white grapes whose berries eventually turn as yellow as *wars*"[598] |
| | or *mayʿah*, | "a tree like the apple with edible fruit larger than walnuts, whose kernels are fatty, liquid storax (*mayʿah*) being squeezed from them" (according to one definition) |
| | or *ghāf*, | "a tree with very sweet fruit" |
| | or *bāsiq*, | "a tasty yellow fruit" |
| | or *rāziqī*, | "long white grapes" |

he would open his mouth even wider and shriek, shout, yell, and clamor yet more, saying, "A woman! A woman! Get me a woman to lick!" and even if you provided him by way of drink

| | | |
|---|---|---|
| 2.14.82 | *raḥīq* mixed with *band*, | *raḥīq* is "wine, or the best-tasting thereof, or the purest, or what is clear" and *band* is "water that intoxicates" |
| | or *salsal* mixed with *salsal*, | *salsal* is "sweet water, or smooth wine" |

| | | |
|---|---|---|
| or *misṭār* with which *ʿaḍras* has been mixed, | *misṭār* is "wine that fells the one who drinks it" and *ʿaḍras* is "sweet, cold water, or ice" | |
| or *isfinṭ* with which *naqiz* has been mixed, | *isfinṭ* is "perfumed grape juice, or a sort of drink, or the finest wine" and *naqiz* is "sweet, clear water" | |
| or *khurṭūm* mixed with *zulāl* water, | *khurṭūm* is "fast-acting wine" and *zulāl* (on the pattern of *ghurāb*) water is "water that is flowing, easy, clear, sweet, cold, and quick to pass down the throat" | |
| or *muʿattaqah* mixed with *furāt*, | *muʿattaqah* is "old wine" and *furāt* is "very sweet water" | |
| or *muthallath*, | "a drink that is cooked until two-thirds of it is gone" | |
| or *faḍīkh*, | "grape juice, or a drink made from split unripe dates" | |
| or *faqd*, | "a drink from raisins or honey; synonym *fuqdud*" | |
| or *maqadī*, | "a drink from honey" | 2.14.83 |
| or *dādhī*, | "the drink of the depraved" | |
| or *jumhūrī*, | "an intoxicating drink, or three-year-old grape wine" | |
| or *khusruwānī*, | "a drink" | |
| or *sakar*, | "wine, or a fermented drink made from dates" | |
| or *ghubayrāʾ*, | "*sukarkah*, which is a drink made from millet" | |
| or *mizr*, | "a fermented drink from millet and barley" | |
| or *kasīs*, | "date wine" | |
| or *bitʿ*, | "a fermented drink made from fortified honey or the best grapes" | |
| or *suqurqaʿ*, | "a drink made from millet or barley and other grains" | |
| or *jiʿah*, | "a fermented drink from barley" | 2.14.84 |
| or *fuqqāʿ*, | "what is drunk when foam rises to its surface" | |

| | |
|---|---|
| or *bādhiq*, | "wine that is cooked as lightly as possible and thus fortified" |
| or *khalīṭān*, | "a fermented drink made of unripe and ripe dates together, or of grapes and raisins, or of the latter plus dates or the like" |
| or *ṣarī*, | "juice of red and yellow unripe dates that they pour onto lote fruit and make into a fermented drink" |
| or *ʿakī*, | "ripe doum-fruit mash" |
| or *aṭwāq*, | "coconut milk, which is highly intoxicating—moderately so, as long as the drinker does not go out into the wind, but if he does go out, he becomes extremely drunk," etc. |
| or *ṣafʿ*, | "a drink made from honey or grapes that are crushed, whose skins are discarded, and whose juice is then boiled" |
| or *nabq*, | "a flour that is extracted from the heart of the palm-tree trunk, that is sweet and is fortified with inspissated juice and then made into a fermented drink" |
| or *salīl*, | "a pure drink" |
| or *maʿmūl*, | "any drink containing milk and honey" |
| or *ṭilāʾ*, | "wine, or *khāthir al-munaṣṣaf*, which is a drink that is cooked until reduced by half" |

he would frown, and scream and shout yet more, saying, "A woman! A woman! Give me a woman to drink!"

2.14.85 Nay, even if you watered him with the waters of al-Faḥfāḥ and al-Kawthar[599] or with fine honey wine with which *tasnīm*[600] has been mixed, and added him to the company "among whom pass immortal youths bearing goblets and ewers and a cup from a spring"[601] and "such fruits that they shall choose and such flesh of fowl as they desire" "mid thornless lote trees and serried acacias and spreading shade and outpoured waters and fruits abounding—unfailing, unforbidden—and up-raised couches," and who have "two gardens abounding in branches, therein two fountains of running water... therein of every fruit two kinds and besides these two gardens... and green, green pastures... and two fountains of gushing water... and fruits, and palm trees, and pomegranates... and maidens good and comely... and fruits and palm trees with sheaths and grain in the blade and fragrant herbs" with among them those who "recline upon green cushions and lovely druggets" and those who "recline upon couches lined with brocade... upon close-wrought couches" who "shall be given to drink a cup whose mixture is ginger, and therein a fountain whose name is Salsabīl; immortal youths shall go about them, when thou seest them one supposest them scattered pearls ... with upon them green garments of silk and brocade, adorned with bracelets of silver," never, even in such a state, will you see him consenting to go without a woman, and I seek refuge with God from such a person: despite all of the foregoing (meaning the availability to the man of food and drink), he will insist upon a woman being present, since the first is created for the sustenance of life and the second to rectify his nature, as mentioned.

The presence of a woman is harder to ensure than that of either 2.14.86
food or drink, demands more effort, and is costlier, for food and drink are to be found in every place and at every time; even the people of hell have food in the form of *zaqqūm*,[602] molten copper, and cactus thorn, and drink in the form of foul pus, and shade from a smoking blaze,[603] but they do not have women in the form of "fire from a smokeless blaze"[604] or from among the demons, and there are no women present on board ship or in a monastery (except occasionally) or available to a man riding a horse or a camel or a mule, or to one running on foot, or to one fighting a war, or to a prisoner, or to a man with an ugly face (unless his money or his pedigree are attractive), or to an unctuous poet even though he flatter them and spend his nights describing their charms and rhapsodizing over them, or to one who has erectile dysfunction, or a tendency to premature ejaculation, premature climax, rapid climax, or early ejaculation, or to come immediately on penetration or to go soft

before it, or one who suffers from weak erections, or from going soft after being stiff, or is too quick to come, or comes just from talking to a woman, or suffers from impotence, or lack of libido, or frigidity, or lack of virility, or thwarted sexual capacity, or lack of sexual interest in women, or lack of sexual drive, or lack of studliness, or lack of manly vigor, or floppiness of the member, or poor performance, or sexual inertia, or sheer inability, or coming too fast, or behaving like a female jerboa, or lack of virility or machismo, or sexual ignorance, or shooting his wad the moment he enters, or indifference to women. If it be said that the toothless man can eat no bread either, I would reply that he can have bread pounded for him until it's soft and then chew on and work it over with his gums, but when you're one of those who come immediately on penetration, or suffer from any consanguine conditions, how are you ever going to find a way to chew over a woman?

2.14.87 In addition, just as confusion reigns over the very nature of womankind and men's minds are at a loss to understand the mystery with which God has endowed her, from the perspective that she is first cause of both the flourishing and the ruination of the universe, for almost nothing of great import takes place in the world but you'll discover when you peep through its chinks that there's a woman standing (or more likely lying) behind it, so likewise muddling and mixing are present in her name. Thus the word *imra'ah* ("woman") in our noble language is derived from the verb *mara'a*, used of food to mean "it was wholesome, healthy, and of beneficial effect,"[605] though in fact a woman is often a food to choke or gag on, one that causes indigestion, spoils one's appetite, and makes one's stomach heave. Furthermore, the glottal stop (*hamz*) in *imra'ah* is for purposes of elison (*waṣl*), and the elision (*waṣl*) in it is for purposes of compression (*hamz*),[606] while its plural is constructed from a different root than that of the singular and has numerous forms,[607] and in one language the word denotes "man's woe" and in another "pudendum."[608]

In contrast, a wife, by which is understood "a woman plus" or "half a woman plus half a man," has been allocated numerous names out of respect, among them *qarīnah* ("consort"), whose etymology is well known,[609] and *ʿāzibah,* which derives from *ʿazaba,* meaning "to distance oneself," because she distances herself from her parents when she goes to her husband or vice versa,[610] or when she goes away from him altogether, etc., and *ḥurmah* ("the protected one"), and also *al-liḥāf* ("the quilt") because she warms the man with the heat of her body, as will be explained,[611] and *ḥadādah*[612] and *niḍr* and *ʿirs*[613] and *ḥalīlah* ("co-dweller") and *al-libās* ("the bloomers") and *jathal* and *ḥāl* ("burden") and *khuḍullah* ("comfort, ease" or "a soft woman") and *shāʿah*[614] and *ḥannah* and *rubuḍ* and *al-naʿl* ("the sole") (though I don't approve of the last and it would be better if it were deleted). It's strange that she is called "the bloomers" and "the quilt" but not "the underdrawers." 2.14.88

A certain scholar has said that if God wishes to do something good on earth, he chooses a woman as the means to its accomplishment, and if the Devil wishes to do something evil, he also uses a woman for his ends. People differ over the interpretation of this statement. The Bag-men believe that the accession of women to the throne of England was an unalloyed blessing,[615] while the Market-men believe it was an infernal evil; similar are the cases of the two queens of England[616] and of Irene, wife of Leo IV, and Theodora, wife of Theophilus,[617] and so on without number. Note here that it has not been the custom to make women popes, metropolitans, heads of armies, ships' captains, or judges, out of fear of their intrepid and powerful natures. What would happen if men, who by nature worship women, were to vacate these high posts and they to assume them? If it be said that the Franks take them as queens and do well, I would respond that it has been decided among them that, if the head of state is a female, the management of the laws and all official work go to a male. This may be one of the most difficult issues relating to women, for the same analysis applies equally to 2.14.89

women being popes or anything else. I may have gone on at too great a length here about women, overlooking the fact that there are to be found among them some who are too short to justify a long discussion. Now, then, it is time for me to divorce myself from them and return to the matter in hand, though I shall come back to them at some other point, God willing.

# Chapter 15[618]

## . . . . . . . . . . Right There! ☞

## Chapter 16

# Right Here!

2.16.1 The pen has refused to obey my command to leave this stimulating spot and talk of the Fāriyāq and his like, and he too indeed, in all likelihood, would rather stay put than talk about himself. Thus there is no help for it but to resume my description of women, without tendering him any apology.

2.16.2 I thus declare: certain of our most eminent scholars have said that the woman is more honorable than the man, more imposing, nobler, more clement, more virtuous, and more generous. The argument for her being more honorable rests on the fact that the two witnesses to her feminity stand in an elevated position, enabling her to see them and to make them seen whenever she wishes, without bowing her head or bending over, and in this lie a pride and a nobility that cannot be concealed. Are you not aware that a certain litterateur has claimed that "the pride of 'No' lies in one's saying it with one's head raised, while the humiliation of 'Yes' lies in saying it with it bowed?" The two witnesses to a man's masculinity, on the other hand, are withdrawn, in a position that allows him to see them only if he bends over and bows down.

2.16.3 The argument for her being more imposing lies in the fact that her legs, which are the columns upon which the mass of the body stands, her belly, which is the nest in which the soul is formed, and her backside, which is a source of paralyzing inaction, are more imposing than the legs, belly, and backside of the man. The argument for her being nobler lies in the fact that she is treated with the respect due to nobility for a period of nine months because of what is cast into her. The argument for her being more clement lies in the fact that the mark of clemency[619] is visible on the two witnesses to her femininity.

The argument for her being more virtuous lies in the fact that she was created from and subsequent to the man and that he was created from dust. She, on the other hand, were she to die (which God forbid), would turn to dust like the man, not to the origin from which she was taken, i.e., would not become either a man or a rib. The argument for her being more generous lies in the fact that she is more tender-hearted, more kindly-minded, and more gentle-natured. If she sees someone to be in need of something she has, she will not begrudge it to him, on which topic it is enough to cite what the eulogist had to say about Mistress Zubaydah when he wrote, 2.16.4

O Zubaydah, Jaʿfar's daughter,
Happy the visitor you reward!
You grant as many wishes with your feet
As your hands accord.

When her attendants reproached him for these words and rose to beat him, she scolded them and thanked him, for she knew that his description was not wrong.[620]

Another eminent scholar has stated that a woman generally lives longer than a man, because her inborn suppleness, childlikeness, and smoothness allow her to face events with patience and deliberateness so that she is flexible with them, meaning that she bends now to this side, now to the other, being in this like the supple branch that bends with the wind and does not snap. Man, on the other hand, given his innate hardness and dryness, holds himself rigid and unyielding in the face of whatever may befall him and is, as a consequence, quickly destroyed by it, being in this like the dry tree in the face of the tempest. Another of her singular charactestics is that 2.16.5

alcohol does not affect her as much as it does the man, and people differ over why this is so. Some believe that there is an attractive force in the woman's blood that overcomes the alcohol and draws it downward so that it doesn't ascend to her brain. Others claim that the woman herself contains a kind of alcohol called *ruḍāb*[621] that is so strong within her that if you mix it with any other drink whatsoever the latter loses its strength; a single drop of this type of alcohol is sold sometimes for an enormous sum of money and sometimes for a man's head or his neck.

2.16.6 Further peculiarities of hers are that her locks are longer than a man's, her lyrics more eloquent, and her likes more precise, and that sleeping with her inside her slip is more fortifying. As to the first, no two will disagree. As to the second, the reason is that, when she makes up verses, she always composes them about a man and as a result it both pleases and affects men through nature, while simultaneously pleasing women through both nature and art. (This may be another of the knotty issues relating to women, for it seems to me that this analysis applies to the man only, for the only thing he composes verse about is women. This may be answered by saying that most of the output of the brilliant poet is directed to activities other than the love lyric, such as dreaming up praises with which to tell lies about some emir or describing a party or a war or something of the sort.)

2.16.7 The third argument may be illustrated by the fact that, if she passes a cloth merchant's store, for example, and catches sight of some translucent, citron-colored fabric, the moment she notices it she'll tell you that it would be perfect for the evening, while your thoughts at the time may be elsewhere—on a book to read or on buying a donkey to ride. If she sees some green silk brocade she'll tell you in the most matter-of-fact way that it would be perfect for winter or, if some extra-fine white linen, she'll assign it to summer. Similarly, if she passes a jeweler's store, or you're besotted enough to take her to one, she'll tell you immediately that that diamond would make a perfect bezel for a signet ring on her little finger, that ruby for one on her fourth finger, that emerald for one on her middle finger, that turquoise for one on her index finger, and that perfect pearl for one on her thumb; that those large pearls would make a collar for her neck, these little ones a bracelet, and those gem-studded gold chains could be placed around her neck next to the necklace so as to hang down to her waist, with a gold watch suspended from them, while those heavy earrings are for the winter, those light ones for the summer, and those medium ones for the spring and fall—during which time your thoughts are still preoccupied with the donkey. If it be objected that the second-person pronoun attached to the word "thoughts" is addressed indiscriminately to all readers and that your book may experience the honor of being read by an emir or other mighty lord, in which case it would be inappropriate to address him in this way, for an emir doesn't think about donkeys, I declare, in Chapter 36 of the Book of Genesis, it says that Anah, descendant of the son of Seir the Horite, used to graze the asses of his father Zibeon, and he was an emir; in fact, in some copies the title "duke" is appended to his name, and a duke is higher than an emir.[622]

Next, she—that is the woman—while contemplating these jewels, will lose no time in dividing the entire population of the cosmopolis into five work groups: 2.16.8

Work Group 1: For the Preparation of Gems and Precious Metals

| | |
|---|---|
| including *tijāb*, | "what is extracted from silver-bearing rock at a single smelting" |
| and *mashkhalabah*, | "white beads in the form of pearls or jewelry made from fiber and beads; also a name that may be applied to a girl because of the beads she has on; there is no other word of this pattern"; I declare, I seem to remember that Ibn al-Athīr cites it as *makhshalab* |
| and *ḍi'b*, | "seed pearls" |

| | | |
|---|---|---|
| | and *qaṣab*, | "any elongated gemstones . . . pearls of the first water or peridot of the first water studded with rubies" |
| | and *yashab*, | ["jasper"] "a stone too well known to require definition" |
| | and *baht*, | ["aetites, eagle stone"] "a stone too well known to require definition" |
| | and *kibrīt*, | "red rubies, or gold, or gemstones whose source is beyond al-Tubbat, in the Valley of the Ants"; under *t-b-t* [in the *Qāmūs*], "Tubbat [*sic*] is a land in the east from which comes the finest musk" |
| | and *yāqūt*, | ["rubies"] "too well known to require definition" |
| | and *dahnaj*, | "a gemstone like emerald" |
| | and *zibrij*, | gems, or an ornament with figures |
| | and *zabardaj*, | "the same as *zabarjad* ['peridot']" |
| 2.16.9 | and *ṣalījah*, | "a purified silver ingot" |
| | and *murjān*, | ["coral"] too well known to require definition; defined in the *Qāmūs* as meaning "small pearls" |
| | and *kharā'id*, | "the *kharīdah* is the pearl, unbored" |
| | and *farīd*, | "a bead made as a spacer between pearls and gold [on a necklace], plural *farā'id*; also any precious stone, or pearls" |
| | and *judhādh*, | "gold nuggets" |
| | and *ballawr*, | ["crystal"] "a gemstone too well known to require definition" |
| | and *tibr*, | "gold and silver, or small pieces of either before being worked; once worked, they are known as *dhahab* ('gold') and *fiḍḍah* ('silver'); or what is extracted from the rock before being worked, or broken glass, or any decorative beads of copper or brass that may be used" |

and *sayrā'*, "pure gold"
and *shadhr*, "pieces of gold extracted from ore without smelting, or beads used as spacers on necklaces, or small pearls"
and *shammūr*, "diamonds"
and *ʿamrah*, "beads used as spacers on necklaces" 2.16.10
and *nuḍār*, "gemstones free of impurities"
and *kharaz*, "gemstones, or anything that is strung as a necklace"
and *filizz*, "white copper . . . any of the gemstones of the earth, or anything that the bellows extracts from any such minerals as have been smelted"
and *hibrizī*, "pure gold"
and *tarāmis*, "pearls"
and *ḥuṣṣ*, "pearl"; synonym *khūḍah*
and *khilāṣ*, "whatever gold or silver one may have purified"
and *dalīṣ*, "gold lacquer"
and *khaḍaḍ*, "small white beads worn by children"
and *thaʿthaʿ*, "pearls, or mother-of-pearl" 2.16.11
and *jazaʿ*, "Chinese beads from Yemen"
and *zaylaʿ*, "a kind of seashell"
and *yanaʿ*, "a kind of carnelian"
and *zukhruf*, "gold, or the perfection of the beauty of something"
and *ṣarīf*, "pure silver"
and *safā'iq*, "the *safīqah* [singular] is a long thin spill of gold and silver or the like"
and *ʿaqīq*, ["carnelian"] "too well known to require definition"
and *khaḍl*, "pearls, or pure pearls, or a certain kind of bead, too well known to require definition"
and *ḥūmah*, "crystal"

| | |
|---|---|
| and *jumān*, | "pearls, or little things with the appearance of pearls made of silver, or beads made white with silver lacquer" |
| and *mīnāʾ*, | "pure glass" |
| and *mahw*, | "pearls, or white pebbles"; also "*mahāh* means crystal" |
| and *nihāʾ*. | "glass (also occurs as *nihā*), or glass vessels, or a white stone softer than marble . . . or a kind of bead" |

2.16.12 Work Group 2: For the Making of Jewelry and Ornaments

including the *buʾbuʾ*, "lid of a kohl-pot"

| | |
|---|---|
| and the *urbah*, | "a necklace" |
| and *arnab*, | "ornaments" |
| and the *miʿqab*, | "earrings"; synonym *raʿthah*, plural *riʿāth* |
| and the *ḥijjah*, | "a bead or pearl hung in the ear" |
| and the *dumluj*, | ["beaded armlet"] "too well known to require definition" |
| and *yāraj*, | "women's bracelets" |
| and the *jāniḥ*, | "the *jāniḥ* is made of pearls, strung to be displayed, or anything one arranges in order" |
| and *dāḥ*, | "a bracelet with multiple strands" |
| and *sanīḥ*, | "pearls, or the thread before they are strung on it, or any jewelry" |
| 2.16.13 and *wishāḥ*, | "two strings of alternating pearls and gemstones with a spacer between each and one string above the other, or a broad piece of leather studded with gems that a woman hangs over her shoulders and that falls to her hips" |
| and *waḍaḥ*, | "jewelry made of silver" |
| and the *fatkhah*, | "a large ring worn on the hand or foot, or a circle of silver like a ring" |
| and the *khaladah*, | "a bracelet, or earring" |

| | |
|---|---|
| and the *zirād*, | "a *mikhnaqah* " |
| and the *ʿiḍād*, | "the *dumluj*; synonym *miʿḍād*" |
| and the *ʿiqd*, | ["necklace"] "too well known to require definition" |
| and the *qilādah*, | "whatever is placed around the neck" |
| and the *minjad*, | "a piece of jewelry edged with bezels consisting of pearls and gold or cloves . . . that occupies the space from the neck to the base of the breasts, worn like a sword belt" |
| and the *masjūr*, | "[a piece of jewelry] made of strung, sagging pearls" |
| and the *safīrah*, | "a neck collar with loops of gold and silver" 2.16.14 |
| and the *shaʿīrah*, | "a trinket fashioned from silver or iron in the shape of a barleycorn," etc. |
| and the *ʿitrah*, | "a neck collar rubbed with musk and other perfumes" |
| and the *ʿamr*, | "the *shanf* " |
| and the *tiqṣār*, | "a neck collar, plural *taqāṣīr*" |
| and the *kusbur*, | "a bracelet of ivory"; synonym *siwār* |
| and *quffāz*, | ". . . or a kind of ornament for the hands or the feet"[623] |
| and the *ḥibs*, | "a silver eyelet placed in the center of a curtain" |
| and the *sals*, | ". . . or decorative earrings"[624] |
| and the *shams*, | "a kind of neck collar" |
| and the *qudās*, | "something made like silver *jumān*" 2.16.15 |
| and the *kabīs*, | "a piece of jewelry that has been hollowed out and filled with perfume" |
| and the *qilādah mukarrasah*, | "pearls and beads are strung on a thread and then joined into segments with large beads" |
| and the *niqris*, | "something made in the shape of a rose that a woman sticks in her head covering" |
| and the *kharbaṣīṣ*, | "a pair of earrings, or something grain-shaped worn as jewelry" |

| | | |
|---|---|---|
| | and the *khurṣ*, | “a hoop of gold or of silver, or the hoop of an earring, or a small hoop worn as decoration” |
| | and the *ḥawṭ*, | “a twisted black and red thread on which are beads, or a silver crescent that a woman wears on her waist so that the evil eye will do her no harm” |
| | and the *simṭ*, | “a neck collar longer than the *mikhnaqah*” |
| | and the *ʿulṭah*, | “a neck collar” |
| | and the *qurṭ*, | “the *shanf*, or an earring hung from the earlobe” |
| 2.16.16 | and the *laṭṭ*, | “a neck collar made of dyed colocynth seeds” |
| | and the *anwāṭ*, | “pendant earrings” |
| | and the *raṣīʿah*, | “a round ornament on a sword, or any round ring on a sword, a saddle, or elsewhere” |
| | and the *shanf*, | “a top earring, or a pendant earring in the upper edge of the ear, or anything suspended from its upper part” |
| | and the *nuṭafah*, | “an earring, or pearl” |
| | and the *waqf*, | “an ivory bracelet” |
| | and the *ḥizāq*, | “a thick bracelet” |
| | and the *ḥilq*, | “a silver finger ring without bezel, or ‘the Ring of Power’”[625] |
| | and the *mikhnaqah*, | “a necklace”; synonyms *minzaqah* and *miʿnaqah* |
| | and the *khawq*, | “the ring of the *qurṭ* or the *shanf*” |
| 2.16.17 | and the *daysaq*, | “any ornament made of pure white silver” |
| | and the *zunāq*, | “anything tied under the chin” |
| | and the *sawdhaq*, | “a bracelet, or a woman’s bracelet” |
| | and the *ṭāriqiyyah*, | “a necklace” |
| | and the *ṭawq*, | [“decorative collar”] “too well known to require definition” |
| | and the *qalaqī*, | “a kind of necklace” |
| | and *masak*, | “bracelets or anklets” |
| | and the *jadīl*, | “a jeweled sash” |

| | | |
|---|---|---|
| and *ḥulbah,* | "a kind of jewelry" | |
| and the *ḥijl,* | "an anklet" | |
| and the *mursalah,* | "a long necklace draped over the breast, or a necklace containing beads" | 2.16.18 |
| and the *sidl,* | "a *simṭ* of pearls that reaches the breast" | |
| and *ashkāl,* | "jewelry made of pearls and silver, each element resembling the next, which women wear as earrings; singular *shakl*" | |
| and the *ṭiml,* | "a necklace (synonym *ṭimīl*), because it is 'impregnated (*tuṭmalu*),' i.e., smeared with perfume" | |
| and the *qabal,* | "a round thing of ivory that shines and is hung on a woman's breast" | |
| and the *qirmil,* | "something a woman ties around her head" | |
| and the *iklīl,* | "something resembling a headband that is decorated with gems" | |
| and *maḥāl,* | "a kind of jewelry" | |
| and *nakhl,* | "a kind of jewelry" | |
| and *tahāwīl,* | "different colors, or decoration in the form of drawn figures and engravings" | |
| and the *barīm,* | "a woman's cord in which there are two colors and which is decorated with gems" | 2.16.19 |
| and *tawāʾim,* | "*tawāʾim* pearls are those that are joined together" | |
| and the *tūmah,* | "a pearl, or an earring containing a large drop" | |
| and the *khātam,* | ["finger ring"] "too well known to require definition" | |
| and the *ʿiṣmah,* | "a necklace" | |
| and the *karm,* | "a necklace, or a kind of work on a *mikhnaqah,* or 'the Daughters of Karm'—ornaments that were made during the Days of Barbarism" | |
| and the *anẓām,* | "any thread on which beads are strung" | |
| and the *thuknah,* | "a necklace" | |

| | |
|---|---|
| and the *jumān*, | "a plaited strip of hide with beads of all colors on it that women wear as a sash" |
| and the *burrah*, | "an anklet" |
| and the *riyy*, | "a necklace, or the thing placed round the neck of a boy" |
| and the *waniyyah*, | "a necklace of pearls" |
| and *khashal*. | "the terminals on bracelets or anklets" |

2.16.20 Work Group 3: For Making Perfume and Concocting Fragrant Pastes

| | |
|---|---|
| including *anāb*, | "musk, or an aromatic substance resembling it" |
| and *jullāb*, | "rosewater" |
| and *zarnab*, | "a perfume, or a sweet-smelling tree" |
| 2.16.21 and *kurkub*, | "a sweet-smelling plant" |
| and *malāb*, | "an aromatic substance, or saffron" |
| and *shathth*, | "sweet-smelling plants used in tanning" |
| and *yalanjūj*, | "aloe wood" |
| and *rabāḥī*, | "a kind of camphor" |
| and *murannaḥ*, | "best-quality aloe wood" |
| and *rayḥān*, | "a [particular] sweet-smelling plant [i.e., 'basil'] or any plant of that nature" |
| and *shīḥ*, | "a sweet-smelling plant" |
| and *ṣayyāḥ*, | "an aromatic substance, or a perfume for washing with" |
| and *naḍūḥ*, | "perfume" |
| and *salīkhah*, | "an aromatic substance like peeled bark, or the fat from the fruit of the ben tree before it is pulped" |
| and *labīkhah*, | "a vesica of musk" |
| and *lakhlakhah*, | "a perfume, too well known to require definition" |
| and *su'd*, | "a perfume, too well known to require definition" |

| | | |
|---|---|---|
| and *rand*, | “a sweet-smelling tree, or aloe, or myrtle” | |
| and *zabād*, | [“civet”] “too well known to require definition”; synonym *zuhm* | |
| and *ʿabd*, | “a sweet-smelling plant” | |
| and *qindīd*, | “amber, or camphor, or musk, or a perfume made from saffron” | 2.16.22 |
| and *nadd*, | [“ambergris”] “a perfume, too well known to require definition” | |
| and *ḥanīdh*, | “an ointment, or a scented wash” | |
| and *kādhī*, | “a tree bearing flowers with which ointment is perfumed” | |
| and *bahār*, | “a sweet-smelling plant” | |
| and *khaṭṭār*, | “an ointment made from oil with aromatic perfume” | |
| and *khumrah*, | “Indian yellow, or various kinds of perfume” | |
| and *dharīrah*, | “an aromatic substance” | 2.16.23 |
| and *zabʿar*, | “a sweet-smelling plant” | |
| and *idhkhir*, | “sweet-smelling grasses” | |
| and *sāhiriyyah*, | “an aromatic substance” | |
| and *ḍaymurān*, | “Persian basil” | |
| and *muṭayyar*, | “aloe, or moistened aloe” | |
| and *ẓafār*, | “a sort of incense, so named because it resembles a fingernail (*ẓufr*) pulled from its root” | |
| and *ʿabīr*, | “saffron, or a mixture of perfumes” | |
| and *ʿabhar*, | “narcissus, or jasmine, or other plants” | |
| and *ʿiṭr*, | “an aromatic substance” | |
| and *ʿamār*, | “the sweet-smelling plants with which the place where men meet to drink is decorated” | |
| and *ʿanbar*, | “the dung of a sea creature, or a substance thrown up by a spring in the sea” | |
| and *gharrāʾ*, | “a scented plant, or it may be that the correct form is *ghurayrāʾ*” | |
| and *fāghirah*, | “a perfume, or cubeb” | 2.16.24 |
| and *quṭr*, | “aloe used for censing” | |

| | |
|---|---|
| and *kāfūr*, | "a scented plant whose flowers are like camomile and palm blossom, or the spadix of the latter, or a perfume too well known to require definition; it comes from trees in the mountains of the Sea of India and from China" |
| and *nisrīn*, | ["eglantine"] "a flower too well known to require definition" |
| and *ʿajūz*, | "a sort of perfume" |
| and *balasān*, | "small trees like those of henna that grow only in ʿAyn Shams, the Cairo suburb, and whose oil is much in demand" |
| and *qalasān*, | "a sweet-smelling plant" |
| and *qanas*, | "a sweet-smelling plant, also called *rāsan*" |
| and *habas*, | "gillyflower, also called *manthūr* and *nammām*" |
| and *mardaqūsh*, | "a perfume a woman puts on her comb" |
| and *ḥuṣṣ*, | "Indian yellow, or saffron" |
| 2.16.25 and *saʿīṭ*, | "the ben tree, or mustard oil" |
| and *qusṭ*, | "Indian or Arabian aloe" |
| and *ḍiyāʿ*, | "a kind of perfume" |
| and *mayʿah*, | "an aromatic substance; synonym *māʾiʿah*" |
| and *naqūʿ*, | "a dye containing sweet-smelling aromatics" |
| and *ʿawf*, | "a sweet-smelling plant" |
| and *khilāq*, | "a kind of perfume" |
| and *raḥīq*, | "a kind of perfume" |
| and *bunk*, | "a perfume too well known to require definition" |
| and *sukk*, | "a perfume made from *rāmik*"[626] |
| 2.16.26 and *misk mashmūʿ*, | [literally, "waxed musk"] i.e., "mixed with amber" |
| and *tatl*, | "a kind of perfume" |
| and *ruʿlah*, | "umbels of basil and myrtle" |
| and *sunbul*, | "a sweet-smelling plant" |

and *qundūl*, “a tree found in the Levant, whose flowers have an oil of excellent quality”

and *mandal*, “aloe, or the best kind thereof; synonym *mandalī*”

and *bashām*, “a fragrantly scented tree”

and *bahramān*, “safflower, or henna”

and *thiwamah*, “a tree more sweet-smelling than myrtle”

and *jayhumān*, “saffron; synonym *rayhuqān*”

and *khuzāmā*, “wild gillyflower” 2.16.27

and *ḍurm*, “a sweet-smelling tree”

and *maktūmah*, “an ointment containing saffron or *katam* (‘boxwood’)”

and *laṭīmah*, “musk”

and *mansham*, “an aromatic substance that is hard work to pound, or *sunbul* pods”

and *nammām*, “a sweet-smelling plant”

and *mahḍūmah*, “a perfume that is mixed with musk and ben”

and *ushnah*, “a white aromatic substance that wraps itself around oak and pine trees”

and *bān*, “a tree the seeds of whose fruits yield a sweet-smelling oil”

and *jafn*, “a sweet-smelling tree”

and *ḥannūn*, “Egyptian privet flower, or the blossoms of any tree” 2.16.28

and *raqūn*, “henna, or saffron”

and *kuthnah*, “something made from myrtle and branches of Egyptian willow, which are spread out and on which sweet-smelling herbs are layered, originally *kuthnā*; or it is something plaited from reeds and supple, leafy boughs bound together inside which a light is placed”; to which I would add that it has a synonym, *kunthah*

| | |
|---|---|
| and *maysūsan*, | "something women put in the wash they use on their heads" |
| and *ghāliya*, | ["galia moschata"] "a perfume too well known to require definition" |
| and *fāʿiya*, | "mint, or henna flowers, or pleasant, sweet odors" |
| and *fāghiya*, | "henna blossoms, or when a henna branch is planted upside down and then produces a flower sweeter smelling than henna itself, this being the *fāghiya*" |
| and *kibāʾ*, | "aloe used for incense, or a kind thereof" |
| and *kādhī*, | "an ointment, and a sweet-smelling plant" |
| and *luwwah*, | "aloe used in censing" |
| and *nadā*. | "something used for perfuming in the same way as incense" |

2.16.29 Work Group 4: For Making Vessels, Tools, Household Articles, and Furnishings

| | |
|---|---|
| including the *gharab*, | "a silver basin" |
| and the *shufārij*, | "a tray on which small dishes are placed" |
| and the *ṣurāḥiyyah*, | "a vessel for wine" |
| and *maṭāfiḥ*, | "ladles" |
| and the *buhār*, | "a vessel resembling a pitcher" |
| and the *ṭirjahārah*, | something like a drinking cup, synonyms *ṭirjahālah* and *finjānah*; a small *finjānah* is called a *sawmalah* |
| and *shawārif*, | "a vessel for wine such as a jar or the like" |

and cups, and pitchers, and bottles, and goblets, and bowls, and drinking scoops, and plates, and utensils, and wine-jars, and crocks, and tuns, and platters, and trenchers, and food trays, and troughs, and tureens, and milk pails, and decanters, and casseroles, and drinking horns, and wine vessels, and beakers, and kettles, and strainers, and jeroboams,

| | |
|---|---|
| 2.16.30 and the *jahmah*, | "a huge cooking pot" |

and the *hayṭalah*, “a brass cooking pot”
and the *mirjal*, “a cooking pot of stone or copper”
and the *kaft*, “a small cooking pot”
and *hiljāb*, “a large cooking pot”; synonym *bisāṭ*
and the *ta'mūrah*, “a pitcher, or a kind of wine receptacle, or a *thamīmah*[627] with a narrow top”
and the *qaʿn*, “a kneading bowl”
and the *jām*, [“silver vessel”] “too well known to require definition”; synonym *ṣāʿ*
and the *makkūk*, “a drinking scoop”
and the *ʿayzār*, “a kind of glass drinking bowl”
and *suʿūf*, “large drinking bowls, or household goods, 2.16.31
or anything, be it a slave, or a valued possession, or a house, that is of quality and value; singular *saʿaf*... and spelled *saʿf* it means ‘... an item of goods’”
and the *warsī*, “a drinking bowl of the best wood”
and the *zawrā'*, “a silver vessel”
and the *fāthūr*, “a basin, or dining table made of marble or silver, or a wine vessel, or a decanter”
and the *qudhmūr*, “a silver dining table”
and the *daysaq*, “a silver dining table”
and the *qarqār*, “a vessel”
and the *mathbanah*, “a purse in which a woman puts her mirror and its accessories”
and the *ʿikm*, “a piece of carpet in which a woman wraps her supplies”
and the *qashwah*, “a palm-leaf basket for a woman's perfumes”
and the *ju'nah*, “a basket lined with hide”; a container for 2.16.32
perfume
and the *ʿatīdah*, “a drum, or a casket containing a man's or a bridegroom's perfume”; synonym *sharīṭ*
and *durj*, “small containers used by women”; singular *durjah*

| | | |
|---|---|---|
| | and the *ṣiwān*, | "the thing in which clothes are kept" |
| | and the *takht*, | "a container in which clothes and the like are kept"; synonyms *ʿaybah* and *mabnāh* |
| | and *asṭān*, | "brass vessels" |
| | and the *abzan*, | "a basin for ablution, sometimes made of copper" |
| | and *shijāb*, | "upright pieces of wood on which clothes are placed" |
| | and the *ghudun*, | "*ghidān* [plural] are bars from which clothes are hung" |
| | and the *qafadānah*, | "an outer covering for a kohl pot, or a leather pouch for solid perfumes and so on" |
| 2.16.33 | and *ḥanājīd*, | "the *ḥunjūd* [singular] is a tall bottle for *dharīrah* , or a receptacle like a small *safaṭ*"; synonym *ḥunjūr* |
| | and *bazz*, | "clothes, or household goods such as clothes and the like" |
| | and *ʿaqār*, | "household goods, or the most prized of these that are only used on feast days" |
| | and *thaqal*, | "anything precious and cared for" |
| | and *batāt*, | "furniture, or household goods"; synonyms *maḥāsh*, *athalah*, *shadhab*, *zalzal*, *aharah*, *rihāṭ*, and *sufāṭah*; the cloth for a tent is called *khāshi māshi*, *qāsh māsh*, and *qarbashūsh* |
| | and *najd*, | "the carpets and spreads with which a house is upholstered" |
| | and the *naḍad*, | "a bed frame on which household goods are placed in layers" |
| | and the *naḍīdah*, | "a cushion, or any other stuffed household item" |
| | and the *būriyyah*, | "a woven mat" |
| | and the *miswar*, | "a rest made of hide" |
| 2.16.34 | and the *ʿabqarī*, | "a kind of carpet" |

| | |
|---|---|
| and *rafraf,* | "green lengths of cloth from which bedspreads are made and which are spread out; . . . or bedding, or cushions, or carpets" |
| and the *zilliyyah,* | "a carpet" |
| and the *namaṭ,* | "a kind of carpet" |
| and the *miskhiyyah,* | "a kind of carpet" |
| and the *irāḍ,* | "a huge carpet of wool or camel hair" |
| and *nusuj,* | "mats" |
| and *zarābī,* | "small cushions, or carpets, or anything that is used to rest one's body on"; singular *zirbī* |
| and *riḥāl,* | "saddlecloths of the kind called *ṭanāfis,* made of cloth from al-Ḥīrah" |
| and *namāriq,* | "small cushions, or silk saddlecloths, or saddlecloths of the kind called *ṭanāfis*" |
| and the *durnūk,* | "a kind of carpet" 2.16.35 |
| and the *wirāk,* | "a cloth with which the place where the rider puts his leg is decorated" |
| and *barāṭil,* | "a *barṭalah* is a narrow sunshade" |
| and *ẓulal,* | "a *ẓullah* [singular] is a covering, or anything used as protection from heat or cold" |
| and *mamāṭir,* | "a *mimṭar* is a woolen cloth used to provide shelter from the rain"; synonym *mimṭarah* |
| and *azfān,* | "a *zifn* is a protective covering that they make over their tents to guard them from the heat of the sea and its dampness" |
| and *surādiqāt.* | "the *surādiq* is what is stretched over the forecourt of the tent, or a tent made of cotton" |

Likewise, *nasīfah* (which are "pitted black stones with which the feet are scraped") must be obtained for the bathhouse. Next, that happy home must be made attractive with

| | |
|---|---|
| *fusayfusā'* and *saranj,* | "*fusayfusā'* are colored beads mounted on the inner walls of houses," and *saranj* are "something crafted like *fusayfusā'*" |

and with beds that are *murammalah*, meaning they have been "decorated with gems and so on," and with curtained bridal alcoves, bridal thrones, couches, trellises, chairs, and small beds made from

| | | |
|---|---|---|
| 2.16.36 | *ʿāj*, | "ivory" |
| | and *sāj*, | "a certain tree" |
| | and *shīzā*, | "a black wood used for trenchers, or it may be the same as ebony, or *saʾsam*, or walnut wood" |
| | and *samur*, | "a certain tree too well known to require definition" ["gum acacia"] |
| | and *nuḍār*, | "wood for containers" |
| | and *ʿayzār*, | "a certain tree" |
| | and *ḍubār*, | "oak" |
| | and *saʾsam*, | "a certain black tree, or ebony" |
| | and *thuwaʿ*, | "a certain lofty mountain tree" |
| | and *shawḥaṭ*, | "a certain tree from which bows are made, or a species of jujube" |
| 2.16.37 | and *ḍabr*, | "wild walnut trees" |
| | and *ṣawmar*, | "grand basil trees" |
| | and *ṣinār*, | "plane trees" |
| | and *salām*, | "a certain tree; someone once said to a Bedouin, '*Salām* ("peace") be upon you,' to which the Bedouin replied, 'And *jathjāth* upon you!' 'What kind of a reply is that?' he was asked, and he said, 'They are both trees with bitter fruits. You wished one on me, so I wished the other on you!'" |
| | and *kanahbal*, | "a certain large tree" |
| | and *baqs*, | "a tree with leaves and berries like the myrtle, or it may be that it is the same as the *shimshādh* ('common box')" |
| | and *nasham*, | "a certain tree used to make bows" |
| | and *ḍāl*, | "the wild lote tree, or a certain other tree" |

| | |
|---|---|
| and *baqsh,* | "a tree, called *khūsh sāy* in Persian" |
| and *nibsh,* | "a certain tree like the pine, harder than ebony" |
| and *shaḥṣ,* | "a certain hard tree" 2.16.38 |
| and *mays,* | "a certain large tree" |
| and *waʿs,* | "a certain tree from which lutes and ouds are made" |
| and *qaṭaf.* | "a certain mountain tree with long-lasting wood" |

Next, it must be made attractive with crystal bottles and with

| | |
|---|---|
| *qiṭr,* | "a kind of copper" |
| and *qilizz,* | "copper to which iron has been added" |
| and *filizz,* | "white copper from which hollow pots are made, or . . ."[628] |
| and *balnaṭ,* | "a thing like marble but harder" |
| and *balaq,* | "stones in Yemen that illuminate whatever is behind them like glass" |
| and *ḥakak,* | "a white stone like marble" |
| and *nihāʾ,* | "a white stone softer than marble" |
| and *muhl,* | "a name that embraces the precious metals such as silver, iron [sic], and others" |
| and *hayṣam.* | "a kind of stones, smooth" |

Next, the finishing touch to this noble place are *withāb* stuffed with *ʿushar* and *ḥuraymilāt* (*withāb* are "beds and bedding," *ʿushar* is "a plant used as a stuffing for pillows and from whose flowers and twigs sugar is extracted," and *ḥuraymilāt* are trees "whose pericarps open to reveal the softest cotton, with which the pillows of kings are stuffed"), though I have committed a grave error here in keeping mention of bedding to the end, the latter being the first thing to enter a woman's mind when she arrives in a country. The furnishings for the house are now *amassed* (and you're still worrying about the *ass*).

2.16.39 Work Group 5: For the Making of Clothes

| | | |
|---|---|---|
| 2.16.39 | The *thurqubiyyah*, | "White garments made from the linen of Egypt" |
| | the *jilbāb*, | "the shirt, or a wide garment for a woman" |
| | the *sakb*, | "a certain garment" |
| | *silāb*, | "black garments" |
| | *qaṣab*, | "soft garments of linen" |
| | the *labībah*, | "a garment like the *baqīrah*" |
| | the *nuqbah*, | "a garment like the *izār*" |
| | the *biẓmāj*, | "any garment one of whose ends is of velvet, or whose middle is of velvet and whose two ends are of a different weave" |
| | the *muʿarrajah*, | "[a garment] with a wavy stripe" |
| | the *mawthūjah*, | "loosely spun and woven garments" |
| 2.16.40 | *habraj*, | "embroidered garments" |
| | the *mutarraḥah*, | "*mutarraḥ* garments are garments that have been well steeped in dye" |
| | *wajiḥ*, | "tightly woven garments" |
| | the *khawkhah*, | "a kind of garment, green" |
| | *walīkh*, | "garments of linen" |
| | the *thafāfīd*, | "a kind of garment" |
| | the *jimād*, | "a kind of garment" |
| | the *muʿaḍḍadah*, | "the *muʿaḍḍad* are certain garments with a mark on the upper arm" |
| | the *firind*, | "a garment, too well known to require definition" |
| | the *muqarmadah*, | "a garment that is *muqarmad* is coated with a substance like saffron" |
| 2.16.41 | the *mujassadah*, | "[a garment] dyed with saffron" |
| | the *maqadiyyah*, | "a garment, too well known to require definition" |
| | the *hurdiyyah*, | "[a garment] dyed with *hurd* roots" |
| | the *lādhah*, | "a garment of Chinese silk" |

| | |
|---|---|
| the *buqṭuriyyah*, | "a certain wide, white garment" |
| the *ḥaṣīr*, | "an embroidered, decorated garment that, spread out, is so beautiful that it captures the heart" |
| the *khusrawāniyyah*, | "a kind of garment" |
| the *dithār*, | "any item of apparel worn over the *shiʿār*"[629] |
| the *sābiriyyah*, | "a delicate, high-quality garment" |
| the *musayyarah*, | "a striped garment" |
| the *ṣudrah*, | "a certain garment, too well known to require definition" ["waistcoat"] 2.16.42 |
| the *ṣidār*, | "a certain garment whose upper part is like a women's head scarf and whose lower part covers the breast" |
| the *ʿabqariyyah*, | "ʿAbqar is a town whose clothes are extremely attractive" |
| the *miʿjar*, | "a certain item of apparel that a woman winds around her head and over which she then dons her *jilbāb*, or a Yemeni garment" |
| the *ʿushāriyyah*, | "a certain garment ten cubits in length" |
| the *ʿuqār*, | "a kind of garment, red" |
| the *qubṭuriyyah*, | "a certain white linen garment" |
| *marmar*, | "a style of tailoring women's clothes" |
| *munayyarah*, | "[cloth] that is woven on two looms" |
| *bāghiziyyah*, | "garments of silk-wool, or resembling silk" |
| the *tawwaziyyah*, | "eponymous" [from Tawwaz, in Persia] 2.16.43 |
| the *mumarʿazah*, | "*mirʿizzā* is the downy fur that is under a goat's hair" |
| the *muṭarrazah*, | a garment with decorated borders |
| the *mafrūzah*, | "a garment that is *mafrūz* has marks like fingerprints" |
| the *qirmiziyyah*, | "a garment dyed with cochineal" |
| the *qahz*, | "garments of red wool resembling the *mirʿizzā* and sometimes mixed with silk" |

| | | |
|---|---|---|
| | the *tinnīsiyyah*, | "Tinnīs is a town from which fine garments are said to come" |
| | the *mudamqasah*, | "*dimqis* is loosely woven cloth, or raw silk, or silk brocade, or linen" |
| | the *qassiyyah*, | "from eponymous Qass, an area of Egypt" |
| | *kirbās*, | "garments of white cotton" |
| 2.16.44 | the *mulaslasah*, | "a garment that is embroidered and striped" |
| | the *narsiyyah*, | "[from] Nars, a village in Iraq" |
| | the *muwarrasah*, | "any garment dyed with Indian yellow" |
| | *akyāsh*, | "fabrics that are re-spun, such as silk-wool and wool" |
| | *mājushūn*, | "dyed garments" |
| | the *muqaffaṣah*, | "a garment with stripes in the shape of a cage" |
| | the *muḥarraḍah*, | "a garment dyed with safflower grains" |
| | the *ʿarḍī*, | "a class of garment" |
| | the *miʿraḍ*, | "a garment in which a girl is displayed" |
| | the *rayṭah*, | "any piece of cloth that is not sewn to another but is all of one weaving and one piece, or any fine, soft garment" |
| 2.16.45 | *sijillāṭ*, | "linen garments embroidered with ornamentations that look like rings" |
| | the *sumṭ*, | "a certain garment of wool; spelled *simṭ* it means an unlined garment, or a *ṭaylasān* ('net shawl')" |
| | *muqaṭṭaʿāt*, | "short garments . . . or embroidered wraps" |
| | the *muraddaʿah*, | "[a garment] on which are traces of perfume" |
| | the *ṣadīʿ*, | "a certain garment worn beneath a coat of mail" |
| | the *muḍallaʿah*, | "a striped *musayyarah*, or one whose ornamentation takes the form of ribs" |
| | the *niṣʿ*, | "a certain white garment" |
| | the *muwashshaʿah*, | "a garment with decorated borders" |
| | the *shurāfī*, | "a certain white garment" |
| 2.16.46 | the *shaff*, | "also *shiff*: a delicate garment" |

| | | |
|---|---|---|
| the *bunduqiyyah*, | "a certain garment of fine linen" | |
| the *muḥaqqaqah*, | "any tightly woven garment" | |
| *khuzrāniq*, | "white garments" | |
| the *dabīqiyyah*, | "Dabīq is a town in Egypt" | |
| the *ritāq*, | "two garments whose edges have been sewn together" | |
| *rāziqiyyah*, | "white linen garments" | |
| the *muzabraqah*, | [a garment] dyed red or yellow | |
| the *ʿilqah*, | "a certain sleeveless garment . . . or a precious garment" | |
| the *lifāq*, | "two garments that have been sewn together" | |
| the *muḥabbakah*, | "a garment that is tightly sewn and striped" | 2.16.47 |
| the *mijwal*, | "a women's garment" | |
| the *khamlah*, | "a certain garment with a nap like the *kisāʾ* ('a kind of cloak') and so on"; synonym *khamīl* | |
| *khāl*, | "smooth garments, or a striped garment of Yemen" | |
| the *diraql*, | "a garment resembling the *armaniyyah*"[630] | |
| the *mumarjil*, | "a garment with images of men on it" | |
| the *mumarjal*, | "a kind of embroidered garment" (the author of the *Qāmūs* lists the preceding word under *r-j-l* and the present word in an entry of its own)[631] | |
| the *murammalah*, | "a thin garment" | |
| the *saḥl*, | "a certain white cotton garment"; synonym *misḥal* | |
| the *musalsalah*, | "a *musalsal* garment is one with striped decoration" | |
| the *ʿaql*, | "a red garment" | 2.16.48 |
| the *mufalfalah*, | [a garment] "decorated as though with peppercorns" | |
| the *qasṭalāniyyah*, | "[a garment] that derives its name from a certain governor"[632] | |
| the *waṣīlah*, | "a striped Yemeni garment" | |

| | | |
|---|---|---|
| | the *muhalhalah*, | “a delicately woven garment” |
| | the *āmmiyyah*, | eponymous[633] |
| | the *mubram*, | “a class of garments, or a garment whose yarn is double-twisted” |
| | the *jahramiyyah*, | “eponymously named [after Jahram, a town in Persia] garments similar to carpeting or made of linen” |
| | the *murassamah*, | “a striped garment” |
| | the *muraqqamah*, | “a striped garment (*raqm* being a kind of decoration), or silk-wool, or wraps” |
| 2.16.49 | the *ʿaqm*, | “a red tunic, or any red garment” |
| | the *qadm*, | “a red garment” |
| | the *qirām*, | “a colored garment of wool with *raqm*-decoration and designs, or a delicate veil; synonym *miqram*” |
| | the *abū qalamūn*, | “a Greek garment of many colors” |
| | the *milḥam*, | “a class of garment” |
| | the *nīm*, | “any bread or garment that is supple” |
| | the *ākhinī*, | “a striped garment” |
| | the *dafanī*, | “a striped garment” |
| | *urjuwān*, | “red garments” |
| 2.16.50 | the *sabaniyyah*, | “a silk garment on which are the likenesses of citrons” |
| | *shatūn*, | “supple garments” |
| | the *shādhakūnah*, | “a thick quilted garment made in Yemen” |
| | the *muʿarjanah*, | “a gament on which palm racemes are pictured” |
| | the *muʿayyanah*, | “a garment whose decoration includes small squares resembling the eyes of a wild beast” |
| | the *mufannanah*, | “a garment of diversified design containing strips made of a different cloth” |
| | the *mufawwahah*, | “[a garment] dyed with madder” (see in the *Qāmūs* under *f-w-h*: “*fuwwah*, on the pattern of *sukkar*, are long thin red roots used in |

| | | |
|---|---|---|
| | dyeing" etc. and under *f-w-y*: "*fuwwah*, on the pattern of *quwwah*, are roots used in dyeing") | |
| the *qūhī*, | "a certain white garment" | |
| the *nahnah*, | "a delicately woven garment" | |
| the *mulahlahah*, | garments described as *mulahlah* are those that are delicately woven; synonym *muhalhal* | |
| *muwajjahah*, | "double-sided fabrics" | 2.16.51 |
| the *miḥsha'*, | "a thick wrap, or a short white wrap which one wraps around one's waist, or a waist wrap in which one envelops oneself" | |
| the *sabīḥah*, | "a black wrap" | |
| the *khasīj*, | "a wrap of wool" | |
| the *iḍrīj*, | "a yellow wrap, or red silk-wool" | |
| the *musabbaḥ*, | "a tough, strong wrap"; synonym *mushabbaḥ* | |
| the *sayḥ*, | "a striped wrap" synonym *musayyaḥ* | |
| the *bijād*, | "a striped wrap" | |
| the *burjud*, | "a thick wrap" | |
| the *jūdiyā'*, | "a wrap" | |
| the *aghthar*, | "wraps made with large quantities of wool" | 2.16.52 |
| the *khamīṣah*, | "a rectangular black wrap with two decorated borders" | |
| the *mirṭ*, | "a wrap of wool or silk-wool; plural *murūṭ*" | |
| the *shamlah*, | "a wrap [similar to but] less [valuable] than the *qaṭīfah*" | |
| the *ṭiml*, | "a black wrap, or a garment thoroughly dyed" | |
| the *mārī*, | "a small wrap with hanging threads" | |
| the *shar'abī*, | "a kind of mantle" | |
| the *'aṣb*, | "a kind of mantle" | |
| *muka''ab*, | "embroidered mantles, or a garment folded into stiff pleats" | |
| the *khilāj*, | "a kind of striped mantle" | |
| the *shīḥ*, | "a Yemeni mantle" | 2.16.53 |
| the *qurduḥ*, | "a kind of mantle" | |
| the *sa'īdiyyah*, | "a kind of Yemeni mantle" | |

| | | |
|---|---|---|
| | the *sanad*, | "a kind of mantle" |
| | the *baqīr*, | "a mantle that is divided in half and worn without sleeves; synonym *baqīrah*" |
| | *ḥibar*, | "a kind of Yemeni mantle; singular *ḥibarah*, on the pattern of *ʿinabah*" |
| | the *ḥabīr*, | "a decorated mantle, or new clothes" |
| | the *sīrāʾ*, | "a kind of yellow-striped mantle, or one mixed with silk" |
| | the *muṭayyar*, | "a kind of mantle" |
| | the *qiṭr*, | "another kind [of mantle]" |
| 2.16.54 | the *mushayyaz*, | "any red-striped garment" |
| | the *murayyash*, | "an embroidered mantle" |
| | the *fūf*, | "a kind of Yemeni mantle; the *mufawwaf* mantle is a delicate mantle, or one with white stripes" |
| | the *naṣīf*, | "a woman's head wrap, or a bi-colored mantle" |
| | the *birkah*, | "a Yemeni mantle" |
| | the *marjal*, | "a Yemeni mantle" |
| | the *muraḥḥal*, | "[a garment] with camel's saddle designs" |
| | the *taḥamah*, | "mantles striped with yellow" |
| | the *atḥamī*, | "a mantle too well known to require definition" |
| | *musahham*, | "striped mantles" |
| 2.16.55 | the *qaṭīfah*, | "a velvet cloak" |
| | the *muṭraf*, | "a cloak of silk-wool, rectangular, with decorated borders" |
| | the *janiyyah*, | "a cloak of silk-wool" |
| | *jīm*, | "silk brocade" |
| | *sundus*, | "a kind of *bizyawn*,[634] or a kind of fine silk brocade" |
| | *istabraq*, | "thick silk brocade, or silk brocade worked with gold, or tightly woven silk garments" |
| | *mushajjar*, | "silk brocade that is *mushajjar* is that which has on it designs in the form of trees (*shajar*)" |

| | | |
|---|---|---|
| the *sibb*, | "a length of fine cloth; synonym *sabībah*" | |
| the *ṭarīdah*, | "an oblong length of silk cloth" | |
| *saraq*, | "oblong lengths of white silk, or of silk generally" | |
| the *batt*, | "a *taylasān* of silk-wool or the like" | 2.16.56 |
| the *sundūs*, | "a green *taylasān*" | |
| the *ṭils*, | "a black *taylasān*" | |
| the *ṭāq*, | "a *taylasān*, or a green *taylasān*" | |
| the *sāj*, | "a green and black *taylasān*" | |
| the *ṣuttiyyah*, | "an enveloping over-robe, or a certain Yemeni garment" | |
| the *shawdhar*, | "an enveloping over-robe, or a mid-leg shift" | |
| the *duwāj*, | "a sheet of cloth worn as a garment" | |
| the *mishmāl*, | "an enveloping over-robe" | |
| the *lifāʿ*, | "an enveloping over-robe, or a wrap, or a mat of hide, or a mantle, or anything that a woman wraps around herself" | |
| the *murajjal*, | "a waist wrap of silk-wool with a decorated border" | 2.16.57 |
| the *mudārah*, | "an embroidered waist wrap" | |
| the *ḥaqw*, | "a waist wrap"; synonym *khiṣār* | |
| the *ṣidād*, | "anything a woman veils herself with; synonym *sitr*" | |
| *fuwaṭ*, | "garments imported from Sind, or striped waist wraps" | |
| the *dithār*, | "any cloth worn over the *shiʿār*" | |
| *ḥulal*, | "singular *ḥullah*, meaning a waist wrap, or a robe, or a mantle, or anything else of the same sort; a *ḥullah* always consists of two pieces of cloth or a single piece with a lining" | |
| the *sirbāl*, | "a shirt, or a chemise, or anything that is worn" | |
| the *qurṭaq*, | "a garment, too well known to require definition" | |

| | | |
|---|---|---|
| | the *yalmaq*, | "a tunic" (Arabized from *yalmah*) |
| 2.16.58 | *qarqar*, | "women's garments" |
| | the *qurzaḥ*, | "a garment that their women used to wear" |
| | the *mifḍal*, | "the *mifḍal*, the *mifḍalah*, and the *fuḍul* are garments which women wear long, so that they trail on the ground, or which they wrap themselves in" |
| | the *ḥiqāb*, | "a thing onto which women hang ornaments and which they tie around their waists; synonym *ḥaqab*" |
| | the *niṭāq*, | "a length of cloth that a woman wears and ties around her middle in such a way that the upper part hangs down over the lower, reaching the ground, and the lower trails on the ground," etc. |
| | the *mijann*, | "the *wishāḥ*" (already mentioined under the rubric of ornaments) |
| | the *itb*, | "a woman's collarless sleeveless mantle split down the sides, or a *baqīrah*, or a woman's shirt" |
| | the *jawb*, | "a woman's *dir*ʿ or shirt" |
| | the *uṣdah*, | "a shirt worn under a garment" |
| | the *khaylaʿ*, | "a sleeveless shirt" |
| 2.16.59 | the *rādiʿah*, | "a shirt that has been splashed with saffron or with perfume" |
| | *qumuṣ sunbulāniyyah*, | "long loose-fitting shirts, or those named after a town in Anatolia" |
| | the *shiʿār*, | "what is worn next to the hair of the body under the *dithār*; also *shaʿār*" |
| | the *qidʿah*, | "the *mijwal*, which is the small tunic split in front" |
| | the *jīd*, | "a small woolen open-fronted tunic" |
| | the *ghilālah*, | "any undergarment; synonym *ghullah*" |

| | | |
|---|---|---|
| *haffāf*, | “*haffāf* shirts are those that are fine and diaphanous, synonym *hafhāf*” | |
| the *shalīl*, | “the undergarment that is worn under the chemise” | |
| the *qarqal*, | “a woman’s shirt, or a sleeveless garment” | |
| the *ghiṭāyah*, | “undergarments that a woman covers herself with, such as the *ghilālah* and the like” | |
| the *farwah*, | “too well known to require definition” [“fur-edged coat”] | 2.16.60 |
| the *sabanjūnah*, | “a coat edged with fox fur” | |
| the *shaʿrāʾ*, | “a fur-edged coat” | |
| the *mustuqah*, | “a fur-edged coat with long sleeves” | |
| the *khayʿal*, | “a fur, or a piece of cloth with unsewn edges, or a shift . . .” etc. | |
| the *miʿqab*, | “a woman’s head covering” | |
| the *niqāb*, | “anything with which a woman covers her face” | |
| the *khimār*, | “a *naṣīf*, which is a turban, or anything with which the head is covered” | |
| *waṣāwiṣ*, | “small face-veils that reveal the eyes” | |
| the *miqnaʿah*, | “anything with which a woman veils her head; the *qināʿ* . . . is wider” | |
| the *ʿiṣābah*, | “anything tied around the head, or a turban” | 2.16.61 |
| the *sīdārah*, | “a protective covering under the *miqnaʿah* and the *miqnaʿ* and the *ʿiṣābah*” | |
| the *ʿamārah*, | “anything worn on the head” | |
| the *ʿamar*, | “a kerchief with which a free-born woman covers her head” | |
| the *khunbuʿah*, | “a small *miqnaʿah* for a woman” | |
| the *bukhnaq*, | “a piece of cloth that a girl covers her face with, tying the two ends under her chin to protect the *khimār* from moisture and the moisture from dust, or a small face-veil that reveals the eyes, or a small cloak” | |

| | |
|---|---|
| the *ṣiqāʿ*, | "a small face-veil that reveals the eyes . . . and a piece of cloth that protects the *khimār* from moisture; synonym *ṣawqaʿah*" |
| the *qunbuʿ*, | "a piece of sewn cloth resembling the *burnus*, or a *khunbuʿah* or something resembling it" |
| the *qunzuʿah*, | "what a woman puts on her head, synonym *qundhuʿah*" |
| the *hunbuʿ*, | "something like a *miqnaʿah* for girls, the front of which is sewn" |
| 2.16.62 the *qurzul*, | "the thing a woman puts on her head; synonym *qunzuʿah*" |
| the *junnah*, | "a piece of cloth a woman wears to cover her head in front and behind but not from the sides and which covers her face and the two sides of her chest; it has two eyeholes cut in it, like the *burquʿ*" |
| *tasākhīn*, | "boots, or things like a *ṭaylasān*" |
| *jarāmīq*, | "the *jurmūq* [singular] is the thing worn above the boot" |
| *kawth*, | "the *qafsh*, meaning short boots, that are worn on the feet" |
| the *rān*, | "a thing like a boot but with no foot and taller than a boot" |
| *jawrab*, | "a wrapping for the feet; one says *jawrabtuhu* meaning 'I put his stockings on for him'" |
| *quffāz*, | "things stuffed with cotton made for the hands that a woman wears against the cold, or a kind of ornament, etc." |

and, to round this out, three hundred and sixty-five *aḥbās* and a similar number of *maqārim* (the *ḥibs* [singular] being a silver eyelet made in the middle of a red curtain, while the *miqramah* [singular] is a bedspread), plus the same number of pairs of underdrawers made of

| | |
|---|---|
| 2.16.63 *arnabānī*, | "blackish silk-wool" |

| | |
|---|---|
| and *sinnā*, | "a kind of silk" |
| and *ardan*, | "a kind of silk-wool" |
| and *ṭārūnī*, | another kind of silk-wool; *ṭurn* is silk-wool |
| and *qatīn*, | "bleached white silk-wool" |
| and *birs*, | "cotton or something similar to it, or papyrus flock" |
| and *sharīʿ*, | "high-quality linen" |
| and *qazz*, | "that is, *ibrīsam* ('a kind of silk'), which is the same as *dimaqs* (also pronounced *diqams* and *midaqs*)" |

though once more the pen has carried me away: underdrawers ought to have come first, so as to give them a place in the *list* appropriate to the underlying *gist*.[635]

Next, if you take her off to the city's open spaces and market- 2.16.64
places, where people gather, as soon as she claps eyes on some handsome well-built young whelp, she'll say, "That one would make a ladies' man and be good for riding fine steeds, buckling on a sword, bracing a spear between leg and stirrup, and thrusting"; or if she sees a blooming boy, she'll say, "That one ought to go to lady-killers school, to realize his potential"; or if an older man, "That one ought to stay at home and take up the composition of love lyrics and saucy songs to prepare for the needs of the pupils of the aforementioned school"; or an old man, decrepit and decomposing, "And that one is fit to give counsel on those matters that perplex its still green graduates; let him exert himself to the utmost in setting them straight, and if no pertinent opinion is to be had from him, let him be rolled up in a shroud and buried." All this, and your thoughts are still preoccupied with the donkey, or its saddle.

As for the argument that sleeping with her inside her slip is more 2.16.65
fortifying, this is because it has become the custom for any of those whose commands and prohibitions must be obeyed, who is growing old, and whose blood had dried and flesh shriveled to the point that he can no longer get warm by cloaking himself in his clothes, to sleep with one of these smooth-skinned beauties inside her slip,

thus substituting her warmth for that of cloak, fire, and hot spices, the best for such purposes being a virgin. There are differences of opinion over the cause and point of origin of this warmth. Some claim that it is the breath from her mouth that warms the chilled, while others object that that same breath must inevitably become embroiled with his mustache and thus cool down. Others would have it that the outlet is obviously the pores, from which sprouts the hair; thus the rising of warmth from a woman, whose pores are open, must be less impeded, in contrast to the situation with a man, whose pores are blocked by his hair.

2.16.66 To this, response was made that the beardless boy is like the woman in terms of his pores being open, but no one has ever claimed that to sleep with one of them inside his slip is more fortifying. Some believe that the breath must come from her nose, while a certain paronomasia-obsessed school claims that it comes from some other place, saying that in the *Qāmūs* it states that "'the man *takawwā* ("cuddled") with his wife' means that he sought comfort in the *ḥarr*/*ḥirr*[636] of her body." I have to point out that, despite the care the author has taken to collect rare and strange vocabulary items, he fails to mention a verb that means "the *woman* sought comfort in the warmth of a *man's* body." It is for this reason—i.e., because the woman's body possesses a warmth not to be be found in the man's—that the lightest of coverings is enough to warm her even in the coldest weather, while at the same time the man is blowing on his fingers and shivering and shrinking, his teeth chattering. Equally strange is the fact that she eats less than a man but has more flesh than he.

2.16.67 Schoolmen have claimed—and skilled physicians agree—that among the gifts that God, glory be to Him, has bestowed on women is the power to persuade their opponents to their way of thinking and lead the misguided to His true religion. As testimony to this, they advance the story of the Muʿtazilī and his wife, when a certain celebrated scholar of this group, who claim that the acts of mortal men are not of God's creation, was debating with certain Sunnis and put to them such arguments and proofs in support of his view that they were at a loss to respond. At this point a sharp-witted Sunni woman upped and said to her co-believers, "Marry me to him and I'll defeat him in a single night, God willing." He spent that night with her as a free-thinker, until such time as he had performed his marital duty, after which he performed a further, supererogatory act, and then an additonal, voluntary, good deed, believing that by so doing he'd earned heavenly reward and deserved a wink of sleep. "And what," said the woman, "of the fourth, fifth, and tenth, you flaccid *poof*?" so he pulled himself together for one more go, after which he said, "There's no more milk left in the milk-skin now, so no blame and no *reproof*." "Such an excuse is *very poor, sir*," replied the woman, "when you claim a mortal's acts are not the creation of the One, the *Enforcer*!" Said the man, "You have brought a fool to his senses, guided one misled to the proper *path*. I hereby relinquish my former way of thinking; God has guided me to the road that averts His *wrath*."

For my part, I declare that a reading of the history books 2.16.68
teaches that to women should go the lion's share of the credit for the introduction of Christianity into the lands of the Franks. A certain witty litterateur once said, "If a woman wants to buy something or requires a service, she has no need to pay the seller or the provider in cash. She can just pay him in kind with a look that's kind, which is why this word has meanings of two kinds."[637] It's a different case with the man: if he wants to get anything, no matter what but especially if it involves any untying of drawstrings, he has to dissolve the knots with puffs[638] of silver and gold.

A further peculiarity of women is that, if one of them craves 2.16.69
something she likes when she's pregnant, the image of what she craves will appear on the child, and a father must therefore inspect his offspring to find out what particular shape appears on their bodies, though if he finds something unacceptable, he'll just have to hold his tongue over it. Further, the woman's creative power is so great that it confers on plants and many other forms qualities that

please her eye and bring her comfort if she sees or touches them. Men have none of these peculiarities.

2.16.70 Another is that a single woman in a gathering of twenty men can bewitch each and every one of them, charming this with a word, that with a look, this with a wink, that with a blink, this with a squint, that with a look through narrowed eyes, this with a nod, that with a sigh, this with a turn, that with a twisting of the neck, this with a sniff, that with a cocking of the head, this by biting her tongue, that by sticking it out, this by moving it back and forth, that by pressing together or parting her lips, this by showing off her profile, that by loosening her hair, this with a smile, that with a laugh, and this with a guffaw, so that all leave well disposed toward her; a woman is at her most brilliant when seated amongst a company of young men who are flirting with her, joking with her, and flattering her.

2.16.71 Another of her peculiarities is that she knows what is in men's hearts, which allows her to bewitch them with her rolling gait and her movements, grieving them and driving them wild, making them sick with love and filling them with anxiety, saddening them and confusing them, sending them into ecstasy and taking over their thoughts, enslaving them and enchanting them, making them love-lorn and distracted, filling them with longing and with terror, occupying their thoughts and putting them through agony, keeping them awake and taking them captive, choking them and setting them on fire, rending their livers and binding them with their spells, plundering them and working them till they can do no more, selling them and buying them, starving them and making them thirst, striking them in their hearts and souls, afflicting them in their lungs and breasts, tearing up their livers and spleens, hurting them in their stomachs and thighs, and beating them on their bellies and bottoms.

2.16.72 Concerning the claims that have been made as to her possessing peculiar skills in terms of the excellent management of such household tasks as sewing, embroidery, and the like, these are mentioned in many a book, and you'll have to look them up yourselves. This concludes our discussion of women for the time being, though let none doubt that I have as much more to say on the subject as al-Farrāʾ has on *ḥattā*.[639] Some idiot of a scholar has said, "Women are pure evil, and the most evil thing about them is that there's no doing without them." I declare: this, like Juḥā's[640] dream, is half true and half untrue, and the half that's true is that there's no doing without them.

## Chapter 17

# Elegy for a Donkey

2.17.1 "Hello there, Fāriyāq! Where have you been and what have you been up to this long while?"—"Writing poems for princes."—"I already knew that. I'm asking you for something new."—"Yesterday I was shocked to lose a donkey of mine. I asked the neighbors about him, but none of them admitted to stealing him, so, for a dirham, I hired a crier who set about crying in the markets, 'Oyez! Today the Fāriyāq's donkey ran away, leaving his shackle on its peg. Has any of you seen him?' but the only response he got was 'How many a donkey has fled from its master's house today!' When he came back to me with this good news, my choler reached its zenith and I swore that from that day forth I'd never again look into the face of a donkey, real or figurative (a leading scholar of the language having said that one of the characteristics that distinguishes our noble tongue from all others is that in it an ignoramus may be called an ass).[641] Then I set to elegizing him in the following lines:

2.17.2 The donkey's gone, leaving the shackle on the peg,
And of it not one soul has seen a trace.
Am I now to ride a peg,
Or is the shackle, though of palm fiber made, supposed to take its place?

How, too, can I return to a house where was once my home
And where he once dwelt as though we shared a familial bond?
I was that fond of him, I fed him, like a child, with mine own hand—
With mine own hand, I say, just like a child I fed him, of him I was that fond.
Barley I brought him, unmixed with diamonds, or even gold,
So concerned was I that he his teeth should keep.
If I o'erslept, his braying would wake me,
Like the voice of a sweetly trilling songbird, from sleep.
How oft did he divert me from some narrow defile
Where, as he saw, the camels on the ground around me their froth did spew
And take me on a road whose sides had been wetted
By the Beauteous with water-of-roses, otherwise known as dew!
How oft did he swiftly run, when some pretty maid's wedding parade
Appeared in the distance, and go flat out!
And, if e'er he spied a funeral bier, he'd ne'er o'ertake it,
No matter how often between his shoulders I gave him a painful clout.
Not a day passed but he closely examined his manger,
Whether he was in a rich meadow or a prairie stripped of vegetation. 2.17.3
His wit was so human, I even thought
He must be the product, as some beasts are, of transmutation.
Ne'er did he complain at a goading, nor did his legs, to take a tour,
However long and whate'er the terrain, e'er tire.
Paralyzed be the hands of him who took him and left me
To slog through this town on foot and sink into the mire!
Doth he know that since he went I've been on tenterhooks,
That separation from him like a fire my liver doth rack,
And that the voice of the crier cries out today,
'Under cover of darkness, put on your saddle and come back!'?

Let not any pampering you may get from the thief, my rival, seduce
you.
He does it only out of envy.
Even for the noble or well-trained steed such things don't last,
As you well know—they're never lengthy.
May every donkey that from willfulness skedaddled,
From exhaustion vociferated,
From effort balked, or whose mind by must was addled,
Every lip-twisting sniffer of old she-donkey pee
Gone dry as jerky, your ransom be!
Long-headed, slender-leggèd, ne'er refusing
When pushed to the limit nor turning off the track,
I swear, a better guide to the roads he'd be
Than his master, were he not curbed by his knotted tack!
Would I had a tress from his tail that his mem'ry ne'er might fade—
I'd gaze upon it as one does upon a cloistered, unwed maid!"

2.17.4 I told him, "Your poetry was as much wasted on that ordinary donkey as your money on the crier." He replied, "The money is truly lost but not the donkey." "How can that be?" I asked, "when the house is devoid of his presence?" "It's my custom," he answered, "if I lose something and then memorialize it in verse, to imagine I've been compensated for it. If I don't do so, I continue to grieve its loss." "And can prose play the same role as verse?" I asked. "Possibly," he replied, "with some people, for I hear that many writers, having tried to achieve pressing goals for which they lacked the wherewithal, wrote books about them and in that way were able to do without them." "Who says so?" I asked. "They themselves," he replied. "It's a pack of lies," I said. "I've written vast numbers of treatises on women and never for a moment felt I'd gained a replacement for one of those I was describing." "Why, then, did you write them?" he asked. "I had no work and no business to attend to," I said, "and found that time lay heavy on my hands, especially at night, when I had nothing to do. So I jotted down whatever came to mind."

"And," he asked, "do you not find pleasure in your writings when you read them now, or hear that others are reading them?" "On the contrary," I replied, "I laugh at how stupid I was in those days, for I exposed my honor to the tongues of those who would vilify me, not to mention that I wasted my time in vain on things that could gain me nothing. I hear that many a married man was upset by what I said about women and my recounting of their wiles, so they tried to defeat me by using a company of scholars, who reproached me for the way my books were organized and found fault with the way they were written. I'd also quoted some of the things that had been said about women verbatim, and they claimed one shouldn't quote things verbatim in books, plus other matters that gave me great cause for regret." "I have heard," he said, "that people never cease attacking a writer as long as he's alive, but when he dies, will go to great lengths to find some saying of his they can pass down. As the poet says, 2.17.5

You'll find one lad denies all merit to another
  While he's alive, but once the man's gone cold
Looks everywhere for a pleasant anecdote
  On him to inscribe in lines of gold."

"What good does such solicitude do one who's dead?" I said. "None," he replied, "except that writing verse provides, in my opinion, great pleasure. No doubt prose is the same, for both emerge from the same source, wouldn't you agree?" I said, "Concerning the pleasures of writing, I'd say that on the one hand the writer knows something others do not, and there can be no doubt that knowledge of true things is a source of pleasure. Opposed to this, however, is a pain that outweighs it, namely, that if the writer is aware of a certain fact and wants to communicate it to others, he'll find that most people turn a deaf ear to it. 2.17.6

"For example, a wise physician who sees the people of his country bathing in cold water when they have a fever may advise them against 2.17.7

so doing, only for them to refuse and say, 'The cold gets rid of the heat.' He is happy then from the perspective that he knows the truth but sad from the perspective that he sees that everyone else is misled, and his personal happiness does not outweigh his sadness on behalf of others. Have you not observed that scholars are, without exception, weak and scrawny, and speak, sleep, eat, and laugh little, while the ignorant are fat, soft, and healthy and get plenty of food, sleep, and everything else that exists to keep the constitution balanced?" "How come, in that case," he said, "that physicians are also fat, when they're the equivalent of scholars in terms of possessing useful knowledge unknown to others?" I said, "The physician doesn't see people when they're eating, drinking, and lying with their spouses. He sees them only when they get sick and, as a result, doesn't grieve over what they get up to. The scholar, on the other hand, observes, at all times and in all places, things that point to the errors and ignorance of the common people. Thus he has no alternative but to sorrow over the stupidity and naïveté from which they suffer." "Do you mean," he said, "that you're in favor of ignorance?" "Good luck," said I, "to those who are resigned to it."

2.17.8 "What do you think of poetry, then?" he asked. I replied, "If it serves some interest of yours, meaning that it will help you survive, it's an excellent thing. But if it's just the product of some obsession and a fondness for the production of paronomasia and other forms of word play at the sight of a beautiful woman, a rose, or a garden, after the manner of most poets, who go to great efforts to compose poetry about everything that crosses their paths, or like your elegy for the donkey just now, then you're better off without it." "But," he said, "the best poetry is the kind that's born of an obsession, meaning spontaneously and not artificially. Thus, when I write a panegyric to the prince, I suffer as must anyone who has to reconcile two opposites, but what I wrote about the donkey wasn't like that: I wrote what I did about him in an hour flat." "On the other hand," I said, "people look only at the outside, so your ode on the ass they'll call asinine, while your lines on the prince they'll call princely."

"If things are as you say," he said, "why have you foresworn writing in general but not about women, which is something that's in abundant supply?"[642] "First," I replied, "because the writer casts himself into the pincers of people's jaws and they proceed to rip his honor and his patience to pieces, as noted above. Secondly, the true meaning of the word *mu'allif* ('author, composer') is dishonorable, for it has the same sense, according to those who know, as *mulaffiq* ('concocter'). Also, most people laugh at the former, believing that it refers to *ta'līf* ('making peace') between two persons,[643] the proper term for one who practices such things being 'shaykh,' which is itself repugnant to some people, especially women.[644] 2.17.9

"The best titles to have here, as far as I can see, are, among the Christians, *qissīs* ('priest') and, among the Muslims, *bayk* ('bey'). *Qissīs* is good because people kiss the priest's hand for blessing. A Coptic woman will go so far as to wash the priest's feet in orange-blossom water with her own hands and then preserve the water in a bottle; and when the priest gets hungry, he lugs his guts over to the house of one of his acquaintances, whose wife receives him with beaming face and does him honor, and how he stuffs them then![645] If he prefers to stay at home because of something that's cropped up, he sends with a note to one of their houses a boy, who returns with a luncheon such as the poets of our day write odes to. As to *bayk*, the bey, even though honored among the people, cannot get the same from their houses as does the priest. This is because it is not easy for him to walk alone. He has to have with him, when walking out, two men, one on his right and one on his left, and these, though they show him deference and respect, harbor grudges in their hearts that impel them to watch his every move and do him harm. The exception is when they wear the costume of a servant, at which time the sight of their dress causes men to look away in awe." 2.17.10

2.17.11 "How unlikely," said the Fāriyāq, "that I'll ever be a *qissīs*! How unlikely that I'll ever be a *bayk*! The profession of priest won't do for me because I don't like bad writing, and I'm not fit for the title of *bayk,* because Eternal Providence has not been pleased to grant me, from before the beginning of time, any possibility of bungling my way into a bey-ship. The only thing left for me then is a shaykh-ship. I'm off!" I told him, "I will let you go only on condition you tell me what happens to you when you get your shaykh-ship." "And so I shall," replied he, "if God wills."

## Chapter 18

# Various Forms of Sickness

Thenceforth the Fāriyāq, being anxious to become known by the title of "Shaykh," devoted himself to writing verse. To that end it occurred to him to study grammar under certain Egyptian shaykhs, for he'd made up his mind that what he'd acquired in his own country wasn't enough for the prince's Panegyricon. In the same month, however, that he declared his intent to study, he was afflicted with a painful case of ophthalmia. When he recovered, he made his first foray into scholarship and studied with Shaykh Muṣṭafā[646] a few small books on morphology and syntax. Then he got a bad case of worms, caused, he was told, by eating raw meat, a well-known custom among Levantines. Whenever his stomach hurt him during the classes, the shaykh would put it down to the wide range of topics and the intensiveness of the analysis. Once he even said to him, "Glory be to God, no one has studied this science at my hands without getting a stomach ache!" to which the Fāriyāq replied, "The stomach ache isn't all from Zayd and 'Amr,[647] Master Shaykh. The worms have a role to play in it too, for there's nothing I eat that they haven't got to before my stomach does." "Never mind," replied the shaykh, "Perhaps the blessings of scholarship will provide some relief." 2.18.1

Around this time, the Fāriyāq happened to be asked by an acquaintance if he could study[648] with the aforementioned shaykh 2.18.2

the book the Christians study on the Mountain, namely the *Baḥth al-maṭālib*.[649] When this acquaintance had gone through it all, he asked the shaykh to write him a certificate allowing him to teach the book in his own country,[650] which the shaykh did, showing the result to the Fāriyāq. When the latter examined it, he found mistakes in the language and the inflections, and he asked his shaykh if he might point the errors out to him. On examining them, the shaykh said, "Tomorrow I shall write him another" and he wrote him another certificate. When the Fāriyāq took a close look at this, he found that it was as bad as the first. He alerted his shaykh to the mistakes, but the latter told him, "You write him whatever you want." This was despite the fact that the shaykh was as well versed in the science of grammar as anyone could be and was capable of devoting a whole hour to the analysis of just part of a sentence. He did not, however, practice prose or verse composition, and, as a result, all his knowledge was in his heart and on his tongue, and he was almost incapable of getting any of it out and into his pen.

2.18.3 After studying grammar in the manner mentioned, the Fāriyāq had a recurrence of eye pain. When he recovered, he decided to study *Al-Talkhīṣ fī l-maʿānī* (*The Epitome on Tropes*).[651] He started on it with Shaykh Aḥmad but had not got far into it before he was struck by pruritis, which he failed to recognize at the onset, which explains why he went on studying. Once, as the shaykh embarked on the explanation of some complex issue, the Fāriyāq's body started itching all over, so he started scratching with both hands. The shaykh turned and, seeing him absorbed in scratching, asked him, "Why are you scratching and, as far as I can see, paying no attention to the 'if-it-be-saids' and the 'answer-may-be-mades'? Are we here to scratch limbs or words?" "Please forgive me," replied the Fāriyāq, "but the relief provided by scratching distracts me from everything else." "You have pruritis?" the other asked. "It may be so," he replied. The shaykh looked at his hands and said, "It is, by God. You must keep to your house and smear your body with dogs' feces, for that is the only treatment." So the Fāriyāq stayed at home and took to smearing his body every day with the aforementioned dogs' feces and sitting in the sun for hours, until he found relief from that torment. Then, when he was cured, he returned to his studies.

After he finished going through that book, he suffered another attack of ophthalmia. Then he conceived the notion of studying al-Akhḍarī's *Sharḥ al-Sullam* (*The Commentary on the Ladder*)[652] on logic, so he started reading it under the direction of Shaykh Maḥmūd and was struck down by the *hayḍah*, which is the disease Egyptians call "the yellow air,"[653] and spent three days oblivious to everything going on around him and incapable of uttering a sound, except that once his servant heard him raving about "the greater affirmative universal"[654] and, thinking he was complaining of the severity of his state, replied that it was indeed "one of the greaters." No one else had then contracted the disease in Egypt but by the time thirty days had passed it had spread throughout the country and become a general affliction, God save us, with thousands dying of it every day. 2.18.4

At this point, the Fāriyāq realized that he had been, to use the language of the logicians, the first term in this disaster, the others the second, and that it was the worms from which he suffered that had expedited his early subjection to this illness. Because of them, then, he moved quickly too and took—the Fāriyāq, that is—to mounting his donkey and touring the markets as though Fate could no longer touch him (note: this wasn't the donkey that merited an elegy and a funeral oration; this one, being still alive, merited a eulogy), and went to a village in the countryside, accompanied by his male and female servant. A local governor, hearing of his presence, summoned him and his servants, the male and the female, and said to him, "Hey, wise guy! Is this a time for dying or a time for knocking people up? What are you doing bringing a girl like this here?" He replied, "I am the prince's panegyrist, and I have come to let my eyes wander over the greenery of the countryside so I can praise it well, after the death of so many, for I have grown tired of the city and was afraid my creative powers would dry up." "So who's 2.18.5

she?" he then said, pointing to the girl servant. "His sister," said the Fāriyāq, indicating the male servant. "And who's he?" he said. "His keeper," he replied, indicating the donkey. The emir turned to the male servant and, finding him comely, said, "Since you're the prince's poet, or his poetaster, you cannot be sanctioned. But you will have to leave this servant with me, for he has the right qualifications to enter my service." "You're the boss," said the Fāriyāq. "Take him!" That night the emir, having had his way with the boy, asked him insistently about the Fāriyāq and the servant told him, "Honestly, my lord, he's a good man, but I think he may not be an Arab because I can hardly understand him when he speaks to me in our language."

2.18.6 When morning came, the Fāriyāq made his preparations for the return journey but couldn't find the donkey, so he decided he must have run off to join the first. He went looking for him and found that he'd gone off with another of the emir's donkeys to an empty patch of ground, where he was bellowing and snorting beneath him. When the Fāriyāq saw him taking the passive role, he couldn't contain his laughter and said, "It says in the hadith, 'People follow the religion of their kings' but no one ever said donkeys should follow the sect of their owners. Anyway, better the ass's ass than the ass's lender's ass!" Then he returned to the house, where he found his serving boy and girl waiting for him. The boy told him, "The emir has released me from his service, because he found my qualifications were good for one night only, so now I'm free."

2.18.7 Then the Fāriyāq, after having paid his respects to the emir and wished him good health, returned to Cairo, where the affliction had died down. He asked after his logic teacher and was told that he was alive and not numbered among the dead,[655] so he went back to him and completed with him what he'd started. When he reached the last step on the *Ladder*, he suffered another attack of ophthalmia and stayed at home. When he recovered, he decided to learn something of jurisprudence and the science of theology, so he started on the *Kanz* (*The Treasure*)[656] and the *Risālah al-Sanūsiyyah* (*The Senoussi*

*Treatise*)[657] and fell ill. A French acquaintance asked why he was so weak, and he told him the story. "I shall cure you," the other said, "God willing, but on condition you teach my son Arabic." "With the greatest of pleasure," he returned, and immediately he started teaching him and taking the medication from his father. This, however, will have to be set out in detail in another chapter, on its own.

## Chapter 19

# The Circle of the Universe and the Center of This Book[658]

2.19.1 This man was a famous doctor in Egypt, but his reputation for causing decease was greater than that for curing it, the reason being that, at an advanced age, he'd married a fresh young girl and fathered on her a daughter and a son. Thereafter he'd ceased to be able to give her her marital rights, so he made it his habit to humor her and flatter her, which is how men usually treat their wives in such cases—falling short of pleasing and satisfying her in this area, he increases his attentions, his demonstrations of affection, and his loving treatment of her, imagining that these will make up in the woman's eyes for the other, and he does the same when he's unfaithful to her and falls in love with another. Likewise, the wife likewise usually increases her demonstrations of love and passion for her husband by giving herself to him to the point that he becomes sated with her and his cup runs over, or she flatters him, if it's she who's being unfaithful.

2.19.2 In keeping with this logic, the doctor told his wife one day, "Good woman, I observe that my key has become too rusty for use in your lock and that your age and blooming good health require you find yourself a copulative instrument to amuse yourself with until my time is done and you marry another. If you don't, I'm afraid you'll come to hate me and fly away and leave me as does the dove. It would be easier for me to lose one part of you than to lose you altogether, for you are the mother of my children and the closest thing to my heart, and I could not bear to be separated from you. Choose whomever you'd like and I'll drag him to you by his horns." (The woman laughed at this.) Then he added, "And given that I am well known in this town to be a doctor, if the neighbors see a man, or even men, coming to me no one will suspect you" (the woman laughed too at his mention of "men") "for people knock on a doctor's door at night—even at midnight" (and here she laughed again). Having talked to her at length in this vein, he ended by saying, "Don't think that I'm the only one who practices this custom. In my country, people like me do the same" (at which, she let out a great whoop of laughter).

His wife's first thought, once he'd finished the rest of his speech along these lines, was that he was trying by this means to discover her inmost feelings and trap her into making a slip, so she wept with rage and said to him, "You must believe I'm a whore to confront me with such words and hold such a low opinion of me." "God forbid!" said he. "I spoke to you simply of what nature requires. Think over what I said in a little while and let me know your answer." The woman left him, scowling and suspicious. A good few days passed and the man neither fondled her nor mounted her nor played with her nor performed his husbandly duties with her. She, becoming worried when the situation promised to *persist*, was too annoyed to have the patience to *desist*, and started thinking about what her husband had said to her. One day, then, she dressed herself in the clothes that pleased him best, made up her face, put on perfume, and set off for his room, telling herself, "Today will be the *watershed*, the dividing line between what's past and what lies *ahead*. If he doesn't treat me like a wife, I'll remind him of his words." 2.19.3

He received her with joy and a beaming face and sat her down at his side, noting that she was aroused, for a redness had suffused her eyes, which glistened, while her voice had a tremolosity, which is to say a shake and a shiver, to it. When she'd settled herself, he started off by asking her if she had thought over what he'd said a 2.19.4

few days before. "Yes," she said. "But don't you have a bit left that would relieve me of this matter?" He replied, "I swear I don't have a drop or a *pottle*, the dregs of a puddle or the lees of a *bottle*, and I've no hope left of improving the situation with any aphrodisiac—not by the rubbing on of flesh of skink or fat of varan, nor by use of ginger or pepper or pan-leaf or saltwort or elecampane or betel-nut or cloves or spikenard or mastic or nutmeg or fennel, or of Spanish pelletory or pinenuts or chickpea or emblic or myrobalans or long pepper or sesame or alpinia or mace or balm-tree oil or ragwort, or in birds' eggs or in iris oil or in colocassia or in narcissus root steeped two nights in milk or in celery whose seeds have been crushed with sugar and clarified butter or in wearing clothes dyed with Indian yellow or in eating mandrake root or in glasswort juice squeezed into fermented milk or in borax mixed with honey or in oil of jasmine or in Indian hazelnut or in fried *hamqāq*[659] or in terebinth or in burdock resin or in musk blended with gillyflower oil or in salvia root or in carrots or in asparagus or in Indian gooseberry or in *mughāth*[660] fruit or in fava-bean greens with ginger or in cassia ground with sesame and kneaded with honey or in mangrove gum or in bdellium or in terebinth fruits or in being censed seven times with lean meat of the Egyptian vulture mixed with mustard seed or in tigernut sedge or in safflower kernels or in rubbed red sand worms or in bananas or in wiping the soles of my feet with bats' brains or in pigeon flesh or in cassia bark; otherwise I would have spurned no possibility of making you happy, for the excessive affection that you know I bear you."

2.19.5 She replied, "If things stand as you say, sir, I choose a priest." "And what wicked tempter has whispered this utterly evil choice into your ear?" he asked. "Firstly," she answered, "it's so that people won't think badly of me when they see him entering my house every day, and secondly because they say that the priest has vital juices in abundance." "You err. Also, I fear what effect he may have on my children, for he may try to seduce them into disobeying me, given that I follow a different creed than he. You had better choose someone else." "You," she replied, "are a doctor and know the sound from the sick, the strong from the weak. Choose me whomever you please, and with whatever contents you I shall be content." "God bless you!" he responded. Then he kissed her, so joyful was he, and promised that he would do as he had promised the following day.

Dawn had hardly broken before he was on his donkey and making his way to one of his friends. When he met with him, he told him, "I have a request to make of you." "Ask away," said the other. "On condition that you don't refuse me," he said. When the other replied, "I shall devote all my effort, God willing, to fulfilling it," he took his hand to seal their agreement. Then he told him, "I want you to succeed me with regard to my wife." "Have you decided to quit Egypt and leave your wife behind?" the man asked him. "No," he said. "You'll succeed me while I'm still here." Offended, the man asked, "Has some doubt got into you as to whether I am truly your friend, making you seek covertly to uncover my innermost thoughts and private affairs?" At this, the man made a clean breast of the matter and urged him to go with him. When they arrived, the deal was contracted in the presence of both husband and wife, and everyone was content, the man calling in daily from that time on at "the caliphal palace."[661] 2.19.6

Things went on this way for a while. Then, when the wife grew bored with the man, the way women do—a situation made apparent to him through her showing a lack of enthusiasm at the sight of him on one occasion and making of excuses on another—he in turn divulged her secret to a friend, the way men do. The latter followed the well-beaten path of others of his ilk, started playing court to her, and took the place of the first. Then she grew bored with him, and he told on her, and another came along, and she accepted him, and then another and another, until they'd become a mighty company. At this, her first lovers returned to her too, and she busied herself changing and exchanging until the doctor's house came to resemble 2.19.7

nothing so much as a watering hole. In the beginning, the affair acquired no notoriety with the neighbors because they thought that all those people were coming to be treated for some illness. Later, however, it got out, because the doctor took a second home outside the country in which to spend the summer and left his wife in the first, where the visitors continued to come and go just as before, so people caught on.

2.19.8 Now, at the very time when all these good folk had been turning up to avail themselves of that cold feast, the poor Fāriyāq had been frequenting the doctor's house to give his son lessons and receive treatment, and, as a result, everyone suspected that he was one of those visitors, a sin they will carry round their necks till the Day of Judgment,[662] for he was hors de combat and wasn't up to doing anything anyway.[663] He went on like that for a while without seeing any improvement from the treatment, as though the doctor wanted to drag out the time till he'd finished teaching his son. Consequently, the Fāriyāq cut short his visits, sought treatment with another, and was cured.

2.19.9 While this was going on, he traveled to Alexandria on some business and there met with a righteous Bag-man, who asked him to go back to Cairo with him to teach some pupils in his house, and this he did, though he was interested only because the Bag-men are prompt in paying those who work for them. During this period too, it occurred to him to study prosody, so he embarked on a reading of *Sharḥ al-Kāfī* (*The Commentary on the Kāfī*)[664] under Shaykh Muḥammad. He barely had time to finish the book before plague broke out in Cairo. At this the Lord caused the Bag-man to feel extreme concern for his own life—out of a desire to ensure the preservation of the Bag-men's interests, as he claimed—and he decided, as a result, to put a little distance between him and the trap that had been dug so he wouldn't find himself buried inside it, thus resulting in a loss that would have inflicted on other Bag-men like him intolerable grief, which would in turn have led to the loss of yet others, for they hold it as a firm belief that extreme sorrow leads to death. He therefore put the Fāriyāq with the graduate Baguettes plus a clever man who had experience in preventive treatment of the bubonic infection, and then gathered to him his own and fled to Upper Egypt, details to follow in the next chapter.

## Chapter 20

# Miracles and Supernatural Acts

2.20.1 The aforementioned Bag-man had living with him a fresh-faced, comely serving girl from his own country. When he resolved to flee, he decided to leave her in his house to look after his things, refusing to take her with him because he was married to a woman less beautiful than she, it being the custom in the lands of the Franks for maids to be, for the most part, superior to their mistresses in form and beauty, though inferior in knowledge and education. It therefore occurred to the wife that, should she fall into the trap before he did, her husband might take the little maid into his bed and find her more to his liking. She recalled too that the first thing a girl learns from her mother before she gets married is how to prevent anything that might lead her husband to do without her, in her presence or in her absence, which is why most Frankish women give their husbands their pictures, even if they be ugly, to wear inside their shirts, or locks of their hair, even if it be red, to wear in a ring.

2.20.2 Then another issue arose, to wit, that if the maid stayed on in the house alone, she would be exposed to the danger of someone climbing the wall to get at her by night, in which case the unthinkable would come to pass, and the once cold oven be *heated*, broken would be the bone that once was set and turned again the tide that had *retreated*, the well once dug would be choked with silt, and what had been stored would be *depleted*, the fallow would be turned, the spells that had protected *deleted*, the seam that had been sewn would be *unpicked*, the pinhead stand *erect*, the pipe once narrow be *rebored*, the grain spilt from the silo where it once was *stored*, the swift, headstrong she-camel be broken to the *rein*, the golden table cleft in *twain*, the cairn *o'erthrown*, the trumpet *blown*, and, as a result, the hornet's stinger *torn*. He therefore saw fit, after first raising his hands to the Almighty in prayerful invocation, to add to her as reinforcement a thin little chit of a man of his country, in the belief that he'd be incapable of performing any of the acts that have drawn in their wake the preceding plethora of rhymes. This is one of a number of scandalous misconceptions that have become widespread, namely that people generally think, without first checking with women or taking their testimony into account, that the thin man isn't up to what the fat man can do; they'd be well advised not to be so opinionated.

The thin man thus stayed with the maid in the utmost felicity. As 2.20.3
for the Baguettes, the one who'd bagged them up (i.e., the one who'd raised them) entrusted their care to that clever man and instructed him to forbid them to leave the house and not to let any of their relatives enter to see them and to employ a man to buy them what they needed from the outside and to accept nothing from him until he had washed it in vinegar, censed it with wormwood, and done the other things that Franks conventionally do to keep away whatever may bring the plague. This agent was a famous scholar of his nation who had, at the beginning of his life, been an infidel, without belief in any religion, despite which he was of noble character and excellent morals. His unbelief, however, had stood in the way of his making a living, and he'd been forced to join sides with the Bagmen of his country, who, delighted at his having found his *Saviour*, bestowed upon him every *favor*. His lighthearted spirit now turned somber and became prey to devilish insinuations and delusions to the point that, in the end, he believed himself capable of performing extraordinary acts and miracles, for a chance to practice which he was always on the lookout.

2.20.4 It now happened that the servant who bought the supplies for the house died of the plague. When the gravediggers came to carry him away, the agent prevented them from entering, and they were afraid to oppose him because he was a Frank, the Franks being regarded by the Egyptians with excessive respect. The man then proceeded to a place where he could be on his own and went down on his knees, praying to the Mighty and Glorious to give him evidence of the truth of his belief. Then he opened the door, came out, threw himself on top of the body of the deceased and put his mouth to his ear, crying, "'Abd al-Jalīl"—the dead man's name—"I call on you in the name of Christ the son of God to return from the darkness of death to the light of life!" He cocked an ear to hear the reply, but no one answered, so he gestured to the gravediggers to be patient and went back to the same place in which he'd prayed the first time and changed his kneeling posture so that his mouth was now between his legs while he mumbled his prayers, after the manner of the Prophet Ilyās when he prayed for the rain to descend after killing the prophets of Baal (who were four hundred and fifty in number, according to 1 Kings 17). There was, however, a difference between the two praying persons, in that the prophet prayed thus after a killing, whereas our man prayed before a resurrection. It would have been more appropriate if he'd carried 'Abd al-Jalīl up into a loft as the aforementioned prophet did with the son of the widow who had been sustaining him, his prayer to God to resurrect the man being, "O Lord my God, hast thou also brought evil upon the widow with whom I sojourn, by slaying her son?"[665] etc.

2.20.5 Next, the man spread out the arms of the corpse to make a cross, sprang happily to his feet, and made haste to throw his body onto that of the deceased, repeating his earlier words in its ear. When no one answered him and he saw that the dead man was still lying there with his mouth open and his eyelids closed and hadn't got up and walked around and about and hadn't sneezed seven times as did the widow's son raised by the Prophet al-Yashu' as mentioned in 2 Kings 4, he went to the kitchen and ordered the cook to make him some broth on the double. When the broth was poured, he took it to 'Abd al-Jalīl and started emptying it down his throat, though the latter was too busy to pay attention as he was talking to Nākir and Nakīr. When all his efforts failed, he ordered the gravediggers to take him away, saying, "It's not my fault I didn't manage to resurrect him, it's his." Then he went to the Fāriyāq's room and said to him, "Excuse me, friend, for failing to resurrect the servant, but the time of resurrection is not yet come. Still, I shall not weaken in my faith that I shall do it next time, God willing." When the Fāriyāq heard this, he lost his composure and his blood rose in fury and sorrow, and on that same day the disease that was making the rounds afflicted him, a ganglion the size of a citron appeared in his armpit, he became feverish, and he got a painful headache. The agent, though, was unaffected, which is one of those mysteries that physicians cannot understand.

During his illness, the Fāriyāq pondered his situation, as a lone stranger with no companion to bring him *cheer*, no doctor to give him *care*. He said to himself, "If I should die now, who will benefit from these books of mine that I have spent so many nights in copying? True, death is hard and hateful under any circumstances, but for a young man like me to die in a strange land is harder still to bear. I have been afflicted in this city, praise God, with every kind of sickness that bears the tint of death. If God should now grant me a reprieve before my time is up, let me not leave this world without the solace of a son and heir, even if my worldly relics consist of nothing but my books. How can it be otherwise when Abīshalūm, son of Our Master Dā'ūd, built himself a wall[666] to be remembered by after his death because he had no children. Let me then marry; if I have no children, there are plenty of bricks in Egypt. God make smooth the path! Your aid, O Generous One, O Compassionate, O Merciful!" 2.20.6

Every time, however, he thought carefully about the married state and pictured the troubles and hardships from the devastating heaviness of whose load he'd seen his friends and acquaintances 2.20.7

suffer and moan, he'd go back on his decision and laugh at how puerile his mind was and at the weakness of its ability to understand the weakness of his body. Then he'd exuse himself on the basis that anybody who had spent his whole life with opinions opposed to everyone else's and believing, when in good spirits, sound of body, and in good health, that all of them were in the wrong and he alone in the right, must inevitably quickly change his mind and reject his former way of thinking when afflicted by some bodily weakness. This is what happened to the philosopher Bion[667] and many other sages and philosophers. Then the Almighty made amends to the Fāriyāq with His *mercy* and granted him relief from *adversity*, and he rose from his bed like one rising from the tomb, went straight to his tambour, and played on it and sang. Leave him now in this state and do nothing to spoil his mood, but gird instead your loins, along with me, and make ready to leap the blazing bonfire that awaits us in Book Three.

*

END OF BOOK TWO

# Notes

1 Buṭrus Yūsuf Ḥawwā: one of a group of Lebanese merchants living in London, on whom al-Shidyāq depended for financial and moral support during his third sojourn there, between June 1853 and the summer of 1857, during which period he was also visiting Paris to oversee the printing of *Al-Sāq*; Ḥawwā provided al-Shidyāq with employment as a commercial agent in his offices.

2 "that house" (*hādhā l-bayt*): i.e., either the Ḥawwā family or the trading house it owned.

3 "the oddities of the language, including its rare words" (*gharāʾibi l-lughah wa-nawādirihā*): works on oddities and rarities of the "classical" or literary Arabic language form a well-established genre of Arabic letters, originally intended to clarify the use of unusual words in the Qurʾān and hadith.

4 "morphologically parallel expressions" (*ʿibārāt muraṣṣaʿah,* from *tarṣīʿ*, literally, "studding with gems"): a device used in rhymed prose (*sajʿ*), e.g., *ḥattā ʿāda taʿrīḍuka taṣrīḥan wa-ṣāra tamrīḍuka taṣḥīḥan* ("until your obscurity reverted to plain statement and your deficient rendering became sound").

5 "substitution and swapping" (*al-qalb wa-l-ibdāl*): on the evidence of his work devoted to the topic, *Sirr al-layāl fī l-qalb wa-l-ibdāl*, the author includes, under *qalb*, not only palindromes (the conventional definition of the term; see Julie Scott Meisami and Paul Starkey, *Encyclopedia of Arabic Literature,* 2 vols. (London and New York: Routledge, 1998), 2:660) but also the substitution of one letter in a word by another without change of meaning (see, e.g., *Sirr* 46, *bāḥah* and

*sāḥah* ("open space, plaza")); by "swapping" the author means variation of the dots used to distinguish certain consonants over an identical or nearly identical ductus to produce different, related, words.

6 Unless otherwise noted, definitions added by the translator have been taken, here and throughout the translation, from Muḥammad ibn Yaʿqūb al-Fīrūzābādhī (= Fīrūzābādī), *al-Qāmūs al-muḥīṭ*, 2nd ed., 4 vols. (Cairo: al-Maṭbaʿah al-Ḥusayniyyah, 1344/1925–26) (see Glossary), from which only one of what are frequently several possibilities has been chosen.

7 *Muntahā l-ʿajab fī khaṣāʾiṣ lughat al-ʿArab*: this work is also mentioned by the author in his *Sirr al-layāl fī l-qalb wa-l-ibdāl* (Mattityahu Peled, "Enumerative Style in *Al-Sāq ʿalā al-sāq*," *Journal of Arabic Literature*, vol. 22, no. 2 (1991), 132); it was multi-volumed and may have been lost in a fire (Mohammed Bakir Alwan, "Aḥmad Fāris ash-Shidyāq and the West" (Ph.D. diss., Indiana University, 1970), app. B).

8 i.e. "space for the avoidance of falsity."

9 The author's implicit claim appears to be that the uncommon "second" or "augmented" form of the quadriliteral verb is associated with intensity.

10 Jalāl al-Dīn al-Suyūṭī (d. 911/1505): a prolific polymath, much of whose 500-work oeuvre compiles material taken from earlier scholars.

11 *Al-Muzhir fī l-lughah*: the full title of the work is *Al-Muzhir fī ʿulūm al-lughah wa-anwāʿihā* (*The Luminous [Work] on the Linguistic Sciences and Their Branches*).

12 Aḥmad ibn Fāris (d. 395/1004), known as al-Lughawī ("The Linguist"), wrote on most areas of lexicography and grammar. It may be that the author's choice of the name "Aḥmad" on his conversion to Islam was an act of homage to this scholar.

13 i.e., the author does not regard such a straightforward figurative usage as a distinguishing characteristic of Arabic.

14 By "the Fāriyāqiyyah" the author has been generally assumed to mean the Fāriyāq's wife, but Rastegar makes the point that, "while the noun is feminine, it is not simply a feminization of his name (which would be Fāriyāqah). Fāriyāqiyyah should more correctly be translated as

'Fāriyāq-ness,' although as a grammatical formulation, it is feminine. Within the text, it is not always clear that it refers to his wife (although at times it clearly does)" (Kamran Rastegar, *Literary Modernity between the Middle East and Europe: Textual Transactions in Nineteenth-century Arabic, English, and Persian Literatures*, 105–6). The Fāriyāqiyyah does not appear again until Volume Three.

15 Rāfā'īl Kaḥlā of Damascus: a litterateur and collaborator of al-Shidyāq's in Paris, who paid for the printing of *Al-Sāq*.

16 "the table enumerating synonyms": i.e., the "Enumeration of Synonymous and Lexically Associated Words in This Book" (in fact, a list of the lists of synonyms, etc.) that occurs near the end of Volume Four and to which the author added further items.

17 See 2.3.3.

18 "had not been mentioned" (*lam takun shay'an madhkūran*): cf. Q Insān 76:1.

19 "dots that shine": perhaps refers to the manuscript writers' tradition of embellishing dots and other diacritical points with colored ink or even gold leaf.

20 "with pulicaria / Plants . . . ." (*bi-l- * rabalāti . . . .*): *Pulicaria undulata* (*rabal*) is a plant with medicinal properties that grows in the region; however, *rabalāt* may also mean "the fleshy thighs of women," in which case it would prefigure "From them will come to you the scent of statuesque slave girls" three lines further on.

21 "statuesque slave girls . . . plump slave girls" etc.: this list of desirable women is not simply a high-flown metaphor for the joys that the book holds, since the same (mostly rare) words used occur also in the main text.

22 "And be not lazy in pursuing and realizing cunsummation" (*wa-lā tatarakhkhā 'an tudrika l-khurnūfā*): the 1855 edition reads *ḥurnūfā*, a word not attested in the dictionaries; we have preferred to read *khurnūfā* (=*khurnūfah*) ("vagina"), supposing its usage here to be figurative, i.e., "the desired goal"; it then parallels the phrase used thirty-four lines later *fa-tukhṭi'a l-khur . . . fah* (the ellipsis is the author's) ("and so miss . . . summation").

23 Shiẓāẓ: a thief of proverbial skill.

24 "I guarantee . . . hunger" etc.: i.e., the book will distract you from all pleasures and keep you awake at night, but everyone will realize that the book is the cause.

25 ". . . summation" (*al-khur . . . fah*): see n. 22 above.

26 "cutting character" (*ḥarf bātir*): or, punningly, "cutting edge."

27 "will pull back from you blinded" (*yakuffu ʿanka kafīfā*): or, punningly, "will pull back from you entirely."

28 "Isn't 'of a certain stamp' the same in meaning as * 'Of a certain type,' with the addition of the thwack of a stick?" (*a-wa-laysa inna l-ḍarba mithlu l-ṣanfi fī l-maʿnā wa-qarʿu ʿaṣan ilay-hi uḍīfā*): *ḍarb* has "blow, stroke" as its basic meaning but also a subsidiary meaning of "type, kind" (synonym *ṣanf*); hence, things that are of a certain *ḍarb* may be conceived of (jokingly) as delivering a certain percussive force. The overall sense of these two couplets seems to be "Do not be offended if the contents of the book, and (perhaps especially) the various lists that I have compiled, is somewhat rebarbative."

29 "It does not strike the noses of mortals": i.e., its injurious consequences harm none but me.

30 "Raising a Storm" (*Fī ithārat riyāḥ*): compare the earlier description of the book as falling "like the wind in the valley when / Stirred up" (0.4.9); the first chapter of each of the four books of which the work is composed bears a title that, like this one, has little to do with the events recounted in that chapter but denotes the initiation of some energetic activity. For further discussion of chapter titles, see the Translator's Afterword (Volume Four).

31 "How many a pot calls the kettle black!" (*wa-muḥtaris min mithlihi wa-hwa ḥāris*): "From many a one such as he does he guard himself though he is himself a guardian," a proverb "alluding to him who finds fault with a bad man when he is himself worse than he" (Edward Lane, *An Arabic-English Lexicon*, 8 vols., London: Williams and Norgate, 1863 (offset ed. Beirut: Librairie du Liban, 1968), s.v. *muḥtaris*).

32 "You've made a bad business worse!" (*ʿāda l-ḥays yuḥās*): "The sloppy date mixture has been made sloppier," said when someone is called

upon to make good something done badly by another and makes it worse (Aḥmad ibn Muḥammad al-Maydānī, *Majma' al-amthāl*, 2 vols. (Cairo: al-Maṭba'ah al-Khayriyyah, 1310/1892–93), 1:316).

33 "Make the most of what you're given!" (*khudh min Jidh' mā a'ṭāk*): "Take from Jidh' whatever he may give you." The pre-Islamic Ghassanid Arabs had been obliged to pay a certain king protection money; when the king died and his son came to collect his money from a Ghassanid named Jidh', the latter beat him with his sword and pronounced the words in question, after which the Ghassanids stopped paying the tax (al-Maydānī, *Majma'*, 1:156).

34 "So what are you going to do about it?!" (*shaḥmatī fī qal'ī*): "My fat is in my shepherd's bag." The wolf, asked what he would do if he came upon sheep guarded by a shepherd boy, replied that he would fear the boy's arrows that were in his shepherd's bag, but when asked, "What if the shepherd were a girl?" replied as given, meaning "I should do with them as I liked" (al-Maydānī, *Majma'*, 1:246).

35 To confound his putative critic, the author produces four impeccably classical proverbs, each of which consists of the words *'alā ẓal'ika* "regarding thy limping" preceded by an imperative verb: *irba' 'alā ẓal'ika* ("Restrain thyself because of thy limping," i.e., "Do not overreach yourself"), *irqa 'alā ẓal'ika* ("Ascend thou the mountain with knowledge as to thy limping," i.e., "Do not make idle threats"), *irqa' 'alā ẓal'ika* (apparently meaning "Be gentle with thyself, and impose not upon thyself more than thou art able to perform . . . or abstain thou, for I know thine evil qualities or actions . . . or . . . rectify thou, or rightly dispose, first thy case, or thine affair"), and *qi 'alā ẓal'ika* ("Be cautious as to thy limping," i.e., "If you live in a glass house, don't throw stones") (see Lane, *Lexicon*, s.v. *ẓala'a*).

36 "Another of Khurāfah's tales, Umm 'Amr!" (*Ḥadīthu Khurāfah yā Umma 'Amr*): Khurāfah was a man of the tribe of 'Udhrah who claimed to have been carried off by the jinn but whose tales of which were, on his return, dismissed as lies; thus *khurāfāt* has come to mean in modern usage "superstitions, fables, fairy stories." Umm 'Amr ("Mother of 'Amr") is an epithet of the hyena; her frequent apostrophization in proverbs and

anecdotes appears to be related to the conventional view of the hyena as "the stupidest of beasts" (see al-Maydānī, *Majmaʿ*, 1:160); thus the sense is something like "It's all a pack of lies, you imbecile!"

37 *abīlīn*, pl. of *abīl*, "one who beats the *nāqūs*," a plank beaten with rods to summon Christians to prayer.

38 "the Great Catholicos" (*al-jāthilīq al-akbar*): the leader of Eastern Orthodox Christians living under Muslim rule.

39 "the Supreme Pontiff" (*al-ʿasaṭūs al-aʿẓam*): the Pope of Rome.

40 "Ascribing partners to God" (*al-shirk*): i.e., polytheism.

41 "pronounce letters like Qur'ān readers" (*tuqalqilūn*): *qalqalah* is "a quality unique to recitation [consisting of] the insertion of [ə] (schwa) after syllable-final [q], [d], [ṭ], [b], and [j]" (Kristina Nelson, *The Art of Reciting the Qur'an* (Cairo: American University in Cairo Press, 2001), 22). Such a pronunciation would sound bizarre in non-Qur'anic contexts.

42 "falter" (*taḥṣarūn*): the repetition is the author's.

43 "tightened" (*mufarram*): cf. the *Qāmūs*, "*al-farm* . . . is a medicament with which a woman becomes narrower" and Lane, *Lexicon*, "*farama* . . . to constrict the vulva with raisin stones."

44 "in two different forms" (*al-ʿakhtham wa-l-khathīm*): while the second word reads in the text *wa-l-khashīm*, this word, which is not found in the lexica, must be a misprint for *wa-l-khathīm*, which the *Qāmūs* gives as a synonym of the former.

45 "the just plain large one" (*al-ʿumāriṭī*): defined in the *Qāmūs* as *farj al-mar'ah al-ʿaẓīm* ("a woman's large vagina").

46 "the buttocks but with a slightly different spelling" (*al-būṣ*): the author has already used *al-bawṣ* above; the *Qāmūs* gives both spellings.

47 *al-ḥāriqah*: literally "the woman who rubs, or burns." The *Qāmūs* gives other possibly appropriate meanings, such as "the woman who is so overcome by lust that she grinds her teeth one upon another out of fear lest that lust take her to the point of neighing and snorting."

48 "the woman whose vagina is wide open and the woman whose vagina is open wide" (*al-khijām wa-l-khajūm*): according to the *Qāmūs*, the two forms are synonymous.

49 "the woman with the tiny vagina a man can't get at (again, but a different word)" (*al-marfūghah*): cf. twenty-one items earlier (*al-marṣūfah*).

50 *al-maṣūṣ*: also (the *Qāmūs*), the "vagina that dries the liquid from the surface of the penis."

51 *al-bayẓ*: also (the *Qāmūs*) "the water of the woman or man."

52 "the clitoris said with a funny accent" (*al-ʿuntul*): "the clitoris (*baẓr*); a dialectal variant of *ʿunbul*" (*Qāmūs*).

53 "a man's practicing coitus with one woman and then another before ejaculating and a man's practicing coition with one woman and then another before ejaculating" (*al-fahr wa-l-ifhār*): the *Qāmūs* states that these two verbal forms from the same root are synonymous.

54 "a little-used word for plain copulation" (*al-nashnashah*): defined in the *Qāmūs* simply as *nikāḥ* ("copulation").

55 "a noun meaning copulation from which no verb is formed" (*al-ʿaṣd*): the definition in the *Qāmūs* runs *al-nikāḥ lā fiʿla lahu*.

56 "dashing water on one's vagina": the next word in the text—*al-ʿaṣd*—has occurred eight items earlier (see n. 55); here the author may have intended *al-ʿazd*, which is synonymous with the former (though it has a verbal form).

57 "the flesh of the inner part of the vulva" (*al-kayn*): this is followed in the text by *al-ṭuʾṭuʾah*, for which no meaning has been found.

58 "the vulva said four other ways": the author supplies four more items (*bizbāz*, *fāʿūsa*, *khurnūf*, *mashraḥ*) that the *Qāmūs* defines simply with the words *farj* and *ḥir* ("vagina" and "vulva").

59 "the flabby vagina": in the text *al-ghuḍāriṭī*, which is not to be found in the *Qāmūs* (or other dictionaries) and is probably a misprint for *al-ʿuḍāriṭī*, in which case it is a repeat from above; this possibility seems stronger, given that the following word is also a repeat (see the following note).

60 "the vagina that dries the liquid from the surface of the penis" (*al-maṣūṣ*): a repeat from above where, however, the second sense given in the *Qāmūs* seems more appropriate.

61 "another name for the vagina" (*al-ṭanbarīz*): defined in the *Qāmūs* simply as *farj al-marʾah* ("a woman's vagina").

62 "the bizarrely spelled" (*al-khafashanfal*): the word, defined simply as "a woman's vagina," is of a particularly unusual form and without related words that might throw further light on its meaning.

63 "the 'nock'" (*al-fūq*): after the notch in the end of the arrow that fits the bowstring.

64 "and the vagina again in another exotic spelling" (*al-qaḥfalīz*): as *al-khafashanfal*, see preceding note.

65 "instruments of erection" (*adawāt al-naṣb*): *adawāt* is a grammatical term (literally, "instruments") applied to particles (prepositions, adverbs, conjunctions, and interjections) that govern other words; *adawāt al-naṣb* (e.g., *an, lan, idhan, kay*) require that words they govern end in a *naṣb*; however, *naṣb*, in its non-grammatical sense, means "lifting up, erecting," and the author puns on this.

66 "the thrower, the catapult," etc.: many of the items in this and the next list appear to be epithets.

67 *khabanfatha*: defined simply as "a name for the anus" (*Qāmūs*).

68 "the fontanel" (*al-rammāʿah*): so called "because of its elasticity" (Jamāl al-Dīn Muḥammad ibn Mukarram al-Ifrīqī Ibn Manẓūr, *Lisān al-ʿArab*, http://www.baheth.info/).

69 "the dry and sweaty smelling" (*al-ṣumārā*): cf. *al-ṣamīr* "the man whose flesh is dry on his bones and who gives off a smell of sweat" (*Qāmūs*).

70 "the draining vent" (*al-ʿazlā* or *al-ʿazlāʾ*): literally, the mouth at the bottom of a waterskin used to drain off the last remains of the water.

71 "the black one" (*al-saḥmāʾ*): in the text this is followed by *al-funquṣah*, for which no meaning has been found.

72 "the bunghole and the butthole" (*al-burʿuth wa-l-buʿthuṭ*): two further words meaning "anus," with no further senses and with no other members to their respective roots.

73 *adawāt al-jazm*: particles (see n. 65) that govern words ending with a closed syllable (*jazm*), e.g., negational *lā, lam*; in its non-grammatical sense, *jazm* means "cutting off or amputation," whence the expression in the *Qāmūs*, *jazama bi-salḥihi* "he voided part of his excrement, part thereof remaining" or simply "he cast forth his excrement" (Lane, *Lexicon*).

74 "another word for the penis": *al-suḥādil* defined simply as *dhakar* ("penis").

75 "the strong, crafty wolf" (*al-ḍabīz*): such is its definition in the dictionaries, with no indication that it may be used figuratively.

76 "the thimble" (*al-qusṭubīnah*): this and the next item refer presumably to the glans penis.

77 "the prick" (*al-qahbalīs*): a word not found in the dictionaries, though the related *qahbalis* occurs, defined in the *Qāmūs* as *zubb* ("penis," a vulgarism).

78 the *qaṣṭabīr*: an orphan word, the only one in its root and cited in only one dictionary (*Qāmūs*), where it is defined simply as "penis" (*dhakar*).

79 "the tassels" (*al-jazājiz*): assuming that their use in the sense of "penises" derives from the underlying meaning of "tassels of colored wools with which the [women's] camel-litter is decorated" (*Lisān*); singular *jizjizah*.

80 *adawāt al-jarr*: particles that govern words ending in *i*, i.e., prepositions that govern the genitive case; in its non-grammatical sense, *jarr* means "drawing toward, attracting," prepositions being so called because the governed word is "attracted to," or governed by, them.

81 "to shtup" (*ʿazaṭa*): described in the *Lisān* as "seemingly a metathesis of" (*ka'annu maqlūbun min*) *ṭaʿaza* (the next to preceding item in this list).

82 "another word of similar form but dubious status" (*ʿazlaba*): the author of the *Lisān* writes, "I cannot confirm it" (*lā aḥuqquhu*).

83 "to bridge" (*qanṭara*): assuming the use of this denominal verb in the phrase *qanṭara l-jāriyah* ("he had intercourse with the slave girl") derives, perhaps via a visual image, from the base sense of the noun *qanṭarah* ("bridge").

84 "to fuck hard" (*qasbara*): assuming the verb derives from the nouns *qisbār* or *qusburī* meaning "a hard penis."

85 "to fill her up" (*qamṭara*): cf. (*Lisān*) "to fill a water skin" and "to tie off a water skin with its thong."

86 "to kick her" (*laṭaza*): if we assume that this sense derives from that of "to kick (its calf), of a she-camel."

87 "and a variant of the same" (*lamadha*): the latter is a dialectal form of the preceding, i.e., *lamaja* (*Lisān*).

88 i.e., beginning with the first letter of the Arabic alphabet and ending with the last.

89 Meaning here the Arabs of the Arabian Peninsula in the days before, during, and shortly after the appearance of Islam, that is, the speakers of the pure Arabic language before its corruption by contact with other peoples and its decadence as the result of the passage of time.

90 The *Qāmūs* equates the two words at the point in its entry from which the author takes this definition; elsewhere, however, he defines *khajawjāh* as "a wind that blows constantly," thus supporting the author's argument.

91 "his 'ocean'" (*qāmūsuhu*): see Glossary.

92 "the *zaqqūm* tree": a tree that grows in Hell and whose fruit are exceedingly bitter (Q Wāqiʿah 56:52).

93 "she is to be excused because she was unaware that I, in fact, was only feigning sleep": the argument seems to be circular, i.e., she is to be excused for not visiting him while asleep because, in fact, he was not asleep.

94 "paronomasia": (*tajnīs* (or *jinās*), literally "making similar"): perhaps the most used rhetorical figure, it consists of deploying in proximity two words that are identical, or almost so, in the ductus but differ in vowelling and diacritics (e.g., حسن "handsome" and خشن "coarse" or أفعاله "his deeds" and أمواله "his money")

95 i.e., Buṭrus Yūsuf Ḥawwā, to whom the book is dedicated.

96 Saʿd al-Dīn Masʿūd ibn ʿUmar al-Taftazānī (d. between 791/1389 and 797/1395) was the author of commentaries (*Al-Muṭawwal*, *Al-Mukhtaṣar*) on al-Khaṭīb al-Qazwīnī's *Talkhīṣ al-miftāḥ* (*The Summary of the Key*) that were accepted for centuries as "the primary authoritative texts for the advanced study of rhetoric" (Meisami and Starkey, *Encyclopedia*, 2:751).

97 Abū Yaʿqūb Yūsuf ibn Abī Bakr al-Sakkākī (d. 626/1229) is best known for his *Miftāḥ al-ʿulūm* (*The Key to the Sciences*). His definitions and

formulations "became standard in the science of Arab rhetoric" (Meisami and Starkey, *Encyclopedia*, 2:679).

98 Abū l-Qāsim al-Ḥasan ibn Bishr al-Āmidī (d. 370/980), whose *Al-Muwāzanah bayna Abī Tammām wa-l-Buḥturī*, which compares the poetry of Abū Tammām and al-Buḥturī, is "one of the most important monuments of Arabic literary criticism" (Meisami and Starkey, *Encyclopedia*, 1:85).

99 Abū l-Ḥasan ʿAlī ibn Aḥmad al-Wāḥidī (d. 468/1076), commentator and literary critic.

100 Abū l-Qāsim Maḥmūd ibn ʿUmar al-Zamakhsharī (467–538/1075–1144), best known for his commentary on the Qur'ān, also wrote in the fields of rhetoric, grammar, lexicography, and proverbs (Meisami and Starkey, *Encyclopedia* 2:820); the author may have had particularly in mind his *Maqāmāt*, which are written in "carefully crafted *sajʿ*" (Devin Stewart, "Maqāma," in *Arabic Literature in the Post-classical Period*, edited by Roger Allen and D. S. Richards, vol. 6 of *The Cambridge History of Arabic Literature* (Cambridge: Cambridge University Press, 2008), 155).

101 Abū Ḥātim Muḥammad ibn Hibbān al-Bustī (270–354/884–965), also known as Ibn Hibbān, was best known as a traditionist, but one of his few surviving works is a literary anthology, *Rawḍat al-ʿuqalāʾ wa-nuzhat al-fuḍalāʾ* (*The Meadow of the Sagacious and Promenade of the Virtuous*) (Meisami and Starkey, *Encyclopedia*, 2:334).

102 Abū l-ʿAbbās ʿAbdallāh ibn al-Muʿtazz (247–96/861–908) was a poet and critic who wrote *Kitāb al-badīʿ* (*The Book of Rhetorical Figures*), the first treatise covering this area of Arabic poetics (Meisami and Starkey, *Encyclopedia*, 1:354).

103 Kamāl al-Dīn Abū l-Ḥasan ʿAlī ibn Muḥammad ibn al-Nabīh (ca. 560–619/1164–1222), a poet, probably included in the list because of his love of morphological parallelism (see, e.g., lines 14 to 18 of the poem starting *afdīhi in ḥafiẓa l-hawā aw ḍayyaʿā* (http://www.adab.com/modules.php?name=Sh3er&doWhat=shqas&qid=55259, accessed March 15, 2012)).

104 The author probably means Jamāl al-Dīn Muḥammad ibn Shams al-Dīn ibn Nubātah (known as al-Miṣrī, "the Egyptian") (686–768/1287–1366), a poet known for his love of punning (*tawriyah*) and a writer on literature and stylistics to whom he refers later (Volume Four, 4.17.5). However, the latter's ancestor, Abū Yaḥyā ʿAbd al-Raḥīm ibn Muḥammad ibn Nubātah (known as al-Khaṭīb, "the preacher") (d. 374/984–85), whose sermons in rhymed prose were regarded as models of stylistics, may be intended.

105 *ghāniyah* ("beautiful woman"): the *Qāmūs* states that the *ghāniyah* may be so called because she is "the woman whose beauty is such that she may dispense with adornment" (*al-ghaniyyatu bi-ḥusnihā ʿan al-zīnah*).

106 "the Fāriyāq": the name of the author's alter ego, formed by combining the first part of his first name and the last part of the last, thus Fāri(s al-Shid)yāq.

107 "monopods . . . monopodettes" (*nisnās . . . nasānis*): according to the dictionaries (which have some difficulty in distinguishing between the two), the *nisnās* is, among other things, "an animal numbered among the monsters, that is hunted and eaten, has the form of a person with one eye, a leg, and a hand, and speaks like a person" (*Lisān*) whereas the *nasānis* may be either the same as, or the plural, or the feminine, of the former.

108 *al-ḥinn*: a species of jinn or their dogs, or half-men half-jinn (see Volume Two, 2.4.44).

109 Kufah and Basra: cities in Iraq from which emerged the two main contending schools of Arabic grammar. The author is unlikely to have meant this to be taken literally.

110 The Arabic letters *ḥ-m-q* used in the text spell out the word *ḥumq*, meaning "stupidity."

111 i.e., in Lebanon.

112 By the Arabic language the author means literary or formal Arabic; Syriac is the liturgical language of the Maronite church.

113 "his Frankish brethren" (*ikhwānihi al-ifrinj*): i.e., the Roman Catholics of Europe.

114 "turning triliteral verbs into quadriliterals and vice versa": in another work the author provides the example of allowing the use of *rafrafa* instead of *raffa* in the sentence *raffa l-ṭāʾir janāḥayhi* ("the bird flapped its wings") (Aḥmad Fāris al-Shidyāq, *Kitāb al-jāsūs ʿalā l-qāmūs* (Constantinople: Maṭbaʿat al-Jawāʾib, 1299/1860–1), 13).

115 For example, by saying *wathiqa fī-hi* ("he trusted him") instead of *wathiqa bi-hi* or *istaʾdhana bi-hi* ("he asked permission to do something") instead of *istaʾdhana fī-hi*.

116 "*Durrat al-thīn* . . .": the author mimics the extravagant rhymed book titles typical of his day.

117 "the country's ruler": Emir Bashīr II al-Shihābī (1767–1850), ruler of Mount Lebanon, with interruptions, from the 1780s until 1840.

118 "Abtholutely not" (*tuʿ tuʿ*): though the lexica do not appear to recognize this item as an interjection, the verb *taʿtaʿa* is defined as *faʾfāʾ* ("lisping") or *ratratah* ("tripping over the letter t"), among other meanings.

119 The interjection *way way* should perhaps be understood here as a reference to the words of the Qurʾān (Q Qaṣaṣ 28:82) *waykaʾanna llāha yabsuṭuka l-rizq* ("Alas we had forgotten that it is God Who increases the provision [of those of his servants whom He will]") (Maududi), where *way* is considered by Sībawayh to be a separable particle meaning *waylaka* ("Alas for you!") (see *Qāmūs* s.v. *way*).

120 "the ten head wounds" (*al-shajjāṭ al-ʿashar*): the significance of the categorization lies in the various penalties owed the victim under the rule of *qiṣāṣ* ("retribution"), the first five requiring no *qiṣāṣ*, the second from five camels to a third of the monetary penalty for murder. Al-Shidyāq in fact increases the number to eleven by adding one category (the first) in an attempt to correct an error in the original, which appears to be the *Lisān* (the *Qāmūs* contains no similar passage).

121 "The Great Christian Master Physician" (*al-sāʿūr al-akbar*): meaning, perhaps, al-Ḥunayn ibn Isḥāq (194–260/809–73), the translator of Galen.

122 "If it be said (*fa-in qīla*) . . . I reply": the author deploys a technique known as *fanqalah* (derived from the preceding Arabic words),

common in Arabic exegetics and literary criticism, by which the author poses, and then responds to and dismisses, an objection to an argument he has put forward.

123 *ṭanāṭīr*: cone-shaped woman's headdresses, singular *ṭanṭūr*; "The height and composition of the tantour were proportional to the wealth of its owner, with the most splendid tantours made of gold and reaching as high as thirty inches. Some were encrusted with gems and pearls. The tantour was a customary gift presented to the bride by her husband on their wedding day" (http://en.wikipedia.org/wiki/Tantour, accessed April 20, 2012, with illustration; see also R. P. A. Dozy, *Dictionnaire détaillé des noms des vêtements chez les Arabes* (Amsterdam: Jean Müller, 1843; offset, Beirut: Librairie du Liban, n.d.).)

124 *qarn*: cf. Latin *cornu*, French *corne*, etc.

125 *ṣābūn*: cf. Latin *sāpon-*, English "soap," French *savon.*

126 *qiṭṭ*: cf. Latin *cattus*, English "cat," French *chat.*

127 *mazj*: not in fact cognate with English "mix" or French *mélange*, etc.

128 Cf. "the horns of the righteous shall be exalted" (Ps. 75:10) and "in my name shall his horn be exalted" (Ps. 89:24), etc.

129 "the word itself is not derived from any verb" etc.: typically, Arab scholars of the classical period regarded nouns as derived from verbs; in this case, however, there is no verb with a meaning related to the noun *qarn* in either its literal or figurative senses.

130 Jirmānūs (Germanus) Farḥāt (1670–1732) was a Maronite cleric, grammarian, lexicographer, poet, and educator from Aleppo; his *Bāb al-iʿrāb ʿan lughat al-Aʿrāb* is an updating of the *Qāmūs.* Jirmānūs's efforts, portrayed as part of a "revival" of literary Arabic are sometimes better understood in the context of the transition from Syriac, the original spoken and literary language of many Levantine Christians. On Farḥāt's life and works, see Kristen Brustad, "Jirmānūs Jibrīl Farḥāt," in *Essays in Arabic Literary Biography 1350–1850*, edited by Joseph Lowry and Devin J. Stewart (Wiesbaden: Harrassowitz Verlag, 2009), 242–51.

131 *Abū l-ʿIbar*, etc.: one of the most famous buffoons and comic poets of his age, whose real name was Abū l-ʿAbbās Muḥammad ibn Aḥmad

al-Hāshimī (ca. 175–250/791–864). Having changed his *kunyah* ("patronymic") from Abū l-ʿAbbās to Abū l-ʿIbar ("Father of Warnings" or "of Tears"), he thereafter added a letter with each succeeding year, ending with the nonsensical appellation given above. His works include a comic sermon on marriage. See further Meisami and Starkey, *Encyclopedia*, 1:37.

132 "from the drain" (*mina l-balūʿah*): the sense is not obvious but perhaps recalls some anecdote concerning Abū l-ʿIbar.

133 The humor of many of the following anecdotes seems to lie in the unexpected and, especially, ridiculous nature of the protagonist's actions and reactions and the crossed purposes at which he always seems to be with his interlocutors.

134 The joke being perhaps that the response fails to answer the question either way.

135 The formulation of the question seems to imply a fuller version, such as "If he grew large, I'd ask him 'Why . . .' etc." This would be ridiculous, since the man cannot control how he grows and hence cannot be blamed for it.

136 The humor may lie in the phrase "to see her" (*li-anẓurahā*), which might be taken to mean "to cast the evil eye on her."

137 "May God be protected from every eye!" (*tabāraka llāhu min kulli ʿayn*): the man confuses the verbs *bāraka* and *tabāraka*.

138 Buhlūl, ʿUlayyān: moralizing "wise fools" of the early Abbasid period (see Naysābūrī, *ʿUqalāʾ*).

139 Ṭuways: Abū ʿAbd al-Munʿim ʿĪsā ibn ʿAbdallāh (10–92/632–711), nicknamed Ṭuways ("Little Peacock"), a celebrated singer and *mukhannath* ("effeminate") of Medina during the early days of Islam, known for his comical sayings.

140 Muzabbid: Muzabbid al-Madanī, a much-cited early Medinan comic.

141 The Fāriyāq: the author seems to have forgotten that the Fāriyāq is already speaking.

142 "waist-bands" (*himyān*): i.e., sashes, in which money was carried.

143 "The Fāriyāq's father was one of those who sought to depose the emir" etc.: Yūsuf, Fāris's father, though employed by Emir Bashīr II

al-Shihābī, became involved in a 1819 Druze revolt against him, led by his relatives Emir Ḥasan ʿAlī and Emir Sulaymān Sayyid Aḥmad and caused by his ever more oppressive tax levies. With the failure of the uprising, Yūsuf fled along with these to Damascus, where he died in 1821 (on the political situation in Mount Lebanon in the early nineteenth century and the Shidyāq family's role in it, see Ussama Makdisi, *The Artillery of Heaven: American Missionaries and the Failed Conversion of the Middle East* (Ithaca: Cornell University Press, 2008)), 72–76, al-Maṭwī, *Aḥmad,* 47–48, and Paul Starkey *Fact and Fiction in al-Sāq ʿalā l-Sāq,* in Robin Ostle, Ed de Moor, and Stephan Wild (eds.), *Writing the Self: Autobiographical Writing in Modern Arabic Literature* (London: Saqi Books, 1998), 36).

144 "a tambour" (*ṭunbūr*): a long-necked fretted lute. According to Starkey, the author uses "the *ṭanbūr* as a symbol of art, of freedom, almost of life itself" (Starkey, *Fact and Fiction*, 36).

145 "their Frankish shaykhs": i.e., the clergy of the Roman Catholic church, with which the Maronite church is in communion.

146 "schlup-flup" (*khāqibāqi*): "the sound of the vagina during intercourse" (*Qāmūs*).

147 "A Priest and a Pursie, Dragging Pockets and Dry Grazing" (*Fī qissīs wa-kīs wa-taḥlīs wa-talḥīs*): the priest is mentioned at 1.5.8, the pursie at 1.5.10; *taḥlīs* does not occur in the dictionaries but may be based on *maḥlūs* (a word already used, see 1.1.6) which, according to the *Qāmūs*, means "scantly fleshed" (of the vagina), in which case it would relate to the figurative use of "pursie" (see n. 10 below) in such sentences as "When my pursie grew light while within your Happy Purlieu, which is to say, when it grew to be a drag . . ." and/or on *iḥlās* meaning "bankruptcy"; *talḥīs* is likewise absent from the dictionaries but may be based on *laḥisat al-māshiyatu l-arḍ* ("the herds grazed the land to the roots"), in which case it would refer to the Fāriyāq's general state of penury.

148 "whose name rhymes with Baʿīr Bayʿar": i.e., Amīr [= Emir] Ḥaydar [ibn Aḥmad al-Shihābī] (1763–1835), cousin of Emir Bashīr II, ruler of Mount Lebanon (see 1.1.20, n. 117). The book referred to in the following lines as "ledgers" is Ḥaydar ibn Aḥmad's *Al-Ghurar al-ḥisān*

*fī taʾrīkh ḥawādith al-zamān*, a history of Lebanon from the earliest times to the Egyptian invasion of 1831.

149 Alphonse de Lamartine (1790–1869), writer, poet, and politician; for these quotations, see Alphonse de Lamartine, *Oeuvres de A. Lamartine: Méditations Poétiques* (Paris: Charles Gosselin, 1838), 21, 23–24, and 25. The author's translations of Lamartine and Chateaubriand that follow are discussed by Alwan, who characterizes them as "smooth, readable, and reasonably accurate" (Alwan, *Aḥmad*, chap. 3).

150 ʿAntar ibn Shaddād: a pre-Islamic poet whose life gave rise at a later date to a popular epic of chivalry.

151 The name of the deity is used to express deep feeling incited by music or poetry.

152 *Poetry's Destiny*, etc.: Lamartine's essay is entitled *Des destinées de la poésie* and contains the words "je vois . . . des générations rajeunies . . . qui reconstruiront . . . cette oeuvre infinie que Dieu a donné à faire et à refaire sans cesse à l'homme, sa propre destinée. Dans cette oeuvre la poésie a sa place." (Lamartine, *Oeuvres* 56).

153 François-René de Chateaubriand (1768–1848): writer, politician, diplomat, and historian, considered the founder of Romanticism in French literature, who lived in America from 1791 to 1792. The originals of the two passages quoted below are to be found at Chateaubriand, *Oeuvres complètes de Chateaubriand,* vol. 6, *Voyages en Amérique, en Italie, au Mont Blanc: Mélanges littéraires* (Paris: Garnier, [1861]), 54 and 62.

154 When Bilqīs, Queen of Sheba, visited Sulaymān from her kingdom in Yemen, he had a splendid pavilion built for her reception (Q Naml 27:44).

155 The verses are by Hammām ibn al-Salūlī (d. 100/718).

156 "a Magian": a Zoroastrian, and thus supposedly a worshipper of fire.

157 "pursies, and other things that have similar-sounding names" (*li-l-akyās wa-li-mā jāʾa ʿalā waznihā wa-rawiyyihā*): literally, "purses, and things that have the same syllabic structure and rhyme-letter"; the author probably intends the Arabic reader to think of *aksās* ("cunts"), just as the translator hopes the English reader will think of "pussies."

158 Mount Raḍwā: a mountain in Medina.

159 "Words... Matter... Form": the terminology is Aristotelian and was adopted by Muslim philosophers writing on physics, psychology, and metaphysics, with "Matter" meaning the substratum from which any entity is formed (thus, the soul is the matter from which the body is formed, wood the matter from which the chair is formed). The application of this analogy to the relationship between speech and meaning may be original to the author, whose intention seems to be to give a twist to the widely accepted notion that man is superior to other beings by virtue of having the capacity to speak, his point being that, if you have little to say, any such superiority is moot.

160 Abū Dulāmah: buffoon poet to the first three Abbasid caliphs (d. 161/777–78).

161 "al-Kuʿaykāt... al-Rukākāt": comic names, meaning "Cookies" and "Simpletons" (or "Cuckolds") and perhaps joking allusions to the village of al-Shuwayfāt (Choueifat)—which is next door to al-Ḥadath, where the author lived in his youth and which has long been a transit point for trade among Beirut, the south, and Mount Lebanon—and another location as yet unidentified.

162 "*cap*ital (and *ass*ets)" (*ra's al-māl wa-dhanabuhu*): literally, "the head of the money (*ra's al-māl*) and its tail," the author playing with the literal meaning of the Arabic expression meaning "(financial) capital."

163 "faces radiant" (*wa-l-wujūhu nāḍirah*): cf. Q Qiyāmah 75:22 *wujūhun yawma'idhin nāḍirah* "Some faces will be radiant on that Day."

164 "those lands" (*tilka l-bilād*): i.e., Lebanon, or Mount Lebanon.

165 "every judge" (*kullu qāḍin*): or "each party to the transaction."

166 "her c..." (*mabā...*): the missing Arabic word is *mabālahā*.

167 Diʿbil: Diʿbil ibn ʿAlī al-Khuzāʿī (148–246/765–860), a poet of invective (*hijā'*) and philologist who lived in Kufa.

168 "'O feeder of the orphans'... etc." (*a-muṭʿimata l-aytāmi ilā ākhirihi*): a reference to the widely cited but unattributed verse *a-muṭʿimata l-aytāmi min kaddi farjihā * a-lā lā taznī wa-lā tataṣaddaqī* ("O you who feed the orphans from the labor of your vagina, * I say to you,

[better that] you neither fornicate nor give alms!"), i.e., it is better to do nothing than to seek to do good through illicit means.

169 "Unseemly Conversations and Crooked Contestations" (*Muḥāwarāt khāniyah wa-munāqashāt ḥāniyah*): alternatively, *Muḥāwarāt khāniyyah wa-munāqashāt ḥāniyyah* ("Inn-style Conversations and Tavern-style Discussions").

170 "which is why it's called *qahwah*": the author links *qahwah* ("wine") to the verb *aqhā (ʿan al-ṭaʿām)*, "to be put off (one's food)," though the roots are different.

171 Daʿd, Laylā: women's names.

172 "his ankleted honies": i.e., the women of his household.

173 "Each day some new matter he uncovers" (*fa-huwa kulla yawmin fī shān*): Q Raḥmān 55:29.

174 "the two best things" (*al-aṭyabayn*): i.e., eating and coitus.

175 Al-Qāsim ibn ʿAlī al-Ḥarīrī (446–516/1052–1122), Iraqi prose writer, poet, and official, wrote fifty immensely popular *maqāmāt*, which he compiled into a work of the same name.

176 "the *Nawābigh*": *Al-Kalim al-nawābigh*, a brief homily written in a mannered, ornamental style.

177 "his grandfather" (*jaddihi*): i.e., his mother's father, Yūsuf Ziyādah Musʿad, of ʿAshqūt (al-Maṭwī, *Aḥmad* 1:49), his father's father, Manṣūr, having died in 1793.

178 "*she . . . degree . . . awry . . . eye*": despite his protestations, the author slips into rhymed prose at this moment of heightened emotion, possibly without noticing, and continues to do so at similar moments throughout the chapter.

179 "she had an eye that was 'dried up'" (*dhābilatuhu*): meaning, presumably, that her eye had lost its moistness by having taken on that "sleepiness" that is said to characterize "bedroom" eyes.

180 "the whole entry . . . too noble to speak of": the entry for the root *ḥ-sh-f* includes words meaning "it (a camel's udder) became contracted and withered" and "dry bread" and "the worst quality of dates," as well as *ḥashafah*, "the head of the penis."

181 "such a contrast . . .": *ṭibāq* ("antithesis"), consisting of the "inclusion of two contraries in one line or sentence" (Meisami and Starkey, *Encyclopedia*, 2:659), is a rhetorical staple of traditional Arabic poetics.

182 "or I do on their behalf": by implying that he wrote the lines himself, the author may be seeking to undermine the sometimes spurious authority lent to ideas stated in prose by topping them off with a couple of lines of verse, a standard technique used by writers of earlier generations.

183 Both are labial consonants.

184 "for a boy I teach": the author refers to the practice of addressing the beloved as though she were a male (*tadhkīr*), a feature of Arabic poetry and song from the earliest times until today.

185 The author deploys two contradictory arguments: that *tadhkīr* is used because some "men who can see no good in women" prefer to do so, and that it reflects an underlying grammatically masculine referent, namely the word *shakhṣ*; thus, according to the second argument, when the poet refers to "he" or "him," he really means "that person" and is thinking of a female. The French and Italian equivalents of *shakhṣ* that the author has in mind are, presumably, *personne* and *persona*.

186 "Ibn Mālik's *Sharḥ al-Mashāriq*": the author's name as given by al-Shidyāq is apparently a mistake for (ʿAbd al-Laṭīf ibn Firishtah ʿIzz al-Dīn ibn Amīn al-Dīn) Ibn Malak (d. after 824/1421), whose *Mabāriq al-azhār (fī) sharḥ Mashāriq al-anwār*, a hadith collection with extended commentary, was regarded as a classic and reprinted several times in the nineteenth century (*Encyclopaedia of Islam*, edited by P.J. Bearman, Th. Bianquis, C.E. Bosworth, E. van Donzel, and W.P. Heinrichs et al., 2nd ed., 12 vols. (Leiden: E.J. Brill, 1960–2005), 2:923–24); it has, however, proven impossible to confirm the reference in the absence of any mention of the hadith from the commentary on which this passage is presumably taken.

187 "Hind . . . Zaynab": generic female names.

188 "the 'novel' style": poetry in the style called *badīʿ*, i.e., that relying largely on rhetorical and technical artifices.

189 "That Which Is Long and Broad" (*Fī l-ṭawīl al-ʿarīḍ*): perhaps an allusion to the long, broad path facing the grammarian.

190 "Zayd struck ʿAmr" (*ḍaraba Zaydun ʿAmran*): Zayd and ʿAmr are generic names used in sentences constructed to demonstrate grammatical rules.

191 "the daughter of Abū l-Aswad al-Duʾalī" etc.: al-Duʾalī (d. 69/688) is known as "the father of Arabic grammar"; the story goes that his daughter said to him *mā ajmalu l-samāʾ* ("What is the most beautiful thing in the sky?") when she intended *mā ajmala l-samāʾ* ("How beautiful the sky is!"), and he corrected her, thus starting the process of the recording and codification of "chaste speech."

192 "'the ship sails' or 'the mare runs'": these are two-step metaphors because the ship is propelled by the wind, which in turn blows at God's behest, while the mare runs because she is made to do so by her rider, who is himself a creature propelled by God.

193 "aeolian" (*ʿiqyawniyyah*): for a definition of the noun *ʿiqyawn* from which this adjective derives, see Volume Two (2.14.43).

194 From this point, the nomenclature leaves the realm of reality and devolves into a series of fanciful and bizarre-sounding terms based largely on onomatopoeia (*farqaʿiyyah*, *qarqaʿiyyah*, etc.) or, toward the end of the list, hapax legomena known only from a single line of ancient verse (*jaḥlanjaʿiyyah*, *ʿuṭrūsiyyah*) or having only a precarious foothold in the language (such as *shunṭafiyyah*, of which the *Qāmūs* says, "a colloquialism, mentioned by Ibn Durayd, who does not explain it").

195 "tongue-smacking" (*ṭaʿṭaʿiyyah*): according to the *Qāmūs*, *ṭaʿṭaʿah* is a sound one makes by "sticking the tongue against the hard palate and then masticating [? *yanṭiʿ*] because of the good taste of something he is eating, so that a sound may be heard from between the palate and the tongue."

196 "panthero-dyspneaceous" (*khuʿkhuʿiyyah*): the word *khuʿkhuʿ* refers to a certain plant and thus does not lend itself to an onomatopeic interpretation; it may, however, be related to the verb *khaʿʿa* "to make a sound from the back of its throat when it has run out of breath running after its enemy (of a leopard)."

197 "the skrowlaceous" (*ʿuhʿukhiyyah*): of this word the *Lisān* says, "Al-Azharī said, 'We heard Khalīl ibn Aḥmad say, "We heard a hideous word, not to be permitted by the rules of word formation: a Bedouin was asked about his she-camel, and he said, 'I left her grazing *ʿuhʿukh*.' I asked reliable scholars, and they denied that this word could belong to the language of the Arabs."'" The *Qāmūs* says that the word, meaning a certain medicinal plant, is a deformation of *khuʿkhuʿ* (see n. 196 above) and, as such, does not offer an obvious onomatoeic association.

198 "skraaaghhalaceous" (*ʿuhkhaghiyyah*): the word is not found in the dictionaries.

199 "the transtextual and the intertextual" (*kashaʿthajiyyah wa-kashaʿẓajiyyah*): the *Qāmūs* says of these words only that they are "recently coined" (*muwalladān*), without definition.

200 "A book's prologue" (*khuṭbat al-kitāb*): the invocation with which pre-nineteenth-century Arabic books usually begin, which weaves a statement of the work's concerns into an encomium of the Prophet Muḥammad, his Companions, etc.

201 "opposition" (*ṭibāq*): al-Ḥillī describes *ṭibāq* as consisting of "using two words of opposite meaning, so that it is as though the poet were opposing (*ṭābaqa*) the one to its opposite" (al-Ḥillī, *Sharḥ* 72).

202 Al-Farrāʾ: Abū Zakariyyāʾ Yaḥyā ibn Ziyād al-Farrāʾ (144–207/761–822), a grammarian of the Kufan school, most famous for his grammatical commentary on the Qurʾān, entitled *Maʿānī al-Qurʾān*.

203 *ḥattā*: a particle (meaning approximately "until") whose usage is complex.

204 "**nna*": a particle (approximately "that") whose initial vowel varies according to environment.

205 "connective *fāʾ*" etc.: on the copula *fa-* (consisting of the letter *fāʾ* plus *a*) and its multiple uses and significations, see e.g., W. A. Wright, *Grammar of the Arabic Language*, 3rd ed., rev. W. Robertson Smith and M. J. de Goeje (Cambridge: Cambridge University Press, 1951), whose index cites ten distinct usages.

206 al-Yazīdī: Abū Muḥammad Yaḥyā ibn al-Mubārak al-Yazīdī (d. 202/817 or 818) was the author of several works on grammar and lexicography; these have not survived, although anecdotes about him abound in anthologies (Meisami and Starkey, *Encyclopedia* 2:812).

207 "connective *wāw*" etc.: on the copula *wa-* (consisting of the letter *wāw* plus *a*) and its multiple uses and significations, see e.g., Wright, *Grammar*, whose index cites five distinct usages.

208 "the right-related . . . uses of *lām*": on the particles *li-* and *la-* (consisting of the letter *lām* plus *i* or *a*), see e.g., Wright, *Grammar*, whose index cites seven distinct usages.

209 al-Aṣmaʿī: Abū Saʿīd ʿAbd al-Malik ibn Qurayb al-Bāhilī al-Aṣmaʿī (122–213/740–828) was one of the most influential early lexicographers and philologists. Sixty of his works are extant, although it is not clear if any dealt with the orthographic issue raised here.

210 "*aw* . . . *am*": two particles that may be translated "or."

211 "[the words] *qāʾil* or *bāʾiʿ*": because the proscribed orthography—*qāyil* and *bāyiʿ*—might be taken to represent a colloquialized pronunciation.

212 "when pronounced without vowels at the end" (*sākinan*): the author implies that most writers do not know enough grammar to use correct desinential inflections and their "concoctions" are therefore less offensive to the ear when read without them, in keeping with the adage *sakkin taslam* ("read without endings and be safe").

213 "the 'doer' and the 'done'": in Arabic grammatical terminology, the subject of a verb is referred to as the *fāʿil* ("doer"), the object as the *mafʿūl* ("done"). In the following, the author plays, as many have done before, on these and other, non-grammatical, meanings of the same words, e.g., "doer" in the sense of "manual worker" and "fucker," and "done" in the sense of "fucked."

214 "'raised' . . . 'laid'": the vowel *u*, called "raising" (*rafʿ*), is the marker of the subject, while *a*, called "laying" (*naṣb*), is, among other things, that of the object.

215 "the doer of the . . ." (*fāʿil al-* . . .): perhaps meaning, in grammatical terms, "the subject of the verb" (*fāʿil al-fiʿl*), which in non-grammatical language would mean "the doer of the (dirty) deed."

216 "who are steadfast" (*min al-qurrā' al-ṣābirīn*): evocative of a number of passages in the Qur'ān, e.g., *sa-tajidunī in shā'a llāhu min al-ṣābirīn* ("and, God willing, you will find me steadfast") (Q Ṣāffāt 37:102).

217 "switching persons" (*al-iltifāt*): a rhetorical figure consisting of an "abrupt change of grammatical person from second to third and from third to second," as in the words of the poet Jarīr "When were the tents at Dhū Ṭulūḥ? O tents, may you be watered by ample rain!" (Meisami and Starkey, *Encyclopedia* 2:657).

218 *māghūṣ*: a nonce-word apparently used to mean "bore, pest."

219 "Faid al-Hāwif ibn Hifām in lifping tones" (*ḥaddasa l-Hāris ibn al-Hithām*): the author substitutes the letter *s* for *th*, *h* for *ḥ*, and *th* for *sh*; without these substitutions, the sentence would read *ḥaddatha l-Ḥārith ibn Hishām*. The name evokes those of the narrators of the best known *maqāmāt* series, by al-Hamadhānī, whose narrator is called ʿĪsā ibn Hishām, and those by al-Ḥarīrī, who names his narrator al-Ḥārith ibn Hammām. At the same time, the name in its "lisped" form may be translated as "Masher, son of Pulverizer."

220 *The Balancing of the Two States and Comparing of the Two Straits* (*Kitāb Muwāzanat al-ḥālatayn wa-murāzanat al-ālatayn*): the title may be intended to evoke the *Kitāb al-Muwāzanah bayna Abī Tammām wa-l-Buḥturī* of al-Āmidī (see 1.1.11 above), although the latter compares not good and evil but the literary accomplishments of two poets and does not employ the "facing tables using a columnar system" referred to below.

221 Abū Rushd "Brains" ibn Ḥazm (Abū Rushd Nuhyah ibn Ḥazm): the name evokes two of the best known writers of the Maghreb—Ibn Rushd, known in the West as Averroës (520–95/1126–98), and Ibn Ḥazm (384–456/994–1064)—although the significance of the choice of these writers is not obvious. *Nuhyah*, literally "mind," is not part of the name of either writer.

222 "by even a jot" (*naqīran*): an echo of Q Nisā' 4:53 and 124.

223 "those who hold to the humoral theory" (*al-ṭabāʾiʿiyyīn*): i.e., those who hold to Galen's theory that one's physical state is determined by

the balance therein of the humors (*al-ṭabāʾiʿ*—phlegm, blood, yellow bile, and black bile).

224 "by insisting on the impossible and making from the non-existent something necessarily existent" (*bi-farḍ al-mustaḥīl wa-jaʿl al-maʿdūm ka-l-mawjūd al-wājib*): the terms "(im)possible" and "necessary" pertain to Aristotelian logic (see also above 1.6.4, n. 159) and were introduced into Islamic philosophy by al-Fārābī (ca. 259–339/872–950). Al-Fārābī postulated that it is inconceivable to posit the impossible (e.g., a square circle), while the author's jurisprudent insists that to do so constitutes the very essence of his trade.

225 "I added him then to the three, making him number four" (*fa-ṣayyartuhu rābiʿa l-thalāthah*): an echo of Q Kahf 18:22 *sa-yaqūlūna thalāthatun rābiʿuhum kalbuhum* "Some will say, 'They were three, the fourth was their dog'" (in reference to "the people of the cave").

226 "mindful men" (*dhī ḥijrin*): an echo of Q Fajr 89:5.

227 "A Sacrament" (*Sirr*): the allusion may be either to the sacrament of confession (1.14.4) or to the secret (also *sirr*) referred to at the end of the chapter (1.14.9).

228 "its number": i.e., the number thirteen.

229 "seized by their forelocks" (*yuʾkhadhu bi-l-nawāṣī*): Q Aḥzāb 33:37.

230 "the 'buttocks' of 'Halt and weep'" (*aʿjāz qifā nabki*): *qifā nabki* ("Halt and weep") are the opening words of the celebrated "suspended ode" (*muʿallaqah*) of the pre-Islamic poet Imruʾ al-Qays; the word "buttocks" occurs later, when the poet says "I said to the night, when it stretched its lazy loins followed by its fat buttocks, and heaved off its fat breast, 'Well now, you tedious night, won't you clear yourself off, and let dawn shine?'" (Arthur J. Arberry, *The Seven Odes: The First Chapter in Arabic Literature* (London: George Allen and Unwin, 1957), 64). The author links, bathetically, the misfortunes of the speaker with those of one of Arabic literature's most heroic figures.

231 *karshūnī*: Arabic written in Syriac script.

232 "soul (*nafs*) . . . breath (*nafas*) . . . breathes (*yatanaffas*)": the author plays with the fact that the words for "breath" and "soul" are spelled

the same when vowels are not indicated, with a resulting potential for confusion; the reference to orifices and "a certain school" may be no more than a joke to the effect that some people count farting, belching, hiccupping, etc. as "points of exit and entry" for the breath.

233 "open his wife's womb": see, e.g., Gen. 30:22: "And God remembered Rachel, and God hearkened to her, and opened her womb."

234 "long converse and closeness in *bed*" (*qurb al-wisād wa-ṭūl al-siwād*—literally, "closeness of pillow and length of converse"): Bint al-Khuss (a semi-legendary figure dating to perhaps the third century before Islam and famed for her ready wit) was asked, "Wherefore didst thou commit fornication?" and this phrase was her response (Lane, *Lexicon*, s.v. *sāwada*; al-Maydānī, *Majmaʿ*, 2:37).

235 "the two *c*s": in the Arabic, "the two *k*s" (*al-kāfayn*). Since there appears to be no conventionally recognized "two *k*s," the meaning is open to speculation. In the opinion of the translator, the phrase is probably code for *al-kuss wa-l-kutshīnah* ("cunt and cards"), the topics of this chapter.

236 The following catalog lists activities, such as gambling, dishonest dealing, speculation, and usury that are forbidden in Islam.

237 "such people": meaning presumably, and presumably ironically, ships' captains.

238 *irtisām* . . . : the following list of 104 words is, in effect, redundant, because all but fifteen of them are repeated, with definitions, in a table at the end of the chapter (1.16.9 ff.); on the author's evolving approach to the formatting of such lists, see the Translator's Afterword in Volume Four. Words that are not repeated in the table, and that thus remain unglossed, are *tashāʾum, taṭayyur, tafāʾul, taḥattum, tayammun, tasaʿʿud, tamassuḥ, kahānah, intijāʾ, ṭalāsim, ʿazāʾim, ruqā, tamāʾim, ʿūdhah,* and *siḥr*; these items are glossed here, in the endnotes. Presumably the author did not regard them as rare enough to need definition.

239 *tashāʾum*: "to draw an evil omen."

240 *taṭayyur*: "to draw auguries."

241 *tafāʾul*: "to draw a good omen."

242 *taḥattum*: "to believe in the inevitability of a thing."

243 *tayammun*: "to draw a good omen."

244 *tasaʿʿud*: "to draw a good omen."

245 *tamassuḥ*: "to seek blessing from holy men by drawing the hands over them" (*Lisān*: "blessing is sought from so-and-so by drawing of the hands [over the object of veneration] (*yutammasaḥu bi-hi*) because of his merit and [the devotedness of] his worship, as if one were drawn closer to God by proximity to him").

246 *ʿāṭis*: defined in the list of definitions at the end of the chapter under *al-ʿāṭūs*, following the *Qāmūs*.

247 "*qaʿīd* or *dākis*": defined in the list of definitions at the end of the chapter under the entry for *kādis*, following the *Qāmūs*.

248 *kahānah*: "soothsaying, divination."

249 *intijāʾ*: the author does not include this in his list of definitions below, nor does it appear in a relevant sense in the dictionaries, but *al-intijāʾ* is described by some of these as synonymous with *al-tanājī*, or "talking to one another in secret," and there may be a reference here to Q Mujādilah 58:9: "O believers, when you conspire (*idhā tanājaytum*), conspire not together in sin and enmity and in disobedience to the Messenger, but conspire together in peace and God-fearing" (58:9; Arthur J. Arberry, *The Koran Interpreted* (Oxford: Oxford University Press, 1982), 570); see also *tanajjā* above and in the list of definitions.

250 *ṭalāsim*: "talismans."

251 *ʿazāʾim*: "spells."

252 *ruqā*: "incantations, charms."

253 *tamāʾim*: "amulets."

254 *ʿūdhah*: "spell."

255 *siḥr*: "magic."

256 *ṣadā*: in the list of definitions at the end of the chapter, this word is defined under the entry for *al-kādis*, following the *Qāmūs*.

257 "those lands" (*tilka l-bilād*): presumably, the lands to which he was bound before the ship turned back.

258 "the *mankūs*": "three lines following one another immediately, then one on its own" (*Lisān*).

259 The wording seems to be the author's, not that of a dictionary, and he interprets *ḥazā* as being of the root *ḥ-z-w* rather than *ḥ-z-y*, an alternative given by the *Lisān* but not the *Qāmūs*; *al-taḥazzī* is the noun formed from the reflexive variant of the verb.

260 "a tree": presumably of the kind also called *ratīmah*.

261 "or etc.": indicating that the entry in the *Qāmūs* continues with other less relevant definitions.

262 "on the pattern of *kataba*" (*ka-kataba*): a word having the same pattern of consonants and vowels as that of the subject of the definition is used to disambiguate its spelling, a necessary procedure given that short vowels and other morphological features are not always indicated in writing and, if indicated, are vulnerable to error; the meaning of the word used (*kataba* "to write") is irrelevant.

263 "the minor magician who claims powers of divination and knocks small stones together" (*al-ḥāzī al-mutakahhin al-ṭāriq bi-l-ḥaṣā*): the *Qāmūs* quotes an authority to the effect that the *ḥāzī* "has less knowledge than the *ṭāriq* ('one who bangs small stones together'), and the *ṭāriq* can scarcely be said to divine; the *ḥāzī* speaks on the basis of supposition and fear."

264 *al-naffāthāt fī l-ʿuqad*: the phrase is taken from Q Falaq 113:4 and means literally "the women who blow on knots."

265 "too well-known to require definition" (*m*): here, as frequently elsewhere, the *Qāmūs* uses the abbreviation *m*, standing for *maʿrūf* ("well known").

266 "a separate book": unidentified, but not, as one might expect, his *Al-Jāsūs ʿalā l-Qāmūs* (the verb *iḥtawā* is dealt with there but in terms of transitivity versus intransitivity, not root-assignment or semantics).

267 Q Insān 76:10.

268 "of moon and of money-wagering" (*al-qamar wa-l-qimār*): perhaps because exposure to moonlight was considered by the ancient Arabs to be hazardous, as, of course, is wagering.

269 "cold talk" (*al-kalām al-bārid*): idiomatically, "rudeness."

270 "an instrument containing drink, or . . . one containing meat" (*adātun fī-hā sharāb . . . ukhrā fī-hā laḥm*): i.e., a bar or a restaurant, amenities

that the author puts on the same level as bed-warmers and hot-water bottles by referring to each as an *adāh* ("instrument, device").

271 "their precipitation is bottom up, or in other words from the heads of people who are themselves ruled to the heads of those who rule" (*lafẓuhā min siflin ilā ʿilwin ay min ruʾūs nāsin masūdīn ilā ruʾūsi nāsin sāʾidīn*): apparently meaning that judges, being themselves subjects of the ruler, cannot impose the law upon him.

272 "a certain vagabond was once the guest of people who failed to honor and celebrate him": perhaps a reference to the author's treatment in Malta, or Egypt, versus that which he received in England or France.

273 "here": i.e., in this book.

274 "Old Testament": see 1.16.2, n. 233.

275 The reference is unidentified.

276 "opener of the womb": the referent has changed, being now the first-born child and not God; for the two different usages, see, e.g., Gen. 29:31 and Exod. 13:2.

277 "the secret's being revealed" etc.: cf. 1.14.9 above.

278 The following list reflects the medical science not of the mid-nineteenth century but mainly of the pre-Islamic and early Islamic periods, whose language provides the corpus for the *Qāmūs*. It thus includes terms not recognized by modern science, some of which are based on medieval understandings of camel and horse, rather than human, anatomy.

279 "the Joker": or "the Liar."

280 "The name of al-Farazdaq's devil": pre-Islamic and early Islamic Arabs believed that major poets had their verses dictated to them by personal devils; Hammām ibn Ghālib al-Farazdaq (ca. 20–110/640–728) identified his demon as bearing the name ʿAmr.

281 "al-Shayṣabān": a name of the Devil (as the two following items), but also the name of a forefather of a certain tribe of the jinn and as such repeated below.

282 "The Corrupter . . . Cut-nose": unlike the preceding, the majority of which are proper names, the following five items are common epithets of Satan.

283 *arḍ khāfiyah*: on *khāfiyah* in the sense of "jinn (collectively)," see further down this list.

284 "with or without nunation" (*wa-qad yuṣraf*): certain indefinite nouns are inflected with terminations ending in the letter *nūn* (n), a feature known as nunation, others with terminations not ending in *nūn*, and a few according to either regime; thus Wabār when fully inflected may be pronounced (in the nominative) either Wabārun or Wabāru.

285 "Wabār ibn Iram": Iram was one of the five sons of Sām, son of Nūḥ; among his descendants was Wabār, forefather of the tribe of ʿĀd, which God destroyed for practicing false belief in the sanctuary of the Kaaba.

286 "The name of one of the jinn who gave ear to the Qur'ān": a reference to "Remember how We sent to you a band of the jinn who wished to hear the Qur'ān and as they listened they said to one another, 'Be silent and listen'. . . ." (Q Aḥqāf 46:29); the jinn heard Muḥammad reciting during his retreat from al-Ṭā'if and became believers.

287 "*mārid*": a sub-species of jinn, literally "the rebellious."

288 "I can't find it in the *Qāmūs*": it does in fact appear there, although without a definition, being glossed simply as synonymous with *ʿaḍrafūṭ* (see below); other dictionaries (e.g., the *Lisān*) define it as meaning "old woman." As the author points out, the word also occurs in the *Qāmūs* as the word used to disambiguate the pronunciation of most of these (in Arabic terms) bizarre-sounding words.

289 "the lexicographer" (*al-m.ṣ.*): an abbreviation for *al-muṣannif*.

290 "fading mirage": and twelve other definitions (in the *Qāmūs*), including "ghoul" and "devil."

291 "the ant mentioned in the Qur'ān": ". . . and when they came to the Valley of the Ants, one ant said, 'Ants! Go into your dwellings lest [Sulaymān] and his hosts inadvertently crush you'" (Q Naml 27:18).

292 "the jumper" (*al-waththāb*): neck-muscle spasm.

293 al-Hirā': "a devil charged with [causing] bad dreams" (*Qāmūs*).

294 "Muḥammad or Maḥmūd": names specific to Muslims, while the emir was a Christian.

295 "unbored pearls": virgins, in conventional poetic imagery.

296 "the letter *nūn*": twenty-nine of the *sūras* ("chapters") of the Qurʾān commence with one or more letters of the alphabet of unknown significance. The Fāriyāq takes the *nūn* preceding the verse quoted here (Q Qalam 68:1) to stand for *naḥs* ("bad luck").

297 "his confidant . . . polemics . . . ecclesiastical bigwig": the "confidant" (*najī*) was his elder brother Asʿad, whom the author visited, with other members of his family, following his adoption of Protestantism and who talked to him at length about his beliefs (al-Maṭwī, *Aḥmad*, 1:69); by "polemics" (*qīla wa-qāla*) the author means "religious controversy and debate"; the "ecclesiastical bigwig" (*aḥad . . . min al-jathāliqah*) must be the Maronite patriarch, to whom Asʿad frankly declared his beliefs in the hope of securing internal reform.

298 "saddlebag" (*khurj*): this introduces the theme of "the Bag-men" (*al-khurjiyyūn*), the author's term for Protestant missionaries (see Glossary).

299 "one of the big-time fast-talking market traders" (*mina l-ḍawāṭirati l-kibār*): see Glossary.

300 "God's horsemen against the *infidel*!" (*yā khayla llāh ʿalā l-kuffār*): the first half of the cry used to assemble the first Muslims before battle and subsequently used as a pious invocation to action on behalf of Muslims in danger.

301 "They shall *roast in Hell*!" (*innahum ṣālū l-nār*): Q Ṣād 38:59.

302 "I shall bring you the little squit 'before ever thy glance is returned to thee'" (*anā ātīka* etc.): the wording evokes the Qurʾān (Q Naml 27:40), when a member of Sulaymān's council volunteers to bring him the Queen of Sheba's throne.

303 "who had a speech defect involving the letter *f* . . . Boss of the the Market Difgwace" (*wa-kāna bi-hi faʾfaʾah*): the defect called *faʾfaʾah* is defined as "repeating and over-using the letter *fāʾ* in speech" and causes the Fāriyāq to say *shaykh al-fusūq* (literally "the Boss of Disgrace") for *shaykh al-sūq* ("the Boss of the Marketplace").

304 "Shouldn't the addition of these eighty require the eighty-lash penalty?" (*fa-lā takun ziyādatu hādhihi l-thamānīna mūjibun li-ḥaddi l-thamānīn*): the addition of *fāʾ* to *sūq* (see preceding endnote)

produces *fusūq*; the numerical value of the letter *fā'* in the counting system known as *ḥisāb al-jummal* is eighty; and the penalty specified in the Qur'an for the *fāsiq* ("committer of *fusūq*" or depravity) is eighty lashes (cf. Q Nūr 24:4).

305 "Emotion and Motion" (*Fī l-ḥiss wa-l-ḥarakah*): both emotion and motion (of the heart) are mentioned in the opening passage.

306 "the Vizier of the Right-hand Side . . . the Vizier of the Left-hand Side" (*wazīr al-maymanah . . . wazīr al-maysarah*): terms derived from popular conceptions of the organization of the courts of the caliphs, but meaning here, presumably, the primary organs on the right- and left-hand sides of the body, respectively.

307 "I came not to send peace, but a sword": Matt. 10:34.

308 "he exerted himself to save the Fāriyāq from the hands of the arrogant": following his brother As'ad's arrest by the Maronite patriarch in March 1826 (see n. 314, below), the author himself sought refuge with the Protestant missionaries with whom As'ad had consorted, and these hid him in Beirut before sending him abroad in December of the same year.

309 "the Island of Scoundrels" (*Jazīrat al-Mulūṭ*): i.e., Malta, normally *Māliṭah*.

310 "the *golden calf*" (*al-ba'īm*, literally, "the idol"): presumably a reference to the "idolatry" implied by the presence of statues of the Virgin Mary and saints in Maronite churches.

311 "ignoble and, beside that, basely *born*" (*'uṭullin wa-ba'da dhālika zanīm*): Q Qalam 68:13.

312 "there is therein no crookedness" (*ghayru dhāti 'iwajin*): an echo of Q Zumar 39:28 ("[an Arabic Koran,] wherein there is no crookedness" (Arberry, *Koran*, 473).

313 "Sh . . . ! Sh . . . !" (*al-khur! al-khur!*): the passenger thinks the Fāriyāq is trying to say "The shit! The shit!" (*al-khur'! al-khur'!*), when, in fact, he is trying to say, in his delirium, "The saddlebag! The saddlebag" (*al-khurj! al-khurj!*).

314 As'ad: As'ad al-Shidyāq (1798–1830), the third eldest brother in the family (the author being the fifth and youngest), became convinced

of the truth of Protestantism after associating with American evangelical missionaries in Beirut and was detained on charges of heresy by Maronite patriarch Yūsuf Ḥubaysh at his palace at Qannūbīn, where he died after some six years of maltreatment. For a detailed account of the events leading to and surrounding Asʿad's death and their significance, see Makdisi, *Artillery*, and Alwan, *Aḥmad*, chap. 1.

315 Qannūbīn: a valley in northern Lebanon, site of numerous Christian monasteries, including a former seat of the Maronite patriarch.

316 Mikhāʾīl Mishāqah (1800–1888 or 1889): first historian of later Ottoman Lebanon, who converted from Greek Catholicism to Protestantism in 1848.

317 "the Mutawālīs": the Twelver Shiites of Lebanon.

318 "the Anṣārīs": a Shiite sect with distinctive teachings and cosmology, with followers in Lebanon, Syria, and elsewhere in the region.

319 "Some of them . . . have written histories": the material that follows, even though attributed below by the author to several writers, appears to be taken mostly—and in some cases word for word—from Voltaire's *Essai sur les moeurs et l'esprit des nations*, chaps. 35–37 (see, e.g., http://fr.wikisource.org/wiki/Essai_sur_les_mœurs, accessed 6 March 2013).

320 "Pope Amadeus VIII, known as the Duke of Savoy": the name and number refer, in fact, not to a pope but to Duke Amadeus VIII of Savoy (1383–1451), who did, however, become antipope, assuming the papal name of Felix V, when elected by the dissident rump of the Council of Basel. The spelling Armadiyūs in the Arabic is an error.

321 "the Council of Basel was convened specifically to depose Pope Eugene": the Council of Basel was convened in 1431 to limit the powers of the papacy. Pope Eugene IV (r. 1431–47) sought to disband the council, a rump of which remained at Basel and elected the antipope Felix V.

322 Nicholas I (r. 858–67) excommunicated the Bishop of Cologne over the latter's support for Emperor Lothar II's petition for an annulment of his marriage that would allow him to marry his mistress.

323 "Ambrose, governor of Milan": Aurelius Ambrosius (Saint Ambrose) (ca. 340–97) became Bishop of Milan after originally being governor

of Emilia and Liguria, with headquarters at Milan. The author's reference to his "unsoundness" of belief may derive from the fact that Ambrose was neither baptized not formally trained in theology when elected bishop by popular acclaim, but his later contributions to theology resulted in his being numbered among the four Latin Fathers of the Church.

324 "Pope John VIII . . . Photius": Pope John VIII (r. 872–82) recognized the reinstatement of Photius as the legitimate patriarch of Constantinople after he had been condemned by Adrian VII. Photius (ca. 810–93) gained, lost, and regained the patriarchate of Constantinople against a background of the struggle between rival candidates for the Byzantine throne, a struggle in which the Western church attempted to intervene. The Western church eventually anathematized Photius, while the Eastern canonized him.

325 "Pope Stephen VII . . . Formosus": under pressure from a leading Roman family supportive of Pope John VIII and opposed by Formosus, then Bishop of Porto, Stephen VI (r. 896–97) had the remains of Formosus (pope, r. 891–96, and Stephen's last predecessor but one) exhumed, put him on trial, and sentenced him to the punishments described.

326 i.e., Pope Sergius III (r. 904–11).

327 Marozia (ca. 890–936): a Roman noblewoman who, with her mother Theodora, was actively involved in the affairs of the papacy, as described in what follows. The accession to the papacy of her bastard son, grandson, two great grandsons, and a nephew has led hostile commentators to refer to the period of her ascendancy as a "pornocracy" (rule by prostitutes).

328 According to most accounts, it was Pope John X rather than Sergius III who awarded Marozia, rather than her mother Theodora, the unprecedented title of senatrix ("senatoress") of Rome.

329 Later, Pope John XI (r. 931–35).

330 "Hugh, King of Arles": i.e., Hugh of Arles (before 885–948), who was elected King of Italy.

331 Pope John X (914–28) was a protégé of Theodora (see n. 327) and perished as a result of the intrigues of her daughter Marozia.

332 i.e., Leo VI (reigned for seven months in 928).

333 i.e., Stephen VII (r. 928 (?) to 931), hand-picked by Marozia as a stopgap until her son could assume the papacy as John XI.

334 "her husband": Alberic I, Duke of Spoleto; it is not usually reported that she poisoned him.

335 i.e., the aforementioned Hugh of Arles, King of Italy.

336 i.e., Alberic II (912–54), who had his mother imprisoned until her death.

337 Stephen VIII: reigned 939–42.

338 "disfigured his face": perhaps a reference to the claim that Stephen VIII was the first pope to shave and that he ordered the men of Rome to do likewise.

339 John XII reigned from 955 to 964, dying at the age of twenty-seven.

340 i.e., Otto I (912–73), who in 962 made a pact with Pope John XII that made the Western Roman Empire guarantor of the independence of the Papal States. Soon, however, the pope, fearful of the power thus bestowed, began to intrigue with the Magyars and the Byzantines against the Western Empire. Otto returned to Rome in 963, convened a synod of bishops, and deposed the pope.

341 Leo VIII was an antipope from 963 to 964, when he was illegally elected by the 963 synod that illegally deposed John XII, and a true pope from 964 to 965, having been legally re-elected following the death of John XII.

342 Crescentius: i.e., Crescentius II (d. 992), son of Crescentius I and not, as the author states, of John X and Marozia, was a leader of the Roman aristocracy who made himself de facto ruler of Rome, was deposed by Otto III, rose again in rebellion, appointed an antipope (John XVI), and was eventually defeated and executed.

343 Benedict: Pope Benedict VII (d. 983); other sources do not confirm that he died in prison; the author appears to have confused him with John XIV (see below).

344 John XIV: pope from 983 to 984, who was imprisoned by the antipope Boniface VII in Sant'Angelo, where he died.

345 Boniface VII: ruled as antipope (974, 984–85) under the patronage of Crescentius and the Roman aristocracy.

346 Gregory: i.e., Pope Gregory V (ca. 972–99), cousin and chaplain of Otto III; although he consistently supported the emperor, his death was not without suspicion of foul play.

347 Otto III (980–1002): son of Otto II, in 996 he came to Rome to aid Pope John XV (985–96) (see below) against Crescentius, whom he eventually killed.

348 "played a trick on him": Otto III promised Crescentius the right to live in retirement in Rome but reneged and had him murdered and hung from the walls of Sant'Angelo.

349 Pope John XV (r. 985–86) succeeded Pope Boniface VII; according to other accounts he died of fever, while it was the antipope John XVI, appointed by Crescentius, who, on the latter's defeat, had his eyes put out and nose cut off before banishing him to a monastery.

350 Benedict VIII: reigned 1012 to 1024.

351 John XIX: succeeded his brother Benedict VIII and reigned from 1024 to 1032.

352 Benedict IX: said by most sources to have been between eighteen and twenty years of age when he succeeded his uncle, John XIX, he is the only pope to have reigned three times (1032–44, 1045, 1047–48) and to have sold the papacy (to Gregory VI in 1045), although he later attempted to reclaim it.

353 Meaning presumably Sylvester III and the restored Benedict IX.

354 "with his concubine" (*maʿa surriyyatihi*): thus the Arabic, although one wonders if *maʿa sariyyatihi* ("with his detachment of soldiers") is not what is meant.

355 "one of the kings of France": i.e., Robert II (972–1032), who was excommunicated by Pope Gregory V when he insisted on marrying his cousin, a marriage denied by the pope on grounds of consanguinity.

356 Gregory VII: reigned from 1073 to 1085. His attempts to strengthen papal hegemony against the Holy Roman Empire culminated in the

Investiture Controversy (over the right to appoint bishops), which led, in 1076, to his excommunication of Emperor Henry IV, who was accused of being behind his brief abduction.

357 Henry IV (r. 1056–1106) had declared Pope Gregory VII deposed at the synod of Worms, held a week before his own excommunication.

358 "Countess Matilda": Matilda of Tuscany (1055–1115), a leading noblewoman and heiress, who supported Pope Gregory VII during the Investiture Controversy.

359 Canossa: Matilda's ancestral castle.

360 Urbanus II (r. 1088–99) in fact succeeded the short-reigning Victor III rather than Gregory VII directly.

361 "the two sons of Henry IV": i.e, Conrad (1074–1101) and his brother Henry (1086–1125), later Emperor Henry V (r. 1106–1125); Conrad joined the papal camp against his father in 1093; Henry was crowned King of Germany by his father to replace Conrad but soon revolted against his father, whom ultimately he deposed.

362 Henry VI (r. 1190–1197) was in fact the son of Emperor Frederick I, while Frederick II was his son.

363 Pope Celestine: i.e, Celestine III (r. 1191–98).

364 Innocent III: reigned 1198–1216.

365 Pope Innocent IV (r. 1243–54) summoned the Thirteenth General Council of the Church at Lyons in 1245 in order to further his attempts to recover from the Holy Roman Empire territories in Italy that Innocent believed belonged by right to the papacy. The Council formally deposed the emperor, although to no practical effect.

366 Frederick II: reigned 1212–1250.

367 Lucius II: during his reign (1144–45), the Senate of Rome established a Commune of Rome that demanded the pope abandon all secular functions; the pope died leading an army against the Commune.

368 "Clement XV": a mistake for "Clement V" (r. ca. 1264–1314).

369 Vienne: on the Rhône in southern France and site of the Council of Vienne, called by Clement V from 1311 to 1312 to address accusations against the Templars, partly in response to the desire of Philip IV of France, Clement's patron, to confiscate their wealth.

370 "Pope Urban": i.e., Urban VI (r. ca. 1318–89), who in 1384 tortured and put to death certain of his cardinals who wished to declare him incompetent.

371 John XXIII: i.e., the antipope John XXIII (r. 1410–15), whose seat, during the Western Schism, was in Rome.

372 John XXIII was deposed, along with other claimants to the papacy, by the Council of Constance, which was called by Emperor Sigismund; he was accused of heresy, simony, schism, and immorality.

373 Sijjīn: a valley in Hell.

374 "over your eyes there is a covering" (*ʿalā abṣārikum ghishāwah*): cf. Q Baqarah 2:7.

375 "the Five Stars" (*al-nujūm al-khamsah*): the planets known to Islamic astronomy (Saturn, Jupiter, Mars, Venus, Mercury), called *khunnas* because they return (*takhnusu*) in their courses.

376 "the *Mijarrah*—'the gateway of the sky, or its anus'" (*mijarratuhā—bāb al-samāʾi aw sharajuhā*): the *Lisān* explains the first part of the gloss by the resemblance of the Milky Way to an arch.

377 "the *rujum*—'the stars used for stoning'" (*rujumuhā—al-nujūmu llatī yurmā bihā*): the stars with which God stones Satan, who is commonly referred to as *al-rajīm* for this reason; in popular belief, shooting stars (see, for Egypt, Lane, *Manners*, 223).

378 "the Two Calves" (*al-farqadayn*): stars γ and β in Ursa Minor (the Little Dipper); also known as Pherkad and Kochab (*al-kawkab*).

379 "all those gazettes" (*fī hādhihi l-waqāʾiʿ al-ikhbāriyyah*): no doubt a reference to *Al-Waqāʾiʿ al-Miṣriyyah*, on which see further n. 132 to 2.11.5 below.

380 "Friends of God" (*awliyāʾ Allāh*): individuals believed to be chosen by God for special favor; sometimes they manifest unusual spiritual powers.

381 "to bring about divorces" (*li-l-taṭlīq*): a reference, perhaps, to the notary (*maʾdhūn*) who gives formal recognition to a divorce.

382 "as a legitimizer" (*li-l-taḥlīl*): if a Muslim man divorces his wife three times—thus irrevocably—and then regrets his act, he may hire a man

(known as a *muḥallil*, approx. "legitimizer") to marry her and then divorce her, rendering remarriage legally possible.

383 Though the references in the following passage are, in some cases, at least, to recognized rhetorical figures, their precise meaning is less important than the impression of erudite obfuscation that they convey.

384 "the method of the sage" (*uslūb al-ḥakīm*): taking advantage of an inappropriate or unanswerable question to open a more important discussion.

385 "person-switching" (*iltifāt*): a rhetorical figure consisting of an "abrupt change of grammatical person from second to third and from third to second," as in the words of the poet Jarīr "When were the tents at Dhū Ṭulūḥ? O tents, may you be watered by ample rain!" (Meisami and Starkey, *Encyclopedia*, 2:657).

386 "tight weaving" (*iḥtibāk*): a rhetorical figure defined, in a widely taught formulation (http://www.alfaseeh.com/vb/showthread.php?t=9355), as "the omission from the earlier part of the utterance of something whose equal or equivalent comes in the later, and the omission from the later of something whose equal or equivalent comes in the earlier"; an example is the Qurʾānic verse "a company that fights for God and a disbelieving company" (Q Āl ʿImrān 3:13), meaning "a [believing] company that fights for God and a disbelieving company [that fights for the Devil]."

387 "an Arabized word": via Latin, from Greek *manganon*.

388 "like common caltrops" (*ʿalā mithāl al-ḥasak al-maʿrūf*): i.e., like star-weed (*Centaurea calcitrapa*), whose spiked seed-cases pierce sandals and feet when stepped on.

389 "a padded outer garment ... a weapon ... thick shields": the confusion as to the word's meaning seems to stem from its foreign, probably Persian, origin.

390 "a device for war worn by horse and man alike": cataphract armor.

391 *al-ʿadhrāʾ*: literally, "the virgin"—"a kind of collar by means of which the hands, or arms, are confined together with the neck" (Lane, *Lexicon*).

392 Jadīs and Ṭasm: related tribes of ʿĀd, a pre-Islamic people destroyed, according to the Qurʾan, for their ungodliness.

393 al-ʿAbbās ibn Mirdās: an early Meccan convert to Islam who burned al-Dimār, the idol of his clan.

394 ʿAmr ibn Luḥayy: a leader of Mecca in the Days of Barbarism, and supposedly the first to introduce the worship of idols into the Arabian Peninsula.

395 "Ilyās, peace be upon him": Ilyās (Elias) is regarded in Islam as a prophet.

396 "ʿUrwah's hadith ʿal-Rabbah'" (*ḥadīth ʿUrwatin al-Rabbah*): the tradition recounts that a recent convert to Islam, ʿUrwah ibn Masʿūd, was refused entry to his home unless he first visited "al-Rabbah" (literally, "the Mistress"), "meaning al-Lāt, which is the rock that [the tribe of] Thaqīf used to worship at al-Ṭāʾif" (see Ibn al-Athīr, *Al-Nihāyah*, 1:56).

397 Dhāt ʿIrq: a place, 92 kilometers north of Mecca.

398 "*Furdūd*, Pherkad . . . *Kuwayy*": names of stars in this list that have accepted English names (all but one of which in fact derive from Arabic) are printed in regular font, while those impossible to identify from the extensive list provided by the Wikipedia article "List of Arabic Star Names" are transcribed in italics.

399 "instruments that . . .": see the Translator's Afterword (Volume Four) on the choice of synonyms in this passage; note that, while the Arabic list contains forty-eight items, only forty-five are represented in the translation, because three (*daghz*, *zazz*, and *waqz*) could not be found in the dictionaries.

400 "headgear of a generic nature" (*ʿimārāt*): *ʿimārah* is defined in the *Qāmūs* as "anything worn on the head, be it a turban (*ʿimāmah*), a cap (*qalansuwah*), a crown (*tāj*), or anything else."

401 "watermelon-shaped . . . cantaloupe-shaped . . . caps" (*bi-arāṣīṣ . . . bi-arāsīs*): while the author, in this footnote, specifies the shape of the former, the dictionaries say of the latter merely that it is "a cap" (*qalansuwah*); however, it seems to be a variant of the first.

402 "judges' tun-caps" (*danniyyāt*): so called from their resemblance to a *dann* or large wine barrel.

403 "antimacassars" (*ṣawāqiʿ*): cloths worn by a woman on her head to protect her veil from grease (*Qāmūs*).

404 "pass their hands over what is in front of the latter" (*yatamassaḥūna bi-mā amāmahu*): the significance is unclear; the *Qāmūs* cites the usage *yutamassaḥu bi-hi* ("people pass their hands over him/it,") and says that it means *yutabarraku bi-hi li-faḍlihi* ("blessing is derived from him because of his/its virtue"). This brings to mind the habit of visitors to certain mosques of passing their hands over the grills enclosing saints' tombs in the belief that they will thus obtain *barakah* ("grace").

405 "*underwear*" (*andarward*): the English word is probably intended; *andarward* may be due to a mishearing by the author or possibly a joke (*andar-ward* "under-roses").

406 i.e., must never stop calling out pious phrases to warn those around him of his presence or that he is "coming through."

407 "As God wills! . . . O God!" (*mā shāʾa llāh . . . Allāh*): typical expressions of delight, pleasure, and appreciation, all of which invoke God's name to protect the one praised from the possible effects of envy.

408 "her peepings through her fingers against the sun to see . . . , her shading of her eyes against the sun to see and her peering through her fingers against the sun to see" (*istikfāfihā . . . wa-stīḍāḥihā wa-stishfāfihā*): all defined in the *Qāmūs* as synonyms.

409 "a fourth way of walking, with further letters changed" (*wa-qahbalatihā*): again, defined in the *Qamūs* as "a way of walking."

410 "a fifth way of walking, with further letters changed" (*hayqalatihā*): again, defined in the *Qamūs* as "a way of walking."

411 "her walking with tiny steps" (*khadhʿalatihā*): the *Qāmūs* defines again as "a way of walking"; however, a second sense given is "cutting a watermelon etc. into small pieces."

412 "her marching proudly (spelled two ways)" (*tabahrusihā wa-tahabrusihā*): synonyms, meaning *tabakhtur* ("strutting"), according to the *Lisān* (s.v. *tabahrasa*).

413 "the same said another way" (*wa-unufihā*): synonym of the preceding item, according to the *Qāmūs*.

414 "two lines": four hemistichs, each hemistich starting here on a new line.

415 The word *muʿqanafishan* has not been found in any dictionary, but cf. *ʿaqanfas*, variant of *ʿafanqas* "ill-tempered, base" (*ʿasir al-akhlāq laʾīm*).

416 "*bardhaʿah*s . . . *ikāf*s . . . *qitbah*s . . . *bāṣar*s": all types of saddle.

417 "with a thread of paper" (*bi-khayṭin min al-kāghid*): perhaps referring to the domination of the bureaucracy by Turks.

418 "leading . . . 'leading' him" (*yaqūdu . . . yaqūdūna lahu*): the author plays with two senses of the verb, *qāda* "to lead" and *qāda li-* "to pimp for."

419 "*bakalım kapalım* ('let's see-bee')": the phrase is constructed by adding a non-existent word *kapalım* to the genuine word *bakalım* ("let's see") thus mimicking such genuine Turkish rhyming couplets as the preceding.

420 "*Ghaṭāliq* . . .": most of the supposed Turkish of the following lines is in fact nonsense, though it does contain distinctive Turkish features, such as the ending *-lik/lıq*; the first hemistich of the last line does make sense in Turkish ("They're like donkeys too, by God!"), and the second hemistich of the same line can be read as near-meaningless Arabic ("Their troubles are their confusions").

421 "head . . . tail": by "head" the author may mean the promontory of Ra's al-Tīn ("the Head(land) of the Figs") and by "tail" the land end of that promontory, where the popular quarter of Anfūshī, home to the city's fish market, is situated.

422 Qayʿar Qayʿār: an invented name that may be translated as something like "Plummy Pompous," from the literal senses of *qayʿar* and *qayʿār*, both of which mean one who "speaks affectedly and from the back of his mouth" (*tashaddaqa wa-takallama bi-aqṣā famihi*). If we follow the clues offered by the similarly coded name Baʿīr Bayʿar (= al-Amīr Ḥaydar (1.5.2)), we may suppose that the first name of this individual may have been Ḥaydar, while the second may have been Bayṭār or another name of the same pattern. However, it is also possible that a European was intended (see next endnote).

423 "the Himyaritic lands" (*al-bilād al-Ḥimyariyyah*): i.e., southern Arabia, though the orthography also allows the reading *al-bilād al-ḥamīriyyah,* meaning "the lands of the donkeys," and it is unclear whether the Fāriyāq is referring to an Arab or a "Frank"; some phrases and topoi in the passage that follows are reminiscent of those used when Franks are lampooned for their bad Arabic, as in the following chapter.

424 "the science of 'subjects' and 'objects'" (*ʿilm al-fāʿil wa-l-mafʿūl*): i.e., Arabic grammar.

425 "chronograms" (*ʿilm al-jummal*): each letter of the Arabic alphabet has a conventionally assigned numerical value under a system known as *hisāb al-jummal.* The construction of chronograms capable of being read both as words and as dates became a common feature of congratulatory poetry starting in the ninth/fifteenth century. For examples, see Volume Four, section 4.20.13.

426 *ʿĪsā*: a proper name, cognate with "Jesus."

427 "within this p'tcher" (*fī hādhā l-kuzz*): *kuzz* appears to be a nonce-word derived from the common word *kūz* by shortening the vowel and doubling the second consonant, the charlatan teacher's idea being that the word needs to contain a doubled consonant (*shadda,* a word conveying the idea of "tightening") to fit with something that is "confined"; the same logic might apply to *zanbīl/zabbīl* below, though both forms in this case are genuine.

428 "*khams daqāʾiq* . . . and not *khamsah daqāʾiq*": the humor lies in the author's attribution of an irrelevant cause to a grammatical rule, the rule in this case being that a feminine noun (here the implied *daqīqah,* singular of *daqāʾiq*) is preceded by the shorter, masculine, number form when counted.

429 "because each is a 'congregator of fineness' (*jāmiʿ al-nuʿūmah*)": the language is that of rhetorical theory, which would claim that the words for "flour" and "minutes" share the same consonantal root (*d-q-q*) because flour consists of finely ground grain while minutes are fine divisions of hours, and the phrase might more accurately be rendered "because they share the common factor of fineness"; however, the

wording is primarily a set-up for the play on words that follows a little later.

430 "The first six have 'parts' at either end" (*al-sitt al-ʾūlā fī-hā farq*): i.e., "have distinct beginnings and endings"; however, *sitt* ("six") also means in the Egyptian dialect "lady, mistress" (from *sayyidah*), while *farq* ("dividing, partitioning") also means a "parting" as a way of dressing the hair; thus, the words are a set-up to allow the joke that follows.

431 "Nuʿūmah Mosque" (*jāmiʿ al-nuʿūmah*): while *jāmiʿ* is, as the shaykh will explain, an active participle, of the verb *jamaʿa, yajmaʿu* ("to gather together, collect, congregate"), it is also used in common parlance as a substantive meaning "mosque."

432 "ʿUdhrah . . . Virgin . . . must be stretched out" (*ʿUdhrah . . . ʿadhrāʾ . . . yajibu madduhā*): the learned monk wrote of a tribe famous for the celebration by its poets of passionate but unconsummated love; however, the ignorant Qayʿar Qayʿār, seeing *ʿUdhrah*, thinks that the monk intended *ʿadhrāʾ* ("virgin"), which should be pronounced with a long vowel at the end (*madd*), though in the colloquial it is pronounced with a short vowel. Thus, while stating a correct grammatical rule (the word for "virgin" should be written with *–āʾ* at the end), he demonstrates that "a little learning is a dangerous thing."

433 "*daʿawtu ʿalayh . . . ṣallaytu ʿalayh*": the use of a preposition after a verb in Arabic, as in other languages, may modify the sense of the verb. Thus plain *daʿawtu* and *ṣallaytu* both mean "I prayed," but *daʿawtu ʿalayh* means "I cursed him" whereas *ṣallaytu ʿalayh* means "I prayed for him."

434 "*tashīl . . . ishāl*": verbs with the consonant-vowel patterns CVC-CVCV (verbal noun form taC1C2īC3) and VCCVCV (verbal noun form iC1C2āC3) may have causative or declarative sense relative to the semantic area of the three-consonant root. Thus, from the root *s-h-l*, associated with "ease," are created the verbs *sahhala* (*tashīl*) and *ashala* (*ishāl*). Each, however, has a different denotation. Thus, *sahhala* means "to make easy, facilitate," while *ashala* means "to be struck with diarrhea."

435 Many of the words used in the letter are double entendres or malapropisms, as follows: "sodomitical"—*ibnī* "filial" may be read as *ubnī* (from

*ubnah* ("passive sodomy")); "penetrated it"—*awlajtu* should mean "I caused to enter" and is often used in connection with sexual intercourse, but here is used intransitively; "the shittiest part"—*ukhrāh* "its end" is both a deformation of *ākhiratihi* and also may be read *akhra'ihi* (from *kharā'* ("excrement")); "excrements"—*al-fuḍūl* may mean either "(bodily) wastes" or "merits, favors"; "creator of pestilence"—*al-fuṣūl* may mean either "chapters" or "plagues"; "a 'congregator' of both the branches of knowledge and its roots"—the word *jāmi'* appears to be used here simply to maintain the running joke relating to "congregator/mosque," which is resumed in the immediately following passage; "long of tongue"—*ṭawīl al-lisān* may intend "eloquent" but idiomatically means "impertinent"; "with 'ands too short to"—*qaṣīr al-yadāni 'an* commits, for the sake of the rhyme, the gross grammatical error of *al-yadāni* for *al-yadayni*; "of broad little brow"—reading *wāsi' al-jubayn* (counterintuitively in the diminutive) for the expected *wāsi' al-jabīn* ("broad of brow"); "wide waistcoated"— reading *'arīḍ al-ṣudar* (from *ṣudrah* "waistcoat") for the expected *'arīḍ al-ṣadr* ("wide of breast, magnanimous"); "deeply in debt"—reading *'amīq al-dayn* for the expected *'amīq al-dīn* ("deeply religious"); and "of ideas bereft"—reading *mujawwaf al-fikar* for *mujawwif al-fikr* ("pentrating of thought"), itself probably a spurious locution.

436 "The Extraction of the Fāriyāq from Alexandria, by Sail" (*Fī-nqilā' al-Fāriyāq min al-Iskandariyyah*): the base sense of *inqilā'* is "to pull up by the roots," but the references to sailing in the first paragraph indicate that the author is simultaneously implying the concoction of a humorous new sense derived from *qil'* "sail," which has the same root as *inqilā'*.

437 al-Ṣāḥib ibn 'Abbād : 326–85/938–95, vizier to the Būyid rulers of Iran; the verses evoke such Qur'anic passages as "And unto Solomon (We subdued) the wind and its raging" (Q Anbiyā' 21:81).

438 The priest substitutes letters he can pronounce for those he cannot. Thus he says *hā'* (*h*) for *ḥ* (*ḥā'*) as in *al-rahmān* for *al-raḥmān* ("the merciful"), for *'ayn* (') as in *hitābukum* for *'itābukum* ("censuring you"), for *khā'* (*kh*) as in *al-mihaddah* for *al-mikhaddah* ("the bolster"), and for the glottal

stop (ʾ) as in *rahzan* for *raʾsan* ("resolutely"); *hamzah* (ʾ) for *ʿayn* (ʿ) as in *al-ʾālam* for *al-ʿālam* ("the world"); *kāf* (*k*) for *qāf* (*q*) as in *akūl* for *aqūl* ("I say"), for *khāʾ* (*kh*) as in *akshā* for *akhshā* ("I fear"), and for *ghayn* (*gh*) as in *mashkūl* for *mashghūl* ("busy"); *sīn* (*s*) for *ṣād* (*ṣ*) as in *nasārā* for *naṣārā* ("Christians") and for *thāʾ* (*th*) as in *akassir* for *akaththir* ("I repeat often") ; *dāl* (*d*) for *ḍād* (*ḍ*) as in *al-hādirīn* for *al-ḥāḍirīn* ("those present"); *tāʾ* (*t*) for *ṭāʾ* (*ṭ*) as in *tūlihi* for *ṭūlihi* ("its length"); and *zayn* (*z*) for *dhāl* (*dh*) as in *lazzāt* for *ladhdhāt* ("pleasures") and for *ẓāʾ* (*ẓ*) as in *mawhizatī* for *mawʿiẓatī* ("my counsel"); *s* for *th* and *z* for *dhāl* are also common "errors" of native speakers. Sometimes the same letter is used with different values in the same word as in *al-akdak* for *al-aghdaq* ("the most bountiful"), or all the letters in a words are changed, as in *al-sukh* for *al-ṣuqʿ* ("the region"). These changes sometimes result in the production of meaningful words (e.g., *kalbukum* ("your dog") for *qalbukum* ("your heart")) but more often in nonsense, e.g., *rahmān* and *rahīm*.

439 "the Arabic-language-challenged . . . Sponging . . . Aleppine" (*al-Ḥalabī al-Bushkānī . . . al-Immaʿī . . .*): names of prominent persons are often followed by a series of attributive adjectives ending in *-ī* (*nisbahs*) indicating pedigree, place of origin, place of residence, legal school, etc.; here only *al-Ḥalabī* ("of Aleppo") is a real *nisbah*; the rest are made by adding *-ī* to words associated with gluttony, parasitism, and ignorance of Arabic.

440 Metropolitan Atanāsiyūs al-Tutūnjī (or Athanāsiyūs al-Tūtunjī) (d. 1874), Melkite bishop of Tripoli from 1836, was dismissed for scandalous behavior and spent some time in England in the early 1840s seeking to promote union between the Anglican and Eastern churches. The author hated him because he denigrated the translation of the Book of Common Prayer on which the author was then engaged for the Society for the Propagation of Christian Knowledge (SPCK) and suggested that he could do better. He did in fact produce a specimen, which al-Shidyāq saw, whereupon he sent the SPCK (in March 1844) "an Arabic Poem expressing the ungenerous behaviours of the Society for Promotion of Christian Knowledge . . . in having employed in my

stead an ignorant person [i.e., al-Tutūnjī]—not withstanding I have addressed them in two letters respecting the numerous grammatical mistakes he has committed" (letter in English in the Church Missionary Society; I am indebted to Geoffrey Roper for this information); subsequently, the SPCK changed its view and reinstated al-Shidyāq as their translator. The author alludes to this imbroglio and a further spat between him and al-Tutūnjī in Book Three (3.18.1).

441 *Al-Ḥakākah fī l-rakākah* (*The Leavings Pile Concerning Lame Style*): we have failed to identify the original of the work whose title is parodied here; according to Georg Graf, al-Tutūnjī wrote only on theological and ecclesiastical matters (see Graf, *Geschichte*, 3:278), but this and further references here (3.5.14, 3.18.1) imply that he was active in the teaching of language and translation.

442 "or . . .": the *Qāmūs* continues "to ʿAdawl, a man who used to make the ships, or to a people who used to camp in Hajar."

443 The verse is attributed to ʿAlī ibn al-Jahm (ca. 188–249/804–63).

444 "their cousins": i.e., the Roman Catholic Maltese.

445 Khalīl ibn Aybak al-Ṣafadī (d. 764/1363): a litterateur whose works include *Lawʿat al-shākī wa-damʿat al-bākī* (*The Plaint of the Lovelorn and Tears of the Disconsolate*), which describes the agonies of love.

446 "his 'stable management (of affairs),' his 'leadership qualities,' and his 'horse sense'" (*al-siyāsah wa-l-qiyādah wa-l-firāsah/farāsah*): the humor lies in the fact that each word has one meaning appropriate to the donkey-boy's supposed elevated state and another appropriate to his actual occupation; thus *siyāsah*, whose original sense is "the management of animals" also means "the management of men," and thence "rule," while *qiyādah* originally meant "the leading of horses, or caravans" and thence "command (e.g., of an army)"; *firāsah* means "horsemanship," while *farāsah* (the two forms being indistinguishable in unvowelled writing) means "intuitive perception."

447 *ʿanmī*: after the red fruit of the *ʿanam* (pomegranate) tree.

448 [?]: *ghurmah*, a word not found in the dictionaries.

449 Sūrat Nūn: i.e., Sūrat al-Qalam (sura 68), which begins with the initial *nūn* and is thus appropriate for a *nūnah* ("cleft in the chin").

450 "I am copying them from one who looked deeply into every veiled face(t)" (*nāqilan lahu ʿamman tabaṣṣara l-wajha l-maḥjūb*): meaning that definitions that the author provides above are those of the author the *Qāmūs*, who, as a lexicographer, has looked deeply into every facet of the meaning of each word just as, as a man, he has looked deeply into the veiled faces of women (*wajh* means both "face" and "facet").

451 "hasn't seen her as did Our Master Yaʿqūb": cf. Gen. 29:10–11 "Jacob saw Rachel . . . and Jacob kissed Rachel."

452 "Professors Amorato . . ." (*al-Ṣabābātī* . . .): given their form, it is clear that these fictitious but contextually appropriate names are intended to represent scholars, as are those a few lines below.

453 "the letter *ṣād* . . . the letter *mīm*" (*al-ṣādī wa-l-mīmī*): *ṣād* (ص) was used conventionally, because of its shape, as a coded reference to the vagina and *mīm* (م) to the anus.

454 Cairo (*Miṣr*): the author uses the word, as Egyptians often do, to refer to the capital city rather than the country as a whole.

455 "answering to the needs of hot-humored men (contrary to what ʿAbd al-Laṭīf al-Baghdādī has said)": in his brief description of Cairo, al-Baghdādī (557–629/1162–1231), a scholar from Baghdad, writes that "you rarely find among them diseases exclusively of the bile; indeed, the most prevalent types are those of the sputum, even among the youth and the hot-humored (*al-shabāb wa-l-maḥrūrīn*)" (al-Baghdādī, *Ifādah,* 18), a comment to which the author gives an insinuating twist not intended by the original.

456 The precise meaning or historical referent of a number of these teasingly described "curiosities" is unclear, and most of interpretations offered in the following notes are tentative.

457 "on the ceiling or the walls": perhaps a reference to depictions of women (or goddesses or nymphs) on the walls and ceilings of buildings done in the European style.

458 "the treatment of the feminine as masculine and of the masculine as feminine" (*tadhakkur al-muʾannath wa-taʾannuth al-mudhakkar*): while the comment appears to refer to a linguistic practice, it is hard to know exactly which, as there is no whole-scale reversal of, for instance,

noun gender in Egyptian Arabic vis-à-vis literary Arabic; perhaps the author has in mind the word *ra's* ("head"), which is most often masculine in literary (and Levantine) Arabic but is feminine in its Egyptian form (*rās*), or the use of *ḥabībī* ("my dear," masculine) as a term of endearment among women or *bāsha* ("pasha") by men as a flirtatious term of address to a woman.

459 "in their bathhouses they constantly recite a sura or two of the Qur'an that mention 'cups' and 'those who pass around with them,'" a reference to either Sūrat al-Zukhruf (Q Zukhruf 43:71 "*yuṭāfu ʿalayhim bi-ṣiḥāfin min dhahabin wa-akwāb*"—"There shall be passed among them platters of gold and cups") or similarly Sūrat al-Insān (Insān 76:15); the author may be implying that the presence in the bathhouses of young boys offering refreshment stimulates the patrons into uttering these verses. Lane, in fact, states that it is considered improper to recite the Qur'an in a bathhouse, as such places are inhabited by jinn (Lane, *Manners,* 337).

460 "many of the city's men have no hearts" etc.: perhaps meaning that they prefer sex to love.

461 "they took to lopping off their fingers" (*fa-jaʿalū yashdhibūna aṣābiʿahum*): perhaps a reference to the chopping off of the index finger of the right hand by young men so as to render themselves incapable of pulling a trigger and hence unfit for military service, which was introduced by Egypt's ruler, Muḥammad ʿAlī, in the 1820s.

462 "veil their beards" (*yubarqiʿuna liḥāhum*): according to the *Qāmūs,* the expression means "to become a passive sodomite" (*ṣāra maʾbūnan*).

463 "Sons of Ḥannā": if the correction of the original from Ḥinnā is correct, this probably is a reference to Copts (Ḥannā is a common name among Christians).

464 "a way of writing that is known to none but themselves": Ottoman financial documents were written in a script known as *qirmah* (perhaps from Turkish *kırmak* "to break"), developed from the *ruqʿah* script, that was indecipherable to the uninitiated and so small that upward of thirty words and figures might be inscribed within an area of 1.5 square centimetres; it was not, in fact, peculiar to Egypt, but

was introduced there by the Ottoman authorities (see El Mouelhy, "Le Qirmeh,").

465 "his family wail and keen over him in the hope that he will return to them": perhaps the author is implying jokingly that such excessive (as he sees it) mourning must be intended to ensure the return of the deceased with gifts from the next world.

466 "ignoble birds . . . may pretend to be mighty eagles" (*al-bughāth . . . yastansir*): a well-known idiom describing presumptuous behavior by the lowly.

467 "the exiguously monied one (meaning the owner of the money)" (*al-muflis ay ṣāḥib al-fulūs*): the author knows that the reader is likely to understand *muflis* in its common sense of "bankrupt," whereas he is using it in its original dictionary definition of "endowed with copper coins (after having owned silver coins)" (*Qāmūs*).

468 "the rise in her fortunes came from her setting herself down" (*ṭāliʿuhā min maḥallihā*): it is supposed that unmarried guests at weddings often to meet their own future spouses there.

469 "'a kind of joking back and forth that resembles mutual insult'" (*mufākahah tushbihu l-sibāb*): this definition of *mujārazah* is from the *Qāmūs*; from the description, *anqāṭ* resemble the twentieth-century pun-based *qāfiyah*, on which see Amīn, *Qāmūs*, 317–18.

470 "Its viceroy" (*wālīhā*): Muḥammad ʿAlī Pasha, who ruled as an autonomous viceroy on behalf of the Ottoman sultan from 1805 to 1848 and laid the foundations of the modern Egyptian state.

471 By the time of the publication of *Al-Sāq*, the author had attracted the favorable notice of the ruler of Tunis by writing odes in his praise and had twice visited the city, in 1841 and 1847 (see 3.18.3, 4.8.2). Later (1857–59), he would take up residence in Tunis and work for its government.

472 "a poet of great skill": identified by one scholar as Naṣr al-Dīn al-Ṭarābulsī (1770–1840), a Catholic from Aleppo who immigrated to Egypt in 1828 and came to direct the Arabic-language section of *Al-Waqāʾiʿ al-Miṣriyyah*, where the author was later employed

(al-Maṭwī, *Aḥmad*, 1:76); elsewhere (2.10.1), the author refers to him as "Khawājā Yanṣur."

473 al-Āmidī: see 1.11.1. Al-Āmidī's detailed comparison of the poets al-Buḥturī and Abū l-Tammām distinguishes between the *maṣnūʿ* ("artificial") and *maṭbūʿ* ("natural") in poetry, but al-Āmidī's concern is style rather than, as here, the motivation of the poet.

474 Āmid: a city in southeastern Turkey, now called Diyarbakır.

475 al-Bustī: Abū l-Fatḥ al-Bustī (335–400/946–1009), poet and prose stylist.

476 Abū l-ʿAtāhiyah: a poet of Baghdad mainly known for his pious and censorious verse (131–211/748–826).

477 Abū Nuwās: one of the most famous poets of the Abbasid "Golden Age," especially in the fields of wine poetry and the love lyric (ca. 130–98/747–813).

478 al-Farazdaq: Tammām ibn Ghālib, known as al-Farazdaq ("the Lump of Dough"), a satirist and panegyrist (d. 110/728 or 112/730).

479 Jarīr: one of the greatest poets of the Umayyad period (ca. 33–111/653–729).

480 Abū Tammām: Abbasid poet and anthologist (ca. 189–232/805–45).

481 al-Mutanabbī: celebrated panegyrist and lampoonist (ca. 303–54/915–65).

482 "Our Master Sulaymān's ring": this magic signet ring, sometimes referred to as a seal, allowed Sulaymān to command demons and talk to animals.

483 "Zayd . . . ʿAmr": Zayd and ʿAmr are names used to demonstrate grammatical points in examples memorized by school children.

484 "a grave offense against him" (*mina l-mūbiqāti lahu*): perhaps because to do so might imply jealousy, or because both beauty and riches are regarded as gifts of God rather than qualities implying merit.

485 "flap of skin" (*zanamah*): the author appears to have in mind the following among a number of definitions of this word given in the *Qāmūs*: "something cut off the ear of a camel and left hanging, done to the best bred."

486 "it is incorrect to refer to the son of a marquis as a 'marquisito' or as being 'marquisate'" (*lā yaṣiḥḥu an yuqāla li-bni l-markīzi muraykīzun aw markīzī*): i.e., it is incorrect to refer to the son of a marquis with a diminutive noun or a relative adjective derived from "marquis," meaning, perhaps, that European titles—which are, unlike oriental titles, hereditary—can be applied to only one holder at a time.

487 On whom see 2.3.5: the Melkites of Tripoli numbered "barely ten" (Graf, *Geschichte,* 3:277).

488 The author's distinction recognizes the fact that such titles are informal terms of respect rather than titles awarded by an authority.

489 "Muʿallim . . . *muʿallim* or *muʿallam*": *muʿallim* means literally "teacher" and is used as a term of polite address to Christians and others; read as *muʿallam*, the same word means "taught."

490 "they apply the term Khawājā to others": i.e., to other Christians (from Persian *khōjā* ("teacher")).

491 "God relieve you (or shrive you or deceive you)," etc. (*maṣaḥa llāhu mā bi-ka . . . aw masaḥa aw mazaḥa . . .*): *sirāṭ* and *zirāṭ* are recognized variants of *ṣirāṭ* ("path"), as *busāq* and *buzāq* are of *buṣāq* ("the best camels"); but *masaḥa* ("to wipe") and *mazaḥa* ("to joke") are not variants of *maṣaḥa* and have unrelated, comically inappropriate, meanings.

492 ʿAzrāʾīl: the angel of death.

493 "*kubaybah . . . kubbah*": both are dishes made of cracked-wheat kernels, with meat, onions, etc., but the first form is Egyptian, the second Levantine ("kibbeh").

494 "*kubbah* . . . patootie . . . *kubbah* . . . pastries!" (*fī ʿijānak . . . kubbah . . . ʿajīnī*): a pair of puns as (1) *kubbah* means, as well as a certain dish, a "boil" or "bubo" and is used in curses, and (2) *ʿijān* ("anus") is from the same root as *ʿajīn* ("pastry"); the foreign doctor confuses the two meanings in the first case and mishears in the second.

495 "like a rugged boulder hurled from on high by the torrent" (*ka-julmūdi ṣakhrin ḥaṭṭahu l-saylu min ʿali*): a hemistich from the *muʿallaqah* of the pre-Islamic poet Imruʾ al-Qays (translation Arberry, *Seven Odes,* 64).

496 "One of these *giaours* (plural of *cure*)" (*aḥada hādhihi l-ʿulūj (jamiʿi ʿilāj)*): the plural of *ʿilāj* ("cure, treatment") is in fact *ʿilājāt*, whereas

*ʿulūj*, though from the same root, is the plural of *ʿilj* ("infidel"); again the doctor confuses the words.

497 "Tell the emir that I am, thank God, a bachelor" etc.: a reference to the exchange at the end of 2.10.3.

498 "his consul's office": in Egypt, legal cases involving a foreigner and an Egyptian could be tried in the foreign plaintiff's consular court.

499 "his turban in Lebanon and its ill-fated fall": see Volume One (1.2).

500 *Baḥth al-maṭālib*: in full *Kitāb Baḥth al-maṭālib fī ʿilm al-ʿArabiyyah* (*The Book of the Discussion of Issues in the Science of Arabic*), by Jirmānūs Farḥāt, a grammar published for the first time under al-Shidyāq's supervision in Malta in 1836; on Farḥāt, see Volume One (n. 130 to 1.3.2).

501 "with no vowel on the rhyme consonant" (*sākinat al-rawī*): see Volume One (n. 24 to 1.11.8).

502 "*wa-ʿawlajtu fī-hā*": the metropolitan's solecism lies in his use of *awlajtu*, a Form IV, or *rubāʿī* (*mazīd*), verb, intransitively, i.e., to mean "I entered," when it should only be used to mean "I caused (something) to enter, I inserted (something)." For the original letter, see 2.2.15.

503 "from *habba* meaning 'to rise'" (*min habba idhā qāma*): the root *h-b-b* is used in two distinct semantic areas: "to rise," as in *habbat al-rīḥ* "the wind rose," and *hibāb*, "soot".

504 "Take heed" etc.: Matthew 24:4–5 in the King James Version, with a difference in the translation of the last clause between the Arabic, reflected above, and the English, though it would seem that the translators of the English were as much in error, from the author's perspective, as those of the Arabic.

505 "Let the deacons be the husbands of one wife": 1 Timothy 3:12: again, the English translators are as guilty as the Arab.

506 "Panegyricon" (*mamdaḥ*): an invented word, literally "a place for eulogizing," by which the author means the offices of the Egyptian government's official gazette and the first daily newspaper to be printed in Arabic, namely *Al-Waqāʾiʿ al-Miṣriyyah*, which was issued for the first time in December 1828 and on which al-Shidyāq worked from January

1829; in its early years, the gazette contained material in both Turkish and Arabic.

507 "neglected" (*uhmilat*): a play on words, as undotted letters are known technically as *muhmalah*.

508 "how can the witness of the instrument itself—the reason for the discounting of its owner's witness—be valid": the speaker implies that musicians are not considered *ʿudūl* (men of probity) and that their testimony cannot be accepted in a court law.

509 "demolish the castles where you store your peddlers' goods, as well as any king's trumpet!": perhaps a reference to the destruction of the walls of Jericho by the trumpets blown at Joshua's command (Joshua 6:20).

510 *Allāh!*: see Volume One (n. 151 to 1.5.3).

511 "his ode known as *Al-Ghabab*": the reference is to a line in an ode in which al-Mutanabbī mocks his former patron, Sayf al-Dawlah, saying, "He who rides the bull after riding fine horses * Ignores its cloven hoofs and its wattle (*aẓlāfahu wa-l-ghabab*)" (Mutanabbī, *Dīwān,* 432).

512 "'nation' ought to have been put in the dual" (*ummatu ḥaqquhā an takūna ummatā*): because the "nation of men-and-jinn" could logically be considered two nations.

513 *al-thaqalayn . . . thaqīlah . . . thiqal*: the author plays with the root *th-q-l*, whose basic sense is of heaviness; *al-thaqalayn* is an idiom meaning "mankind and the jinn," an appellation explained as being "because, by the discrimination they possess, they excel other animate beings" (Lane, *Lexicon*).

514 "the rule of *taghlīb*": *taghlīb* ("awarding of precedence") is a stylistically elegant usage according to which the dual form of one noun is used to indicate both that noun and another with which it is closely associated, e.g., *al-qamarān* (literally, "the two moons"), meaning "the moon and the sun" and *al-aṣfarān* (literally, "the two yellow things"), meaning "gold and silver"; the argument here, therefore, turns the convention upside down and claims that, since *māshiyayn* ("two persons walking on foot"), were it an example of *taghlīb*, would give precedence to the prince, the singular (*māshiyan*) may be assumed to mean "the prince and others."

515 "the body (singular) of each of the two" or "the bodies (plural) of each of the two," (*jismuhumā aw ajsāmuhumā*): i.e., the prince and the squadron should be regarded as consisting of either two entities with one body each or of two entities with a plurality of bodies. Objection may be made that it would be simpler and more natural to take *sariyyah* as the feminine singular equivalent of *sarī*, in which case the translation would run, "The prince repaired with *the princess*" etc. To this the riposte would be that, had the critics entertained this possibility, they would have proposed the dual form of the noun (*jismāhumā*) as being (along with the singular) the "more chaste" option, rather than the plural (*ajsāmuhumā*).

516 "the poet": ʿAdī ibn Zayd al-ʿIbādī (d. ca. AD 600).

517 "Objection was made that *aẓāfir* should not be inflected" (*fa-ʿturiḍa ʿalay-hi ṣarfu aẓāfir*): i.e., *aẓāfir* is normally diptote (i.e., should be read here as *aẓāfira*) but in these verses has to be read as triptote (*aẓāfirin*), a bending of the rules that is permitted, as the author says, for the sake of the meter (Wright, *Grammar,* 2:387) and which is determined by the form of the following word, (*ẓafirat*).

518 "for the sake of the paronomasia": i.e., because *aḥlas* and *malḥūs*, while having different meanings, share the same triliteral root (*ḥ-l-s*).

519 "Except for the words 'in glory'": *tanawwarā*, repeated at the end of each hemistich of the first line ("to reveal a brighter fate" and "was made depilate"), is an example of both "perfect paronomasia" (identicality of form with difference of meaning) and "antithesis" (the use of two contrasting ideas in one line); *al-shiʿr* ("poetry") and *al-shiʿrāʾ* ("pubic hair") are examples of near-perfect paronomasia and antithesis; *mafkharā* ("in glory") stands out as neither paronomasia nor antithesis.

520 "the word *qaḥaba*": this, in the unchaste or vernacular language, means "to whore."

521 "the repetitive form" (*al-takthīr*): i.e., *fassā* versus *fasā*, the former indicating repeated performance of the action indicated by the latter.

522 "*ẓallām li-l-ʿabīd*": the phrase occurs several times in the Qurʾan (e.g., Q Āl ʿImrān 3:182); *ẓallām*, from *ẓālim*, is the nominal equivalent of the verbal intensive.

523 This apparently irrelevant aside may perhaps be explained by the fact that the author contracted a venereal disease while in Malta.

524 "at this point": i.e., at the thirteenth chapter of each book.

525 "Hie ye to security!" (*ḥayya ilā l-falāḥ*): a phrase in the call to prayer.

526 "a turban of different fashion": in Egypt, men of different religious communities wore turbans of different colors and, sometimes, shapes (see Lane, *Manners*, 31).

527 "pilgrims from 'Arafāt": the gathering on Mount 'Arafāt outside of Mecca is the final rite of pilgrimage, after which the pilgrims disperse to their separate countries.

528 "You are to me as my mother's back!" (*anti 'alayya ka-ẓahri ummī*): i.e., "intercourse with you is as forbidden to me as it is with my mother," a pre-Islamic divorce formula; the "back" is specified rather than the belly because intercourse with a woman is likened to riding an animal (see Lane, *Lexicon*, s.v. *ẓāhara*).

529 "Your nose-rope is on the top of your hump!" (*ḥabluki 'alā ghāribiki*): meaning "Go wherever you want" because when a she-camel that is wearing a nose-rope is sent out to graze, the rope is thrown on top of her hump, for if she can see the rope, she will not want to eat anything (al-Maydānī, *Majma'*, 1:132); the expression is associated with divorce.

530 "Return to your covert!" (*'ūdī ilā kināsiki*): as though she were a gazelle or an oryx that had made itself a shelter against the heat.

531 "(un)buckle to her will and her every demand fulfil" (*yuwāṭi'ahā 'alay-hi wa-yujāmi'ahā*): the verbs *wāṭa'a* and *jāma'a* both mean both "to agree with" and "to copulate with."

532 "legal dalliance" (*al-mut'ah*): a marriage legally contracted for a set period, usually short.

533 "How many a heart has been tied to the rack . . . or gold coins expended" (*wa-la-kam taṣadda'at qulūb . . . wa-danānīra nuqidat*): evocative of Q Takwīr 81:1–14.

534 "Verily . . . it is a great woe" (*innahā la-iḥdā l-kubar*): Q Muddaththir 74:35.

535 "ill you answered though well you heard!" (*asa'ta jābatan ba'da an aṣabta sam'an*): a distortion of the proverb *asā'a sam'an fa-asā'a jābatan*, "he answered ill because he heard ill."

536 In fact, none of the obscure words explained in this chapter occur in the preceding.

537 The author uses the double entendres implicit in the terminology of grammar (*fāʿil* "actor/subject of a verb"; *mafʿūl* "acted upon/object of a verb"; *fiʿl* "act/verb"; *rafʿ*, literally "raising," i.e., the vowel ending *-u* when used to mark the nominative case; *naṣb*, literally "erecting,") i.e., the vowel ending *-a* when used to mark the accusative case to describe sexual acts (a common conceit). The thrust of the argument laid out below is that there is no word for marriage that does not derive from other words that originally refer to something else; thus, the rites and institutions that have developed around it are historically contingent and further (2.14.5), religion's, or the state's, interference in what is a private contract is without justification.

538 Abū l-Baqāʾ: Ayyūb ibn Mūsā Abū l-Baqāʾ al-Kaffawī (ca. 1027/1618 to ca. 1093/1682); his *Kitāb al-Kulliyyāt* is a dictionary.

539 "noun *nikāḥ*" etc.: the issue here is that this word, which is the preferred legal term for sexual congress, is regarded by some as embarrassingly direct.

540 "mysterious letters" (*asrār*): letters of unknown signification that occur at the beginning of certain suras of the Qurʾan (see Watt, *Bell's Introduction*, 61–65).

541 "*Nūn*. By the Pen and all that they write!" (*nūn wa-l-qalami wa-mā yasṭurūn*): Q Anfāl 8:1.

542 *kāf-hāʾ-yāʾ-ṣād*: letters occurring at the beginning of Sūrat Maryam (Q Maryam 19:1).

543 *alif-lām-fāʾ*: letters occurring at the beginning of Sūrat al-Baqarah (Q Baqarah 2:1).

544 *ḥāʾ-mīm*: letters occurring at the beginning of suras 40–46.

545 "an active participle of the verb *ḥ-y-y* . . . an imperative verb formed from *kāna*": i.e., if نكاح is written backwards the result, حاكن, may be broken down (ignoring short vowels) into حا, to be understood according to the orthography used here as حاي ("alive, quick," an epithet of God) from حَيِي (or حَيَّ) and كن ("Be!") from كان.

546 "the letter *nūn* followed by the letter *kāf*": i.e., *nik*, meaning "fuck!"

547 "the *alif* and the *ḥā'*": i.e., *āḥ*, which could also be understood as the exclamation "Ah!"

548 "by keeping only the end" (*bi-ḥaythu yaslamu l-ṭaraf*): i.e., by removing the initial syllable *nik-* from *nikāḥ*, leaving (by re-interpretation of the remaining ductus) *aḥḥ*, which is an "exclamation expressing . . . pleasure during sexual intercourse" peculiar to women (Hinds and Badawi, *Dictionary*).

549 "*mustaqbiḥah* and *mustafẓiʿah*": see 2.5.5 above; in fact, it is heads rather than bonnets that are so described.

550 On ʿUlayyān, see Volume One (n. 138 to 1.3.13); however, no anecdote involving a chicken occurs in al-Nīsābūrī.

551 "bag" (*haqībah*): literally, "a bag carried behind the saddle" and also, punningly, "posterior."

552 "well-known": the *Qāmūs* defines a girl who is *raṭbah* as being *rakhṣah* and defines *rakhṣ* as "smooth."

553 "mentioned under *burquʿ*": there is no entry for *burquʿ*; however, *shanab* ("lustrousness of the teeth") is referred to in the earlier passage describing the charms of *al-mutabarqiʿāt* ("women who wear the *burquʿ*") (2.4.5), as are *khanas* and *dhalaf*, which are likewise linked below to *burquʿ*.

554 *ʿanaṭ* and *ʿayaṭ* are synonyms.

555 "synonym *abārīq*": thus in the text, but, as the *Qāmūs* makes clear, *abārīq* is in fact the plural of *ibrīq*, which is synonymous with *barrāqah*.

556 "having a certain quality welcomed in a woman during copulation": this definition of *ḥārūq* is explained in the definition of *al-ḥāriqah* that precedes it in the *Qāmūs* and to which the author has referred earlier; see Volume 1 (n. 47 to 1.1.6).

557 Ṣāliḥ is a prophet referred to in the Qur'an (e.g., Q Aʿrāf 7:77); the People of the Cave (*ahl al-kahf*) are mentioned in the eponymous eighteenth sura of the Qur'an.

558 "or . . .": the entry in the *Qāmūs* continues "a house roofed with a single piece of wood, synonym *azaj*."

559 "or . . .": the entry in the *Qāmūs* continues "a place where people gather and sit for so long as they are gathered there."

560 "they": i.e., pastoralists of the Arabian peninsula.

561 "or . . .": other definitions given in the *Qāmūs* are "a village, or a granary, or flat land, or houses of the Persians in which are drink and entertainment."

562 "or . . .": the entry in the *Qāmūs* continues "for the harvester of truffles."

563 "a kind of building": according to the *Lisān*, "a house built in elongated form, called in Persian *ūsitān*."

564 "or . . .": the *Qāmūs* continues "a day on which they eat and drink."

565 al-Muqtadir: i.e., the Abbasid caliph Jaʿfar al-Muqtadir (ruled three times between 295/908 and 317/929).

566 "a pool of lead" (*birkatun mina l-raṣāṣ*): more often described as having been of mercury.

567 Al-Nuʿmān: i.e., al-Nuʿmān ibn Imruʾ al-Qays (r. AD 390–418), king of al-Ḥīrah, in the area of ancient Babylon in Iraq; the palace in question was named al-Khawarnaq.

568 Uḥayḥah: Uḥayḥah ibn al-Julāḥ was a pre-Islamic leader of the Aws tribe of Yathrib (now Medina).

569 al-Mutawakkil: an Abbasid caliph, r. 232–47/847–61.

570 Dawmat al-Jandal: a town in northwestern Arabia.

571 Khayzurān: mother of the caliph Hārūn al-Rashīd.

572 ʿAmr ibn al-ʿĀṣ: a leading general of the Muslim conquests in the time of the Prophet Muḥammad and after (b. before AD 573).

573 Wajj: a wadi east of Mecca and northeast of al-Ṭāʾif.

574 "on which Adam . . . fell": i.e., after being cast out of heaven, the mountain being situated in modern Sri Lanka.

575 al-Jazīrah: the plain lying between the Tigris and the Euphrates, in Upper Mesopotamia.

576 "the lote-tree beyond which none may pass" (*sidrat al-muntahā*): see Q Najm 53:14; this tree "stands in the Seventh Heaven on the right hand of the throne of God; and is the utmost bounds beyond which the angels themselves must not pass; or . . . beyond which no creature's knowledge can extend" (Sale, *Koran*, 427 n. 1).

577 Ibn Hishām: ʿAbd al-Malik ibn Hishām (d. 218/833), an Egyptian scholar of South Arabian origin, who wrote, in addition to the authoritative

*sīrah*, or biography, of the Prophet Muḥammad, for which he is best known, a collection of biblical and ancient Arabian lore entitled *Kitāb al-Tījān fī mulūk Ḥimyar* (*The Book of Crowns concerning the Kings of Ḥimyar*); in the *Qāmūs* the name of the dead queen is given as Tājah, in the Tāj as here

578 Ḥimyar: a kingdom of ancient Yemen that flourished between the first and fourth centuries AD.

579 "the battle of Badr": Ramaḍān 17, 2/March 13, 624, a victory for the Muslim forces of Medina over the pagans of Mecca.

580 ʿAlī: ʿAlī ibn Abī Ṭālib (d. 40/660), the Prophet Muḥammad's cousin, foster-brother, and son-in-law.

581 ʿĀd: an ancient people of Arabia, mentioned in the Qur'an (Q Aʿrāf 7:65, Hūd 11:59, etc.).

582 "*nās*, *nasnās*, and *nasānis*": since *nās* ordinarily means "people" the implication is that there are three kinds of humanoid—(ordinary) people, *nasnās*, and *nasānis*.

583 Yājūj and Mājūj: Gog and Magog.

584 "or the remainder of the bearers of the Proof, which no part of the earth is without" (*wa-baqiyyatu ḥamalati l-ḥujjati lā takhlū l-arḍu minhum*): a Tradition mentioned by al-Jawharī (see *Lisān*, s.v. *r-b-ḍ*).

585 "an ant who spoke to Sulaymān" (*namlatun kallamat Sulaymān*): a reference to Q Naml 27:18 "when they came on the valley of the ants, an ant said . . . ."; since the ant did not in fact address Sulaymān directly, the verb has to be taken as meaning "spoke in the presence of."

586 "the ant mentioned in the Qur'an": see Q Naml 27:18.

587 "Ibn Sīnā . . . the *Shifā*'": ʿAbdallāh ibn Sīnā (d. 428/1037), a philosopher of medieval Islam, known in the west as Avicenna.

588 "cup his ears with his hands": in the manner of a muezzin making the call to prayer.

589 "'Waḍḍāḥ's Bone'" (*ʿaẓmu Waḍḍāḥin*): "A certain game of the Arabs . . . in which they throw in the night . . . a white bone and he who lights upon it overcomes [sc. beats] his companions" (Lane, *Lexicon*).

590 "*ʿuqqah*": the dictionaries offer no further definition.

591 "on which one plays" (*yuḍrabu bihi*): i.e., not *ʿūd* in any of its other senses (such as "stick" or "a certain perfume").

592 "honey" (*ʿasal*): all references to "honey" (in its complete form *ʿasal abyaḍ* or "white honey") may be taken in the alternative sense of "molasses" (in its complete form *ʿasal aswad* or "black honey").

593 "*ḥays*": dates mixed with clarified butter and curd.

594 al-Maʾmūn: Abbasid caliph, r. 189–218/813–33.

595 "fatty dishes or . . .": the author appears to have misread the *Qāmūs*, which gives a different definition for *makhbūr* (*al-ṭayyib al-idām* or "good-tasting condiments") and in which *khubrah* is not a synonym of *makhbūr* but constitutes a new lemma, with *tharīdah ḍakhmah* as one of its definitions.

596 "*sikbājah*": not in the *Qāmūs* but presumably the same as *sikbāj*.

597 "*ruṭab* dates": i.e., dates that are fresh but soft and sugary (and neither fresh and astringent nor dried).

598 "*wars*": a plant, *Memecylon tinctorium*, grown in Yemen, from whose roots a yellow dye ("Indian yellow") is made.

599 al-Faḥfāḥ and al-Kawthar: rivers in Paradise.

600 "*tasnīm*": the beverage of the blessed in Paradise.

601 "among whom pass immortal youths . . . .": a collage of verses taken from three chapters of the Qurʾan, namely al-Wāqiʿah, al-Raḥmān, and al-Insān (Q Wāqiʿah 56:17–18, 20–21, 28–34; Raḥmān 55:46, 48, 62, 64, 66, 68, 70, 11–12, 76, 54, 15 (note that here the author incorrectly writes *furushin* for *sururin*); Insān 76:17–19, 21); the translation is Arberry's, with minor adaptions.

602 "*zaqqūm*": see Volume One (n. 92 to 1.1.9).

603 "and shade from a smoking blaze" (*wa-ẓillin min yaḥmūmin*): Q Wāqiʿah 56:43.

604 "fire from a smokeless blaze" (*mārij mina l-nār*): Q Raḥmān 55:15.

605 "it was wholesome, healthy, and of beneficial effect" (*ṣāra marīʾan hanīʾan ḥandīda l-mighabbah*): the quotation is from the *Qāmūs*, though the designation of the verb as the etymon of the noun appears to be the author's.

606 “the glottal stop (*hamz*) in it is for purposes of elision (*waṣl*) and the elision (*waṣl*) in it is for purposes of compression (*hamz*)” (*hamzuhā li-l-waṣl wa-waṣluhā li-l-hamz*): the author plays with orthographic terminology, exploiting the fact that *imra'ah* begins (unusually for a concrete noun) with a glottal stop (*hamz*) that is elided when preceded by a word ending in a vowel and as such is distinguished from its non-elidable cousin by a sign called *waṣl*, while *hamz* also has the non-grammatical sense of “compression,” here to be understood as “sexual intercourse.”

607 “its plural” etc.: no plural is made from *imra'ah*; words for “women” are from the root *n-s-w* and have different forms (e.g., *niswah*, *nisā'*, *niswān*).

608 “in one language the word denotes ‘man's woe’ and in another ‘pudendum’”: i.e., in English, “woman” is a phonetic anagram of “man's woe” and in Ottoman Turkish the word for both “woman” and “pudendum” was عورت (realized in modern Turkish as *avrat* for the former, *avret* for the latter).

609 “*qarīnah* . . . whose etymology is well known”: probably an allusion to *qarn* (“horn”), from the same root, and its figurative reference to cuckoldry.

610 “or vice versa”: i.e., perhaps, when she returns to her parents' home in a fit of anger at her husband.

611 See 2.16.65 below.

612 “*ḥadādah*”: a word whose semantic link to others with the same root is left unexplained by the lexicographers; thus *ḥadādatuka* means “your wife” (*Qāmūs*), but why it does so is not clear. The same is true of *niḍr*, *jathal*, and *ḥannah* below.

613 “*‘irs*”: from the verb *‘arisa bi-* meaning “to cleave to.”

614 “*shā‘ah*”: because, according to the *Qāmūs*, she takes her husband's part (*li-mushāya‘atihā l-zawj*).

615 “the accession of women to the throne of England was an unalloyed blessing”: perhaps because the reign of Elizabeth I witnessed the irreversibility of Protestantism as the national creed.

616 "the two queens of England": presumably, Mary and her successor Elizabeth I, the first queens regnant of England, the first of whom was Catholic, the second Protestant.

617 "Irene, wife of Leo IV, and Theodora, wife of Theophilus": Irene was Byzantine empress regnant from AD 797 to 802, while Theodora was regent for her son from AD 842 to 855. The significance of their being opposed here is not clear, since both, as anti-iconoclasts, took the same position with regard to the most important theological issue of their day.

618 Chapter 15: the dots seem to imply a silent dialogue between the author and his pen, in which the former tries to persuade the latter to move on to a new topic while the latter refuses, insisting that the renewed discussion, instead of taking place "at some other point" (*fī mawḍiʿin ākhar*) as promised at the end of the preceding chapter, should, in fact, take place "right there" (*fī dhālika l-mawḍiʿ*), as indicated by the hand, namely immediately, in the following chapter. The extreme shortness of the chapter, the dots, and the pointing hand have been noted by scholars as examples of the influence of Laurence Sterne's *Tristram Shandy* (see, e.g., Alwan, *Ahmad,* chap. 3, sect. 11).

619 "the mark of clemency" (*simat al-ḥilm*): a pun, in that the phrase may also be read as *simat al-ḥalam* ("the mark of the nipple").

620 Zubaydah daughter of Jaʿfar (d. 216/831) was cousin and wife of Hārūn al-Rashīd, fifth Abbasid caliph; this poem, which appears in many classical anthologies, is interpreted in those as illustrating (on the poet's side) the danger of misusing a rhetorical feature and (on Zubayda's) insight and generosity; thus, al-Nuwayrī (667–732/1279–1332) writes in his *Nihāyat al-arab fī funūn al-adab*, "When the poet recited the above, the slaves leapt up to beat him, but Zubayda said, 'Let him be! He must be rewarded well, for he who means well and makes a mistake is better than he who means evil and is correct. He heard people saying, "Your nape is comelier than others' faces and your left hand more generous than others' right hands," so he supposed that what he had written was of the same sort. Give him what he hoped for and teach him what he did not know'" (http://www.alwaraq.net/, accessed 8

July 2012). The author's different interpretation ("his description was not wrong") implies that Zubaydah accepted the validity of the poet's comparison, in the sense, perhaps, that even with the tips of her toes she gave more than others gave with their whole hands.

621 "*ruḍāb*": literally, "saliva."

622 Genesis 36:20, "These are the sons of Seir the Horite, who inhabited the land; Lotan, and Shobal, and Zibeon, and Anah"; 36:24 "And these are the children of Zibeon; both Ajah, and Anah: this was that Anah that found the mules in the wilderness, as he fed the asses of Zibeon his father"; 36:29 "These are the dukes that came of the Horites; duke Lotan, duke Shobal, duke Zibeon, duke Anah."

623 ". . . or a kind of ornament for the hands or the feet": the entry in the *Qāmūs* reads "*quffāz* . . . : something made for the hands that is stuffed with cotton and that women wear against the cold [sc. 'gloves'], or a kind of ornament for the hands or the feet," etc.

624 ". . . or decorative earrings": the entry in the *Qāmūs* reads "*sals* . . . : the string on which the white beads worn by slave girls are strung, or decorative earrings."

625 "the Ring of Power" (*khātam al-mulk*): a magic ring by which jinn and other forces may be commanded.

626 "*rāmik*": described in the *Qāmūs* as being "something black that is mixed with musk."

627 "*thamīmah*": defined in the *Qāmūs* as synonymous with *ta'mūrah*.

628 "or. . . .": the *Qāmūs* continues with further unrelated definitions.

629 "*shiʿār*": defined in the *Qāmūs* as "any item of apparel worn under the *dithār*."

630 "*armaniyyah*": literally, "the Armenian [garment]. but not further defined."

631 "in an entry of its own": i.e., under *m-r-j-l*; in fact, available editions of the *Qāmūs* do not include *mumarjil* but read, under *r-j-l*, *al-mumarjal —thiyābun fīhā ṣuwaru l-marājil*; for more on the confusion around these and similar terms, see Lane, *Lexicon,* s.v. *mirjal.*

632 "from a certain governor": i.e., from a provincial governor whose name was al-Qasṭalānī ("the Castilian").

633 Cf. *Qāmūs* (s.v. *a-w-m*): "*Ām*, a town whose name is used to describe clothes."

634 "*bizyawn*": defined in the *Qāmūs* as "a kind of *sundus*."

635 "so as to give them a place in the *list* appropriate to the underlying *gist*" (*li-yuṭābiqa l-dhikru l-fikr*): i.e., because they are put on before anything else.

636 "*ḥarr/ḥirr*": with the first vowelling, the word means "warmth," with the second, "vagina".

637 "in kind . . . kind . . . kinds" (*al-ʿayn . . . mina l-ʿayn . . . bi-l-maʿnayayn*): the author plays with two senses of *ʿayn*, namely "kind" (as opposed to "cash") and "eye," and rhymes the word with *maʿnayayn* ("two senses").

638 "he has to dissolve any knots with puffs" (*yaḥulla ʿuqdatahu bi-nafāthāt*): a reference to Q Falaq 113:1–4— *qul aʿūdhu bi-rabbi l-falaq min . . . sharri n-naffāthāti fī l-ʿuqad* ("Say, 'I seek refuge with the Lord of the daybreak . . . from the evil of those who blow on knots'"), the Qur'anic reference being to witches who performed magic using this method.

639 "as al-Farrā' has on *ḥattā*": Yaḥya ibn Ziyād al-Farrā' (144–207/761–822) was a leading grammarian; *ḥattā* is a conjunction and preposition with multiple functions.

640 "Juḥā's dream": Juḥā is the protagonist of jokes and anecdotes, in which he often plays the role of the "wise fool." A version of this story goes: "Juḥā told the following story: 'When sleeping I had a dream the first half of which was true, the second half untrue.' 'How can that be, O Abū Ghuṣn?' he was asked. He said, 'As I slept I seemed to behold myself come across a purse full of gold, silver, and golden coins, and when I picked it up, I defecated on myself from the effort of lifting it, it was so heavy. When I woke up, I found I was covered with filth and wetness, and the purse was no longer in my hands!'" (http://www.belkhechine07.com/joha.doc, accessed on 27 June 2012).

641 "a leading scholar of the language . . .": i.e., Jalāl al-Dīn al-Suyūṭī (see Volume One, 0.4.10).

642 "why have you foresworn writing [in general] but not [writing] about women": in what follows, the author answers that first part of the question but appears to forget the second.

643 "most people . . . [believe *mu'allif*] refers to *ta'līf* ('making peace') between two persons": *mu'allif* in the sense of "author" etc. was a nineteenth-century neologism.

644 "repugnant to some people, especially women": because "shaykh" also means "old man."

645 "and how he stuffs them then" (*fa-zaʿabahā ayya zaʿbin*): the phrase could also be understood "and how he stuffs her then!"

646 Shaykh Muṣṭafā: according to one scholar, a teacher at the mosque-university of al-Azhar but not further identified (al-Maṭwī, *Aḥmad*, 1:79), the same applying to the Shaykh Aḥmad, Shaykh Maḥmūd, and Shaykh Muḥammad mentioned later (2.18.3, 2.18.4, 2.19.9); however, it is possible that the author simply chose these common names to hide the identity of little-known scholars, as one might say "Tom, Dick, and Harry."

647 "Zayd and ʿAmr": two characters used to illustrate points of grammar; for example, the sentence *ḍaraba Zaydun ʿAmran* ("Zayd struck ʿAmr") illustrates the typical verb-subject-object order of the Arabic sentence.

648 "happened to be asked . . . if he could study": presumably, the Fāriyāq's acquaintance asked him for an introduction to the shaykh.

649 "*Baḥth al-maṭālib*": see n. 126 to 2.11.3.

650 "to write him a license to teach the book" (*an yaktuba la-hu ijāzata iqrā'ihi*): traditionally, scholarly knowledge was acquired through the study of individual books at the hands of a shaykh, with the student reading the work out loud to the teacher, who corrected and commented. When the student had acquired full mastery of the text, the shaykh would write him a licence (*ijāzah*) to teach it in the same fashion to others, just as the shaykh had earlier received a licence from his teacher, and so on.

651 *Al-Talkhīṣ fī l-maʿānī*: probably the commentary of Masʿūd ibn ʿUmar al-Taftazānī (d. between 791/1389 and 797/1395) on the *Talkhīṣ al-miftāḥ fī l-maʿānī wal-l-bayān wa-l-badīʿ* by Jalāl al-Dīn Muḥammad ibn ʿAbd al-Raḥmān al-Qazwīnī, known as Khaṭīb Dimashq

(666–739/1268–1338), the "basic textbook for rhetorical studies in the *madrasas* of the later Middle Ages up to modern times" (Meisami and Starkey, *Encyclopedia,* 2:439).

652 "al-Akhḍarī's *Sharḥ al-Sullam*": ʿAbd al-Raḥmān ibn Muḥammad al-Akhḍarī (920–83/1512–75) wrote this commentary on his own *Al-Sullam al-murawnaq fī l-manṭiq*.

653 "the yellow air" (*al-hawāʾ al-aṣfar*): summer cholera.

654 "greater affirmative universal" (*kulliyyah mūjibah kubrā*): presumably meaning, in the terms of Aristotelian logic, a "universal" statement of the form "all S are P."

655 "and not numbered among the dead" (*wa-lam yaqḍi mina l-qaḍāyā*); or, punningly, "and had not yet run out of syllogisms."

656 "the *Kanz*": probably the *Kanz al-daqāʾiq* of ʿAbdallāh ibn Aḥmad al-Nasafī (d. 710/1310).

657 "the *Risālah al-Sanūsiyyah*": probably the *Ḥāshiya* (marginal commentary) of Ibrāhīm ibn Muḥammad al-Bājūrī (or al-Bījūrī) (1189–1276/1784–1859) on the *Matn al-Sanūsiyyah* of Muḥammad ibn Yūsuf al-Sanūsī (after 830-95/1426–90).

658 "the Center of This Book": as the thirty-ninth chapter of a work consisting of eighty, this section is, in fact, slightly off-center.

659 "*hamqāq*": according to the *Qāmūs*, "seeds found in the mountains of Balʿamm that are fried and eaten to increase the capacity for intercourse."

660 *mughāth*: *Glossostemon bruguieri*, a plant with therapeutic and nutritional properties.

661 "the caliphal palace" (*dār al-khilāfah*): i.e., the place where, like the caliph, or successor to the Prophet Muḥammad, the man in question carries out his duties.

662 "everyone suspected ... a sin that they would carry ... till the Day of Judgment" (*fa-ẓanna l-nās ... wa-taqalladū ithmahu ... ilā yawmi l-dīn*): the passage evokes the words of the Quran *inna baʿḍa l-ẓanni ithm* ("Indeed some suspicion is a sin") (Q Ḥujurāt 49:12).

663 "for he was hors de combat and wasn't up to doing anything anyway" (*fa-innahu kāna muʿaṭṭalan wa-fiʿluhu mulghan ʿani l-ʿamal*): probably

an allusion to the fact that he was receiving treatment for a venereal disease (see n. 149 to 2.12.18).

664 Probably *Al-Qawl al-wāfī fī sharḥ al-Kāfī fī ʿilmay al-ʿarūḍ wa-l-qawāfī*, a commentary by ʿAlī ibn ʿAbd al-Qādir al-Nabtītī (d. ca. 1065/1655) on a work by Yaḥyā ibn ʿAlī al-Tabrīzī (421–502/1030–1109).

665 "a loft . . .": see 1 Kings 17:19–20.

666 "a wall" (*judāran*): "Now Absalom in his lifetime had taken and reared up for himself a pillar, which is in the king's dale: for he said, I have no son to keep my name in remembrance: and he called the pillar after his own name: and it is called unto this day, Absalom's place" (2 Sam. 18:8).

667 Bion: Bion of Borysthenes (ca. 325–250), who is said to have attached himself to all the contemporary schools of philosophy in succession and to have attacked everyone and everything.

# Glossary

*Abīshalūm* Absalom.

*Abū Nuwās (al-Ḥasan ibn Hāni' al-Ḥakamī)* a poet (ca. 140–98/755–813) of the Abbasid period.

*al-Andalus* those parts of the Iberian Peninsula that were under Islamic rule from the seventh to the fifteenth centuries AD.

*Bag-men (khurjiyyūn)* the author's term for Protestant missionaries in the Middle East, whether the American Congregationalists of the Board of Commissioners of Foreign Missions, with whom he first came into contact in Beirut, or the British Anglicans of the Church Missionary Society, for whom he worked later in Malta, Egypt, and London. The Congregationalists established their first mission station in Beirut in 1823 (Makdisi, *Artillery*, 81, 83). In December 1823, when their intention to proselytize became clear, Maronite patriarch Yūsuf Ḥubaysh (1787–1845), who had initially received them cordially, ordered his flock to avoid all contact with what he referred to as "the Liberati" or "Biblemen" (Makdisi, *Artillery*, 95–97).

*Bilqīs* Queen of Saba' (Sheba) in Yemen, the story of whose visit to Sulaymān (Solomon) is told in the Qur'ān (Q Naml 27:22–44).

*cubit (dhirāʿ)* 0.68 m.

*Dā'ūd* David.

*Days of Barbarism (The) (al-Jāhiliyyah)* the period in Arabia before the coming of Islam.

*Druze* a monotheistic religious community found primarily in Syria and Lebanon.

*emir (amīr)* a title (lit., "commander" or "prince") assumed by local leaders in the Arab world; as used in Book One, the term refers most often to the emirs of the Shihābī dynasty of Mount Lebanon.

*Fāriyāq (The)* the hero of the events described in the book and the author's alter ego, the name itself being a contraction of Fāri(s al-Shid)yāq.

*Himyar (Ḥimyar)* a kingdom of ancient Yemen that flourished between the first and fourth centuries AD.

*Iblīs* the Devil, Satan.

*Ilyās* Elias.

*Khawājā* a title of reference and address afforded Christians of substance.

*kuttāb* a one-room school in which children are taught reading, writing, and numeracy.

*maqāmah, plural maqāmāt* "short independent prose narrations written in ornamented rhymed prose (*sajʿ*) with verse insertions which share a common plot-scheme and two constant protagonists: the narrator and the hero" (Meisami and Starkey, *Encyclopedia,* 2:507). The thirteenth chapter of each book of the present work is described by the author as a *maqāmah*, the plot-scheme in these *maqāmāt* being a debate. See further Zakharia, "Aḥmad Fāris al-Šidyāq."

*Market Boss (The) (shaykh al-sūq)* the author's term for the Maronite patriarch.

*Market-men (sūqiyyūn)* the author's term for the Maronite and Roman Catholic clergy, or the Maronite and Roman Catholic churches in general.

*market trader (ḍawṭār, plural ḍawāṭirah)* the author's term for a member of the Maronite upper clergy.

*Maronite* of or pertaining to the Maronite Christian community, whose historical roots lie in northern Syria and Lebanon and whose church, while using Syriac as a liturgical language, is in communion with the Roman Catholic church.

*mawwāl* a form of vernacular poetry, often involving complex rhyme schemes and word play.

*Mountain (The)* Mount Lebanon, a mountain range in Lebanon extending for 170 kilometers parallel to the Mediterranean coast and the historical homeland of both the Maronite and Druze Lebanese communities.

*Muʿtazilite* follower of a school of theology that appealed to reason as a basis for understanding the truths of Islam.

*Nākir and Nakīr* angels who question the deceased in the grave concerning his or her faith.

*Nūḥ* Noah.

*Numrūdh* Nimrod.

*People of the Cave (ahl al-kahf)* believing youths who, as recounted in the eighteenth *surah* (chapter) of the Qur'an (Q 18, Sūrat al-Kahf), were caused by God to fall asleep in a cave for many years and then revived and who had no knowledge of how many years they had passed there.

*Qāmūs (al-)* *Al-Qāmūs al-muḥīṭ* (*The Encompassing Ocean*), a dictionary compiled by Muḥammad ibn Yaʿqūb al-Fīrūzābādī (d. 817/1415) that became so influential that *qāmūs* ("ocean") eventually came to mean simply "dictionary." The author later published a study of the *Qāmūs* entitled *Al-Jāsūs ʿalā l-Qāmūs* (*The Spy on the Qāmūs*).

*Qāyin* Cain.

*Recoiler (The) (al-Khannās)* Satan, so called because he recoils at the mention of the name of God.

*rhymed prose (sajʿ)* "artistic prose, subject to certain constraints of rhyme and rhythm . . . Etymologically, the word referred to the cooing of pigeons" (Meisami and Starkey, *Encyclopedia*, 2:677). First used by pre-Islamic soothsayers, the form developed, often in combination with other types of parallelism, until it became virtually de rigueur by the tenth century AD, and it remained in use into the early twentieth century, "by which time, however, the modern revolt which has now largely swept away this sort of artifice was already growing strong" (idem). The author uses *sajʿ* in the title of the work and most of his chapter titles, in short scattered bursts in the midst of unrhymed prose (especially at moments of drama), and sometimes, as in the four preceding chapters, in sustained blocks. For further discussion of *sajʿ* in this work, see Jubran, "Function."

*Sām* Seth son of Noah.

*Sībawayhi* Abū Bishr ʿAmr ibn ʿUthmān ibn Qanbar Sībawayhi (or Sībawayh) (second/eighth century), the creator of systematic Arabic grammar. By the fourth/tenth century, his only work, Kitāb Sībawayhi, was firmly established as the foundation of a grammatical system that has remained essentially unchanged to the present (Meisami and Starkey, *Encyclopedia*, 2:718).

*Sulaymān* Solomon.

*Surra Man Raʾā* Samarra, a city in Iraq, capital of the Abbasid caliphate from 836 to 892; the name may be interpreted as "A Joy to All Who See It".

*Suyūṭī (al-), Jalāl al-Dīn* a prolific polymath (d. 911/1505), much of whose 500-work oeuvre compiles material taken from earlier scholars.

*Waqāʾiʿ al-miṣriyyah (al-)* the Egyptian official gazette (and the first newspaper issued, partially, in Arabic), established in December 1828.

*Yashuʿ (al-)* Elisha.

*Yūnus* Jonah.

*Yūsuf* Joseph.

*Zabbāʾ (al-)* Zenobia, queen of Tadmur in Syria during the third century AD.

# Index

ʿAntar, 57
aphrodisiacs, 394
Arab nationalism, xxiv
"Arab rediscovery of Europe," xi, xxiii–xxiv
Arabic journalism, xx
Arabic language, *Baḥth al-maṭālib* (*The Discussion of Issues*), 270; distinguishing feature of, 380; the Fāriyāq as teacher of, 390, 396; Frankish pronunciation of, 221–25, 445n423; love and, 90–91; Maronite patriarchs, 35; oddities, 6–10, 403n3; priest's pronunciation of, 221–25; Qur'an revealed in, 213; rare words, 9, 48, 133–41; students from the Mountain and, 270–71; synonyms, xxxi–xxxii, 6, 11, 30–31; translations into, 272
Arabic literature, literary modernity, x–xi, xxvi, xxxv; *maqāmāt*, xxviii, xxix, xxx, xxxv–xxxvi, 110; renaissance in (*see Nahḍah*); *riwāyah* ("novel"), xxv; *sajʿ* (rhymed prose), xxviii–xxxi, 86, 99, 130, 403n4; translation and philology to, xi; tropes, 192–93. See also rhymed prose
Arabic poetry, 77, 431n280
Arabic publishing industry, xxiv–xxvii, 35, xliiin47
Arabic script, 317
Arabs, 30, 57, 77, 211–13, 246, 251, 291
ʿAshūr, Raḍwā, xxix
al-Aṣmaʿī, 98
aromas/perfumes, words for, 354–58
asses, 174, 233–34, 389–91
Atanāsiyūs al-Tutūnji, 224, 261–62, 448–49n440
atheists, 133
attire, 69
authors, 144, 147
ʿAwaḍ, Luwīs, xxix
*Bāb al-Iʿrāb* (*Gateway to Grammar*) (Jirmānūs Farḥāt), 43
the bag, Bag-man/Bag-men's preoccupation with, 220; the Fāriyāq's burden, 256, 271–72; point of, 230
bag, women's, 294–95, 460n551
Bag-man/Bag-men (Protestant missionaries), in Alexandria, 219–18; the bag, preoccupation with, 220; in Cairo, 232, 243; damage done by, 195–96; English queens, 341; the Fāriyāq and, 162, 168, 219–20, 226–28, 230–31, 232, 253, 275, 396–97; indifference to people's troubles, 202; influence, xxiii; language, 231; Market-men, 171, 181–85; Market-man/Market-men, feuds with, 219–20, 229, 231; Market-woman/Market-women, 228–29; payment by, 396; pork-eating, 226–27; prototype of, 219; saddlebags, 202, 433n298; serving girl/maid, 398–99; tools of the trade, 192, 200; weeping, instruction in, 170; wife beating by, 218; wife of a, 398
Baguettes, 397, 399
*Baḥth al-maṭālib* (*The Discussion of Issues*), 270, 388, 455n500
Baʿīr Bayʿar, 56, 58–63, 107
Basra, 34, 414n109
bawdiness, 77
*bayk* ("bey"), 385
beardless boys, 376
Benedict VII, Pope, 177
Benedict VIII, Pope, 177

girl, 389–90; garments for, 366, 373, 374; Khayzurān, 312; love of, 88; milk for fattening, 330; monks, 107–8; neighboring, 48–49; veils, 211; on wedding days, 75; words for, 295, 297–306, 347
God, 105–6, 109, 123–24, 160
good, 115
Gospels, xvii
grammar, works on, 98–99
grammarians, 98–99
grammatical studies, 94–100
Grand Panjandrum of the Panegyricon, 276
Great Catholicos, 24
Great Christian Master Physician, 40
greed, 51, 70
Greek Orthodox church, 174
Gregory VII, Pope, 177
*al-Ḥakākah fī l-rakākah* (*The Leavings Pile Concerning Lame Style*) (Atanāsiyūs al-Tutūnji), 224, 261–62, 449n441
al-Hamadhānī, xxvii, xxxv, xln31, 426n219
handkerchiefs, 182, 184
handwriting, 38, 54
happiest trade, 78–85
al-Ḥarīrī, xxxv, 86, 117, 421n175, 426n219
hashish, 248
al-Hāwif ibn Hifām (character in Leg over Leg), xxxv, 110, 283, 288–89
Ḥawwā, Buṭrus Yūsuf, xvi, xxxixn19, 5, 403n1
head wounds, 40
headwear, in Alexandria, 207; Frankish, 207, 218, 247; market traders', 203–6; of Market-men of the Levant, 228; tarbush, 246–47
health, 115
heart, 164–65
heaven, words for, 314
Henry IV, King of Germany, 177–79
Himyaritic lands, 214, 445n423
Hind, 45, 93, 290
*History of Arabic-Language Literature, A* (Jurjī Zaydān), xiv
horns, 40–41, 53; bulls', 276–77; dragging men by their, 393; husbands', 285; rams with and without, 263
Hosea, 167
hospitality, 218, 250, 269
household items, words for, 358–62
houses, words for, 310–12
Hugh, King of Arles, 175
humanity, common, 201
hunger, 200, 202, 227–28, 231, 233, 293
husbands, 74, 75
Ibn al-ʿAbbād, al-Ṣāḥib, 221, 447n437
Ibn al-Athīr, 347, 442n396
Ibn Aybak al-Ṣafadī, Khalīl, 232, 449n445
Ibn Hishām, 315, 461–62n577
Ibn Mālik, 90
Ibn Manẓūr, xix
Ibn al-Muʿtazz, 32
Ibn al-Nabīh, 32
Ibn Nubātah, 32
Ibn Sīnā, 319
idiots, language attributed to, 102
idols, words for, 196–99
ignorance, 122, 126
ignorant, the, 109, 169; scholars compared to, 384
Ilyās, 198, 400, 442n395

monks, 102–9, 216, 271; abbots, 132, 134; age at becoming one, 108–9; blameworthiness, 180; bread baked by, 102–3, 104, 105, 121; donkeys among, 144; escaped monk, 109, 121; at feasts, 107; frightening, 17; girls, 107–8; happiness of, 79; ignorance, 126; lentils eaten by, 103–5, 106, 109, 121; monasticism (*rahbāniyyah*), 104–8; *Qāmūs* (al-Firūzābādī), 104, 109; scholarship, 107, 108
Moses, 167
Mountain, the (Mount Lebanon), 271; borrowing by people of, 103; Emir of, 167; the Fāriyāq's father, 52; music and other arts, 52; women of, 40–42, 76–77
*Muʿallim* (term of address), 262, 454n489
Muhammad ʿAlī (of Egypt), xvii, xxiv, xlii
Muḥammad ʿAlī Pasha, 452n470
Muḥammad, Shaykh, 396
*mujārazah*, 251
*Muntahā l-ʿajab fī khaṣāʾiṣ lughat al-ʿArab* (*Wonder's Apogee concerning Every Arab Linguistic Particularity*) (al-Shidyāq), 6
musical instruments, words for, 324–25
*Muslim Discovery of Europe, The* (Lewis), xxiv
Muslims, Christian imitation of, 227, 251; Copts and, 252; divorce, 284–87, 440–41n382; of the Levant, 250; titles (honorifics) for, 385
Muṣṭafā, Shaykh, 387–88, 468n646
al-Mutanabbī, 255, 277, 453n481
Mutawālīs, 174
Muʿtazilite, 376
Muzabbid, 48
*Nahḍah*, [Aḥmad] Fāris al-Shidyāq, xviii; Arabic literary modernity, xxvi; meanings/translations of the term, x; "new age" as subject, xii; participation in global processes, xxvi–xxvii; print market, xxiv–xxvii; social and literary change, xxii; *tamaddun*, xxvi–xxvii; tradition, xxvi; Western literary and cultural models, xxi–xxii
Nākir and Nakīr, 247, 401
*Nawābigh* (al-Zamakhsharī), 86
Nestorian church, 174
new goods *vs.* old goods, 157–58, 165
New Testament, 271
Nicholas I, Pope, 175–76
Nicholson, John, xvi
Nile River, 10, 245
nominative case, 95
non-Arabic languages, 90
non-Arabs, quick-witted woman on, 223
non-Jewish writers, 41
Nūh (Noah), 198, 307, 318
*nūn*, 233–34
nuns, 121–22, 271
Nuʿūmah Mosque, 215, 446n431
Occidentals, 260
Octavianus, 176–77
Old Testament, 130, 148, 168
Orientalist scholars, xxxii, xxxv
Otto I, 176
Otto II, 177
Otto III, 177
Ottoman Empire, xxii, xxiii
pain, 111

Panegyricon, 272, 276, 387, 455–56n506
panegyrics, 255, 278, 281, 384
panegyrist, a prince's, 389
parasites, undercapitalized, 166, 170
Paris, xvi, 403n1
paronomasia, xxvii, 32, 101; al-Bustī, 273; in the Fāriyāq's poetry, 279; perfect paronomasia, 457n519; poets, 273; solecisms, 281
passion, 119
peddler, roving, 157–58
Peled, Matityahu, xxix
penises, 26–27
people, diversity of, 192–93
People of the Cave, 307, 460n557
Perceval, Caussin de, xvi
perfumes/aromas, words for, 354–358
persecution, 173
Persian(s), 219, 246
Photius, 175
physicians, 40, 48, 179. See doctors/physicians
pigs, 227
pigs' snouts, 53
pious, the, 24
places, words for various, 312–13
plants, sprouting of, 96, types of, 290
pleasure, 111, 116
poetry, about blessings, 66; about forgiveness, 25; about gazelles, 59; about knives, 66; about men and women, 99–100; about sin, 25; about verse, 88; Arabic poetry, 77, 431n280; about divorce, 289; about veils, 211; elegy for a donkey, 380–82, 384; by the Fāriyāq, 49, 67, 76–77, 77, 115–16, 154–57, 276–82, 289, 387; the Fāriyāq on, 43, 48; by Franks, 77; love poetry, 49, 119–21; *mawwāl*, 246, 251; by men, 346; to Mountain residents, 52; priests on, 119–21; for princes, 276–82; Proem, 14–20; prose compared to, 383–84; by slim poets, 118; as a means of survival, 384–85; by women, 118, 346
*Poetry's Destiny* (Lamartine), 57
poets, anecdotes about, 43–47; in Cairo, 244, 245, 253–57; celebrity, 273; characteristics, 253–54; crows and, 165; diversity among, 91; drooling by, 239; emirs, 265–68; on leisure compared to wretchedness, 114; the manner of most, 383–85; need for critics, 273; paronomasia, 273; personal devils, 431n280; by trade vs. by nature, 254; women, 339
popes, French authors on, 174–79
pork, 145, 227, 230
price lists, 181, 185
priests, adultery with a merchant's wife, 130–31, 148; Arabic-language sermon by, 221–25; Baʿīr Bayʿar's daughter, 60–61; blameworthiness, 180; deference to, 385–86; doctor's wife's choice of, 394; extorting secrets from wives, 55; the Fāriyāq's conversation with, 119–22; in Frankish lands, 134; gambling by, 133; language attributed to, 102; large-nosed priest's tale, 123–34; as lovers, advantages of, 394; on Malta, 228 on poetry, 118–20; praise for, promised, 120–21; repartee, good, 102; threats based on calling in, 55; women serving, 134

# About the NYU Abu Dhabi Institute

The Library of Arabic Literature is supported by a grant from the NYU Abu Dhabi Institute, a major hub of intellectual and creative activity and advanced research. The Institute hosts academic conferences, workshops, lectures, film series, performances, and other public programs directed both to audiences within the UAE and to the worldwide academic and research community. It is a center of the scholarly community for Abu Dhabi, bringing together faculty and researchers from institutions of higher learning throughout the region.

NYU Abu Dhabi, through the NYU Abu Dhabi Institute, is a world-class center of cutting-edge research, scholarship, and cultural activity. The Institute creates singular opportunities for leading researchers from across the arts, humanities, social sciences, sciences, engineering, and the professions to carry out creative scholarship and conduct research on issues of major disciplinary, multidisciplinary, and global significance.

## About the Translator

Humphrey Davies is an award-winning translator of some twenty works of modern Arabic literature, among them Alaa Al-Aswany's *The Yacoubian Building* and Elias Khoury's *The Gate of the Sun*. He has also made a critical edition, translation, and lexicon of the Ottoman-period *Hazz al-quḥūf bi-sharḥ qaṣīd Abī Shādūf* (*Brains Confounded by the Ode of Abū Shādūf Expounded*) by Yūsuf al-Shirbīnī and compiled with a colleague an anthology entitled *Al-ʿāmmiyyah al-miṣriyyah al-maktūbah: mukhtārāt min 1400 ilā 2009* (*Egyptian Colloquial Writing: selections from 1400 to 2009*). He read Arabic at the University of Cambridge, received his Ph.D. from the University of California at Berkeley, and, previous to undertaking his first translation in 2003, worked for social development and research organizations in Egypt, Tunisia, Palestine, and Sudan. He is affiliated with the American University in Cairo, where he lives.

# The Library of Arabic Literature

*Classical Arabic Literature*
Selected and translated by Geert Jan Van Gelder

*A Treasury of Virtues,* by al-Qāḍī al-Quḍāʿī
Edited and translated by Tahera Qutbuddin

*The Epistle on Legal Theory,* by al-Shāfiʿī
Edited and translated by Joseph E. Lowry

*Leg over Leg,* by Aḥmad Fāris al-Shidyāq
Edited and translated by Humphrey Davies

*Virtues of the Imām Aḥmad ibn Ḥanbal,* by Ibn al-Jawzī
Edited and translated by Michael Cooperson

*The Epistle of Forgiveness,* by Abū l-ʿAlāʾ al-Maʿarrī
Edited and translated by Geert Jan Van Gelder and Gregor Schoeler

*The Principles of Sufism,* by ʿĀʾishah al-Bāʿūnīyah
Edited and translated by Th. Emil Homerin

*The Expeditions,* by Maʿmar ibn Rāshid
Edited and translated by Sean W. Anthony

*Two Arabic Travel Books*
*Accounts of China and India,* by Abū Zayd al-Sīrāfī
Edited and translated by Tim Mackintosh-Smith
*Mission to the Volga,* by Ahmad Ibn Faḍlān
Edited and translated by James Montgomery

*Disagreements of the Jurists,* by al-Qāḍī al-Nuʿmān
Edited and translated by Devin Stewart

*Consorts of the Caliphs,* by Ibn al-Sāʿī
Edited by Shawkat M. Toorawa and translated by the Editors of the Library of Arabic Literature

*What ʿĪsā ibn Hishām Told Us,* by Muḥammad al-Muwayliḥī
Edited and translated by Roger Allen

*The Life and Times of Abū Tammām,* by Abū Bakr al-Ṣūlī
Edited and translated by Beatrice Gruendler